V&R

Gunther Wenz

Introduction to Wolfhart Pannenberg's Systematic Theology

Translated by Philip Stewart

Vandenhoeck & Ruprecht

Bibliographic information published by the Deutsche Nationalbibliothek
The Deutsche Nationalbibliothek lists this publication in the Deutsche Nationalbibliografie;
detailed bibliographic data available online: http://dnb.d-nb.de.

ISBN 978-3-525-56014-3
ISBN 978-3-647-56014-4 (e-book)

© 2013, Vandenhoeck & Ruprecht GmbH & Co. KG, Göttingen/
Vandenhoeck & Ruprecht LLC, Bristol, CT, U.S.A.
www.v-r.de

All rights reserved. No part of this work may be reproduced or utilized in any form or by any
means, electronic or mechanical, including photocopying, recording, or any information storage
and retrieval system, without prior written permission from the publisher.
Typesetting by Konrad Triltsch Print und digitale Medien GmbH, Ochsenfurt
Printed and bound in Germany by Hubert & Co, Göttingen

Printed on non-aging paper.

Foreword

Wolfhart Pannenberg influenced the history of Christian theology and philosophy of religion in the second half of the 20th and beginning of the 21st century both decisively and lastingly, far beyond the German-speaking world. His works, many in number, have been translated into many languages and there is a tradition of international reception. They are exceptional in their theoretical concentration, the breadth of their topical horizon, their interdisciplinary nature and their ecumenical openness, which is aimed towards the unification of Christianity.

Pannenberg is one of the great thinkers of our time. He has offered multiple studies to the history of problems in modern Christian theology, to the relation of theology and philosophy, to the natural sciences and the humanities, and on foundational questions of dogmatics and ethics. His works "Revelation as History", "Jesus: God and Man", "Theology and the Philosophy of Science", "Anthropology in Theological Perspective", and the magnum opus, his three-volume Systematic Theology, have become classics of the theological science.

My introduction to Wolfhart Pannenberg's systematic theology orients itself thematically to the structure of the Systematic Theology, but takes also into account the monographs, and as such, offers a foundation for the study of the entire Pannenbergian concept of theology. The first edition of the book, published in 2003, was dedicated to my honored teacher and predecessor in office not only in its content, but also formally. This dedication shall remain for the English edition, the existence of which I thank Philip Stewart for heartily. He has, in a selfless manner and on his own authority, applied his great linguistic and theological competence, that this introduction might be available to the English-speaking public. He is also to be thanked for the selection of secondary literature at the end of the volume.

The bibliography in this volume includes the works of Pannenberg which have been published since 1998. The list of publications from 1953 to the beginning of 1988 can be found in: Vernunft des Glaubens. Wissenschaftliche Theologie und kirchliche Lehre. (Festschrift W. Pannenberg), ed. by J. Rohls and G. Wenz, Göttingen 1988, 693 – 718. The years 1988 – 1998 are bibliographically documented in KuD 45 (1999), 143 – 154.

Munich, 15 July 2012   Gunther Wenz

Foreword to the German Edition

He wouldn't require of anyone that he read his work, opined Karl Barth in his preface to Otto Weber's introduction to Barth's Church Dogmatics. He, however, who would wish to speak of Barth, must have read his work – and it would not be asking too much that he (be the reader not a journalist, but a serious person, or indeed a serious and not a dilletante theologian) have read his work entire. The same can be said with reference to Wolfhart Pannenberg's theology. The text before you, which comes from class material, makes of course no pretension of replacing a more thorough and detailed reading of the original. At best, it offers help in bringing structure.

At the end of the book, one will find a bibliography of selected secondary literature as well as an extended bibliography of Pannenberg's works from 1998 – 2002. Mirjam Rose executed both of these; to her many thanks for her careful work. Additional thanks to Katrin Wirth for her assistance in proofreading and quote-checking. A list of Pannenberg's publications from 1953 to the beginning of 1988 can be found, compiled by Bernd Burkhardt, in: Vernunft des Glaubens. Wissenschaftliche Theologie und kirchliche Lehre. Festschrift W. Pannenberg, hg. v. J. Rohls und G. Wenz, Göttingen 1988, 693 – 718. A continuation for the years 1988 – 1998 from Friederike Nüssel can be found in KuD 45 (1999), 143 – 154. Additional suggestions for the amendment of the selected bibliography would be received with thanks by the Institut für Fundamentaltheologie und Ökumene der Evangelisch-Theologischen Fakultät der Ludwig-Maximilians-Universität München (Schellingstraße 3/III VG, 80799 München).

On the occasion of the 2nd of October 2003, this book is formally dedicated to my honored teacher and predecessor in office; and that not merely in reference to its content.

Translator's Foreword

The sheer breadth of Wolfhart Pannenberg's thought can be daunting. The arc of development can be traced from his early works into his magnum opus, and there is no easy entry point into Pannenberg's corpus. For this reason, I am pleased to have been part of the task of bringing Professor Gunther Wenz's introduction to Pannenberg's system into English. More than an introduction into the three volumes of Systematic Theology, it is an overview of Pannenberg's systematic theology – the theology of decades of teaching, research, and writing – by none other than a former student and current successor. Such a volume as an entry point into perhaps the greatest systematic theologian of the late 20th century may, I hope, prove invaluable.

The reader may notice some inconsistency in the translation – due to the various translators of Pannenberg's works into English, he often seems to speak with a different voice. I have attempted to keep references in the main body as unified in terminology with the quotations as possible, nonetheless, Pannenberg may sometimes "distinguish" and sometimes "differentiate", sometimes speak of "fellowship" and "consummation" and sometimes of "communion" and "completion" in this volume. Additionally, some quotations retain British English conventions, while this volume uses those of American English. I have followed the original text very closely, and where ambiguity could occur unintentionally, the German term is given in parentheses. Many of the translations, when quoted, took on a different tenor than the original work – where this has occurred, I have placed a footnote with alternate understandings, or, where necessary, a correction of the original translation so as to preserve both the words of Pannenberg and the context within this volume.

Additionally, the capitalization of nouns has not been consistent throughout the translations; I have made no effort to reconcile these to the main body of Professor Wenz' volume. In a language where all nouns are capitalized, a translator must choose what convention to follow in English for words such as Trinity and Christology, as well as with regard to the use of pronouns referring to God. I have often endeavored to refer to "humanity" rather than to man, where possible; especially some of the older translations retain "man" as a common designator.

The selection of secondary literature at the end of this volume limits itself to works in English and works of substance – reviews, even in English, have been left out in preference for articles and monographs. The intent was to create a manageable list.

I thank Professor Wenz for working so closely with me on this volume, and for his availability to answer questions regarding his intent. Any error in the representation of his thought remains mine. I thank also my wife, Karin, without whom this translation would have remained merely a well-intentioned idea.

Munich, 1 August 2012   Philip Stewart

Guide to Abbreviations of Pannenberg's Works

Anthr.	Anthropology in Theological Perspective
BSTh 1	Beiträge zur Systematischen Theologie. Bd. 1: Philosophie, Religion, Offenbarung
BSTh 2	Beiträge zur Systematischen Theologie. Bd. 2: Natur und Mensch – und die Zukunft der Schöpfung
BSTh 3	Beiträge zur Systematischen Theologie. Bd. 3: Kirche und Ökumene
BQiTh	Basic Questions in Theology. Collected Essays Volume 1
BQiTh	Basic Question in Theology. Collected Essays Volume 2
EuE	Ethik und Ekklesiologie. Gesammelte Aufsätze
GSTh 2	Grundfragen systematischer Theologie. Gesammelte Aufsätze Bd.2
JGM	Jesus, God and Man
M	What is Man? Contemporary Anthropology in Theological Perspective
MIG	Metaphysics & the Idea of God
Probl.	Problemgeschichte der neueren evangelischen Theologie in Deutschland. Von Schleiermacher bis zu Barth und Tillich.
RaH	Revelation as History
ST I,II,III	Systematic Theology Volumes I, II, III
ThPS	Theology and the Philosophy of Science
ThuPh	Theologie und Philosophie. Ihr Verhältnis im Lichte ihrer gemeinsamen Geschichte.

Contents

Introduction (Revelation as History)

Wolfhart Pannenberg was born on the 2nd of October 1928 in Stettin an der Oder. He began his university studies in theology and philosophy in 1947 in Berlin, continuing in Göttingen and Basel, and finishing in Heidelberg. His most influential philosophical teachers were Nicolai Hartmann, Karl Jaspers and Karl Loewith; the theologians who left the greatest impression upon him were Gerhard von Rad, Karl Barth, and Edmund Schlink. The latter, with whom Pannenberg spent time as an assistant, brought home to him the ecumenical problems within Christianity, and, at the same time, convinced him of the necessity of interdisciplinary dialogue, in particular dialogue with the natural sciences.

He achieved his doctoral title in 1953 in Heidelberg; the topic of his dissertation was the dogma of predestination in the thought of Duns Scotus. The dissertation was published in the following year.[1] During his preparation of his as yet unpublished *Habilitationschrift* on the history of the term of analogy in the doctrine of the knowledge of God,[2] he undertook further research in the medieval Scholastics as well as intensive studies on various general topics of systematic theology.[3] The year 1955 brought his ordination as

---

1 Die Prädestinationslehre des Duns Skotus im Zusammenhand der scholastischen Lehrentqickung (= Forschungen zur Kirchen- und Dogmengeschichte Bd.4), 1954. Cf. in this context also: Der Einfluß der Anfechtungserfahrung auf den Preädestinationsbegriff Luthers, in: KuD 3 (1957), 109 – 139. Regarding his youth and time at university, cf. W. Pannenberg, An Autobiographical Sketch, in: C.E. Braaten/Ph.Clayton (ed.), The Theology of Wolfhart Pannenberg, Minneapolis 1099, 11 – 18.

2 Analogie und Offenbarung. Eine kritische Untersuchung der Geschichte des Anaologiebegriffs in der Gotteserkenntnis, 1955 – typewritten *Hablitationsschrift*. Cf. also Pannenberg's first publication: Zur Bedeutung des Analogiegedankens bei Karl Barth. Eine Auseinandersetzung mit Urs von Balthasar, in: ThLZ 78 (1953), 17 – 24. A significant result of Pannenberg's *Habiliationsschrift* is the demonstration that the epistemic strength of analogy, instead of the claimed middle position between univocal and equivocal speech, in fact depends on the sameness of the logos analogans. Among medieval theologians, at the latest Duns Scotus and William Ockham had made specific their recognition that analogy itself presupposes a univocal element. With this it was impossible to miss the fact that the spiritual access which should succeed in analogizing, i. e. the organization of the unknown within the schema of the already known, was inappropriate when used in reference to God (cf. in reference to this "Analogie und Doxologie", in: W. Joest und W. Pannenberg [Hg.], Dogma und Denkstrukturen [FS für E. Schlink], 1963, 96 – 115; reprinted in BQiTh 1, 212 – 238, esp. 222 ff.).

3 Cf. the great number of lexical articles on this topic which Pannenberg published during this period. Among others are: Art. Abendmahl, II. Dogmengeschichtlich –dogmatisch in: EKL, I, 6 – 11; Art. Analogie, in: EKL I, 113 f.; Art. Das Böse, in: EKL I, 559 – 561; Art. Johannes Duns Scotus, in EKL I, 980 – 982; Art. Gnade, III. Dogmengeschichtlich, IV. Dogmatisch, in EKL I, 1607 – 1614; Art. Gnadenmittel, in: EKL I, 1615 – 1617; Art. Analogie, in: RGG³ I, 350 – 353; Art. Christologie,

well as a lecturing position in systematic theology. In 1958 he accepted a call to the Kirchliche Hochschule Wuppertal, where he taught as Professor for Systematic Theology until 1961, where he changed to the Universität Mainz in the same function.

The relocation to Mainz was concurrent with the publication of the programmatic work "Revelation as History," with which a new conceptual design for theology was announced within German Protestantism. This new concept differentiated itself from both of the leading methods of Wort-Gottes-Theologie, drawing distinct borders from both the existential hermeneutics of the Bultmann school and the religion-critical concept of revelation of the Barthians. The a-historical subjectivity of faith, which, according to Pannenberg's judgment was the indicator of both of these interpretations of dialectical theology, was to be overcome through the rediscovery of universal history as the medium of God's revelation, and through the demonstration of an inherent rationality to faith which trumps all irrationalism and decisionism. Principally, a reconstruction of the history of Christianity was intended, whose origins should be passed on along with its present. As a leading category of interpretation, the history of Christianity was to serve as the thought of universal history which enclosed future events, and was thus eschatologically oriented. In this manner the contingence of each individual occurrence would be taken into account on the future whole. With this insight into the unfinished nature of the course of history, the history of Christianity was to be connected with the awareness of the preliminary nature of all history and all historical representation.

The orientation upon universal history present in the hermeneutic method attempted to avoid the dissolution of theology in a simple theory of faith-speech, and demanded instead the development of a theology based in religious history, a theology which examined the history of revelation with the scientific means of the historical-critical method. Christianity, with its eschatological message of the coming and in Jesus of Nazareth already initiated Kingdom of God, was understood in the context of the historical transmissions from Israel, particularly that of the Jewish apocalyptic literature. The assumption that the end of history and the future of the world had, through God, anticipatorily occurred in the resurrection of Jesus Christ as confirmation of his claim to power was considered a unique aspect

II: Dogmengeschichtlich, in: RGG³ I, 1762–1777; Art. Dialektische Theologie, in: RGG³ II, 168–174; Art. Erwählung, III. Dogmatisch, in RGG³ II, 614–621; Art. Gott, V. Theologiegeschichtlich, in RGG³ II, 1717–1732; Art. Ontologie, in EKL II, 1689–1691; Art. Maimonides, in EKL II, 1218; Art. Glaube, IV: Im prot. Glaubensverständnis, in: LThK² IV, 925–928; Art. Jesus Christus, II: die prot. Christologie, in: LThK² V, 961–964; Art. Person, in: RGG³ V, 230–235; Art. Prädestination, IV. Dogmatisch, in: RGG³ V, 487–489; Art. Natürliche Theologie, II: Im ev. Verständnis, in LThK² V, 816–817; Art. Thomas von Aquin, in: RGG³ VI, 856–863; Art. Schleiermacher, Friedrich Daniel Ernst, in: Encyclopaedia Britannica 14 Edition, Chicago-London-Toronto 1962 ff. Vol XX, 72–73; from 1967–1973 Vol. XIX, 1165–1166.

present only in Christianity. Pannenberg's theology represented an attempt to justify this assumption within the forum of a general awareness of truth. The rationality of faith, in particular in regard to the structure of the "openness to God" of humanity, was to be demonstrated anthropologically. At the same time, the claims of the Christian faith were understood as a hypothesis which posited a theory to make sense of everything; a theory whose final validity remained undecided, such that theology received a foundation within the framework of general philosophy of science and could present itself as rational theology.

The foundational concepts which were laid out in "Revelation as History" had already been anthropologically and christologically developed during the time Pannenberg was in Mainz, during which he also spend time as a visiting professor at the University of Chicago, Harvard, and the Claremont School of Theology. Noteworthy during this period are the works "Was ist der Mensch? Die Anthropologie der Gegenwart im Lichte der Theologie" from 1962,[4] "Grundzüge der Christologie" from 1964,[5] and the collected essays published under the title "Grundfragen systematischer Theologie" (volume I 1967; volume II 1980).[6] The continuation of these exists in Pannenberg's intensive research activity and significant literary production since 1968 at the newly-founded Evangelsich-Theologischen Fakultät in Munich, where he remained, despite multiple renowned calls to other universities and invitations to positions elsewhere, for 26 years, teaching until his emeritus status in 1994. Of the publications in the Munich years, "Wissenschaftstheorie und Theologie"[7] from 1973, "Anthropologie in theologischer Perspektive"[8] from 1983 and the essay collection "Ethik und Ekklesiologie" are of particular import. In addition to these were multiple studies and articles, of which (analogous to the monographs) many were published in English and/or translated into other languages. A bibliography of Pannenberg's works extends today to well more than 600 titles, and the amount of secondary literature is also legion.

The imposing number of students also bears witness to the success of Pannenberg's efforts. His teaching career has, over many years, opened the way into systematic theology to generations of students, and given the a theological foundation for their future service, be that as university professors, pastors, religious education teachers or even in other careers. In relation to this it is particularly worth mentioning that Pannenberg, in opposition to an individualistic narrowing of the Christian faith, always

---

4 In English as "What is Man? Contemporary Anthropology in Theological Perspective", Fortress 1970.

5 In English as "Jesus, God and Man", Westminster Press 1968.

6 In English as "Basic Questions in Theology. Collected Essays Volume 1", Fortress 1970 and "Basic Questions in Theology. Collected Essays Volume 2", Fortress 1971; these are pages 1–201 and 202–398 of Pannenbergs first 1967 volume.

7 In English as "Theology and the Philosophy of Science" Westminster Press 1976.

8 In English as "Anthropology in Theological Perspective" T&T Clark 1985.

emphasized the connection between faith and culture implicitly present in the message of Jesus about the coming kingdom of God, a connection which characterizes the history of Christianity even today in its form that is more or less exposed to the secular world. Overcoming the isolated privacy of piety, a state caused at least partially by the confessionalization of Christianity in the modern age, was for Pannenberg not least of value in his efforts towards the unity of the churches – a unity without which, according to Pannenberg, the unity of a society grounded in the foundation of Christian culture was not, in the long run, sustainable. In this sense, his thought represents not only a theology oriented on the common rational criteria of science, but rather equally a church doctrine marked by ecumenism.

The ecumenical nature of Pannenberg's thought and work comes to light particularly in the founding of the Ecumenical Institute in Munich, which he also led. Equally, his research in the so-called Jaeger-Stählin-Circle reaching back into the fifties, which he also co-led for many years as the Protestant counterpart, makes this apparent. This research was, among other things, during the time in which the study on the dogmatic rejections[9] was undertaken. His leading role in the Commission for Faith & Order in the World Council of Churches, where he served as delegate of the Evangelische Kirche in Deutschland from 1975 to 1990 is also indicative of this, as he was significantly involved in the development of the "Lima Text" as well as the study "Towards Sharing the One Faith." In addition to his ecumenical work, Pannenberg took worked with a great number of interdisciplinary institutions and took part in many such dialogues, with a focus on the intersection of philosophy and theology. One to be mentioned here is the research circle "Poetik und Hermeneutik."

There was no absence of honors for Pannenberg: He is a founding member of the Academie Internationale des Sciences Religieuses. In 1977 he was voted a regular member of the Bavarian Academy of the Sciences, in their philosophical-historical division. In 1993, he was subscribed as a corresponding member to the British Acadamy. He received honorary doctorates from the University of Glasgow (1972), the University of Manchester (1977), Trinity College Dublin (1979), The University of St. Andrews (1993) and the University of Cambridge (1997), as well as from the University Comillas in Madrid (1999). In 1987 he received the Order of Merit of the Federal Republic of Germany, first-class, in 1993 the Bavarian Order of Merit, and in 1995 the Bavarian *Maximiliansorden*. His greatest honor, however, was given by himself, in crowning his life's work with the completion of his three-volume Systematic Theology. The first volume was published in 1988 by Vandenhoeck

---

9 Lehrverurteilungen – kirchentrennend? I. Rechtfertigung, Sakramente und Amt im Zeitalter der Reformation und heute, hg. von Kerl Lehmann und Wolfhart Pannenberg (= Dialog der Kirchen Bd. 4), 1986. Können die gegenseitigen Verwerfungen zqischen den Reformationskirchen und Rom aufgehoben werden? In: Lehrverurteilungen.

& Ruprecht, with volume 2 to follow in 1991 and volume 3 in 1993. This opus magnum was expanded by a study on the relation of philosophy and theology in the light of their common history[10] in 1996, a history of theological problems in Germany from Schleiermacher through Barth and Tillich[11] in 1997, and through three volumes of collected articles in contribution to systematic theology which appeared in 1999 and 2000.[12] Additionally, a series of sermons has been published.

What follows is an introductory examination of the three-volume Systematic Theology, presented with the goal of demonstrating the structure of Pannenberg's thought by focusing on the systematic baselines of the arguments. This is emphatically for the purpose of assisting the reader as one engages with Pannenberg's original works. The significant monographs on Christology, Philosophy of Science, and Anthropology (including "What is Man?") as well as the considerations present in "Metaphysics and the Idea of God" will be taken into account at the appropriate locations in the structure of the Systematics. The collected essays and shorter studies, due to their volume, will only be able to be considered in places of direct bearing and in footnotes. As an introduction to the whole, we turn now to a brief characterization of the two terms which make up the title of the 1961's "Revelation as History",[13] as a conceptual understanding of these two terms provides a preliminary understanding of the design of the whole Systematics.

Revelation and History

The philosophy of German Idealsim, and in particular Hegel, is decisive for the significant role which the thought of revelation has played in the modern age, for it is "…the present consensus that revelation is, in essence, the self-revelation of God" (RaH, 4). Revelation does not refer to the manifestation or communication of supernatural truths, rather, the completion of God's disclosure of Himself in His being. As God's being is, however, one, in the strict understanding of self-revelation questions of the unity and uniqueness are already decided. Along with this thought, the idea of a direct and incommunicable self-disclosure of the sole God in the unity of His being is to be rejected as biblically unjustified. Neither through His name, nor His Word, nor even through Law and Gospel is God directly revealed (cf. RaH

---

10 Studien zum Verhältnis der Theologie und Philosophie im Lichter ihrer gemeinsamen Geschichte. See Chapter 8.1 of this work.

11 Problemgeschichte der neueren evangelischen Theologie in Deutschland. Von Schleiermacher bis zu Barth und Tillich. See chapter 8.2 of this work.

12 Beiträge zur Systematischen Theologie (I. Philosophie, Religion, Offenbarung; II. Natur und Mench – und die Zukunft der Schöpfung; III. Kirche und Ökumene).

13 English 1969.

8 ff.). His self-disclosure is instead completed in an indirect manner, through God's action in history. Corresponding to this is the first of seven theses offered on the doctrine of revelation: "The Self-Revelation of God in the Biblical Witness is not of a Direct Type in the Sense of a Theophany, but is Indirect and Brought About by Means of the Historical Acts of God" (RaH 125, section title). These "dogmatic theses" are proposed as the result of the exegetical studies from Rolf Rendtorff ("The Concept of Revelation in Ancient Israel", RaH 23 – 53) and Ulrich Wilckens (The Understanding of Revelation in Primitve Christianity", RaH 55 – 121), included in the volume.

Among the types of history through which God is indirectly revealed, one is only to think of individual events under specific conditions. For, one wishes "…to understand the indirect self-communication that resides in every individual act of God as revelation, then there are as many revelations as there are divine acts and occurrences in nature and history. But this destroys the strict sense of revelation as self-revelation of God. Only then is it possible to understand the totality of God's action – and if God is one then that means everything that happens – as his revelation." (RaH 16)[14] In this manner of thinking, two possibilities of understanding are available: one might, in the manner of the classical philosophy of the ancient Greeks, understand the entirety of reality in its cosmic planning as the as the indirect revelation; one might otherwise understand the whole of reality in its temporally extended context of universal history as the indirect revelation of the true God. The latter path is that which was taken by German Idealism, the path taken by such as Lessing, Herder, and Hegel, who "gave a systematic formulation to the conception of universal history as an indirect revelation of God in connection with his explication of the concept of self-revelation" (RaH 16 – 17).

Pannenberg examines the theological problems of God's indirect self-revelation in history in two particular points, the first of which has already been intimated: 1. When it is the case, that history is the self-revelation of God only in its context of universality, and thereby in its entirety, how can a particular event, such as the history of Jesus Christ, have the character of revelation in the strict sense? 2. If the reality of God, which determines all other reality, reveals itself first in the entirety of world history, is the incompleteness of world history a fact which necessary excludes the absolute meaning of Jesus Christ and the completed salvation in his name? Would the openness of all occurrences to the future reduce the history of Jesus Christ and its effects to the status of merely preliminary? The answer to these two tightly interwoven questions is the central thesis of "Revelation as History", according to which,

---

14 the final sentence quoted from Pannenberg is perhaps better understood when rendered "It can thus only be valid, that one understand the totality of God's action – and when one is dealing with the One God, then that means everything that happens – as His revelation" (*Es kann also nur gelten, das Ganze des Gotteshandelns – und das heißt, wenn es um den einen Gott geht, das Ganze alles Geschehens – as Offenbarung Gottes zu verstehen*). – Trans.

in the fate of Jesus Christ "the end of all events is anticipated" (RaH 139, section title). As a proleptic anticipation of the eschaton, the history of Jesus Christ is the universal revelation of the Godhood of God.[15]

In grounding and explicating this central thesis, Pannenberg interweaves historical and systematic arguments in a manner characteristic for his entire project. The systematic assumption implied in the thought that God's self-demonstration is indirect, namely, that revelation occurs at the end of the history which is revelation rather than at its beginning (thesis two), is not only confirmed through reference to the eschatological character of the sending of Jesus Christ, but is also historically derived from it. In the same manner, the eschatological character of the sending of Jesus Christ proves itself to be so far in continuity with the Judaic-Old Testament history of tradition, as the primacy of eschatology is not to it foreign. The contrary is, in fact, the case, as Pannenberg makes clear in the foreword to the fifth edition of RaH[16] over against the retractions made by Rendtorff: the scope of the entire Old Testament is an eschatological one. From this both the meaning and the content of the fifth thesis are made clear. It is within this thesis that the meaning of the apocalyptic nature of the tradition is recognized. This thesis claims that the revelatory sense of the history of Jesus is first understandable from the perspective of the traditions of Israel: "The Christ event does not reveal the deity of the God of Israel as an isolated event, but rather insofar as it is a part of the history of God with Israel" (RaH 145, chapter title, Thesis 5).

If then the single, and in its unity unique, self-revelation of God does not refer "*exclusively* to the figure of Jesus Christ"[17], it is at the same time the concrete history of Jesus Christ in its own particularity which is the anticipatory occurrence of the whole of history and which brings history to unity. Within this, the history of the people of Israel within the consequence of the determination put upon them is transferred into the human history of the

---

15 The foundational importance of eschatology for the idea of history was handled two years prior to the appearance of "Revelation as History" in the article "Heilsgeschehen und Geschichte", (*Kerygma und Dogma* 5, 1959, pgs. 218 – 237 and 239 – 288) published as "Redemptive Event and History" in BQiTh pgs. 15 – 80. It begins with the foundational sentence: "History is the most comprehensive horizon of Christian theology." (BQiTh 15). The majority of the motifs which make up Pannenberg's conception of theology can already be found in this article. In one important aspect, however, Pannenberg quickly changed his view: the thesis that history is the occurrence in tension between promise and fulfillment. In the place of the simple corres-pondence of promise and fulfillment, Pannenberg developed a perspective on the history of tradition in the study "Kerygma und Geschichte" (in: Studien zur Theologie der alttesta-mentlichen Überlieferungen, ed.R. Redtorff and K. Koch (Festschrift for Gerhard von Rad), 1961, 129 – 140), published as "Kerygma and History" in BQiTh, 81 – 95. This perspective views the promises handed down as to be newly interpreted in the light of each new historical experience. The maxim which drives this is that "the history of the transmission of traditi-on…has to be seen as a deeper concept of history generally." (BQiTh 93)

16 Unfortunately, the English translation is based on the third edition, and thus one must be referred to VIII ff. of the German fifth edition for the foundation of this claim. – Trans.

17 XI of the German fifth edition of RaH.

world. The own particularity of the history of Jesus Christ, in its turn, is brought into the light of Easter, and appears in light of his resurrection from the dead. In this, the eschatological sending is confirmed, and the eschaton is anticipated. Indeed, the universality and finality of the eschatological self-disclosure of God in the resurrection of Jesus Christ from the dead could be expressed in gentile Christendom through ideas of revelation which were influenced by Gnostic or other Jewish-external sources (cf. thesis 6); the advantage lies with the Jewish-apocalyptic horizon of interpretation and understanding not merely for historical, but also for systematic reasons. This is the case not least because the execution of the proleptic anticipation which is revealed as completed in the history of Jesus Christ allows the sense-structure which permeates all events to be recognized. All historical conceptual grasping is executed as anticipatory understanding, as "all knowledge takes place in view of the anticipation of its results and receives its impulse from this, although the anticipated results that are to establish faith seem to have an undercurrent of an extremely self-critical testing" (RaH 157, note 15 to pg. 139).

It is in this context that one must understand the thesis that the historical revelation of God is, due to its universal character, "open to anyone who has eyes to see it" (RaH 135, section title, Thesis 3). The events of the historical self-revelation of God are not of themselves hidden and require no additional to content or event in Word-revelation, rather they are laid out in their nature to be recognized. "When these are taken seriously for what they are and in the historical context to which they belong, theny they speak their own language, the language of facts. God has proved his deity in this language of facts. Naturally, these experiences are not to be treated as naked facts, but are to be seen in a way different from what would naturally emerge. That these and also other events are veiled from many men, indeed, from most men, does not mean that this truth is too high for them, so that their reason must be supplemented by other means of knowing. Rather, it means that they must use their reason in order to see correctly. If the problem is not thought of in this way, then the Christian truth is made into a truth for the in-group, and the church becomes a gnostic community." (RaH 137)[18]

In an afterword to the second edition of "Revelation as History", Pannenberg defends these implementations, as well as the thesis that the foundation of faith must lie in the knowledge of God's revelation within the history which proves His Godhood. The thought of "anticipation of the end" is there explicitly referred to as the "salient point" of the newly conceived term for revelation. Additionally, Pannenberg also makes valid his point that "the

---

18 The final sentence is *very* freely translated in the English edition of RaH, as Pannenberg does not make any reference to gnostic community, but rather says that "…one would make the Christian truth into a matter for the conventicle." (…*dann würde man die christliche Wahrheit zu einer Konventikelangelegenheit machen*. Offenbarung und Geschichte, 100). – Trans.

proleptic structure of the existent as such and particularly of intellectual acts [is to] become intelligible in the light of the prolepsis of the Christ event" (RaH 194), as well as the reverse. A future theology of reason has this challenge to prove. It would, in the understanding of Pannenberg, "describe reason, not as *a priori* capacity, but in its historical structure of sketching and reflecting, but thus also in its essential (not however always factual) openness to a truth always presupposed but never grasped in the act of thinking out the sketch" (RaH 192). In the three volumes of the Systematic Theology, Pannenberg integrates the concept of a theology of reason, and carries it out as well, though one must presuppose the results of the monograph "Theology and Philosophy of Science." This monograph may not, also, be ignored when the system of the Systematic Theology should be understood, and moreover, when one wishes to understand the content of the first chapters, when Panneberg speaks of the truth of Christian dogma as the theme of systematic theology.

§1 The Thematic Content and Scientific Character of Systematic Theology (ST I, Chapter 1)

1. The Truth of Christian Doctrine as the Theme of Systematic Theology

The title of Pannenberg's systematic theology is to be "taken quite literally" (ST I, x) and has no desire to avoid the incriminating term "dogmatics": "We shall be expressing the subject matter of dogmatics in all its variety as the unfolding of the Christian idea of God" (*ibid.*) Not one bit less conceptually important is the program which is demonstrated already in the title, the resolution to develop a portrayal of the dogmatic topics in constant awareness of their historical contexts. In this methodology, it is also the case that the methodology itself is determined by its object, and not to be abstracted from its specific features. This characteristic interaction of historical and systematic work, which is indicative for Pannenberg's entire systematic conception, is an expression of the conviction that the systematic results only make sense in connection with the historical process of their establishment. Dogmatics can only be done properly in the differentiated unity of systematic terminology and historical analysis – this leaves behind the abstract ideas of an ahistorical reason and a relativizing historicism. Two aspects in the Foreword make this foundational assumption apparent: 1. Systematic theology is directed at the rationality of faith; nonetheless, the task of philosophical theology is, in Pannenberg's judgment, "to fix its intellectual point of departure in the historical revelation of God." (ST I, xii) 2. Pannenberg nowhere denies the confessional background of his theological design, nor its geographic background in Europe; this notwithstanding, it is for Pannenberg a matter of "simply the truth of Christian doctrine and the Christian confession."[1] (ST I, xiii)

The exposition of this decision to present the content of dogmatics as the unfolding of the Christian idea of God begins with an examination of the term

---

1 This method is grounded as necessary both historically and systematically: "As a reform movement …the Reformation sought not to ground its own separated form of Christendom, but to bring the central core and foundation of Christian faith to its place of honor in all of Christianity, to free it from distortions in theology as well as in the life of the church. This means: to ask after the particular principles of Protestantism, in contrast to the nature of Christian faith in general, is quite simply un-Protestant, so long as the idea of Protestantism finds its measure in the Reformation." (Das protestantische Prinzip im ökumenischen Dialog, in LM 30 [1991], 125–129, reprinjted in BSTh 3, 186–193, here 188)

"theology". Despite its historical ambiguity, one should note the fact that the traditional Christian and pre-Christian term "theology" refers not only to human epistemological effort, but also always and primarily to the message about God which is revealed and communicated by divinity itself: "...the knowledge of God that is made possible by God, and therefore by revelation, is one of the basic conditions of the concept of theology as such. Otherwise the possibility of the knowledge of God is logically inconceivable; it would contradict the very idea of God." (ST I, 2) If it is the case that theology, due to the dependence of human knowledge of God on divine revelation, constituted by God as its central and comprehensive object, then the differentiated fullness of the Christian traditions can only be unitarily and theologically perceived when God is recognized as both the organizational middle and the central point of reference. This insight cannot be relinquished in the face of the independence of the different theological disciplines. Theology is, in its being, never a discipline simply of cultural studies; the truth of theology is measured only against the question, what right does theology have to speak about God?

In dogmatics as a theological discipline, the truth of Christian speech about God becomes an explicit topic, as dogmatics is the science of dogma.[2] "The Greek word *dogma* can denote both a subjective opion as distinct from certain knowledge and also a legally binding opinion or 'judgment'" (ST I, 9) The truth claim of dogma or dogmas is, according to Pannenberg, is given warrant neither through legal (that is, through judicially authoritarian determination and the obligation to believe) nor though the bare fact of an existing consensus in the church. Rather, warrant is given to its truth claim alone through its subject matter. The subject matter of dogma is developed only through the process of testing, a matter which is not able to be finalized under earthly conditions. "The exposition and testing of dogma in this sense constitutes the task of dogmatics. Dogmatics inquires into the truth of Dogma. It asks whether the church's dogmas express God's revelation and are therefore God's own dogmas. It pursues this inquiry by expounding dogma." (ST I, 16–17) The task of dogmatics is, then, to "not only unfold the content of church teaching but also attend to the question of the truth of dogma." (ST I, 17)

Dogmatics undertakes this task in the carrying out of *systematic theology*. The system of systematic theology consists primarily in "systematic

2 The doxological and proleptic structure element of dogmatic statements is discussed in the article "Was ist eine dogmatische Aussage?" in: KuD 8 (1962) 81–99, in English as "What is a Dogmatic Statement?" BQiTh 1, 182–210. Cf. also "Analogie und Doxologie", in: w. Joest und W. Pannenberg (eds.), Dogma und Denkstrukturen (Festschrift for E. Schlink), in english as "Analogy and Doxology" BQiTH 1, 211–238. For the ecumenical aspect of the dogmatic task, cf. "Dogmatische Theologie in ökumenischer Perspektive" in: E. Schockenhoff und P. Walter (eds.), Dogma und glaube. Bausteine für eine theologische Erkenntnislehre (Festschrift for Walter Kasper), 1993, 152–164. A quote from pg. 152 is translated here: "Catholicity is a characteristic trait of Christian theology and the Church in general, not a particularity of the specific Roman Catholic tradition and Church.

presentation itself as a connection is shown between the various Christian doctrinal statements and also between these statements and whatever else is regarded as true. Hence the systematic presentation of the content of Christian doctrine is already related as such to its truth claim. It tests the truth of what is presented. If truth can only be one, the things that are regarded as true will not contradict one another, and they can be united with one another." (ST I, 19) Coherence is then the necessarily implied condition of each claim to truth. Foundational for the system of a dogmatics whose representation of doctrine is constituted by the systematic demands of such a question regarding truth, indeed, a question which is posed by its very content, is the "recognition of the basic principles of identity and contradiction" (ST I, 21), without which no argumentation is possible, even in theology. "These principles have always been especially presupposed in efforts to present the systematic unity of Christian doctrine. The scientific nature of theological work rests on their thorough application[.]" (*Ibid.*) Although the coherence of the presentation of doctrine according to this principle, in which contradiction is avoided, is indispensable, the systemtatic reconstruction of Christain doctrine cannot definitively decide the question of its truth. Consensus of judgment and coherence of interpretation do not guarantee correspondence to the way things are, that is to say, to that comprehensive correlation of the interpretation with the facts of the matter which is essential for such an accord. This fact is due at least partially to the priority of the object of theology, which is only graspable in an anticipatory manner. This does not, however, change the fact that "*presupposed* truth can be grasped only in the medium of knowing it *as* truth." (ST I, 24)

If, then, the truth of the topics of Christian doctrine can only be regarded in the execution of perception and coherence-discursive treatment, dogmatics must "renounce the claim to a prior guarantee of its truth" (ST I, 48). The meaning of this for the so-called prolegomena to dogmatics is developed by Pannenberg in wide-ranging historical excursuses, with particular attention to the theme of scripture, the term "religion", and the consciousness of faith. It is in this latter that the foundations of Pannenberg's theo-historical conception comes to light. The continuous point of the development is, to repeat, the consistent criticism of the attempt to establish "the truth of Christian doctrine…in advance of all discussion of its content" (ST I, 47). This criticism is based not only on the previously mentioned priority of the content to the act of perception, but equally on the connected interminability of the process of experience. Both aspects, as one can easily see, belong together. Insofar it is valid that "[i]n fact we can validate and appropriate as true only that which our experience confirms." (ST I, 47) However, individual experience never conveys "absolute, unconditional certainty. At best it can offer no more than a certainty which needs clarification and confirmation in an ongoing process of experience. This subjective certainty does indeed expereice the presence of truth and its unconditionality, but only in an ongoing process. The conditionality of all subjective certainty is part of the finitude of human experience." (*Ibid.*)

If it is then the case that the truth of Christian doctrine cannot be verified in the manner of prior assertion and decisiveness (as its creditability depends on its own content), the question of truth can only be appropriately posed and answered in the context of the dogmatic portrayal itself. This requires that the world-enclosing universal coherence, which is demanded by the truth-claims of Christian doctrine, to be aware of the disputability of God in the world and to find its grounding in God himself, rather than to fossilize in the prejudices of faith. "Christians especially should have such confidence in the truth of their faith that they can let its divine truth shine forth from the content without any need for preceding guarantees." (ST I, 52) The term *hypothesis* holds a leading function in Pannenberg's argumentation, along with the ideas of proleptic anticipation, the doxological, and the relation between relative/absolute (Cf. ST I, 54 f.), finite/infinite, part/whole (Cf. ST I, 54) – these ideas are inextricably connected with one another. In order to understand this correctly, one must go beyond the corresponding sections of the *Systematic Theology* (in particular ST I, 49 – 61), which are to be recommended for close reading; one must also take into consideration Pannenberg's understanding of theology on his philosophy of science.

2. Philosophy of Science

The method which Pannenberg judges to be required by the content of dogmatics comes characteristically forth in Pannenberg's manner of argumentation. This method is none other than an advancing sublation of preliminary abstractions through the development of a thought. This method likewise marks the discussion in the first half of his work "Theology and the Philosophy of Science", which appeared in 1973.[3] This work aims at both a

---

3 "Wissenschaftstheorie und Theologie" Frankfurt am Main 1973. In English as "Theology and Philosophy of Science", 1976 Darton, Longmann & Todd Ltd. Published by The Westminster Press, Philadelphia, Pennsylvaina (ThPS). For the internal relevance of this work for Pannenberg's overall concept, cf. among others the foreword of "Glaube und Wirklichkeit. Kleine Beiträge zum christlichen Denken" (München 1975), where the author underscores the initial opinion, "that the Jewish and Christian faiths have grown out of historical experience and the consideration of the meaning of that experience, an experience whose present conception and testing initially demands perusal on account of its content, and one which is insofar a matter of historical knowledge and insight into its consequence" (8 f.) Pannenberg continutes: "I judge, however, differently today regarding the degree of theoretical certainty which is achievable through such excercises than many of my former formulations might suggest. In the intervening time, the insight is increasingly important (although it was indeed present in less than its full consequence before) that the provisionality of our knowledge of the revelation of God in history, and the plurality which that provisionality brings with it, are themselves a part of the content-

critical and constructive treatment of the current discussion in philosophy of science, intending a "new conception of a scientific discipline" (ThPS, 4) and thus a "new self-understanding of science in general" (ThPS, 4). The current *discussion in the philosophy of science* has been spurred on by the "models...proposed by analytical philosophy (logical positivism and critical rationalism).[4] These models rely on a [*sic.*] unitary concept of science which contrasts with the approach of the 'moral' or 'human' sciences (*Geist-eswissenschaften*), which have built methodological foundations of their own on hermeneutic and on a distinction between the methods of historical and natural science. The two concepts of science conflict most strongly in the social sciences, which may explain[5] why in recent decades it has been representatives of the social sciences who have been particularly active in seeking a solution to the problems of philosophy of science. The analytical theories take their model from the natural sciences, but hermeneutic and dialectical social science, on the other hand, are based on a distinction between the natural or physical sciences and what they call the 'human' sciences, the sciences of culture and society, for which they claim methodo-logical autonomy. For this reason the problems raised by the distinction between 'natural' and 'human' sciences are treated in[6] this book immediately after analytical theories of science. This forms a transition to the consideration of the hermeneutical and dialectical accounts of the human or social sciences, and of attempts to analyse them in terms of systems theory." (ThPS 21)

This is an excellent description of the first division of "Theology and the Philosophy of Science". Without going into detail regarding the content of the volume, one should note that that which was made clear at the beginning has been emphasized: Pannenberg's argumentation regarding the philosophy of science, as it develops in the demonstration and examination of the various positions, occurs through an advancing sublation of abstractions which were unavoidable at the beginning. It is in this sense that Pannenberg begins with Positivism. On one hand, such a beginning merely not only convenient; there is no alternative, as the epochal importance of Positivism is a simple fact. The positivist model of science, based on the natural sciences and with a term "science" whose claim to validity is made regardless of the subject treated, has

---

structure of revelation" (9; the articles published in this collection are from the years 1960–1974 and are connected thematically under the topic of the connection between the question after God and one's understanding of reality).

4 These three are listed separately in the German addition, and should not be read as if the latter two are exhaustivley descriptive of the former for Pannenberg. – Trans.

5 The German version cited in the original words it as "there is no coincidence that..." (*Es ist kein Zufall, dass...*). – Trans.

6 The German version contains no reference to the work iteslf, and should be understood as demonstrating a self-evident move from the treatment of analytical philosophy of science to this distiction. – Trans.

factually prevailed. The repristination[7] of traditional philosophies of science, such as those of transcendental-philosophical provenience, simply cannot take this fact off the table. On the other hand, the discussion cannot end where it began, with Positivism's "monopolisation of the concept of science as such by methods simply generalised from the procedures of the natural sciences." (ThPS 27) In this process, one can only rationally oppose a positivist claim on the concept of science "only if it is essentially connected with internal difficulties which, when followed up, force us to go outside the original concept of science." (ThPS 27) The discussion regarding Logical Positivism (as the continuation of older forms of Empiricism and Positivism) is based on the demonstration that this is, in fact, the case. The point at which Logical Positivism is forced to go outside its own concepts and which leads to a critical Rationalism is the following: the justified doubt of the clarity of facts in their independence from an observer. Furthermore, scale at which knowledge can be said to be controlled by the mere presence of facts as such drives one out of the merely empirical realm.

This process, in which the demonstration of internal aporias drives a position on the philosophy of science outside its own limits, is not exhausted in the transition from Positivism to Critical Rationalism (cf. ThPS 29 – 71). This method shows its strength also in the context of a critical reconstruction of the process of the emancipation of the human sciences from the natural sciences (cf. ThPS 72 – 155). This process leads to an understanding of hermeneutics as a method of understanding sense – a method which is continually followed in the process of reaching this goal, and within which a proper term for theology as a science is brought to light. Foundation for this hermeneutic methodology of understanding sense is the insight that each individual referent only has specific meaning within the context of a sense-totality, a "whole"[8], to which

---

7 Restoration to an original condition. – Trans.
8 Pannenberg's understanding of categories and in particular his understanding of the category of the whole are developed in relation to Hegel in the text reprinted in English as "Theology and the Categories 'Part' and 'Whole'" in MIG 130–152. The following insight is fundamental for the whole of the argument: "But neither can the whole be absolute, as therefore it cannot be God, at least not if it, as the whole of its parts, not only itself constitutes the being-as-part of its parts, but conversely is also dependent on the parts whose whole it is this means that the whole cannot be conceptualized as self-constitutive. As the whole of its parts, it is a unified unity that presupposes some ground of itself as *unifying unity*. As the unifying unity of the world, God is distinct from the totality of the finite, though not again absolutely distinct. If God were merely distinct in relation to the totality of the finite, then he himself would be finite and would consequently have to be conceived as a part of that totality o the finite that we think of as world. As the unifying unity of the totality of the finite, God is indeed necessarily distinct from it. Yet at the same time, he is just as necessarily immanent to the world of the finite (given that its existence is already pre-supposed) as the continuing condition of this unity. He is this condition either as the ground of this unity, which then independently continues to exist, or as the force which continuously effects the unity o the parts and thereby remains immanent to the world of the finite and present to its parts." (143) In distinction from Hegel, Pannenberg insists on the anticipatory character of the knowledge of the whole in the world, which is itself not yet completed and has its eschatological

every attempt to represent the conditions for the possibility of understanding must move. This is valid also for the methodically regulated and systematic scientific understanding – indeed, not merely the human sciences, but also the natural sciences, a distinction which Pannenberg emphatically refuses to make into a division. The dualism between human and natural sciences and the reification of their methodological opposites as "explaining" and "understanding" are untenable, as even the "explaining" of the natural sciences takes place in the classification of the individual within the meaning of the whole. The topic of the study of meaning, then, is not the realm of the human sciences, whose particularity is that they "can only be described in themes of their special form of perception of [the] common object. This special form is a concentration on the historical character of the formation of meaning, which is intimately connected with its mediation by individual perception of meaning." (ThPS 134 – 135) In this manner, the human sciences' understanding of meaning shares an anticipatory-hypothetical character of its statements with the theory-development of the natural sciences. This has to be taking into account for philosophical and theological sentences as well, insofar as these wish to raise a claim to be considered as scientific.

Without attempting to work out an encyclopedia of the individual sciences, Pannenberg's philosophy of sciences gives us some indications of the differentiated internal constitution of the sciences. Within this, the narrow sense of science is differentiated from a wider sense. The narrow sense is that science whose statements are restricted to a specific, formalized realm, including that restriction of empirically provable data, and which is constituted by its interaction with that realm of objects. The wider sense of science, however, is marked by the specific characteristic of unrestricted reflection (cf. ThPS 221 – 222). Taken together, their aim is "producing systematic interpretations in the form of models of meaning which are intended to be free form internal contradiction and contain no more than what can be shown to be logically necessary for the explanation of networks of phenomena." (ThPS 221) This commonality makes the unitary term, and makes up the scientific nature of the sciences – for it is in this that they differ from myths and mythologies. These latter deliver also a complete and explicit explanation of meaning, but unlike the sciences they do not subsume their assertions to the criteria of rationality or systematic logic. At this point, one should note that these general criteria of science are also valid for theology, insofar as theology is to be understood as a science. Pannenberg accepts

future before it. Dilthey is given particular importance for the mediation of this insight, "because his analyses of the structure of meaning in human experience in regard to the meaning of individual moments in the context of the whole, and in particular a whole which is in the process of its history and not yet completed for those experiencing it, reach particularly deep and are foundational for the modern situation in discussion." (Sinnerfahrung, Religion, und Gottesfrage, in: ThPh 59 (1984), 178 – 190; reprinted in BSTh 1, 101 – 113, here: 109) explicity, in contrast to Karl Barth, the minimal conditions set out by Heinrich Scholz in 1931, in "Wie ist eine evangelische Theologie als Wissenschaft Möglich?"[9] The postulates of propositions, coherence, and control are, along with the postulates of independence and concord (cf. ThPS 270 f.), to be fulfilled by a scientific theology. This is even more so, as these postulates are simply "the explicit formulation of the implications of statements." (ThPS 326) To relinquish the use of these would be for theology to relinquish its relevance entirely.

In all sciences, the systematic presentation of context meanings has the function of locating individual facts consistently within the theoretic whole. This theoretic consistency is the criterion for being a science. It is the characteristic nature of *philosophy* to transcend the formal borders and the content of the sciences, beginning a process of unrestricted reflection. This nature is also shared with theology. The limits set, on one hand by mathematics and logic and on the other hand by the sciences themselves in the constitution of their characteristic nature upon their content, are transcended through this reflection, an unlimited reflection within which direct sense-experience causes further reflection. The process cannot end prior to the conception of the comprehensive meaning of experience in its totality. As a consequence of this, philosophy and its results are themselves necessarily objects of philosophical reflection, a reflection which proves itself to be as incompletable as it is unlimited. In the individual sciences, as sciences in the narrow sense, continual reflection is pragmatically limited and the totality of meaning is systematically blended out for the sake of the investigation of the particular object which makes the science a singular science. For philosophy, and in the same manner for theology, the infinitude of reflection and the anticipation of the whole are characteristic. Nothing is excluded, but is rather to be absolutely enclosed into the terminology.

Philosophy is the theory of the absolute, and theology is the science of God. In order to take these as their respective objects without doing either an injustice, and indeed, in the very confirmation of these as their objects, they must know themselves as differentiated from their respective object and not set their idea – be it even the idea of ideas – equal to that object. This would be in both cases a "false dogmatism." (ThPS 223) This false dogmatism can only be avoided when the following is true: Philosophical analysis of meaning can operate only by systematically describing the totality of meaning which guides its reflection, although a systematic account of this sort is itself no more than an anticipation of the implicit and only partly defined totality of meaning of all experience, to which it is related and in which it possesses its truth. It can demonstrate its truth only by its ability to integrate, and so illuminate, actual experiences of meaning. It may be assumed in advance that the situation of theology will prove to be similar. Theology also deals with the totality of

9 How can Protestant theology be a science? – Trans.

meaning of experience and us be aware of this if it is to know what it is saying when it talks about God." (ThPS 224)

3. Theology as the Science of God

The scientific self-understanding of theology is the topic of the second half of "Theology and the Philosophy of Science". This self-understanding must, like every other science, "must always have two aspects. On the one hand it seeks to establish and external relation to other disciplines on the common basis of their scientific character. On the other, it must consider its own internal organisation." (ThPS 5) In this particular case, the latter is a matter of the internal divisions of theology. In order to treat the *self-understanding of theology as a scientific discipline* in the differentiated unity of its subdisciplines, Pannenberg outlines the most important forms it has taken throughout history since the introduction of the claim of a scientific character. (cf. ThPS 7 – 14) The conception of theology as a derived science (cf. ThPS 228 – 231) and as a scientia practica (cf. ThPS 231 – 241) in the manner of the medieval scholastics and protestant orthodoxy is presented. Following this, Pannenberg offers an in-depth examination of the modern concept of theology as a positive science, in which he gives particular attention to Schleiermacher's 1811 encyclopedic outline.

Schleiermacher had grounded the unity of theology through the common orientation of the subdisciplines upon the necessities of church government. However, one can find points in Schleiermacher's thought with which one can ground the connectedness of the theological disciplines "not merely from the need for training clergy but also from the essence of Christianity" (ThPS 254). Pannenberg builds upon this in his initial description of theology as the science of Christianity. A science of the Christian religion, however, cannot operate in a manner that presupposes the truth of Christianity positively, in the sense of a direct axiom. "The truth of the Christian tradition can function only as a hypothesis in any theology which proceeds scientifically." (ThPS 261) Beyond this, the Christian tradition cannot be restricted to the positive nature of Christianity as an historical entity, as the tradition of the Old Testament proves. Alone this is reason enough to go beyond a definition of theology as the positive science of Christendom. Additionally, the truth claims of Christianity themselves force the transcendence of such a definition of theology, in order that the truth which is claimed might stand the test in the competition of religions and worldviews. This endurance can, in turn, only prove itself true when the question of absolute truth as the truth of God is posed. "This is so because Christianity claims to be not just Christianity but Gods revelation, or at least to be based on God's revelation. If this appeal to revelation is treated not just as a presupposition but as a theme of theological reflection, then theology must go beyond Christianity in its description and interpretation of Christianity. It must go beyond Christianity as a religion among and beside other non-religious areas of culture and also beyond Christianity as a revealed religion in contrast to natural human life." (ThPS, 264) Brought to a point, the science of Christianity can only be theology when it goes beyond the simply positive definition and understands itself as the science of the truth of God, and not merely the science of positive Christian religion. "This is how theology in fact saw itself in the periods of its classical development at the time of the early church and in the middle ages. It was teaching about God and the things that happened through his divine ordinance (*oikonomia*). A 'science of Christianity' must also be concerned with this." (ThPS, 265) The term theology and its history prove in themselves, that God must be considered the actual object of such a science.

"Karl Barth with his own peculiar determination has impressed a whole generation with the idea that theology is about God and his revelation and not primarily the science of the Christian religion." (*Ibid.*) However, Pannenberg doubts that Barth succeeded in understanding the dogmatic effort regarding God and his revelation as something other than subjective assumption. Barth presupposed the incommunicable givennness of the positive revelation – and in doing so, did not give a true alternative to theological subjectivism, but rather demonstrated its "furthest extreme" (ThPS, 273): "Whereas other attempts to give theology a foundation in human terms sought support from common arguments, Barth's apparently so lofty objectivity about God and God's word turns out to rest on no more than the irrational subjectivity of a venture of faith with no justification outside itself" (*Ibid.*)[10] The outcome of Barth's controversy with Heinrich Scholz regarding the criteria of the scientific nature of theology is for Pannenberg a confirmation of the appropriateness of this assumption as well as the fact that "a view of theology based on the positive nature of revelation is untenable." (ThPS, 275–276)

Pannenberg sees in Barth's revelation-positivism a subjectivism which manages to do without its own grounding. In order to avoid such a subjectivity, Pannenberg must understand the topic of God as located in the context of the subjectivity of the theologian, within the context of the tradition in which that theologian works, rather than direct and incommunicable. This is the reason which "with the passing of dialectical theology the hermeneutical problem has become the centre of theological discussion." (ThPS, 277) In order to solve this, it must be shown "whether the primacy of God and his revelation over all that is human and relative, which Barth restored as the theme of theology, can, through reflection on its self-mediation in the process of the Christian tradition, be stated in such a manner that, although of course it still requires faith, it does not require the positivity of basing theology on an

---

10 Perhaps better would be "to give theology an anthropological foundation"; *anthropologischer Begründung der Theologie* (Wissenscahftstheorie und Theolgie, 274). – Trans.

arbitrary venture of faith on the part of the theologian." (ThPS, 277) A decisive aspect of the connection between hermeneutic topics and the idea of God proves itself not only in the totality of the process of understanding, but also in the totality of meaning which is implied as a historical whole within each interpretation of experience. In particular at this point, Pannenberg considers the theological concepts of Ebeling, Moltmann and Sauter (among others), using the herementical methods of Gadamer[11] and Dilthey. At the end of this, he develops the fundamentals of his own understanding of theology as a science, a theory determined largely by his understanding of the history of Christian tradition.

God is the reality which determines everything. This claim is internal to the term "God" and is nothing more than the nominal definition of the same (cf. ThPS 302 ff.) As this reality which determines everything, God is drawn upon in every statement – indeed, independently from whether the term "God" is explicitly used or not. This applies for every statement which has any reference to the totality of meaning presupposed in each individual experience of meaning in its context. It is the task of theology as the science of God to test these statements for their appropriateness to the topic, as these statements occur not only explicitly in the religions, but also as they take more or less systematic form. In doing so, however, theology cannot "dogmatically" presuppose the principle or principles which it is testing. Such an action would necessarily lead to an aporia of ideological positivism or decisionistic faith-subjectivism, as has been shown. The only appropriate manner, then, is one which tests the idea of God present in this system "on its own

---

11 The importance of H.E. Gadamer's work (in particular Wahrheit und Methode. Grundzüge einer philosophischen Hermeneutik, 1960) for Pannenbergs universal-history theory oft he process of understanding is presented in "Hermenutik und Universalgeschichte" in ZThK 60 (1963), 90 – 121, reprinted in English as "Hermeneutic and Universal History" in BQiTh 1, 96 – 136. For his critique and constructive continuation of Gadamer's concept the foundational principle is decisive, that the task of a theology or philosophy of world history may not be relinquished for the sake of a hermeneutic ontology within the horizon of speech, as this falls prey to the accusation that it brings the occurrences into abstraction fro the statement-character of speech. This sort of task can only be fulfilled by a concept of universal history "that, in contrast to Hegel's, would preserve the finitude of human experience and thereby the openness of the future as well s the intrinsic claim of the individual. The task thus formulated might seem like that of squaring the circle, since the totality of history could only come into view from the perspective of its end, so that there would then be just as little need to speak of a further future as there would be to speak of the finitude of human experience. But the Hegelian conception of history is not in fact the only possible one, because the end of history can also be understood as something which is itself only *provisionally* known, and in reflecting upon this provisional character of our knowledge of the end of history, the horizon of the future could be held open and the finitude of human experience preserved. It is precisely this understanding of history as something whose totality is given by the fact that its end has become accessible in a provisional and anticipatory way that is to be gathered today from the history of Jesus in its relationship to the Israelite-Jewish tradition. Hegel was unable to see this because the eschatological character of the message of Jesus remained hidden to him, as was the case with the New Testament exegesis of his time." (BQiTH 1, 135)

implications" (ThPS, 300, cursive in Pannenberg): "In other words, the idea of God as, by definition, the reality which determines everything must be substantiated by the experienced reality of man and the world. If the substantiation succeeds, it does not depends on something external to the idea if God; rather, the successful method turns out to be identical in form with the ontological proof of the existence of God, the self-proof of the existence of God. However, while the result of the testing of the idea of God against empirical reality is still undetermined, which is the situation of finite knowledge, the idea of God as a mere idea in contrast with empirical reality remains a hypothesis. It is part of the finite nature of theological knowledge that even in theology the idea of God remains hypothetical and gives way to man's knowledge of the world and himself, by which it must be substantiated. On the other hand, as the *theme* of theology, God by definition includes the empirical reality by which the idea of God must be tested, and so defines the object of theology." (ThPS, 300) That God "is the object of theology only as a problem, not as established fact" (ThPS, 300), gives also the result in its confirmation that the reality of God "is therefore accessible to theological reflection not directly but only indirectly." (ThPS, 301) The object of scientific theology can thus be God – differently than in religious consciousness – only in a communicable, and not in an incommunicable manner. It is the case that the means of transmission of the topic of God, in the sense of the nominal definition of God as that reality which determines everything questions basically everything. It is, however, in the conditions of modern though not the reality of the world, but rather the reality of humanity in which the thought of a totality of meaning and thus the thought of the divine has its primary *Sitz im Leben*. Modern thought gives to anthropology, rather than cosmology, a role in fundamental theology. Indeed, alone through anthropological arguments, one cannot "provide...a sufficiently firm idea of what is meant by postulating God as reality. Such a postulate carries conviction only if, and to the extent that, the *idea* of God derived from consideration of the human self-understanding illuminates experience of the world. To this extent experience of the world and the search for the power that ultimately determines it is even today essential to any attempt to gain knowledge about the reality of God. Access to the idea of God, however, is no longer possible directly from the world, but only through man's self-understanding and his *relation* to the world." (ThPS, 309)

Anthropology wins a fundamental function for theology through the insight that the reference to totality of meaning is constitutive for being human – in the same manner in which it is manifested in religious experience and explicit in the systems of the religions. Insofar as religion is an anthropological universal, the relation to God is an inherent part of being human. The human relation to the totality of meaning brings with it, to a greater or lesser degree of explicitness, the relation to God. This does not mean, of course, that the reality of God is a given as such and incommunicably. It is "always present only in subjective anticipation of the totality of reality, in models of the totality of meaning presupposed in all particular experience. These models, however, are historic, which means that they are subject to confirmation or refutation by subsequent experience." (ThPS 310, italics in Pannenberg) While the insight into the historicity human of the attempts to discover meaning, attempts which are necessarily referential to the totality of meaning, must of itself have catastrophic consequences, according to Pannenberg it can and could be understood as a consequence of the topic of theology itself (cf. ThPS, 311). This is due to the fact that the Jewish-Christian tradition is characterized by the perception of the historical nature of God's self-revelation, in contrast with the *Kosmos*-piety connected with unchanging time.

The human is reliant on an anticipated totality of meaning in all current experience, thought and action; that which appears in the present is the proleptic presence of that which is future. It is the future from which the present comes.[12] In the various religions, as said, this relation is explicit. They alone are the form of human life in which it is valid that "an understanding of reality as a whole is articulated" (ThPS, 313). Consequentially, the fundamental examination of anthropology must be brought into a theology of the religions and their history, as Pannenberg does. This theology of the religions and their history is for Pannenberg the absolute foundational science of theology, insofar as Christian theology is defined as theology of the Christian religion and subjugated to the context of comparative studies of religion. The task of the study of religion can, of course, never occur from an external, psychological, sociological or phenomenological standpoint. Rather, it requires a theology of religion, which tests "religious traditions by the standard of their own understandings of divine reality." (ThPS, 320) Such "testing by the standard of the particular tradition's own understanding of divine reality does more than see how far the rest of the contents of the tradition agree with its understanding of God. In addition it tackles the more important question of whether the particular tradition has fulfilled in one historical situation, or now fulfils, the claim implicit in its talk of a God with power over reality. Does it, in other words, provide an interpretive approach to reality which gives insights into the way it is experienced in practice?" (*Ibid.*) A decisive criterion for the appropriateness of this method to its topic is thus the capacity for development of a religion. While the Judeo-Christian religion as "religion of history" (ThPS, 314) is able to integrate its own internal changes, religions "which are dominated by the idea of an allegedly unsurpassable mythical Golden Age and a corresponding world-order are swept away by the changes produced in them in the course of history" (*Ibid.*).

---

12 The thought that the present is essentially an anticipation of its future in its appearance has been explicated by Pannenberg in the lecture "Erscheinung als Ankunft des Zukünftigen" in Studia Philosophica 26 (1966), 192–207. Appearance is in this sense revealing. With this it is also said that the difference from the appearance and the one appeared to is that which constitutes the thought of the appearance itself.

4. Theological Encyclopedias

Under the term "encyclopedia", one understands the idea of a system of all knowledge, organized by the internal structure of knowledge. An encyclopedia of the sciences thus deals with the internal divisions of the *universitas litterarum*, and a theological encyclopedia must deal with the internal organization of the theological disciplines in the context of the *universitas litterarum* (cf. ThPS 14 – 20). Within the theological disciplines, the theology of the religions is, as already mentioned, in a fundamental position due to the acceptance of the fundamental insights of anthropology for theology. Simply put, theology is, in differentiated unity, a *theology of the religions*. In order to act as such, especially when theology should be systematic, it must proceed historically and be also a theology of the history of religion. It is, after all, the case that the explicit forms of the religions are undeniably historically influenced, up to the awareness of historicity present in Christianity. The relationship between the historic and systematic tasks of theology (cf. ThPS 346 – 358) is definably only as an inseparable interconnectedness. Just as the theological dimension of an historical religious phenomenon must be uncovered "as a historical phenomenon" (ThPS, 3419, italics in Pannenberg), so is such a phenomenon only perceived as such when it is systematically referred to the totality of meaning, and thus to the idea of God. The differentiation of historical and systematic theology into separate disciplines, specific to the modern period, cannot overlook this foundational interconnectedness, regardless of the pragmatic advantages and regardless of how easily the desire for the emancipation from one another might be understood (as they have developed throughout the last centuries).

Due to the fact that the actual topic of the religions is formed by their message of divine reality as it takes form in history, the study of religions can only handle this topic as a theology of religion. It can be replaced neither through psychology, sociology, or phenomenology of religions, as important as these disciplines are as aids. The latter is particularly the case because they take a "position midway between empirical investigation and conceptual systematization" (ThPS, 368 – 369). The theory of the Christian religion can build upon this mediation as an indispensible characteristic of the proper study of religions, as it is necessary for a comparison between the general (and thus abstract) idea of religion raised by the philosophy of religion and the concrete histories of particular religions. Christian religion can take this as a point of interaction because it can understand history as itself as the term which Christianity has from itself. As the religion of history, Christianity is, in a certain sense, the unity of that which the philosophy of religion and the history of religion conceive of differently. This can be seen in its lifting of the theology of religions to a fundamental discipline of theology. This casts light upon the relationship between the theology of religions and Christian theology; it is not a relationship of subsumption (in whatever manner one might conceive this) but is to be thought of as a relationship of mutual open-mindedness, indeed of mutual self-interpretation.

Regarding the *theology of the Christian religion* as that which integrates as well as is integrated by the religions, it is only this theology which can appropriately deal with its object, namely, with the differentiated unity of historical and systematic work, and in the universal theory of Christian tradition. It is in this that the Christian religion finds its unity, a unity which cannot be endangered by the independence of the theological subdisciplines. Pannenberg puts great emphasis on this, especially in the relationship between New Testament and Old Testament studies. Any tendency to separate the two must be met with a biblical theology, which of course does not mean to restrict one's thoughts only to the canon, as important as it is. The biblical theology is necessary to represent the true perfection and claim of finality of the revelation of God in Jesus Christ. The goal of biblical theology and the center of both its research and teaching must be an in-context "account of the history of the transmission of the tradition of Israel and primitive Christianity which includes both political and institutional history" (ThPS, 390) and it must strictly avoid the fatal opposite of a "a descriptive *history* of the religion of Israel or primitive Christianity with no theological basis" to a "*theology* of the Old and New Tesaments" (ThPS, 389).

The work of church history connects itself to this continually. Indeed, in a certain manner of thinking, church history can be understood as the discipline which conceives of the entire process of Christian tradition. A biblical theology relates to this, then, in the same manner as it does to the theology of religion, as a special discipline. As the history of the religion of Christianity, church history is able to grasp "beyond its formal boundaries into biblical theology on the one side and dogmatics and practical theology on the other." (ThPS, 392) In this it is able to represent the context of Christian theology as a whole. Church history is confronted with the question of the relevance of religion for the understanding of history in a manner which no other historical discipline faces. Its topic is, after all, the history of a religion, which is characterized by the belief in a God who takes action in history. In working out this concept, the tension between Christianity and the church within Christian history has to be taken into account, without forgetting that "[o]nly in the church does Christianity acquire an institutional expression of its existence." (ThPS, 402)

The tradition history of Christianity, as it is understood by church history in concert with New and Old Testament studies, is founded on meaning in the present which demonstrates the future. This meaning is to be interpreted in, with, and among the tradition of the history of religion. The meaning of Christian tradition for the present process of its reception is determinative, and is the "function of the work in systematic and practical theology, using the results of historical theology" (ThPS, 381), even when this task does not *prima facie* break free of the framework of a self-referential historical theology. The perception of the systematic task of theology has been relegated in the framework of organization to the special task of systematic theology, however, Pannenberg judges that it can do this task well "the more it realises that the investigation of the nature and truth of Christianity is not a specialised *area*, but the shared responsibility of Christian theology as a whole, and the more it combines the systematic and the historical in its own activity. And conversely, the less willingness the systematic theologian shows to penetrate the *historical* phenomenon of Christianity in systematic terms, the more subjectively contingent and arbitrary elements his models will contain." (ThPS, 421 – 422)

The *internal organization of systematic theology* must occur under the conditions of the modern organization of theological disciplines. The anthropology which searches for religious and theological implications builds the foundation, though one must keep in mind the "questions of man's relationship to the non-human world, question of natural philosophy or ontology on one hand and of epistemology on the other." (ThPS, 422) "On the basis of general anthropology the theology of religion first elaborates, by way of introduction, the concept of religion (philosophy of religion) and then subsumes it in the actual movement of the history of religion. Because it is a *theology* of religion it is concerned in the history of religion with the history of the apparition of the reality of God as well as that of man. It therefore includes the topics contained in the traditional doctrine of God as well as christology, ecclesiology, and ethics. All four of these groups of themes, however, can also be treated independently, the question of God in connection with the problem of mind in the immediate context and of the theme of religion, christology in its connection with general anthropology, which is indicated by the doctrine of the incarnation, and ecclesiology in connection with the need for a philosophy and theology of human society: ethics, finally, can be studied both as a general science of action with a basis in anthropology and with regard to the dependence of the objectives of action on the context of the experience of meaning and ultimately ton the religious understanding of meaning in its concrete historical form at any given time." (ThPS, 423) Ethics is that which at the same time provides the connection point "connects systematic theology with practical theology, which can also be understood as a specialised branch of ethics, the ethics of action *in the church.*" If practical theology were to be widened beyond church praxis, it would become a general Christian ethic, "in which case the social nature of Christian action, which is characterised by the forming of a church and acting in a church, will be a particular sub-division." (ThPS, 438)

§2 The Religious Nature of Humanity and the Self-Revelation of God (ST I, Chapters 2 – 4)

1. The Human as Self-Transcending Historical Being

Anthropology is, according to Pannenberg's judgment, the *foundational science of the modern age.* It was metaphysics in previous centuries which delivered the foundation of the sciences, through the organization of all beings into the *kosmos,* however, instead of the modest interest in the human condition as a microcosm, the modern human declares humanity and human freedom to be the basis of all truth. The indexing label for the modern age is subjectivism. Of course, cosmology is, in a certain sense at least, not completely ignored. Instead, it is interpreted through the schema in which the human relates to and is determined by the world. The traditional trend of cosmologizing anthropology is increasingly being replaced by the reverse, an anthropologization of cosmology, and it is a trend which seems to hold strong: the leading scientific role in the *universitas litterarum* belongs to anthropology. From this, it would follow that both philosophy of religion and theology must seek their own foundation in their respective anthropological conceptions, at least when they wish to remain in the conscious consideration of the modern public. Equally, they must found themselves in this manner in order to preserve the initial plausibility of their content, in particular in the face of the modern atheism which is, itself, grounded in anthropological conceptions. Indeed, Pannenberg acknowledges anthropology to be the *fundamental leading science* in his conception. This does not, of course, occur such that the doctrine of man functions as the furthest premise of theology. Rather, anthropological phenomena are viewed for their religious and theological implications from the beginning. The goal of this procedure is to demonstrate the fact that the religious nature and referentiality to God are constituent parts of being human. The following foundational principle of method applies: analogous to the progress of human research in general, anthropology must develop itself through going beyond the initial, abstract conceptions and become a continually more concrete concept.

Due to the fact that humans are necessarily creatures in community, one must retain the provisionality of the first aspect under which humanity is viewed in Pannenberg's concept. Nonetheless, it is the individual for himself who relates to nature and differentiates himself from the world of animals. Initially, of course, the form of the human body and the natural differences from animals are the object of observations; afterward one must look at human activity and behavior. This task is not least worthy of attention, and indeed quite helpful, due to the ability to make a distinction between body and soul as a derived principle. The sort of differentiation between body and soul, or analogous ones such as between *res cognita* and *res extensa*, is then not applied without ground, but derived from the observed behavior of humans. The second major aspect is a concretization of this investigation of human behavior, such that individuals are not viewed as for themselves, but in the context of a unity of individuals, and of society. Failing to take these into account leads one necessarily into abstractions. To reverse these abstractions, that is, to view the constitutive sociality of each human individual, comes one step closer to the concrete human. Despite this, the structures of the social relationships remain themselves too abstract without insight into their genesis. The communal character of human existence is demonstrated in the sociological perspective which includes both the biological aspect and the aspect of individual behavior. This sociological perspective must itself be included in the larger context of human history, a history which follows the concrete changes of human and humanity, a history which marks the tip of the anthropological pyramid.

This outline of the process of the progressive inclusion of anthropological abstractions, ending provisionally in historical examination, is the methodical presupposition of Pannenberg's view, in the same manner as in the monograph treatment "Anthropology in Theological Perspective" from 1985, as it is in the eleven lectures on theological anthropology published as "What is Man?" in 1962.[1] "The anthropological sciences with their pictures of man never arrive at man in his concreteness. Neither biology nor cultural anthropology, neither sociology nor the anthropology of rights, and certainly not existential ontology arrives at man in his concreteness. Their pictures of man are abstractions. To be sure, abstract consideration is the condition without which a person can say nothing at all about man. In order to accentuate this or that feature of human existence, a person initially must set aside all other aspects. Certainly, however, the diverse abstract aspects can mutually supplement one another. While no science can avoid beginning with individualized, abstract discoveries, progress in study still consists in tying the diverse abstract points of view together. In this way the abstraction is undone, so that a concrete picture emerges to an increasing degree. This is also the case in anthropology." (M, 137)

Regarding the biological nature of humanity, Pannenberg links up with philosophical anthropology by regarding it primarily under the concept of "openness to the world" (M, 1). As a part of this, the human differentiates itself from animals and all extra-human creatures in "a more profound distinction" M, 8). As a being open to the world, the human does not merely transcend this

---

1 N.B., the translation varies sometimes strongly from the German text, to an extent which cannot be corrected here. – Trans.

or that connection, rather "is completely directed into the 'open.'" (M, 8) The exocentric striving of humanity has no limit, and goes beyond the world into the infinite. The human openness to the world must consequently be thought of as human openness to God. "What the environment is for animals, God is for man. God is the goal in which alone his striving can find rest and his destiny be fulfilled." (M, 13) The plumb line of world-opnenness which is defined in the first lecture is then extended to the cultural world of language, a human element ruled by the ability to imagine. This is done in order to emphasize the fact that God appears "not only as the goal of man's striving in his openness to the world, but also as the origin of man's creative mastery of the world." (M, 27) Then, it is demonstrated that the human, as a limitlessly open being, can live neither without a reason for trust in the facticity of the world and the self which itself is infinite, nor without hope for life after death. If a human seeks the constituting and preserving ground of being in himself rather than finding it in God, then he necessarily curves into himself necessarily all of his acts of will and consciousness, thereby failing to fulfill the human purpose. The hamartiological problems and soteriological needs of humanity which are indicated in this sentence are explicated through individual examinations of the attachment to ego and purpose of humanity as well as reflections regarding time, eternity, and judgment. The social aspects of human being-in-the-world, without which one cannot appropriately conceive of the individuality of the single human, are also examined from the viewpoint of personal relations of recognition. It is through this which justice becomes flexibly temporally extended, by finding the fulfillment of these in love. This is examined and demonstrated at work in the cultural process, in whose historical progression the natural relationship of the human to itself and to the world of things is progressively transformed through cultural relationships. These cultural relationships are, for Pannenberg, to be placed beyond mere reaction and revolution.

This series of anthropological lectures ends according to the methodology outlined in its introduction: with the consideration of humans in their historicity. As beings open to the world, humans are "by nature historical." (M, 139) This is valid first for the individual, whose purpose is not a natural function but a cultural task for which one is inalienably reliant on God, as the entirety of one's being does not stand under one's own control. It is also valid for humanity, which is not a mere natural factor but rather an object of historical development whose culture is inconceivable without religious relationships. Culture is unthinkable without religion insofar as the history of humanity does not find its ground and unity within itself, but is rather able to receive the eschatological future of God.[2] The knowledge of this eschatological

---

2 Eschatology is not merely a single doctrine, but is determinative for Pannenberg's entire system (cf. in particular "Theology and the Kingdom of God" [1969]). There is also a task for a theological aesthetic: "the aesthetic metamorphosis of the object represented in the work of art may

future is thus decisive for the self-knowledge of the human, in particular the human in history. It is first relatively late, through the Judeo-Christian tradition, that "the awareness of man's historicity first arose" (M, 143). Pannenberg comes from this to the conclusion which completes the fundamental-theological role of anthropology by integrating it into Christian historical theology, the historical fact that "men's destiny is…determined by their relationship to the God of Israel and his revelation in Jesus of Nazareth." (M, 148)[3] With this the scope of both the explanation of the term "God" and question of the truth of His existence as well as the investigation of the reality of God and the gods in the experience of the religions demonstrated – the topics of the second and third chapters of the Systematic Theology.

2. The Idea of God and the Question of Truth

Although dogmatics has as its task the explanation of the idea of God within all of its subtopics, it cannot simply begin directly with the reality of God. This is due to the fact that the reality of God is only present in a human manner, namely in human conceptions, words, and thoughts. This indirect and mediated manner in which the divine reality presents itself is analogous to the manner in which Pannenberg brings forth his introductory examinations of the term "God", the idea of God, the proofs of God's existence, and the human religions. These latter receive the results of an anthropology from a religious perspective and thus mark the context of discovery of systematic theology, a context which is carried over into the foundations of dogmatics as it proceeds into a doctrine of God based on revelation.

In pre-modern cultures, the word "God" (or the "gods") referred clearly and unambiguously to the final foundational instance of all reality. This is no longer the case in the modern age. Despite this, Pannenberg wishes explicitly to keep hold of the term. In this context, he rejects attempts to understand the idea of God solely, or even primarily, as an interpretative paradigm for

---

stand in a relation to the eschatological transformation of our earthly lives, a transfiguration which includes judgment as well as glorification in itself. In the greatest works of its history, Christian art has presented this transfiguration of its objects and thus made something of the eschatological hope of Christians present. One need not speak here of the dangers that such daring opens one up to. Indeed, the renewal of the awareness of a connection between aesthetic perception and Christian eschatology could be one of the tasks of future theological work in this topic." ("Die Aufgabe christlicher Eschatologie", in: ZThK 92 [1995], 71–82; reprinted in BSTh 2, 271–282, here: 280 f.)

3 "Christian speech about God proves itself in relation to the limit-transcending openness of human existence, which is disclosed in its depths in this light and then in turn points back to the God of the Bible as its ultimate, unsurpassable fulfillment" ("Die Frage Nach Gott", in: EvTh 25 [1965], 238–262; reprinted in English as "The Question of God" in BQiTh 2, 201–233, here: 233)

religious experience (ST I, 65 – 66). The word "God" brings man before "the singular whole" of his own being and all reality, as Pannenberg states along with Karl Rahner (ST I, 71). It is characterized foundationally in humanity in a unique manner and that in a very general gestalt (metaphysical term "God"), without which one could not begin to define the specific Christian under-standing of God. It is in this context that the remark "that the recourse to experience in clarification of talk about God does not succeed because the word "God" is one of the most important keys to interpretation if we are to understand the content of religious experience. The importance of the reference to religion and religious experience lies elsewhere, namely in the question of the reality, if any, what corresponds to the concept of God" (ST I, 69) is at home. If then, the concept of God is prior to all religious experience as the content of that experience, then it follows that "[t]he tradition of philosophical theology is more helpful as regards the general content of the concept than is recourse to specific experiences." (ST I, 70) The object of philosophical theology, on the other hand, is God as the foundation for the unity of the world, something which Pannenberg opines is one of the original functions of the term, namely, to give "an ultimate explanation of the being of the world as a whole" (ST I, 70 – 71).

If it is the case that the relationship between philosophical and revelatory theology is not one of alternatives (as Pannenberg shows historically in his demonstration of the reliance of early Christian theology on the Greek concept of God [cf. ST I, 71 – 73]), then the so-called *natural knowledge of God* and the correlating *theologia naturalis* cannot be denied a truth claim, at least in a momentary sense, which has meaning for revelatory theology – even which the term "natural theology" proves itself inappropriate. This general right to a truth claim exists primarily in the assumption of a general human knowledge of God. This is, of course, to be differentiated from "natural theology" as a historically specific phenomenon in the sense of an argumentatively developed philosophical doctrine of God (cf. ST I, 76 – 77). At the same time, the necessary connection of early Christian theology with the philosophical idea of God in the intended statement that the Christian God is "the one true God of all peoples." (ST I, 79) If Christian theology had to face the demands of philosophical theology in that manner, it required a "critical reformulation of the formulas of philosophical theology" (*Ibid*). "The revision, however, had also to justify itself by philosophical arguments if it was to claim the universality with which the one and only God must be declared." (*Ibid.*) Still for Augustine, the Christian doctrine of God could be identical with "a purified form of true natural theology, i.e., theology commensurate with the nature of God." (ST I, 81) Pannenberg is beholden to a similar conception, for all its differences, though he significantly remarks, "Stress on the perversion of sin should not be pushed so far theologically that we are no longer claimed as creatures of God. This means, however, that there is always a correspondence between human nature and its Creator." (ST I, 82)

The function of natural theology depends, by its own nature, on the existence of the object which it treats. Whether the existence of God can be known with certainty "on the basis of us and our nature is the problem of the proofs of God which have thus become a critical point in the modern form of natural theology." (ST I, 82) Pannenberg concentrates first on the cosmological proof, without which the ontological proof lacks a grounded starting point (cf. ST I, 84). The cosmological proof is characterized in that it "move on from the world to God as its origin." (ST I, 86) The reasons for which the cosmological proof as modified by Leibniz from the third Thomisitc way became determinative for the modern age (in opposition to the proofs from movement and first cause, which lost importance) is connected to the introduction of the principle of inertia, in particular through Descartes and Newton. "In a mechanistic worldview the concept of God was no longer needed to explain natural events" (ST I, 88), which became the occasion for Descartes and those following him to make an anthropological turn in the proof for God's existence, a turn which, of course, brought with it an endangerment of the objectivity of the concept of God. It is manifest with Kant, when he critically refers to all rational theology as "the expression of a need of reason with no objective validity." (ST I, 90) At least Kant also saw "the necessity of the rational idea of such a being" (*Ibid.*). Hegel, following this, assigned the various proofs to the steps of the development of the religions and progressively developed them into his theory of the Absolute; Feuerbach reduced the proofs of the existence of God to a mere expression of subjective desire. In opposition to this, it would be the task of an *anthropological proof for God's existence* to show "that the concept of God is an essential part of a proper human self-understanding, whether in relation to human reason or to other basic fulfillment of human existence." (ST I, 93)

Though it is indispensable for theology, no anthropological argument is able to "prove God's existence in the strict sense." (*Ibid.*) It cannot be an actual proof for God's existence (aside from the fact that it might prove the necessity of the phenomenon of human self-transcendence) "There can be no strict proof because the existence of God would have to be proved in relation not only to us but above all to the reality of the world." (ST I, 93 – 94) That is the staying power of the cosmological proofs, which themselves are founded anthropologically insofar as "the demand of human reason for a final explanation of the world's existence underlies them." (ST I, 94) It is in the demonstration of the necessity of the lifting up of human thought above the coincidence of all finite to the thought of an *a se* origin which makes up the essential and lasting meaning of the argument from contingence, indeed in the specific, modern formulation given to it by Leibniz. It cannot, however, achieve a strict "proof" of the existence of God. That is confirmed by the theological insight that "God can only be known through God himself." (ST I, 94; cf. fn. 102 regarding Hegel's ontological proof)

To remember the fact, or respectively, to bring to the fore of the consciousness, that knowledge of God is possible not "on the sole basis of philosophical reflection (*Ibid.*)" but rather "only by revelation of the divine reality" (ST I, 94–95) can be taken as the essential function of a theological critique of natural theology, including the proofs for God's existence. Despite this, the arguments of *theologia naturalis* retain "significance as descriptions of the reality of humanity and the world which make talk about God intelligible and can thus establish criteria for it." (ST I, 95) Pannenberg makes this explicit in the face of various theological attempts to disconnect philosophical theology, exemplified in the historical sketch of the theological criticisms of the so-called natural theology in Schleiermacher, Ritschl, and Barth. The philosophical term "God" is indispensable for theology, as it builds a critical framework, the "minimal conditions for talk about God" (ST I, 107). "an independent knowledge of the existence and nature of God – independent of the reflection of the philosophy of religion on the truth claims of the positive religions – is no longer to be expected from philosophical theology today." (*Ibid.*) Thus, according to Pannenberg, the term "natural theology" should be rejected. "But the impossibility of a theology that is based on pure reason does not answer the question as to the possibility and actuality of a natural knowledge of the God whom the Christian message proclaims." (*Ibid.*)[4]

The "natural" human knowledge of God in the sense of *cognitio Dei naturalis insita* ensures for Pannenberg that, among other things, the Christian message to humanity can be a witness to the truth even when it is factually present in a manner contrary to its own nature. The central indication for such a natural knowledge of God is often taken to be the phenomenon of the conscience (cf. ST I, 111). In referring to this, Pannenberg does not wish to limit the idea of conscience to the sphere of morality, nor does he wish, in the sense of syndresis, to unite it with self-awareness and I – Identity. For the genealogy of the conscience, the assumption of a direct, unthematic and pre-reflective presence of the entirety of life is of extreme importance (cf. terms of "feeling" and "eternity"); this is what Pannenberg interprets as an "unthematic knowledge of God". Pannenberg does not identify this with a religious a priori, nor with the questionable character of human existence in the sense of a time-invariable existential structure. As unthematic knowledge of God, the unthematic presence of the whole of life is not already in the primordial state of feeling, rather it is in the passage of time and in the progression of reflection – that of the individual, or of humanity as a while – and thus it is perceived after the fact.

---

4 The English translation leaves out the phrase *dem Menschen als solchen immer schon eigenen* – that is, that this natural knowledge is inherent to humans and has always been so. – Trans.

3. Theory of Subjectivity and Metaphysics of the Absolute

As this sketch of the second chapter of the Systematic Theology can indicate, but in no wise exhaust the content, it is perhaps helpful to examine the philosophical implications of the question regarding the truth of the concept of God. The opportunity to do this is offered by five studies published in 1988, with an appendix,[5] under the title "Metaphysik und Gottesgedanken".[6] This appendix (cf. MIG 113–129: *Atomism, Duration, Form: Difficulties with Process Philosophy*) is dedicated to Process Philosophy, which is primarily a factor in the USA, a system of thought which Pannenberg views as "this century's most significant contribution to metaphysics." (MIG xiv)[7] Pannenberg's criticism is aimed particularly at Whitehead's concept of radical creativity in each elementary event; in contrast to this, the constitutive meaning of the whole of the process for individual moments is underscored. If the goal of this examination of Process Philosophy is "more critical than systematic" (*Ibid.*), in the previous texts his critique is in the service of a systematic-constructive intention which runs through all the lectures. The topics of those lectures are as follows: 1. The End of Metaphysics and the Idea of God (cf. MIG 3–21); 2. The Problem of the Absolute (cf. MIG 22–42); 3. Self-Consciousness and Subjectivity (cf. MIG 43–68); 4. Being and Time (cf. MIG 69–90); 5. Concept and Anticipation (cf. MIG 91–109)[8]

Pannenberg argues for a continuation and *renewal of the tradition of metaphysical thought*, especially in the interest of theology, against the common opinion within philosophy and theology that the era of metaphysics has ended and that the current time is a post-metaphysical one. Without metaphysical statements, the theological self-explication of the Christian faith must exhaust itself in subjectivism. All general truth claims would be for naught, as the absence of metaphysical reflection would require, with its absence, the absence of an idea of the world. After a critical examination of diverse and often diverging arguments for the end of metaphysics, Pannenberg determines their common chord to be Onto-Theo-Logic, which is to say, that "first Philosophy" stands in constitutive connection with religion and the theme of God which determines religion. The historical appearances of the

---

5 In the English version, the appendix, along with two additional essays, comprises the second section of the collection. The additional essays are present only in the English version.

6 In English as "Metaphysics & the Idea of God" Eerdmans 1990, trans. Philip Clayton.

7 The German version of the original (pg. 6) is *"den bedeutensdsten, wenn auch zu Kritik herausfordernden Beitrag"*, that is, the contribution is not only the most important, but also a contribution which challenges one to criticize it. This aspect of necessary criticism has been lost in the translation. – Trans.

8 The English version contains two additional essays: "Theology and the Categories 'Part' and 'Whole'" (cf. MIG 130–152) and "Meaning, Religion, and the Question of God" (cf. MIG 153–170).

truth in religion is to be terminologically examined, however, this examination cannot replace or control the reality which it examines. This dependence of metaphysical thought upon religious tradition does not exclude philosophical critique, or even criticism, of religion. On the contrary, the original task of philosophy is precisely to apply the criteria for truth which religious traditions themselves claim to those traditions, to examine their claims about all-encompassing and all-determining reality, and in this manner to examine them in light of the experienced world. At the same time, philosophy can only carry out this original task when it does not fixate upon finite objects of experience or consciousness (which themselves relate to finite objects of experience), but rather when it develops a critical-constructive pattern of thought examining the search for meaning grounded in the nature of humanity. This drive to find meaning transcends the foundational relationship of "I" and "the world" which comes from empirical experience. In contrast to an awareness which – not mindful of the transcendental relation foundational to humanity – exhausts itself in day-to-day interaction with the finite world of experience, philosophy converges with religion and theological reflection, even with the noted differences.

The remaining difference between philosophy on the one hand and religion and theology on the other hand explains itself, for Pannenberg, through the fact that religion and theology generally start from the point of revealed divine reality, that they view the self and the world from that perspective, while "within philosophy the main focus is on justifying one's opposition to the natural consciousness and on moving away from the experience of life that is based on it. As a result, philosophers stress the requalifying of the objects that we encounter in our consciousness of the world, rethinking them from the perspective that is achieved by going beyond the finite givenness of the world." (MIG, 15 – 16) Indeed, in the form of a metaphysics of the absolute, philosophy can aim at a presupposition which presupposes itself, that is, one that precedes as a condition all finitude. One might say with this that the finite can only be properly thought of as the self-differentiation of the absolute. However, philosophy is bound to the One by its methodology of propaedeutic introduction, that same One which transcends the finite experience of self and world.[9]

The idea of the One names, for Pannenberg, the theme of the metaphysical "rising above", above the multiplicity of finite givens in the awareness of self and world. The One must rise above the historical point of origin, or the difference between being and Being, and must do so without the claim that it is

---

9 The demand to think of finitude not merely from the concepts of religious awareness, but also from the philosophical concept-formation and its historical considerations in the estimation of its truth value gives for Pannenberg a series of consequences which are listed under seven aspects in "Offenbarung als Kategorie philosophischer Theologie", in M. Olivetti (ed.), Filospifa della revelazione, in: Archivo di filosofia 62 (1994), 867 – 874; reprinted in BSTh 1, 238 – 245.

the highest and most complete conception of the Absolute. For, although the idea allows both a metaphysics of finitude as well as a metaphysics of infinitude to be conceived of, it remains undetermined on what grounds each individual for itself is "one" as well as what makes up (in contrast and comparison) the unity of the absolute One. With the concept of the One, which is the topic of the second study, the Problem of the Absolute is rather first posed, rather than solved. In the process of the argumentation, the idea of the infinite, which Pannenberg sees as intuitively present in every experience of finitude, has an essential mediating function. It is to be assumed of the idea of the finite, which can be characterized noetically as well as ontically: "We can understand the finite ontologically as implying a real ending in space and in time, as being limited by another, noetically, insofar as every 'something' is what it is in its particularity only by being differentiated from an other. This demarcation of one thing from another (or from all others) is what constitutes its concept." (MIG, 24)[10] With the thought of limit, however, is that which is limited already in a relationship to something else,[11] a relationship which transcends the limit. "Now the other, in demarcation from which the finite is what it is, is either another finite thing of *the* other of the finite as such, that is, the Infinite. Both of these are suggested by the border that is contained within the very notion of the finite: the finite in is specificity suggests the other finite form from which it is distinguished; and the finite as finite per se, in its generality, suggests the infinite. The notion of the finite as such can therefore not be thought without already thinking the Infinite at the same time" (MIG, 24–25).[12]

Pannenberg praises Hegel for having shown this in a convincing manner in his *Logic*, with the caveat, that transcendence beyond one's own finitude is not already to be acknowledged as the "something" in the *Seinslogik*. This is true as the transition from finitude to the concept of infinite cannot be understood as the agency of the "something", rather, it is brought about by human reflection (though this reflection is spurred on by that "something") (cf. MIG, 91 ff.). We have Hegel to thank, that the concept of the truly infinite, as he calls it, can be clearly separated from the mathematical infinite. This latter, to speak with Descartes, is not an actual infinite, but rather an indefinite, a differentiation which Pannenberg counts as "the most important result of the Hegelian treatment of the Infinite as the Absolute." (MIG, 35) As a result of such differentiation, it is shown that infinity can only truly be thought of as infinite when it does not base itself upon the abstract opposition of infinitude-finitude, but rather encompasses itself the very difference between finite and infinite. "As long as the Infinite is thought of only in opposition to the finite, its

---

10 Pannenberg has "ontically", *ontisch* rather than "ontologically". – Trans.
11 I.e., that which is outside of the limit. – Trans.
12 Pannenberg's language is stronger, in that he claims these are "given with" the finite (*mit...gegeben*), and not merely suggested by. – Trans.

essence remains limited through its opposition to the finite as its other – which is precisely what characterizes things that are finite. Any infinity that we can conceive as only abstractly transcendent, as standing in opposition to the finite, is itself finite. In order to truly be conceived as infinite, the Infinite must not only be set in opposition to the finite but must at the same time overcome this opposition. It must be conceived both as *transcendent* in relation to the finite and as *immanent* to it." (MIG, 36) For religious speech about God, the critical consequence follows: "from now on, the only understanding of God that can be called monotheistic in the strict sense will be that which is able to conceive the one God not merely as transcending the world; at the same time this 'God beyond' must be understood as immanent in the world." (*Ibid.*)

With this insight, the theological potential of Hegel's philosophy is in no wise exhausted. Pannenberg follows the internal logic of the system to the developed conception of spirit, in which the concept of infinity is, as a mediation of the category of the Absolute and according to its own reflexiveness, sublated. First with the concept of Spirit is the content of this idea of the Absolute fully explicated, insofar as now the condition for the unity of the Absolute and the other is thought, for "the content of the Infinite is first fully explicated in the concept of Spirit, insofar as that concept mediates the opposition between infinity and finitude, as we already saw to be demanded by the concept of the true Infinite." (MIG, 38) Pannenberg agrees with Hegel to this point, however, they part ways on the assumption of achieved (or yet to be achieved) sublation of religious imagination into the concept of concepts. The demand of absolute conceiving, as in Hegel's absolute conception, fails to recognize the provisionality of all rational understanding and the finitude of philosophical thought, which can only correspond to the infinitude of the object when it avoids all self-totality through constant self-differentiation from its ground. For Pannenberg, the programmatic conclusion follows that is developed in the last of the five studies: "the philosophical concept will reveal itself to have the structure of anticipation." (MIG, 94; further to Hegel cf. in particular 101 ff.)[13]

---

13 Cf. the remark in "On Theological and Historical Hermeneutics" in BQiTh 1, 137 – 181; here 172: "…in distinction from the Hegelian philosophy of the concept, a type of thought that understands itself as anticipation, and thus as an intrinsically reflected anticipation, would not be able to be self-constituting. Rather, as anticipation, it would always refer to something preliminary, in relation to which all thought and knowledge prove also to be once again *mere* anticipation, which can never be overtaken or superseded by means of a type of thought that itself has anticipatory structure. That applies not only to any anticipatory concepts one pleases, but also to the very form of anticipation itself. A form of thought that understands itself as a mere foreconception of the truth does not have the truth in itself but is rather the process that strives beyond itself toward it. This process can be maintained only on the presupposition that existing being itself is not what it is, i. e., has not yet attained its own essence." – That the reduction of the concept to an anticipation is not an external antithesis to Hegel's thought has been presented by Pannenberg in "Die Bedeutung des Christentums in der Philosophie Hegels" in Gottesgedanke und menschliche Freiheit, Göttingen 1972, 78 – 113).

Insofar as Pannenberg's anticipatory understating of the philosophical concept of the Absolute connects metaphysics to religious tradition, he denies to philosophy the claim to complete itself in the wise self-consciousness above the world and above all finitude.[14] Of course, philosophy retains the task of critically testing religious tradition, but cannot replace it, as without religious form the priority and thus absoluteness of the Absolute cannot be preserved. Where such an idea of philosophy is present, not only is philosophical terminology robbed of its ability to describe, but also it fails to appropriately handle the idea of subjectivity and self-consciousness, to which the third study is dedicated, with particular consideration given to Kant.

Kant's critical philosophy occurs essentially in the reflection upon the implications of the awareness of experience. In this, the unity of the ego, which has achieved awareness of itself in the identical movement of self-awareness, becomes the condition of possibility for all empirical experience. The ego marks the *conditio sine qua non* for the connection of each perceptive act within one's own awareness of experience: The fact that I think must accompany all thoughts. Indeed, Descartes also built upon the certainty of the *cogito,* though he made the concept of the "I" prior to the concept of the infinite; that same infinite which should mediate and ground the differentiated unity of self and world. According to Pannenberg, it was Kant who declared the awareness of the identity of the "I" to be the condition of possibility for all experience of objects and thus to ground all empirical knowledge upon the foundation of the I-awareness. This epochal step brings a great deal of reservations with it. It is true that Pannenberg does not deny the meaning of the theorem of transcendental apperception for the formulation of the modern conditions of the empirical knowledge of the world and the self: "Because the awareness of knowing, in contrast to simple perceptual awareness, always includes an awareness of the subject of such knowing, the unitary consciousness that underlies the unity of argumentation is characterized by a unity of *self*-consciousness. This unity need not be present in the sense of the identity of the individual empirical ego, but it must be positive at least as an identity of the subject that is engaged in doing science. Empirical subjects take part in the scientific view of the world to the extent that they fulfill these conditions. Hence, the unity of self-consciousness always underlies the activity of arguing about various subjects and drawing connections between them." (MIG, 56) Regardless of this, it is precisely as necessary to determine the limits of a theory of transcendental subjectivity.

The assumption of a transcendental subject prior to all experience which

---

14 Only where philosophy knows itself to be connected to religion is it able to accurately understand the primacy of the infinite not only from all finite determinations b, but also the reflective thematizing of its own concept. The lasting importance of religion and Christendom for a post-Kantian metaphysic that is aware of its own historicity is offered by Pannenberg in "Religion und Metaphysik", in: D. Henrich un H.P. Horstmann (eds.), Metaphysik nach Kant? Suttgarter Hegelkongress 1987, Suttgart 1988, 728–741; reprinted in BSTh 1, 45–57.

enables that experience is, for one thing, directly opposed to the thesis of the genesis of the "I" in the process of experience, which has been held at least since David Hume. This theory claims that the awareness of self-unity is first mediated to the individual through the empirical relationship to the world, and thus cannot function as an instance of a priori identity. Also, the "I" cannot be seen as a stable instance *realiter*, even after the formation of identity, without limitations. "The idea that an existing and enduring ego is the condition for the unity of conscious experience must for this reason be judged to be an idealized construction – however well it serves to provide unitary basis for the modern scientific description of the world as encountered within the secular empirical sciences." (MIG, 57)[15] Thirdly, the discoveries of the cultural history of humanity speak clearly for the fact that the unity of the experienced world was historically founded through the communal awareness of religiously grounded order and a cultural memory, which themselves orient on the given context of the *a posteriori* world of experience, and not primarily upon the individual. "A consciousness of the subjectivity of one's experience arises only to the extent that one experiences a deviation from the common framework. This sort of stable world has often had its basis within religion. Only when the basis was destroyed, as in Europe in the seventeenth century, did it become necessary to derive a new way of establishing the world. Thus, Western thinkers began to seek a foundation for the social order in the concept of the unity of human nature, and a foundation for the multiplicity of experiences of the world in the unity of self-consciousness." (MIG, 54–55)

It would appear that Kant's theory has now been relegated to history, but Pannenberg asserts that an entire series of current issues speak for the idea that the method of transcendental reflection should be applied to a method of thinking which concerns itself with the ground of all possible experiential knowledge, and not merely the implicit conditions thereof. With this, one would call also upon the resources of the pre-Kantian tradition of metaphysics back to the antique traditions, that one might catch sight of the priority of the infinite to each finite experience. The fact that Kant himself did not give priority to the infinite over the finite is not a timeless advantage of his system, but rather the historically-caused limitation which can only be overcome when the idea of totality as *omnitudo realitatis* is thought constitutively as a part of the experiencing and defining the individual objects of experience. It cannot be relegated to a mere transcendental ideal of pure reason without an elementary relationship to the beginnings of world-experience. This is made clear by example in the examination of Kant's conception of space. For the conception of time, the same is done in a separate process of argumentation entitled "Being and Time". In this latter, Pannenberg makes explicit the reason why the unity of time is grounded in the eternality of God and not in the

---

15 Pannenberg merely has "in the service of" (*im Dienste*) rather than "however well it serves". – Trans.

identity of the individual, with reliance on Plotinus and Augustine. The identity of the individual can only be self-aware of the whole of our being through the presentation and representation of anticipatory participation in eternity.

Despite his criticism of Kant's theory of transcendental subjectivity, whose aporia is evident in the failure of Fichte's doctrine of the I positing itself,[16] Pannenberg's judgment is that it is no mere coincidence and no accident, but rather a consequence of the tradition history of Christianity, that *subjectivity* became the *epochal index of the modern age.* Under Christian conditions, the absolute and infinite One must indeed be thought of as that which the finite subject has as its object and at the same time is its own end. The idea of the independence of the subject as subject is not problematic, rather simply the movement of independence away from the Absolute for reasons of "emancipation". Such becoming independent is, however, counter-productive for the self-preservation interests of the subject, as its constitution and individual preservation cannot be guaranteed through mere world- and self-reference. Rather it is solely through the religious relationship with the Absolute. The Absolute is only appropriately conceived of as Absolute and as the Christian God when it is not a mere causal reason for and final end of the world, but rather when perceived in concert with these ideas the foundation and highest good of subjectivity.

4. The Reality of God and the Gods in the Experience of the Religions

In his examination of the relationship between philosophy and religion in "Metaphysics & the Idea of God", Pannenberg asks "Can the metaphysical ascent toward the concept of the One fully grasp the reality of the absolute on the basis of independent philosophical reflection, and can it sufficiently establish its conclusions?" (MIG, 18) The given answer is clear and explicit: it is true, it can show "the necessity of extending reason to include the idea of God. It does not show that the existence of God, prior to all human consciousness and to the existence of the world, can be proved. Bound up with this result is the fact that metaphysics has always had difficulties in conceiving the absolute One as person and therefore as 'God' at all." (MIG, 19)[17] Metaphysics thus cannot replace religions, but remains tied to their factual and historical experience, though without clinging to them naively. "These limitations notwithstanding, the ascent to the absolute One can be effective as a critical corrective to the images of the divine within the religious traditions.

16 Which lives on in the exaggeration concept of action in modern anthropology and sociology.
17 Pannenberg's original language is that of "explanation" or "elaboration" (*dartun*), not "demonstration" or "proof" – Trans.

In fact, this corrective function may go so far in individual cases that basic elements in the traditions' understanding of God become untenable." (MIG, 19 – 20) This does not change anything about the fact that metaphysics can clarify the content of religious traditions, but can principally neither catch up nor overtake said traditions. It is to be noted that explicit speech about God in philosophy "belongs perhaps more appropriately to the philosophy of religion than to metaphysics – unless, of course, the metaphysics of the Absolute should itself turn out to be connected to the philosophy of religion." (MIG, 21)

That is as may be: replacing religion with philosophy lies outside the possibilities open to philosophy, because the absolute ground of thought cannot be conceived of in a manner other than the religious. Only the religious form guarantees the truth of the Absolute, whose absolute priority makes itself known through revelation. Again, due to this, "[t]he result of our inquiry for the philosophical concept of the Absolute and its relationship to the God of religion is clear: philosophical reflection can lead to the formulation of criteria for presenting the understanding of God within a religion tradition. But it cannot actually replace the tradition." (MIG, 41 – 42) This result coincides with the result of the considerations on the concept of God and his truth in the second chapter of the Systematic Theology; it is valid that the proofs for God's existence, like natural theology as a whole, cannot provide knowledge of God independent from the positive religions, but rather stand solely on "the possibility of proving an anthropological need for rising above the finite to the thought of the infinite and absolute" (ST I, 106), as is indispensable for the truth claims of all religious speech about God. The thought "God" has reality "only in the positive religions." (*Ibid.*) This assumption conforms to the insight in the historical character of reason, and marks the transition to the treatment of the reality of God and the gods in the experience of the religions.

Pannenberg operates with the assumption that the term *religion* has become the foundation of theological systematic in the newer protestant theology,[18] at least since the decline of the doctrine of verbal inspiration. "The

18 To the fundamental anthropological function of the concept of religion and its changes, to the relation of philosophical theology and religion, to the conflict of religious truth claims as an area of responsibility for a theology of religions, to the relation of Christian theology to the conflict and dialogue between religions and to their participation in salvation in the perspective of Christian theology cf. "Die Religionen als Thema der Theologie. Die Relevanz der religionen für das Selbstverständis der Theologie", in: ThQ 169 (1989), 99 – 110; reprinted in BSTh 1, 160 – 172. – to the foundation-crisis of modern Protestant theology, as given in the dissolution of the doctrine of Scripture, cf. the considerations on "The Crisis of the Scripture Principle", reprinted multiple times and in English in BQiTh 1 – 14. The crisis of the principle of Scripture occurred on the historical-critical side as well as the hermeneutical. The result is "that theology cannot continue as a special science of divine revelation on the basis of Holy Scripture. Precisely in endeavoring to understand the biblical writings it will be led back to the question of the events they report about, and of the meaning that belongs to them. Theology can, however, understand the meaning of these events as deeds of God only in relation to universal history, because statements about the origin of all events can be defended only with a view to the totality of all

concept of the Christian religion, or Christianity, became a criterion whereby to judge what is binding doctrinal truth in the content of the biblical writings and what may be regarded as time-bound and no longer relevant today." (ST I, 120) This process culminated in that knowledge of God itself was "not the basis of religion, but its function or even its product." (ST I, 123; cf. already 120) The breakthrough in protestant theology of the 19th century was the "mediation of the knowledge of God by the subjectivity of religion" (ST I, 123). In the 18th century, there remained two hurdles for this development, to say nothing of the pre-modern development of the idea of religion, which are presented in the examples of Cicero and Augustine (cf. ST I, 120 ff.). The first hindrance was the founding of the knowledge of God on Holy Scripture, the second the "linking of the concept of natural religion to the natural theology of reason. This combination ensured not merely the universal validity of the subjective awareness of God in natural religion but also the primacy of the knowledge of God in or even over against religious practice." (ST I, 124) The first hindrance fell away with the dissolution of the old protestant doctrine of scripture inspiration, the latter when "the ideas of the primacy of natural religion and the theoretical validity of natural theology came under the criticism of Hume and Kant" (ST I, 125). "Religion, including the awareness of God, now became no more than an expression of our practical needs in our capacity as rational beings." (*Ibid.*) One could no longer speak of an "independence of the knowledge of God vis-à-vis the anthropological aspect of religion." (*Ibid.*) "Only on the sure foundation of anthropology could the idea of God have the high rank that it does for the phenomenon of religion." (ST I, 127)[19]

---

events." (BQiTH, 12) – Regarding the place of the doctrine of Scripture in the total context of his systematic theology, Pannenberg has expressed himself in summary in "Zur Begründung der Lehre von der Schriftinspiration" in: M. Seitz and K. Lemkühler (eds.), In der Wahrheit Bleiben. Dogma – Schriftauslegung – Kirche (*festschrift* for Reinhard Slenczka), Göttingen 1996, 156 – 159; reprinted in BSTh 1, 246 – 248. He assumes "that dogmatics cannot simply presuppose the grounding of the authority of the Bible in an inspiration of the biblical documents through the Spirit of God as the starting point of its argumentation, in order to present Christian doctrine as grounded from this sort of formal authority. Much more, the claim of inspiration made by the apostolic writings of the New Testament to be grounded and tested against the content of the Gospel of Jesus Christ. Thus, this topic does not belong in the prolegomena, but rather first after the doctrine of the person and work of Jesus Christ, in connection with the doctrine of the Gospel as the word of reconciliation and prior to the doctrine of ecclesiology, where one is to connect the doctrine of the ecclesiological office called to the Gospel to the authority of the Gospel. It is here that the place for the presentation of the precedence of Holy Scripture to all later ecclesiological doctrine formation and tradition, in the Reformation sense of Scripture as the rule and norm of all doctrine." (BSTh 1, 247). The importance of the Old Testament for Christian faith is made clear in an article of the same name, in: JBth 12 (1997), reprinted in BSTh 1, 255 – 256. The concept of a theology of only the Old Testament, however, is rejected: cf. "Problems in a Theology of (Only) the Old Testament" in: H.T.C. Sun and K.L. Eades (Eds.), Problems in biblical Theology. Essays in honour of Rolf Knierim, 1997, 275 – 280; reprinted in BSTh 1, 249 – 254.

19 For the limitation of the concept of the idea of meaning as foundation for the concept of religion

Barth and Pannenberg protest against the anthroplogizing of theology in unity. Pannenberg opines, however, that one can only protest against such effectively in the manner of "a discussion of the problem which from the time of the Enlightenment has led to the domination of the concept of religion as a foundation for dogmatics." (ST I, 127) The task of systematic theology – which Pannenberg judged that Barth had not sufficiently perceived – is then: "How can theology make the primacy of God and his revelation in Jesus Christ intelligible, and validate its truth claim, in an age when all talk about God is reduced to subjectivity, as may be seen from the social history of the time and the modern fate of the proofs of God and philosophical theology?" (ST I, 128) Prior to the explicit treatment of this question, the implicit problem must be examined; the implicit problem which the fact of the plurality of religions causes for the idea of religion as well as for the claim of absoluteness which Christianity makes. The starting point of Hume's demonstration of the priority of the positive religions in opposition to the so-called natural religion. The result of this detailed examination, which contains detailed examinations of the positions of Schleiermacher, Hegel, Otto Pfleiderer and Ernst Troltsch, is that there is a necessary differentiation between anthropological foundations and concrete religions. This differentiation itself is related to the question regarding the relationship between religions and the reality of God or of the gods. The goal is to emphasize the primacy of divine reality in religious experience in opposition to a purely anthropological conception of the religious phenomenon.

The claim that religious awareness is explicitly of such a nature that divinity precedes and preempts it is brought to bear against a purely anthropological definition of the idea of religion. This purely anthropological concept is that such as in the sense of Paul Tillich, that which directly concerns me. This argument is also differentiated through the observation, that the unity of the idea of religion as a compilation of different religious behaviors presupposes a "unity which transcends the phenomena on the side of divine reality." (ST I, 144) This brings Pannenberg to the following conclusion: "As religion in general, according to the self-understanding of the religions, is grounded in the working of the gods, so the unity of the religious object must have its basis and origin in the unity of the deity. According to the modern view, early in the cultural history of the race the sense of a unity of deity dominating the plurality of manifestations is implied, if not definitely present, in the tension between the one and the many. If this is so, it is natural enough to regard the

as apart from the concept of the meaning of actions, cf. "Macht der Mensch die Religion, oder macht die Religion den Menschen? Ein Rückblick auf die Diskussionen des religionstheoreti- schen Arbeitskreises", in T. Rendtorff (ed.), Religion als Problem der Aufklärung. Eine Bilanz aus der religionstheoretischen Forschung, 1980, 151–157; reprinted in: BSTh 2, 254–259. For the basic anthropological relevance of religion, cf. further the article "Religion und menschliche Natur", in: W. Pannenberg (ed.), Sind wir von Natur aus religiös?, 1986, 9–24; reprinted in: BSTh 2, 260–270.

history of religion as a history of the manifestation of the unity of deity which God himself controls on the path of self-revelation. A view of this kind presupposes, off course, the standpoint of the monotheistic religions. It takes not of all the religions but relates them to the general understanding." (ST I, 149) This thought is connected to the idea of the unity of humanity, and rounded out: "Where the world of religion is viewed as a unity on the basis of the concept of the unity of God, there is no incompatibility with religion's understanding of itself. The ambivalence of the unity and plurality of deity which marks the thinking of early cultures is simply merged into a sense of the unity which raises up the plurality into itself." (ST I, 151)

The continuation of this thought is found in the consideration of the *truth of religion*, or the religions. This has been systematically improperly recognized in functional theories of religion (cf. ST I, 151) and explicitly denied by the genetic critique of religion (Marx, Feuerbach). Theology has encountered such attacks not seldom with recourse to the factual nature of religious experience. This recourse is, however, "hampered by the basic difficulty that the deity which is claimed to be the author of religious experience inevitably seems to be a positing of this religious sense. But this difficulty in no way characterized the religious sense as such, which can never think of surrendering its subjectivity as an guarantee of the reality of its object." (ST I, 154) It was first in the secular culture of the modern west that the dependence on subject steadied the content of religion; it was in any case so that religion was usually ascribed a constitutive meaning for the humanity of man in the sense of a religious disposition, valid as an anthropological universal. Schleiermacher is named as a classic example of this position. Under Schleiermacher's own conditions, on cannot speak of a positing of religion by human consciousness, even when he himself did not develop the idea of religion from the primacy of its object. As a consequence of this, the radical criticism of religion and the thesis that "religion is not a constitutive part of human nature" (ST I, 155) are confronted with the principle that exactly this is the case, in one way or another. As an indicator for the foundation of anthropology through religion, Pannenberg names the general presence of religion since the earliest beginnings of humanity, and, in association with this the "universal occurrence from the very beginnings of humanity" of religion, "and especially its basic importance for all cultures and probably also for the origin of speech." (*Ibid.*) This corresponds with the that unique factor of human behavior which is described with self-transcendence, ex-centricity, and world-openness, in the manner in which this is constitutive in the life of the individual; the original trust upon the strength of which the "I" leaves itself and undergoes the process of building personality in the concretion of life history.

One can speak validly in anthropological terms about a religious disposition of humans. Religion is constitutive for the humanity of the human. This result is not sufficient to establish the truth of religious claims, but it is indispensable. To put it theologically: "If the one God is to be the Creator of the human race, then as self-conscious beings we must have some awareness, however inadequate, of this origin of ours. Our human existence necessarily bears the mark of creature-hood, and this cannot be totally hidden from our awareness of ourselves." (ST I, 157) However, the proof of religion decides, as mentioned, for itself as an anthropological universal as such, but says nothing about the *truth-content* of religion. "Hence the question as to the truth of religious statements about God finds an answer in the sphere of experience of the world, as the world, including humanity and its history, shows itself to be determined by God." (ST I, 159) With this task and the meaning which comes to the idea of the world in the context of perception, one indeed cannot gain the upper hand over the anthropological referentiality; however, the limit of religious anthropocentrics is defeated. The demonstration of the God-determined nature of the world occurs, according to Pannenberg, "not…in the form of the cosmological proof which by inference from the world, and especially from the contingency of everything finite, postulates a self-existent Origin or Author of the world. For religious belief in God the concept of God is already the starting point for the appeal to experience of the world. This experience has the function of either confirming or not confirming the truth which is already claimed in the religious concept of God, namely, that God is the all-determining reality." (*Ibid.*) This criteria is in the following passages combined with the fact that world-experience is not yet finished. Additionally, the fact that experiences continually contain a constructive-fictional element[20] plays a role. From these follow both the contentiousness of religious content as well as the plurality of the same. In the face of this, the question must be posed whether the criteria of protection (or, respectively, non-protection) of religious content comes to grips with the experience of the world.

Pannenberg insists first once again that the claims of religious content are note mere functions and epiphenomena of other contexts – such as the political-economical context. (cf. ST I, 162). Thereupon he notes that "[o]bviously, changes in secular experience do not automatically bring with them religious changes." (ST I, 164) This leads to the question, in what manner religious claims relate to the content of world-experience "that we do not have purely subjective interpretations which may be exchanged at will and which are outside experience itself? This seems to be possible only if there are implications of meaning in the actual contents of experience – implications which become thematically explicit on the plane of religious statements but which might be missed by such statements." (*Ibid.*) The content of this

---

20 Pannenberg shows that an abstract criticism of the fictional as important for religious awareness is itself an expression of a reduced awareness of reality in "Das Irreale des Glaubens" in: D. Heinrich and W. Iser (eds.), Funktionen des Fiktiven (= Poetik und Hermenutik Bd. X), München 1983, 17–34; reprinted in BSTh 1, 114–131.

determination is explained with reference to Tillich, as well as the conceptions of Schleiermacher and Hegel. In particular the treatment of Hegel plays an important role for Pannenberg's own understanding, insofar as Pannenberg draws the following conclusion from Hegel's critique of Schleiermacher: "If religious perceptions thematize the implicit relation of the contents of experience to the infinite, the question arises whether they do justice to the full complexity of the relation." (ST I, 167) Put simply, "religious perceptions are…exposed to the question whether they properly fulfil their function of bringing to light the infinite in the finite." (*Ibid.*) Or, said differently, "the gods of the religious must show in our experience of the world that they are the powers which they claim to be." (*Ibid.*)

If the decision about the truth of the religions is made "in the process of experience of the world and the struggle to interpret it" (ST I, 168), then in this context the observation is also important that (first) in Israel "the experience of historical change itself became a medium of awareness of God" (ST I, 169). "In the process an awareness also necessarily developed that each confirmation of faith in God in a historical situation, each experience of new acts of God, not only sets all that precedes in a dew light but also itself proves to be provisional. There thus arises the question of a future definitive self-demonstration of the deity of God, a question which arose in Israel especially in exilic prophecy and was later taken up by apocalyptic into expectation of end-time events." (*Ibid.*) For Pannenberg's own conception, this is insofar foundational as he wishes to understand history, especially the history of religion, as the history of the appearance of divinity (cf. ST I, 170 f.).[21]

---

21 Pannenberg does not deny that his theology of the history of religions is conceived from a Christian perspective. This is not to say "that such a point of view needs to argue from a standpoint of faith instead of appealing to the actual phenomena in the history of religions. The notion of understanding the history of religions as the history of the appearances of the divine mystery indeed did not arise by chance. If this perspective, as I hope, comes closer than others to the logic of the essential content of the phenomena of the history of religions, it is nevertheless not produced by these phenomena; rather, it is this perspective that first allows the phenomena to be discovered. And reducing it to its proper concept, could hardly be accomplished without commitment to the god of the Bible and his eschatological revelation in Jesus Christ." (BQiTh, "Toward a Theology of the History of Religions", 65 – 118, here:112). This also indicates the fact that makes the Judeo-Christian tradition special among the other religions: it is open to the future of its own metamorphosis. – Theological considerations on the idea of dialogue with the world religions can be found in "Religion und Religionen" in: A. Bsteh (ed.), Dialog aus der Mitte christlicher Theologie (=Beiträge zur Religionstheologie 5), 1987, 179 – 196; reprinted in BSTh 1, 143 – 159. After a differentiated determination of the context of religion and revelation, Pannenberg explicates the relation of Christianity to the world religions (with particular view to Judaism and Islam on one hand, Buddhism and Hinduism on the other). Cf. also: "Das Christentum – eine Religion unter anderen?" (1996), in: BSTh 1, 173 – 184 as well as "Das christliche Gottesverständis im Spannungsfeld seiner jüdischen und christlichen Wurzeln" in: Der christliche Glaube und seine jüdisch-griechische Herkungt (EKD-Texte 15), 1986, 13 – 22; reprinted in BSTh 1, 266 – 277. Further to the dialogue with Buddhism cf. " Auf der Suche nach dem wahren Selbst. Anthropologie als Ort der Begegnung zwischen christlichem und buddhistischem Denken", in A. Bsteh (ed.), Erlösung in Christentum und Buddhismus, 1982, 128 –

Prior to developing his own understanding of revelation, Pannenberg summarizes the elementary parts of religious behavior: foundational for all forms of religious worship, when not its highest gestalt, is the awareness of God. "For the truth of religion as worship of God rests on its correspondence to the true God and his revelation." (ST I, 172) With this is presupposed the "fact that hand in hand with awareness of the divine reality goes awareness of our own finitude in our distinctness form God" (*Ibid.*), which is implied in the religious relation. With reference to Hegel, this is broken down: "For Hegel the cultus overcomes the distance from God in which we find ourselves." (ST I, 173; cf. the idea of sacrifice, myth, etc.) Pannenberg is convinced of the superiority of the Hegelian description of religious relationship, as opposed to a phenomenology "which can find in the religious phenomenon only expressions of human behavior" (ST I, 175). He is thus able to accept the metaphysical idea of absolute infinity as the condition for all experience of the finite, which, although it lacks the character of the personal or personally encountered power, converges in the rest with the idea of God present in the monotheistic religions. The personal deficit, when one can call it that, brings Pannenberg ultimately to "regard the Absolute of metaphysics as only an approximation of the reality that is meant in religious ideas of God, although it is so, of course, from the standpoint of rational universality." (ST I, 176)

It is thus repeated, what has already been said about the relationship between rational, "natural" theology and the positive religions. Pannenberg also reflects on the deficiency which comes to light in the religious relationship itself, as well as the criticism against Judeo-Christian religion. : among other things, the accusation of an inadmissible making-finite of the infinite (cf. ST I, 180 – 181), as well as the idea of power over God for the sake of the self-security of the human (cf. ST I, 182 – 183). It is in this context that magic is labeled a declined form of religion, and the myth or the idea of mythic awareness is criticized. Despite this, it is important to see "that myth is not eliminated in Christianity but integrated and transcended. This is in keeping with an understanding of God which is not determined exclusively by his function in originally establishing the order of the world but which is also not antithetical to this function, believing that God as Creator, Reconciler, and Redeemer of the world embraces all the dimensions of the reality of life and abolishes the distinction of sacred and profane in terms of the eschatological consummation. What is normative for the Christian understanding of God, then, is not the awareness of myth but the event of revelation, of the self-demonstration of the deity of God in the process of salvation history." (ST I, 187)[22] The task set

---

146; reprinted in BSTh 2, 175 – 190 (cf. also: Christliche Spiritualität. Theologische Aspekte, 1986, 82 – 98).

22 For the concept of myth as an archetypal original event, cf. Späthorizone des Mythos in biblischer und christlicher Überlieferung, in M. Fuhrmann (ed.), Terror und Speil (= Poetik und Hermenutik IV), 1971, 473 – 525; independently printed as "Christentum und Mythos", 1972,

for further consideration comes from this: "It will have to be shown that the making finite of the Infinite which characterizes the religious relation of humanity to God, while it is not overcome in the cultic practice of Christians, is transcended in the event of the revelation of God. To the extent that this overcoming of the perversion that takes place in the religious relation to God works itself out, through the consciousness of faith, in the life of Christians and the church, the human relation to God is set right by faith. But this does not protect the members of the church, as the experiences of history show, against the perversion of religion into magic" (*Ibid.*)

5. The Revelation of God

Because God can only be known as He gives Himself to be known, knowledge of God is only possible through revelation. With this principle Pannenberg defines the theological function of the idea of revelation (cf. ST I, 189 ff.)[23], although he makes with this no statement about the manner of revelation though which God gives Himself to be known. The following differences are to be considered first:

1. Only such communication as mediates the first instance of knowledge of the divinity can be considered revelation (cf. ST I, 195 f.)
2. "Nor should we expect that every form of revelation will have God himself as its content or even its author." (ST I, 195)
3. "Finally, we have to consider that even where the biblical God declares himself and thus makes himself known in many places his deity is shown

reprinted in GSTh 2, 13–65. "Die weltbegründende Funktion des Mythos und der christliche Offenbarungsglaube" are viewed in their relation in the article of the same name in: H.H. Schmid (ed.), Mythos und Rationalität, 1987, 108–122; reprinted in BSTh 1, 185–199. With this, "not only the difference, but also the positive relevance of mythical forms of thought in relation to the Christian understanding of revelation and the process of its tradition" (BSTh 1, 9) are worked out. Cf. further the early writing: Mythos und Wort. Theologische Überlegunen zu Karl Jaspers' Mythusbegriff, in:ZThK 51 (1954) 197–185. – Pannenberg sees the "falling asleep" of the debate over Bultmann's demythologization program rather a a result of a certain exhaustion and turn to other current topics than as the result of a solution pleasing to all parties. "In the course of theological discussion, a continual unfolding of the great problems of theology rarely finds expression. The topic of myth is, however, too earnest, that it may simply be seen as handled with the turn to other theological interests. In the question of the mythical in the biblical tradition is collected all of that which makes a critical handling of the biblical text regardless of all temporal conditions, also in regard to its religious theme, as if it were the burning point at which also the modern awareness focuses, when it does not deny its own Christian mediation." (GSTh 2, 8).

23 To the complex terminological and material result, cf. "Offenbarung and 'Offenbarungen' im Zeugnis der Geschichte" in the handbook for fundamental theology volume 2 1985, 84–106 (eds. W. Kern, H.J. Pottmeyer and M. Seckler); reprinted in BSTh 1, 212–237.

only as the mightily transcendent deity of the God of Israel, known only to his people and its members, not a universal deity for all humanity." (*Ibid.*)

These enclosing differences are demonstrated individually in a historic manner. Pannenberg does this with a particular view to the tradition of the Israelites. This brings exceptional meaning to the witness of Deutero-Isaiah, insofar the future of God's self-proof and the terminological content of revelation are connected, and insofar as emphasis is placed upon the uniqueness and universality of the revealed God. In this tradition, Pannenberg makes systematic connections to the function of eschatological self-revelation of the one true God, that the idea of revelation which is encountered in such variety in the Bible becomes concentrated on this revelation for the entirety of humanity, and for the world.

It is with this goal in mind that Pannenberg turns to the *complexity of the biblical idea of revelation.* He notes explicitly and prior to beginning that the development of the biblical ideas of revelation "will make the transition from the phenomenology of the experiences of revelation which are richly attested to in the religious world to the theme of the revelation of the deity of the God of Israel as the one God of all people." (ST I, 196) The methodical consequence of this transition for the further explication of the truth-question regarding the Christian message about God are presented in such a manner, that one is allowed good insight into the whole conception (ST I, 195 – 198). In particular, the question is once again repeated, why it is that a systematic theology whose theme is the question after truth cannot directly begin with a reconstruction of Christian doctrine by building on the claim of the historical revelation of God. Interesting and important is also the observation, that and under what conditions the method chosen for the development of Christian doctrine can be applied to other religions (cf. ST I, 197 f.).

The presentation of the complexity of the biblical idea of revelation is next aimed to "refute the idea that experiences of revelation involve a first-time knowledge of deity." (ST I, 199) Against this view, it is shown to be valid that "Deity was not so much the content of experiences of revelation as the source of information concerning what was hidden in everyday life." (*Ibid.*) This is not the place to examine these empirical issues; however, it is desirable to note the summary, which is given first with a view to the Old Testament (cf. in particular ST I, 206) and later for the New Testament. Worth noting is also the lack of a unified terminology of revelation. Further, the idea of a self-revelation of God in the sense of a communication which aims to reveal itself is not an explicitly biblical manner of speaking. Despite this, the thought is present since the concentration of the exile prophecies on the word of God's self-proof through His deeds, and this is also contained in the New Testament exegesis of the revelation of the divine plan of history (mysterion).

The chapter on revelation in the Systematic Theology aims at a differentiated, new formulation and new foundation of the thesis from "Revelation as History", in which one should understand revelation biblically as the indirect self-revelation of God. On one hand, this does justice to the fact that the Old Testament contains a multiplicity of revelatory formulations, analogous to its religio-historical environment. On the other hand, the transition from this multiplicity of religious phenomena to the specific biblical understanding of revelation as the self-revelation of God in God's historical action is demonstrated in the development to the prophetic word of divine self-proving. This concept of revelation eventually flows into the New Testament thought of revelation as a divine plan for history (mysterion). The terminological situation in the New Testament is also first examined in the Systematic Theology.

Although the idea of revelation as the (indirect) *self-revelation of God* through his action in history is present in the biblical text, it is only gradually within the history of theology an important topic; it is first in modern times thematically central. The reason for this requires an explanation from historical theology. This is given in the context of extensive considerations regarding the function of the term "revelation" in theological history. "In patristic theology the concept of theology did not yet have the basic function in the presenting of Christian teaching that it took on in the Latin Middle Ages and especially in modern theology." (ST I, 214)[24] Pannenberg displays the reasons for this upon the background of detailed examinations of the patristic idea of revelation (cf. ST I, 214–217).[25] While this was rather "the basis of the argument but the goal" (ST I, 218), this is quite different in "the European Middle Ages, in which the church had long since become an authority for the peoples, and the church for its part vouched for the authorities on which it relied, namely, the teaching and writings of the apostles. Augustine had prepared the ground for the dominance of the idea of authority in the Latin Middle Ages. In the new grouping, in which authority based on divine revelation confronted reason and experience, the concept of revelation acquired a basic theological function in close connection with the authority of scripture." (ST I, 218–219)

The critique of authority present in the Enlightenment brought an additional and significant change in the idea of revelation. Pannenberg follows this process, with particular attention to the concept of Carl Ludwig Nitzsch and his "differentiating and interrelating of an outer revelation, of a public manifestation of God in the events of history, and of inspiration as the effect and interpretation of these events in the subjectivity of the biblical witness" (ST I, 221). In this he takes the "idea of a historical revelation that is distinct from inspiration" to the point at which it meets the thought "that

---

24 This error is a clear editorial oversight; it should read "the concept of revelation" (*Offenbarungsbegriff* in the original). – Trans.

25 Cf. also "Revelation in Early Christianity" in the *festschrift* for Henry Chadwick: Christian Authority, ed. G.R. Evans, Oxford 1988, 76–85.

revelation has God not merely as its subject but also as its exclusive content and theme." (ST I, 222) Thereupon, Pannenberg examines the history of the concept of "God's self-revelation in this strict sense" (ST I, 222), with the result, that it is first German Idealism that has thought of "the self-revelation of God in the sense of the strict identity of subject and content." (ST I, 222–223) This gain in meaning for the thought of God's self-revelation in philosophy and theology at the turn of the 19th century is explained by "[a] first reason…the decay of the older Protestant doctrine of the authority of scripture which viewed revelation as divine inspiration. A second reason was the decay of the natural theology of the Enlightenment." (ST I, 224) Under these conditions, the idea of the self-revelation of God must, at the same time, become the foundation for the assertion of the reality of God (cf. *Ibid.*). The manner in which this thought connects with the idea of an external revelation, as developed by Carl Ludwig Nitzsch, is examined thereupon, with particular attention to the thought of Richard Rothe (cf. ST I, 224 f.). Rothe's thesis, that the "external" revelations as manifestations of God must also be accompanied and expanded by an event of inspiration, is particularly important (cf. ST, I 225). The so-called word revelation thus "determines the character of the historical acts of revelation." (ST I, 226) The examples of Kähler and Barth allow Pannenberg to examine this situation as the (biblically inappropriate) "reduction of the revelation of God to divine speaking" (ST I, 227), that he can thereupon develop his own position in contrast, coming from the 1961 "Revelation and History". The criticism of this work, primarily from the camp of the dialectic theologians, centered on the "supposed alternative of the Word of God and history" (ST I, 228), thus Pannenberg turns to a concluding section with the topic "Revelation as History and as Word of God" (ST I, 230).

The factual requirements of his idea of revelation and the criteria of his evaluation are formulated as follows at the end of the previous section: the conception of *revelation as history* makes not only possible "to abandon the restriction of the historical self-demonstration of God to exceptional miraculous events" (ST I, 229), but also allows one "to overcome the antithesis between revelation as manifestation and a supplementary inspiration insofar as the dawning of eschatological reality in the coming and work of Jesus implies that the expectation of the final revelation of the deity of God to the whole world that is bound up with the eschatological future of history is already fulfilled in Jesus, although only by way of anticipation." (*Ibid.*) The judgment regarding the correctness of this concept, in turn, must "be made according to two criteria, first, by whether the different biblical views of revelation are successfully integrated, and second, by whether the presuppositions are systematically plausible on which the proposed solution rests." (*Ibid.*) Pannenberg takes care to deal with the proof of truth in both senses in what follows. First, he deals with the criticism of a historical theology, as it was presented in 1963 from James Barr. In this context, the primary point of importance is the definition of the biblical idea of history as that of the action of God, which "embraces all human action" (ST I, 231), as well as the comparison with the so-called profane idea of history. Also important is Pannenberg's interest in "the realistic intention of the bibilical accounts" (*Ibid.*). This is the ground for his insistence on the necessary facticity of the events reported in the bible and his plea for the theological essentiality of historical verification. It is equally the ground for his decided retention of the term "history" as opposed to "story". Thereupon, Pannenberg's concentrates on the "replacement of the idea of revelation as history by the old idea of a revelation by word" (ST I, 233), as it was suggested by Barr, and in the manner in which it was made valid by many theologians. He considers first the British discussion, followed by the German Word-of-God theology, in particular that of Barth (cf. ST I, 235 f.), Jüngel (cf. ST I, 236 ff.), and Ebeling (cf. ST I, 238 ff.). Following this, he examines the reasoning, why it is that the idea of the Word of God "has gained a great deal of plausibility and is largely taken for granted by Christians, especially in the Protestant world." (ST I, 240) Next, he notes his reservations regarding the "simple and naïve understanding of God's self-revelation as the Word of God." (ST I, 241) The renewed reference to the multiple nature of the biblical idea of revelation gives then the opportunity to introduce the thesis of "the indirectness of God's self-revelation", insofar as this "has the systematic function of integrating the various experiences of revelation to which the biblical writings bear witness." (ST I, 243)

A systematic treatment of this thesis follows the biblical founding: the indication of the "majesty of God in the revelation of his deity" (ST I, 244)[26] is important for the consideration, as well as the retrospective character of the knowledge of revelation (cf. ST I, 244 – 245).This latter observation is one in which Pannenberg connects a comparison of the *heilsgeschichte* thought in Israel to the mythic traditions with the central thought of God's self-proof at the end of history. He then immediately connects this to a fundamental, Christological principle, when he writes "The future of God is not merely disclosed in advance with the coming of Jesus; it is already an event, although without ceasing to be future." (ST I, 247) In this particular sense, one can "speak of an anticipatory revelation, in Christ's person and work, of the deity of God that in the future of his kingdom will be manifest to every eye." (*Ibid.*) Additionally, "[t]he realism of eschatological expectation of the future is the basis of the primitive Christian understanding of revelation as it was also the presupposition of Jesus' proclamation of the coming of God's kingdom and the frame of reference for the apostolic message about Christ." (ST I, 247 – 248) The question, whether the early Christian eschatological expectation can be combined with the modern worldview remains unexamined, after the point is made that this very question cannot be avoided. The answer is to be found first

---

26 The German original refers to the secret of the majesty of God in the revelation of his deity", (*Geheimnis der Erhabenheit Gottes in der Offenbarung seiner Gottheit*, page 268 in the German version) – Trans.

in Pannenberg's eschatology, though its development begins in his doctrine of creation. However, the question regarding the form of knowledge of revelation is to be answered here (cf. ST I, 249), that is to say, the question regarding eschatological evidence unique to the Christ-event (cf. ST I, 249–250).

The thesis regarding the knowable or recognizable nature of the eschatological Christ-revelation without additional inspiration, already present in "Revelation as History", has (in Pannenberg's own words) its peak in the fact that the revelation develops from its own content (as spirit-filled).[27] "The eschatological revelation of God does not need to be manifested by outside supplementary inspiration as a principle of interpretation, for the reality of the Risen Lord itself sheds forth the Spirit that makes hum known as the fulfilment of the divine promises." (ST I, 250) Of course, this knowledge remains disputed under certain conditions. Furthermore, the argument is concentrated on the question how "we are to understand more precisely the need which the content of apostolic proclamation imposes to communicate it in the form of the Word" (ST I, 252). This answer is also postponed; here only "more radically[,] the function of the Word as 'report' for the mediation of the content of relation" (Ibid.) is handled. With reference to Ebeling and "a theologically deepened understanding of human speech" (ST I, 254) as well as with the use of a comparison of the biblical understanding of the Word of God with the word of myth (cf. ST I, 254–255), Pannenberg asks this question with the result that "the idea of the Word of God remains a mythical category and an instrument of unproven claims to authority" (ST I, 256) without the historical theology of the bible and its presence in the idea of revelation.[28]

27 For this the article "Einsicht und Glaube" in ThLZ 88 (1963), Sp. 81–92; reprinted in BQiTh 2, 28–45 is helpful. In this, Pannenberg deals more precisely with the questions of the relation of the knowledge of revelation to faith and the Holy Spirit, which were brought up regarding "Revelation and Histroy" by Paul Althaus (Offenbarung als Geschichte und Glaube. Bemerkungen zu Wolfhart Pannenbergs Begriff der Offenbarung, in: ThLZ 87 (1962), 321–330).

28 The implication oft he thought of the self-revelation of God in His historical Word which is Jesus Christ in person is explicated in the doctrine of the Trinity. Cf. ST I, 281.

§3 The Trinitarian God and the Creation of the World (ST I, Chapters 5–7)

1. The Trinitarian Nature of the Revealed God

In the course of the Systematic Theology, the move from the end of the chapter on revelation also occasions a methodological change. The idea of progress through continual hypotheses, each closer than the last, was the plumb line for the topic until now; everything that follows is, however, presented in under the aspect of the explication of God's self-revelation in Jesus Christ. The explicit presentation of the Christian truth-claim couldn't be placed at the beginning of a systematic-theological examination, according to Pannenberg, in order to avoid the suspicion of building on either an authoritarian dogmatism or a subjective decisionism. Introductory examinations of the idea of God as a result of human language use and human though were required, as was an analysis of the anthropological relevance of religion as a theme in human lives. This allowed Pannenberg to examine the religious evidences of divine reality, which, of course, are in the reality of the world disputed, as a context for the examination of the biblical idea of revelation. It is this idea in whose context "human historical experience becomes an express theme in demonstration of the power and deity of the gods, and the related claim is made that the God of the Bible will prove himself to be the one God of all people, or has already shown himself to be this on God in Jesus Christ. At this point, then, the question of the truth fo the Christian message has to be the question whether this claim may be coherently made, and the testing of this claim must take the form of a systematic reconstruction of Christian teaching from its starting point in the historical revelation of God which it asserts." (ST I, 196)The argumentative demands on the previously-mentioned principle of coherence are thus not least extraordinary due to necessity of showing that "this transition took place in the history of religion itself and not just in modern theological reflection" (*Ibid.*) in the process of the "turn in our examination of the truth question to the reconstruction of what is said about God in the tradition of Christian doctrine." (ST I, 197) The Trinitarian understanding of God as revealed in Jesus Christ is decisive for this demonstration.

The consideration of the Trinitarian God are connected directly to the doctrine of historical revelation, fittingly so, as such is the order of theological knowledge.[1] Pannenberg begins with the name of God as Father, which was a

---

1 The biblical understanding of God in the Old and New Testament and the understanding fo reality

distinguishing mark not merely for the message of Jesus, but already foundational for Israel's history of covenant and election. Of course, this explicitly contradicts the assumption that "the words 'God' and 'Father' are…just time-bound concepts from which we can detach the true content of the message." (ST I, 263) That is already not the case because the *self-differentiation of Jesus from God*, already contained within the act of calling Him "Father", is constitutive for his own theological importance. Pannenberg connects the already-developed idea of indirect revelation with considerations arising from a theology of the Trinity. The deciding thesis notes that the unity of Jesus with God is achieved precisely through the strict self-differentiation of Jesus from God. The Son is, in this sense, precisely as the one differentiated from the Father, the real figure in which He appears. "Here is one of the starting points for the history of primitive Christian Christology and also for that of the doctrine of the Trinity which arose out of primitive Christology." (ST I, 264)

Pannenberg follows this with a treatment of a few initial points in the Christological statements of the early church which lead to the thought of the full Godhood of the son: the conception of pre-existence, and furthermore, the assumption of the Spirit of God as "the medium of the communion of Jesus with the father and the mediator of the participation of believers in Christ." (ST I, 266) The latter point leads to the thesis that "the fellowship of Jesus as Son with God as Father can obviously be stated only if there is reference to a third as well, the Holy Spirit." (ST I, 267) Pannenberg evaluates the historical and content-based reasons for the perception of the Spirit as an independent hypostasis, differentiated from the Father and from the Son, as well as the constitutive importance of the Spirit for the Father-Son communal relationship. Following this, he turns to the particular problem of the unity and correct

---

as history build the context upon which Christian theology focuses. The question of God and that of the meaning and truth of history can indeed be distinguished, but not separated. The key to a differentiated answer to both questions in their commonality is delivered by the doctrine of the Trinity, which Pannenberg sees as bringing the general doctrine of God into itself and thus also including the doctrine of God's being, nature, and attributes. As the doctrine of the Trinity thinks of the God revelaed in the history of Jesus Christ, it opens up the insight into the relation of God to history as such, for it identifies the God revealed historically in Jesus Christ as the Creator of the worl of humans and the future of their salvation. The connection of historical and Trinitarian theology are given, for example in "Der Gott der Geschichte. Der trinitarische Gott und die Wahrheit der Geschiche" in KuD 23 (1997), 76–92; reprinted in GSTh 2, 112–128. The argument of this article is prepared by the following studies: 1. "Person und Subject (NZSTh 18(1976) 133–148; reprinted in GSTh 2, 80–95), 2. "Die Subjektivität Gottes und die Trinitätslehre. Ein Beitrag zur Beziehung zwischen Karl Barth und der Philosophie Hegels" (KuD 23 (1977), 25–40; reprinted in GSTh 2, 96–111. The first „connects a treatment of the subject-theoretical view of modern philosophy, in particular of German Idealism, with a terminological explanation. Through this, the critical dismissal is possible of an anthropomorphic 'psychology' of the one God into the doctrine of the Trinity, as was introduce by Latin scholasticism and as it became acute in modern theology. This makes the second step possible, to work out the problematic common denominator of the interpretation of the Trinity by Barth and Hegel." (GSTh 2, 8)

differentiation between Father, Son, and Spirit and the problem of the correct perception of the Spirit and the solutions to these problems. The relevant principle is: "One can know the inter-Trinitarian distinctions and relations, the inner life of God, only through the revelation of the Son, not through the different spheres of the operation of the one God in the world. Only subsequently can one relate specific aspects of the unity of the divine working in the world to Trinitarian distinctions that are known already." (ST I, 273) This is an indication of both organizational and factual importance in dogmatics, insofar as it refers to the inseparable connection between the Trinity and the Christ-event. The inter-Trinitarian differences are founded in "one and the same event, in the message of Jesus concerning God and his coming kingdom." (ST I, 272)

Without dealing with a more precise Christology at this point, Pannenberg turns to the question, whether and to what extent the Christian doctrine of the Trinity "harmonize[s]…with the monotheistic character of the biblical belief in God and the tradition of philosophical theology." (ST I, 273) The peak of the argumentation is in the decided claim, that monotheism can only be grounded and maintained in a Trinitarian manner. In the context of the thesis of Trinitarian monotheism the "essential transcendent reality of the one God and the modes of his manifestation" (ST I, 277) play a key role. Pannenberg follows the theological determinations of this relationship first from the perspective of the history of dogma, with particular attention to the logos-speculation. He comes to the result that the dogmas from Nicaea and Constantinople have not sufficiently solved the Trinitarian problem, for which reason it was to be passed on to other theological generations.

In contrast to the process common since high scholasticism (and which was kept after the Reformation), "the procedure of beginning with the question of the existence of the one God, then dealing with the nature and attributes of this God, and only then handling the doctrine of the Trinity" (ST I, 280–281), Pannenberg begins with the trinity. The reasons for this are developed in detailed interaction with the tradition, which divided the doctrine of God into "De Deo uno" and "de Deo Trino", giving the former a theologically foundational function. Critical attention is given to the question, whether the tri-unity of the divine persons is to be derived from the divine unity, as the traditional method would seem to approve as appropriate. The conception of Augustine finds a special place in these considerations (ST I, 283 ff.). Furthermore, Pannenberg handles the relevant conceptions of Pseudo-Dionysius the Areopagite, Anselm of Canterbury, Richard of St. Victor, Gilbert de la Porrée, and Thomas Aquinas (cf. STI 285 ff.). "Reformation theology lost the tighter systematic structuring that the doctrine of God had achieved in High Scholasticism because it took seriously its declaration that the trinity is known only by revelation." (ST I, 289)

The decline of Trinitarian thought, as it proceeded towards the goal of full dissolution in the time of the Enlightenment and rationalism, is increased

with the antitrinitarian criticism of Socinianism and (moderated) Armi-
nianism; it is founded in their lack of negotiating properly between the idea
of the personal difference of God with the thought of the unity of the divine
being. It is first with Lessing and the philosophy of German Idealism that a
renaissance in the doctrine of the Trinity arises: "In Hegel's philosophy of
the absolute Spirit the renewal of the doctrine of the Trinity in terms of self-
conscious spirit took classical form." (ST I, 292) However, Pannenberg raises
the objection against Hegel and the Hegelian theological tradition that "to
derive the Trinitarian distinctions from the self-differentiation of the divine
Spirit in its self-awareness is to subsume the threeness of the persons into the
concept of a single personal God...For all the differentiation in the self-
consciousness, the God of this understanding is a single subject. The
moments in the self-consciousness have no subjectivity of their own." (ST I,
294 – 295) this difficulty is also present in Karl Barth's doctrine of the trinity
and its speech of three "modes of being" (cf. Isaak August Dorner) instead of
three persons present and unresolved. Indeed, Barth does not derive the
Trinitarian differences from the idea of self-awareness or *Geist*, but rather
from the formal idea of revelation. "This model of a Trinity of revelation is
easily seen to be structurally identical with that of the self-conscious
Absolute, especially when God's revelation has to be viewed primarily as a
self-revelation." (ST I, 296)

Pannenberg has similar reservations regarding the derivation of the
Trinity from the thought of divine love, as he demonstrates in his analysis of
Jüngel. This is due to the fact of the necessity of the idea of a pimary subject
of love, whose product is the other persons (cf. ST I, 297 ff.). This leads to the
following conclusion: "Any derivation of the plurality of trinitarian persons
from the essence of the one God, whether it be viewed as spirit or love, leads
into the problems of either modalism on the one hand or subordinationism
on the other. Neither, then, can be true to the intentions of the trinitarian
dogma." (ST I, 298) "To find a basis for the doctrine of the Trinity we must
begin with the way in which Father, Son and Spirit come on the scene and
relate to one another in the event of revelation. Here lies the material
justification for the demand that the doctrine of the Trinity must be based on
the biblical witness to revelation or on the economy of salvation. On this
approach there is no material reason to append the doctrine of the Trinity to
that of God's essence and attributes. The latter can be relevantly dealt with in
the context of the trinitarian revelation of God as Father, Son, and Holy
Spirit.

It is true that Christian talk of Father, Son, and Spirit, and especially Jesus'
addressing of God as Father, must always presuppose a prior understanding of
God. This is not, however, the understanding of philosophical theology but
that of religion, and in particular it is the understanding of the God who
revealed himself to Israel as the one God. This view for its part was the result of
a process of struggle between Israel and the surrounding religions, as we

showed in the discussion of revelation in chapter 4 above. It was implicitly modified in the relation of Jesus to the Father, and the modification found explicit expression in the Christian doctrine of the Trinity.

Christian statements about the one God and his essence and attributes relate to the triune God whom we see in the relation of Jesus to the Father. They can thus be discussed only in connection with the doctrine of the Trinity. Rightly this was Barth's procedure in *Church Dogmatics*. But because Barth subordinated his doctrine of the Trinity to a pre-trinitarian concept of the unity of God and his subjectivity in revelation, he could not see what is the function of the doctrine of the essence and attributes of God for the doctrine of the Trinity, namely, that it is only with the question of the essence and attributes of the trinitarian God that the unity of this God becomes a theme, and we are thus enabled to avoid the confusions which inevitably arise when we try to derive the trinity from the person of the Father or the unity of the divine substance." (ST I, 299)

Pannenberg makes an explicit theme of the *differentiation and unity of the divine persons* on this basis, namely, on the result of "a systematic grounding and development of the doctrine of the Trinity... [beginning] with the revelation of God in Jesus Christ, just as the historical past to the construction of the doctrine in Christian theology started with the message and life of Jesus and the apostolic preaching of Christ." (ST I, 300) By beginning with the revelation of God in Jesus Christ, Pannenberg requires first the "fact that the revelational Trinity is inseparable from the essential Trinity...as God reveals himself, so he is in his eternal deity." (*Ibid.*) The decisive question in this context is how the Trinitarian idea of God can be founded in the revelation of God in Jesus without an explicit scriptural evidence for the Trinity (cf. ST I, 300 ff.). Pannenberg finds the starting point in "the relation of Jesus to the Father as it came to expression in his message of the divine rule." (ST I, 304) While Barth derives the idea of Trinity merely from the "formal concept of the self-revealing God" (*Ibid.*), placing the initial point with the father-relationship of Jesus makes the content of revelation the foundation which grounds the doctrine. After indicating the Christological ("The NT statements about the deity of Jesus all presuppose his divine sonship and are ultimately grounded in his relation to the Father. The relation of his message and work to the Father forms the foundation of the confession of the divine sonship of Jesus by the Christian community in the light of the divine confirmation of his fullness of power by the Easter event." ST I, 304; cf. 307) and pneumatological ("As a Son Jesus both differs from the Father and is related to him. This fact is the presupposition for the understanding of the Spirit as a third figure which is distinct from both Father and Son and yet closely related in fellowship with them." ST I, 304–305) implications, Pannenberg makes his judgment regarding the terminology which the classical doctrine of the Trinity "worked out to describe the relations among Father, Son, and Sprit." (ST I, 305) His critique is aimed primarily at the fact that the mutuality and self-differentiation of Father, Son, and Spirit was not appropriately taken into consideration.

For the thought of mutual self-differentiation between Father, Son and Spirit as the concrete gestalt of the Trinitarian relations, the insight that "Jesus shows himself to be the Son of God precisely in his self-distinction from God" (ST I, 310) is foundational: "The self-distinction of Jesus as man from the Father is constitutive not merely for his fellowship with the eternal God in distinction from the first Adam, who wanted to be as God (Gen. 3:5) and in this way separated himself from God. As Jesus glorifies the deity of the Father by his sending and in his own relation to the Father, he himself, in corresponding to the claim of the Father, is so at one with the Father that God in eternity is Father only in relation to him. This distinguishes Jesus from all other human beings who follow his call and by his mediation share in his fellowship with the Father. When this happens it is always on the premise that it is he in whom they have access to the Father. As the one who corresponds to the fatherhood of God, Jesus is the Son, and because the eternal God is revealed herein as Father, and is Father everywhere only as he is so in relation to the Son, the Son shares his deity as the eternal counterpart of the Father. We have here an aspect of the reality of the person of Jesus which is his as the eternal correlate of the deity of the Father and which precedes his human birth. The eternal Son is first, however, an aspect of the human person, and decisive for his appearing is the self-distinction of Jesus from the Father, who for him, too, is the one God. Hence self-distinction from the Father is constitutive for the eternal Son in his relation to the Father.

The transition from the relation of Jesus to the Father to the thought of the eternal Son, and consequently the difference between Father and Son in God's eternal essence, depend upon, and take place in, the fact that God as Father is manifest in the relation of Jesus to him and therefore also in the eternal encounter with Jesus as Son. The eternal God cannot be directly thought of as from eternity related to a temporal and creaturely reality unless this is itself eternal, as a correlate of the eternal God, and thus loses its temporal and creaturely nature. A distinction has thus to be made between the relation of Jesus to God's eternal deity, as the correlate of the Father, and his human, creaturely reality. This is the root of the differentiation between a divine and human aspect, or two 'natures,' in the person of Jesus. We shall have to examine the implications when we turn to christology." (ST I, 310–311)

This intentionally extensively quoted passage is, without question, a key to the entire work, which requires a differentiated and precise individual exegesis. As this is not possible here, a quote from the next section is offered, where Pannenberg writes: "If the self-distinction of Jesus from the Father is constitutive for the fact that even I the eternal God there must be a counterpart to the Father, i. e., the Son, then the question arises whether the same can be said about the relation of the Father to the Son, so that on the Father's side the distinction from the Son is posited by a self-distinction of the Father. The further question also arises whether the relation of the Spirit to the Father and the Son rests on mutual self-distinction of the same kind." (ST I, 311) Before Pannenberg begins with the evaluation of this question, he remarks that "the self-distinction of Jesus from the Father applies not merely to the Father as a person in the unity of the divine life, but also to the Father as the one God from whom Jesus distinguishes himself. If precisely herein Jesus is the eternal Son of the Father, it follows that in the act of self-distinction he receives his deity from the Father. Might there be anything similar on the Father's side in his relation to Jesus?". Pannenberg answers this question in the affirmative. If "genuine mutuality in the relation of the Trinitarian persons" appears excluded because "it has the order of origin running irreversibly from Father to Son and Spirit", Athanasius does say to the Arians "that the Father would not be the Father without the Son" (ST I, 311 – 312). Pannenberg echoes this with the following argument: "In the handing over of lordship from the Father to the Son, and its handing back from the Son to the Father, we see a mutuality in their relationship that we do not see in the begetting. By handing over lordship to the Son the Father makes his kingship dependent on whether the Son glorifies him and fulfils his lordship by fulfilling his mission. The self-distinction of the Father from the Son is not just that he begets the Son but that he hands over all things to him, so that his kingdom and his own deity are now dependent upon the Son. The rule of kingdom of the Father is not so external to his deity that he might be God without his kingdom." (ST I, 313)

These explanations are expanded by considerations "of the trinitarian relevance of the cross of Jesus" (ST I, 313 – 314) as well as through a observation of the *new determination of the idea of self-differentiation*, which consists in the following: "The term 'self-distinction' has been used in trinitarian theology since the 19th century but almost always in the sense of the bringing forth of a second and third divine person by the Father. Starting with the self-distinction of the Son from the Father, however, we can use the term in a different sense, namely, that the one who distinguishes himself from another defines himself as also dependent on that other." (ST I, 313, fn. 167) Thereupon, Pannenberg turns to the open question of "whether the relation of the Spirit to the Father and the Son rests on mutual self-distinction of the same kind." (ST I, 311) This question is also answered affirmatively, a fact which has its primary reason in the Easter effect of the Spirit. With reference to Jesus' resurrection, one may say that "the Father and the Son are referred to the working of the Spirit." (ST I, 315) As the Spirit glorifies the Son of the Father in the Easter event, the Spirit carries out a self-differentiation which "constitutes the Spirit as a separate person from the Father and the Son and relates him to both." (*Ibid.*) One might say summarily, "that the Spirit finally has a place in the eternal fellowship of the Father and the Son because he is the condition and medium of their fellowship. Only on this basis may the imparting of the Spirit to believers be seen as their incorporation into the fellowship of the Son with the Father. On the other hand the personhood of the spirit, which comes out most clearly in what John's Gospel says about the coming of the Paraclete, is a necessary premise of his work in the fellowship of the Son with the Father." (ST I, 316) Without examining the additional pneumatological differentiations, the Filioque-debate is such that the firm thesis that the Spirit has His origin in the Father and proceeds from Him (cf. ST I, 317 f.) does not eliminate either the intended mutuality of the Trinitarian relations nor the criticism of the one-sided understanding of simple relations of origin.

Under the subtitle "Three Persons but Only One God" (cf. ST I, 319), Pannenberg picks up the central problem of his entire Trinitarian theology, where the central thesis is: "If the Trinitarian relations among Father, Son, and Spirit have the form of mutual self-distinction, they must be understood not merely as different modes of being of the one divine subject but as living realizations of separate centers of action." (ST I, 319) While he postpones the question of "whether we must also view these centers of actions as centers of consciousness" (Ibid.), he attempts to make explicit "that self-distinction does not mean exactly the same thing for each of the three persons" (ST I, 321), rather, each having a different form. A presupposition for this is that which is noted precisely as the "point of the self-distinction of one person from one or both of the others" (Ibid.), that namely "the self distinction of each of the persons from the others relates also to the deity and/or its attributes." (ibid.) "The mutuality and mutual dependence of the persons of the Trinity, not merely as regards their personal identity but also as regards their deity, do not mean that the monarchy of the Father is destroyed. On the contrary, through the work of the Son the kingdom or monarchy of the Father is established in creation, and through the work of the Spirit, who glorifies the Son as the plenipotentiary of the Father, and in so doing glorifies the Father himself, the kingdom or monarchy of the Father in creation is consummated." (ST I, 324) Thus is "the monarchy of the Father [is] itself mediated by the trinitarian relations" (ST I, 325); though because this mediation through the Son and the Spirit cannot be external to the monarchy of the Father, the Christian doctrine of God cannot begin directly with the idea of monarchy, but rather must develop, in a Trinitarian manner, "the doctrine of the unity of the divine essence in the trinity of persons." (TT I, 326) Pannenberg connects this with the indication, which is not unimportant for his entire concept, that "even in the preparation in religious history for the knowledge of God as Father which Jesus mediated, the Son was already at work even though he definitively took human form only in the incarnation." (ST I, 327)

With the thesis that "the monarchy of the Father is not established directly but through the mediation of the Son and the Spirit" (Ibid.), the topic has already been raised that will be handled in the section on "the unity of the divine lordship [having] its essence in the form of this mediation" (Ibid.), namely: the relationship (to speak scholastically for a moment) between the immanent and the economic Trinity. In determining this relationship, the primary question is that of "the dependence of the deity of the Father upon the course of events in the world of creation" (ST I, 329). Pannenberg emphasizes "the person of the Father is thus implicated also in the course of salvation history, and indeed in such a way that the progress of events decides concerning his deity as well as the deity of the Son." (*Ibid.*) However, as much emphasis is given to the refutation of the "idea of a divine becoming in history, as though the Trinitarian God were the result of history and achieved reality only with its eschatological consummation." (ST I, 331) The thought of eschatological retroactivity has an important role to play in this context. Not less important is the following principle: "Viewing the immanent Trinity and the economic Trinity as one presupposes the development of a concept of God which can grasp in one not only the transcendence of the divine being and his immanence in the world but also the eternal self-identity of God and the debatability of his truth in the process of history, along with the decision made concerning it by the consummation of history." (ST I, 333) To think this single thought in its uniqueness is the task of the doctrine of God and the divine attributes. "Only with this discussion can we bring the doctrine of the trinitarian God to a provisional conclusion." (ST I, 335) – Pannenberg notes, however, that this cannot be an attempt to derive the Trinitarian tri-unity out of the unity of the divine being: "The task is simply to envision as such the unity of the divine life and work that is manifest in the mutual relations of Father, Son, and Spirit. This requires a concept of essence that is not external to the category of relations. But it does not require in any sense a derivation of the trinity of Father, Son, and Spirit, which we know from the event of revelation, from the concept of the one essence of deity. As forms of the eternal God, Father, Son, and Spirit cannot be derived from anything else. They have no genesis from anything different from themselves. The unity of the essence may be found only in their concrete life relation." (*Ibid.*)

2. The Unity of the Divine Being and the Divine Attributes

Prior to dealing with the individual aspects of the doctrine of God's being, nature, and attributes, Pannenberg evaluates the concept of rationally defending speech about God in the face of divine majesty. "Although God's majesty transcends all human concepts, it does not follow that we do better to be silent about God than to speak about him, or that nothing definite is conceivable in our talk about God." (ST I, 337) The false opinion that one can know nothing of God is rejected emphatically and with reference to Hegel. This, of course, is not the opposite of the *ineffability of God*. Pannenberg refers to Luther's distinction between *deus revelatus* and *deus absconditus* in order to explain this more precisely. This distinction means that one must cleave to the Son, when one wishes to know the unknowable God. "The many-faceted concept of the *deus absconditus* (cf. Isa. 45:15) embraces the hiddenness of God from sinners, whether in salvation or in judgment, the unsearchability of his counsels, and the incomprehensibility of his essence. By his revelation in the Son the essence of the otherwise incomprehensible God is disclosed. It is disclosed in such a way that the hidden God himself is manifest." (ST I, 339–340) This differentiation between the hidden and revealed God is connected to the relationship between the Father and the Son. Not such that "the Father is the hidden God and the incarnate Son the revealed God. In the event of revelation the hidden God is revealed as the Father of Jesus Christ. The unity of the hidden and revealed God is manifest in the unity of the Father and the Son." (ST I, 340) Pannenberg continues: "If for Luther the unity of the hidden and revealed God will be definitively manifest only in the light of eschatological glory, this means that the unity of the trinitarian God himself is still hidden in the process of history. The trinitarian distinctions of Father, Son, and Spirit are not hidden. They characterize the divine reality that discloses itself in the event of revelation. What is hidden is the unity of the divine essence in these distinctions." (ST I, 341) This accords to the fact that the central problem of the Christian doctrine of the Trinity has traditionally not been that of God's threeness, but that of God's oneness (cf. ST I, 342). In this context it is not only the indication towards the connection of the incomprehensibility of God with God's infinitude and the infinite unity of God's being which is important, but also the comment, that the unity of the divine being is a "unity in difference", that is, a unity in which difference does not disappear into sameness. To what extent this is valid for the relationship of God's nature and attributes is explicated in the context of the determination of the relationship between being, nature, and attributes.

First, Pannenberg deals with the *differentiation between the existence and being of God*. I will skip here the extensive examination of the proofs for God's existence and their history, and merely note the comment that the idea of the infinite, in opposition to the thought of a prime cause or an uncaused cause, is given importance for the doctrine of God. The interpretation of Descartes earns particular interest Descartes had founded – as Gregory of Nyssa before him – the idea of God on the idea of the infinite in opposition to the derivation of statements about God's nature from first causes (cf. ST I, 351–351). Pannenberg follows this line of thought. Although he holds Descartes' arguments to be lacking, it is only because "it did not work out the difference between a confused sense of what reflection calls infinite and the developed concept of the infinite as such." (ST I, 353) Pannenberg puts the following twist on Descartes' conception of infinitude: "the original confused intention the infinite is not an idea of God as Descartes thought, although from the standpoint of a philosophical idea of God which is determined by the concept of the infinite we let ourselves be told that God is already present to our mind in the original intuition of the infinite as the condition of the idea of every object." (*Ibid.*)[2]

The theological evaluation of the inherent intuition of infinitude, which is the condition of all finite objectification, creates a problem for how one understands the experience of the existence and being of God in the process of knowledge of God. This problem is, how it can be that this intuition of infinitude "aims" at the idea of God without representing that idea already. The question is, "In knowing God, then, does an experience or knowledge of the existence of God precede and awareness of the nature of his essence in distinction from all else, but in such a way that this experience or knowledge of the *existence* of God is not a knowledge that this is the existence of *God?*" (ST I, 354) Pannenberg answers this question by using an "undetermined that" as a reference point for thinking of the being of God, which as a "that" can first be understood in its existence as explicitly existing through its "what" (being). Thus it is first through the idea of God that the undetermined "that" of the infinite is known as the existence of God. "Only when we decide on the concept of essence, the whatness of what is, do we know that it is already the existence of this essence even when we have not yet grasped it as such. Much in our experience exists in this indefinite way before we 'discover' what it is. Present reality is always more than we can grasp or name. in the same way, as we can say in the light of explicitly religious knowledge, God is always present already in all human life. He is there for us and our world even thought he is not known as God. He is there as the undefined infinite which is formed by the primal intuition of our awareness of reality, as the horizon within which we comprehend all else by limitation." (ST I, 355–356) As "God", the undetermined infinite becomes such that "[w]e can and do call it God in the process of concrete revelation, religious experience, and interpretation of the world, and in the history of the conflict between the gods of the religions the definition of the undefined mystery that is present and active in our lives progresses – of the mystery that embraces all things and that never comes to an end within the march of time." (ST I, 356)

Pannenberg develops this thought along two lines: the being is, according to our previous definition, first such that "[w]e must not think of God's existence as simply transcendent, as an existence outside this world. We must think of it as an active presence in the reality of the world, we can and must think of it as an existence transcending the world and worldly thingy only when the essence of God is recognized to be eternal and thus high above the perishability of created things. This is important for the link between the revelatory reality of salvation history on the one side and the eternal essence of God on the other, in correspondence with what the doctrine of the Trinity has to say about the unity of the economic and the immanent Trinity.

---

2 A slightly better reading of this would be "we can indeed say that God is already present to our mind" (*dann in der Tat sagen läßt, dass Gott...*) pg 383 in the German version. – Trans.

When we name the essence of what exists indefinitely and distinguish it from all else, another aspect of the relation between essence and existence is present. The existence is now the specific existence of a specific essence. If the essence is not restricted to a single existence but is present in pother moments of existence in time and space, the essence and the specific existence are separate. The moment of existence is separate from the essence even though identical with it for a time. The essence simply finds manifestation or appears in it. Only the sum total of the moments of existence is coincident with the unity of the essence.

If the essence of God – and therefore also the sum total of his moments of existence – transcends finite things and their world – a point that we shall have to clarify when examining the attributes of God – then the individual moments of his active presence in the world and in human life, to the extent that they are known to be moments of the existence of God, are moments in which the essence of God finds a manifestation.

The individual manifestation is different from the essence inasmuch as the latter, thought manifested in it, can be fully defined only in terms of the sum total of its manifestations and existence. If the manifestations are viewed as a series, their totality can be defined only in anticipation of the completed sequence, and in the case of a finite series only in the light of the final member. We can overlook this factor, of course, when the essence is the same in each of its manifestations. But even then we can reach a conclusion only by anticipating the rest of the series. At any rate, we can accept as revelation of the essence only the sum total of the manifestations or a single manifestation that is constitutive for this total." (ST I, 357 – 358) This process of thought is given a final Trinitarian twist, so that Pannenberg may close with the following concept, important for the entire work: "the specific form of the existence of God as Father, Son, and Spirit is identical with the unlimited field of God's nonthematic presence in his creation." (ST I, 359)

Moving from the relationship between existence and being, Pannenberg turns to the *relationship between the being and attributes of God*. The principle here is: "The essence of things comes to manifestation in existence as a specific essence which is distinct from all others. It distinguishes itself from others by its attributes. Thus God finds manifestation in the working of his power, and we know the distinctiveness of his essence, and differentiate it from others, by the characteristics of his working." (*Ibid.*) The central question in this context is: how do the multiplicity of attributes expressed in the actions of God relate to the unity of God's being? Pannenberg reflects on this in intensive excurses through the history of thought, finally leading from the aporias of the traditional doctrine of God's being and attributes to the idea of God as cause of the world. It is then not far removed to think of God, or God's being, as "in its own unrelated and transcendent self-identity apart from all relation to the world." (ST I, 365) In the theological use of the term "substance" and its relationship with the category of "relation" this is demonstrated: "The scientific undermining of the older concept of substance found principial formulation in Kant's subordination of the category of substance to that of relation." (ST I, 366) The development continues with Hegel. According to him, "it was part of the concept of essence to be self-related to something else. The relation between substance and accident thus became a special instance of the relational structure of essence." (*Ibid.*) Pannenberg draws the following conclusion from this: "The changes in modern thought regarding the concept of essence and its position vis-à-vis that of relation have inevitably had implications for theology, and especially for theological ideas of the essence of God. The divine essence can no longer be thought of as unrelated identity outside the world. It has to be recognized that an idea of this kind is contradictory because the idea of transcendence itself expresses a relation. This recognition need not mean that God's transcendence vanishes panthe-istically in the infinity of nature, as in Spinozism, nor that it is simply an element in the divine process of producing and dissolving the world, as in Hegel, nor finally that it is just a correlate of the concept of the world, as in the metaphysics of Whitehead. Nevertheless, theological thinking now faces the task of revising traditional ideas of God. It cannot escape this challenge if it is to remain in intellectual dialogue with modern criticism of the traditional doctrine of God and with atheism, and if it is not to fall back upon loose symbolical language in its statements about God." (ST I, 367)

After showing the possible theological advantages of the "introduction of relation into the concept of substance" (*Ibid.*), that is, regarding the relation between divine being and Trinity as well as the God-world relationship, Pannenberg turns to the later problem with the question of the manner in which God's in-the-world-ness relates to His transcendence. The solution to this question is to be found in the *concept of divine action*. Pannenberg sketches the concept first, and then defines it more precisely in relation to the knowledge, will, and spirit-nature of God. The central problem is whether and to what extent God "is a self-consciously acting and in these sense 'personal' being." (ST I, 370) For the sake of this solution, Pannenberg turns first to the concept foundational to the traditional Christian understanding, that of a highest reason (cf. ST I, 371 ff.). he notes that the biblical concept of spirit does not correspond with reason or consciousness (cf. ST I, 373), that much rather "[the] penetration of the narrower view of *pneuma* as rational soul and consciousness is connected with the rise of the Platonic school in the 3rd century and the decision of Christian theology in favor of the Platonic transcendental view of God rather than Stoic pantheism." (ST I, 374) In this context, a critique and counter-critique of the idea of an absolute conscious-ness are evaluated and problems for anthropology are found: if it is the case that the difference in human consciousness between the I and the Self are an expression of the fact that we are simply not identical with ourselves, then the relationship of the Trinitarian persons to one another must assume a completeness of identity which makes it questionable if the form of their self-relationship can still be referred to as consciousness. In any case, Pannenberg agrees with the judgment of Spinoza, "that it is just as metaphorical to speak of the intellect of God as to call God the 'rock' of our salvation" (ST I, 379). Thus he comes to the conclusion that the metaphorical speech about "God's knowledge" means "that nothing in all his creation escapes him. All things are present to him and are kept by him in his presence. This is not necessarily knowledge in the sense of what is means by human knowelge and awareness." (ST I, 379 – 380)

Analogous to this is the argument regarding the divine will (cf. ST I, 380 ff.). Pannenberg understands the idea of divine will, in connection with anthropological-religious considerations, as a "connection between God's will and the Spirit, giving concrete form to the dynamic of the Spirit" (ST I, 382). In this, he characterizes the biblical concept of spirit as a field of forces, the powerful presence of God. This connects with the field theory of modern physics, which itself is a development of the stoic *pneuma*-doctrine. Thus there result "astonishing possibilities…for a new understanding of the relations between the trinitarian persons and the divine essence that is common to all of them. The autonomy of the field demands no ordering to a subject such as is the case when the Spirit is understood as nous. The deity as field can find equal manifestation in all three persons." (ST I, 383) One can, in the end, expect a solution to the ancient problem of Trinitarian theology from the idea of the field, that is, to what extent the Spirit can be referred to as the common being of the Godhead on one hand, and the third person of the Trinity next to Father and Son on the other. "As a field, of course, the Spirit would be impersonal. The Spirit as person can be thought of only as a concrete form of the one deity like the Father and the Son. But the Spirit is not just the divine life that is common to both the Father and the Son. He also stands over against the Father and the Son as his own center of action. This makes sense if the Father and the Son have fellowship in the unity of the divine life only as they stand over against the person of the Spirit. Precisely because the common essence of the deity stands over against both – in different ways – in the form of the Spirit, they are related to one another by the unity of the Spirit. If the union is to include the spirit as a person, it must be assumed that the personal Spirit, as he glorified the Son in his relation to the father and the Father through the Son, knows that he is united thereby to both. A self-relation is proper in different ways to the personal of the Father and the Son as well. We shall have to discuss this in the last section of this chapter." (ST I, 383 – 384) Pannenberg refers already in this context to the fact that the particularity of the self-definition of each Trinitarian member is communicated though their relation to the two other persons, and closes with the question, whether speech about divine action remains justified when one does away with the idea of *nus* as the subject of divine action and assumes that the living being of God has rather the manner of a field than that of a subject.

The Trinitarian persons remain the locus of action when referring to divine action (cf. ST I, 384 f.), as they are the "modes of being of the one divine life" (ST I, 385). First, the question must be answered, how it is that the communal action "of the divine persons... [relates to] their living union in the unity of the divine essence." (*Ibid.*) "The commonality of action of the Father, Son, and Spirit can only be a manifestation of the unity of life and essence by which they are always linked already."(*Ibid.*) After demonstrating the multiple problems and errors in the idea of God as an acting subject, and after presenting the Kingdom of God in the world as certainly the monarchy of the Father, but such that it is transmitted by the Son and the Spirit, Pannenberg emphasizes once again that the subject of divine action "[are] the three persons of Father, Son and Spirit...by their cooperation their action takes form as that of the one God" (ST I, 388), continuing: "The action of the Father, Son, and Spirit in the world is thus ascribed not merely to the three persons of the Trinity but also to the one divine essence. Only for this reason can we ascribe to God the qualities of his being on the basis of his action in the world. The one God is thus the acting God, the subject of his action. But this being as subject is not a fourth in God alongside the three persons of Father, Son, and Spirit. It does not precede the persons and find development in the trinitarian differentiation. It expresses their living fellowship in action toward the world." (ST I, 389) In reference to this, Pannenberg can speak of a "repetition" of God's eternal divinity in relation to the world, and even of a "self-actualization" of God." one cannot speak of self-actualization with humans, because then "[t]his would demand that from the beginning of its action the acting I would be identical in the full sense with the determination that is the result of its action." (St I, 390); nonetheless, this condition is fulfilled in (and only in) divine actions: "God actualizes himself in the world by his coming into it. For this his eternal existence in the fellowship of Father, Son, and Holy Spirit is presupposed and his eternal essence needs no completion by his coming into the world, although with the creation of a world God's deity and even his existence become dependent on the fulfillment of their determination in his present lordship." (ST I, 390)[3]

On the basis of the divine actions in the world, as it takes shape in the cooperation between Father, Son, and Spirit, one can predicate *divine attributes* not only to divine persons, but to the common divine being as well: "These attributes may be seen equally in the divine works of creation, reconciliation, and redemption, thought they are articulated differently. From the identity of the attributes we may see that the God who acts in the creation, reconciliation, and consummation of the world is one and the same God." (ST I, 392) Pannenberg does admit that a pre-term of divine being, to which the attribution of characteristics is made, is and must be used, in order that such attribution can even take place. However, the idea of divine being is first determined concretely by the attribution of those characteristics. "Apart from

---

3 Alternatively, "in the presence of his lordship" (*in der Gegenwart der Gottesherrschaft*). – Trans.

these it is incomplete" (ST I, 393), though one must add, that even the philosophical concept of God, which includes the minimal conditions for referring to something as God, must not be confused with the concrete reality of God: "hence the Christian doctrine of God has a critical function in relation to the conditions of consistent talk about God which philosophy has formulated....Christian theology can only weaken such these if even from the standpoint of the biblical revelation is moves only on the basis of physical argument." (ST I, 395)

It is upon this background and with this constellation of problems that the question is posed which founds everything that follows, "whether the initial concept of the divine essence as modified by the thought of the Infinite does in fact correspond to the biblical understanding of God" (ST I, 395) in such a manner that it matches up with the sentence that God is love. One must add that this sentence goes beyond the idea of God as Spirit, without contradicting it ("Also and precisely in the event o his love God is Spirit in the sense of the living dynamic of the OT view of God as Spirit." [ST I, 396]). The strategy that Pannenberg takes in answering this question is analogous in structure to the previous ones: he intends to show, that the abstract, general moments of conceiving of "God at all" is taken up into the concrete love-*gestalt* of the being of God, and can be demonstrated as such (cf. ST I, 396). The central task is thus named for the doctrine of attributes, which are now individually examined.

Pannenberg begins with making the theologically anticipatory idea of infinity more concrete. In his opinion, the "thought of infinity as *God's* infinity needs the statement of his holiness for its elucidation" (ST I, 397). The relationship between infinitude and holiness in God is particularly important in the following observations: "The Infinite that is merely a negation of the finite is not yet truly seen as the Infinite (as Hegel showed), for it is defined by delimitation from something else, i.e., the finite. Viewed in this way the Infinite is a something in distinction from something else, and it is thus finite. The Infinite is truly infinite only when it transcends its own antithesis to the finite." (ST I, 400) The thought of the holiness of God and the understanding of the being of God as Spirit nears to this. Without examining the consideration of eternity and omnipresence individually, we merely note that "[w]hereas God's eternity means that all things are always present *to him*, the stress in his omnipresence is that he is present *to all things at the place of their existence*." (ST I, 410) Of course, omnipresence is closely connected to omnipotence, which is not the enforcement of the own will against an "other", but the omnipotence of the Creator, who brings forth every creature. The result of the individual considerations is the assertion that "More detailed discussion of the omnipotence of God demonstrates that it can be thought of only as the power of divine love and not as the assertion of a particular authority against all opposition. That power alone is almighty which affirms that which is opposite to it in its particularity, and therefore precisely in its limits, which affirms it unreservedly and infinitely, so that it gives the creatures the opportunity by accepting its own limits to transcend them and in this way itself to participate in infinity." (ST I, 422)

The latter considerations prepare the way for *the concept of divine love as the epitome of theology*, to which the final section of the first volume of the pannenbergian systematics is dedicated. First, the Trinitarian understanding of the theological term "love" is examined. One should note in this context especially the statements regarding the personality of the Holy Spirit and the specific differences of the Trinitarian persons among one another. Regarding he attribute of divine love, one should take note of the initial and final "sentences"[4] of the relevant passage: "As they are summed up in Exod. 34:6 (cf. Ps. 103:8; 145:8) and in the NT witness, the attributes of God's essence as they are disclosed in his revelatory action may be understood through and through as the attributes of his love. They differ in for from the attributes that we discussed in §6. The difference is not that of the abstract from the concrete. The attributes are concrete aspects of the reality of divine love. Whereas infinites is defined by holiness as *God's* infinity, eternity, omnipresence, and omnipotence specifically describe the divine Spirit, and the Spirit is materially defined as the divine love, the goodness, grace, righteousness, faithfulness, wisdom, and patience of God do not take us beyond the thought of divine love but describe different aspects of its reality. In relation to them love is not an abstract master concept but the concrete reality itself which unites all the aspects." (ST I, 432) The final "sentence" is "Only the future consummation of God's kingdom can finally demonstrate that the deity of God is definitively revealed already in the history of Jesus and that the God of love is truly God. On the way to this ultimate future the truth claim of the Christian message concerning God remains unavoidably debatable. Theology can do nothing to alter this. Theology cannot replace faith. Bt it can try to show how far faith, in keeping with the truth claim of Christian proclamation, is aware of being in alliance with true reason." (ST I, 442)

With the question "whether the reality of the world as it is may even be thought of as the creation of the God of the Bible" (*Ibid.*), Pannenberg announces "The next chapters of this systematic theology, first the doctrine of creation and anthropology, but also Christology, ecclesiology, and eschatology, will have to take up this question, for they will show that the world and humanity as they are do not fully correspond to the loving will of the Creator but stand in need of reconciliation and consummation." (*Ibid.*) First, though, the problem of divine unity crops up again. In this context, it is such that "by the love which manifests itself in his revelatory action God's unity is constituted the unity of the True infinite which transcends the antithesis to what is distinct from it.

---

4 The number of thoughts in a German sentence often requires that it be translated into multiple English sentences. – Trans.

If the unity of God this finds nuanced and concrete form only in the work of divine love, then the other attributes of the divine being may be shown to be either manifestation of the love of God or to have gtrue meaning only insofar as their concrete manifestation is taken up into the sway of divine love. The latter is true especially of the qualities of God's infinity." "ST I, 445) The infinitude of God, as formulated by Pannenberg after a critical examination of Hegel (cf, ST I, 445 – 446), "is the unity of God with his creature which is grounded in the fact that the divine love eternally affirms the creature in its distinctiveness and thus sets aside its separation from God but nott its difference from him." (ST I, 446) Furthermore: "As love gives concrete form to the divine unity in its relation to the world, it also represents the taking up of the plurality of the divine attributes into the unity of the divine life." (ST I, 446 – 447) Thus it follows that "the thought of love makes it possible conceptually to link the unity of the divine essence with God's existence and qualities and hence to link the immanent Trinity and the economic Trinity in the distinctiveness of their structure and basis. This is because the thought of divine love shows itself to be of trinitarian structure, so what we can think of the trinitarian life of God as an unfolding of his love. It is also because the thought of live permits us to think of God's relation to the world as grounded in God.

What we have not yet shown, however, is how God's relation to the world is to be understood in the light of the trinitarian understanding of God." (ST I, 447) It is with this problem that the further parts of the dogmatics deal, as they find their closure in eschatology. Thus, one expects from those parts a "more nuanced understanding of what it means that God is love." (ST I, 448)

3. The Creation of the World as a Free Act of the Trinitarian God

The doctrines of God as Creator and the world as creation determine one another. "This mutual conditioning of our understanding of God and the world does not rule out our giving precedence to the concept of God in understanding humanity and the world, nor vice versa. Any serious talk about God implies the requirement that we think of the reality of humanity and the world as determined by God and established through him. Conversely, the possibility of an integrated interpretation of the world, including humanity and its history, in terms of the concept of God will already be a test of the possible truth of this concept even though the interpretation of the world may be debatable at many points. The more such a presentation is in harmony with the data of knowledge derived from experience, the more illuminating it will be for the truth claim which the relative understanding of God is making. At all events it will carry with it a proof of the way in which the function of constituting a concept of the world that is in some way implicitly bound up with the concept of God is capable of a more or less detailed presentation." (ST II, xv) In this sense, Pannenberg's doctrine of the creation of the world is divided into two pars. First, the creation of the world is described and presented as the free act of the Trinitarian God, that is, how the divine act of creation relates "to the divine activities of the preservation and overruling of the world" (ST II, 59). Then, the world of creatures comes into view, that one might "interpret it as a work of the Trinitarian God. We have here a theme of the utmost importance for the question for the truth of the Christian faith. Only if we understand the world as the creation of the biblical God and God himself as its Creator can we raise a truth claim for belief in the sole deity of God." (Ibid.)

The doctrine of creation as explication and proving of the Christian understanding of God remains abstract and unspecific, if the protological aspect were not connected thoroughly with an eschatological perspective."As the Author and Consummator of the actual world, including humanity, the God of the biblical revelation can be understood as its Creator only from the standpoint of a reconciliation of the world to himself." (ST II, xv) For the proof of the Christian understanding of God in His relationship to the reality of the world and the human, creation and redemption are inseparable, thus in a certain sense "creation will be complete only with the eschatological consummation of the world." (ST II, xvi) In a third section, the pannenbergian doctrine of the creating of the world is thematised according to the differentiated context of creation and eschatology. This is done in such a manner that the unity and difference in the act of creation and the eschaton are valid at the same time. "Creation and eschatology belong together because it is only in the eschatological consummation that the destiny of the creature, especially the human creature, will come to fulfillment. Yet creation and eschatology are not directly identical, at least from the creature's standpoint. For the creature, its origin is in the past, in which it has the roots of its existence. It is thus inclined to orient itself to the past. This is true of humans in the early stages of the history of their self-awareness, as we see from its mythical form. For the creature, the future is open and uncertain. Nevertheless, creatures that are awakened to independence (i.e., living creatures) open themselves to the future as the dimension from which alone their existence can achieve content and fulfillment. In the creature's experience, however, the origin and the consummation do not coincide. They form a unity only from the standpoint of the divine act of creation. Even in this regard the structure of their unity demands more precise explanation." (ST II, 139)

The foundational initiatives of such a clarification are already contained in the considerations regarding the *creation as a divine act*, with which Pannenberg begins his doctrine of the creation of the world. The unity of the divine act of creation is, as is the unity of God, differentiated in a Trinitarian manner without damaging that unity, insofar as the three Persons of the Trinity bring forth the reality of a creaturely world different from God commonly. From an economic perspective, the Trinitarian act of creation presents itself according to the inter-Trinitarian differentiation of divine unity, in the connected but different aspects of creation, conservation, and governance of the world. Thus it is proved that "the concept of creation relates to the overarching unity of the divine act...the concept of preservation relates the existence of creatures to their beginning and...the divine rule aims at the future consummation" (*Ibid.*). One can explain from the fact that the idea of creation is not merely a partial aspect, but the world-initiating act of God, in which the world as world has its own unity, that this idea has become the epitome of the doctrine, even when this doctrine and its unity can only be examined under its various aspects and in various manners. The unity and inner-connectivity of the doctrine of Creation in the difference of its aspects are, for Pannenberg, significantly indicated through the concept of an act of God. Through this concept primarily it is that the existence of the world can be traced back to God as origin, and only so can the world be called "creation": "The world is a product of an act of God." (ST II, 1) In order to recognize the creative act of God in its own inherent freedom as well as the inherent contingency of the world (regarding contingency, cf. ST II, 66 fn. 161),[5] one requires a clear difference between the world-creative action of God as a communal action of the divine persons externally from the also active (since the Latin Scholastics) innertrinitarian relations of God. The rule for this differentiation is: "*Opera trinitatis ad intra sunt divisa, opera trinitatis ad extra sunt indivisa*" (cf. ST II, 3).

It must be "sharply differentiated" (ST II, 3) between the relational act of the Trinity, which is characteristic and constitutive for the differentiation of the divinity of God, and the singe undifferentiated work of God externally, as it is completed in the inseparable unity of the divine persons. Noticeably, it is relatively late in the process that Pannenberg judges the expansion of the idea of divine action into the intertrinitarian relationship of Father, Son and Spirit;

---

5 A precise explanation of the idea of contingence can be found in "die Kontingenz der ge-schöpflichen Wirklichekit" in ThLZ 119 (1994), 1050–1058; reprinted in BSTh 2, 69–81. The result: "Contingent is not only that which is, but is not necessary; all that is, that is not impossible but could not be and actually is, is contingent. Not all that is not impossible actually exists. What is not impossible is possible. But what is not impossible, i.e., is not necessarily not, and which also exists, although it could be not, is contingent: to this belongs the strictly unique and thus underivable as well as the regular and that which occurs with necessity according to natural law." (BSTh 2, 80). Already in a study regarding contingency and natural law from 1970, Pannenberg defined the idea of contingence (differently than normal) as that which factually exists that is not necessarily not. At that time, he had "however not explicitly made clear, that this description refers to that which factually is, although it could be not. This is as such already contingent. Only its relation to the necessary is expressed, that it is not necessary, and not that it is not necessarily not. Also that which occurs with (natural law) necessity is contingent in the sense, that it could also be not, in the case that no occurrences occur upon which the context of natural law results manifest. Within the concept of contingence, then, is all that is although it could be not. Only that which is from and through itself, such that nonbeing would be unthinkable, would be not contingent." (*Ibid.*)

despite possible misunderstandings, Pannenberg sees this principally positive. The assumption of intertrinitarian *opera* or *operationes* or *actiones*
allows one to think of God as active in a manner such that He does not require
the world to be active. In contrast to the current relationships between Father,
Son, and Spirit, the world and its creation are not constitutive for the life of
God. The creation of the world is a free act of God, thus the world as creation is
not a divine emanation, but a contingent putting-into-being. Further
theological insight is made possible by the expansion of the idea of divine
action into the intertrinitarian relationships due to the fact that it allows one to
think of the world-God relationship of Creator, Redeemer, and Completer in a
Trinitarian manner, "so that the reciprocal action of the persons always lies
beyond the relation of the one God to creatures and the relation of creatures to
the one God. The action of the one God in relation to the world is not wholly
different from the action in his trinitarian life. In his action in relation to the
world the trinitarian life turns outward, moves out of itself, and becomes the
determinative basis of relations between the Creator and the creatures." (ST II,
5) The mutuality and unity of the internal relationship is expressed in the
external action of the Trinitarian persons.

The thought of a Trinitarian understanding of divine action *ad extra* means
that one has not only to deal with the potential problem of a means-to-an-end
structure in relation to divine action, rather it is also decisive for the correct
understanding of the relationship of the *unity and difference of divine work*.
"[T]hat what is new is that the sequence of the divine action, and therefore its
multiplicity, is grounded in the trinitarian plurality of the divine life.
Therefore, the unity of this divine action in the economy of God's history with
his creation is not lost by reason of the plurality of events." (ST II, 8 – 9) If it is
the case that the Trinitarian God is active in a different and yet unique manner
in all His actions, then a wide sense of the term "creation" can also include the
concept of the completion of creation, as God proves Himself creative in all His
actions. In the narrow sense of the work of God in providence, redemption and
completion, the concept of creation communicates primarily the fact of the
freely chosen cause which brought the world, as other-than-God, into being.
The unlimited freedom of the divine causal act in creation is, according to
Pannenberg, analogous to the freedom of the historical action of the God of
Israel, and characteristic for the biblical idea of creation. This idea is
illustrated through the assumption of a creation of the world, and emphasized
by the formula "*creatio ex nihilo*", which is first encountered in 2 Maccabeus
7:28 (cf. Romans 4:17, Hebrews 11:3). Foundational is the rejection and
exclusion of any concept which sees the world as dualistic. The world is "not
the result of any working of God with another principle" (ST II, 15), but rather
the exclusive product of an act of God. This does not imply, from the biblical
witness, a monistic idea of act of creation. "The reason that the biblical belief in
creation that found classical expression in Gen. 1 could not make any
concession to a dualistic cosmogony also differentiates it from the opposite

view of the relation of God to the world in the act of its creation. If a dualistic view of the world's origin limits the Creator's freedom in his almighty working, the divine freedom in the systems of a philosophical monism falls victim to an iron necessity governing the cosmic process subsequent to its origin. On this view God himself seems to be tied to the logic of his own nature, the logic that everything has to happen as in fact it does." (ST II, 17) Pannenberg illustrates this through the antique idea of *heimarmene* as well as through Hegel's doctrine of creation, which he criticizes as manifestly monistic.

In contrast to both dualism and monism, the Christian understanding of creation turns on the thought of the divine freedom in the act of creation. In order to distinguish this from both caprice and necessity, the Trinitarian origin and Trinitarian authorship are to be kept constantly in mind. Thus, it is characteristic for Pannenberg's concept that he does not view the theology of creation abstractly as the province of the first person of the Godhead, associating an undifferentiated unity of God with that. Rather, Pannenberg argues from the self-differentiation of the Son from the Father, where he sees the foundation for the existence of the world as creation in its difference from the Creator. The basis for this knowledge is the self-differentiation character-istic for Jesus' appearance, which proves him to be the personal incarnation of the eternal Son. The eternal Son, as revealed in Jesus, is the mediator of creation in His unity with the Father and in the self-differentiation through the power of the Spirit. He is the generative principle of the world as other than God, as well as the variety of the creaturely reality. As the Logos of creation, the eternal Son represents not merely an intelligible cosmos of ideas, but He is the one who makes difference possible as a principle, which He Himself is. He makes it possible that the other-than-God in its difference from God can appear *realiter*, and in that same difference He can take on bodily form. "In the free self-distinction of the Son from the Father the independent existence of a creation distinct from God has its basis, and in this sense we may view creation as a free act not only of the Father but of the Trinitarian God. It does not proceed necessarily from the fatherly love of God that is oriented from all eternity to the Son. The basis of its possibility is the free self-distinction of the Son from the Father; even as the Son moves out of the unity of deity, he is still united with the Father by the Spirit, who is the Spirit of freedom (2. Cor. 3:17). The Father sends the Son but thereby lays on him no compulsion to follow a command of fatherly love as though by outer constraint. In a free act of fulfilling his sonship, the Son himself moves out of the divine unity by letting the Father alone be the one God. That even in this act of freedom he is one with the will of the Father can be understood only in the light of a third thing, namely, that we have here an expression of the fellowship of the Spirit that unites the two. Thus creation is a free act of God as an expression of the freedom of the Son in his self-distinction from the Father, and of the freedom of the fatherly goodness that in the Son accepts the possibility and the existence of a creation distinct from himself, and of the freedom of the Spirit who links the two in free agreement." (ST II, 30)

From this passage, one can observe many aspects, among which is that the Son and Spirit take part in the work of creation each in a different manner, yet nonetheless an inseparable manner. The creative working of the Logos as the eternal Son of the Father is universally to be thought of in connection with the work of the Spirit as third person of the Trinity, and vice-versa. Pannenberg describes the creative cooperation of the Son and the Spirit as follows: "For the independence and distinction of the creatures relative to God goes back to the self-distinction of the Son, but the Spirit is the element of the fellowship of the creatures with God and their participation in his life, notwithstanding their distinction from him." (ST II, 32) By opening the possibility of transcendence to God to the creatures in the process of the continual internalization of their created disposition toward self-transcendence, the Spirit is the internal dynamic of the creative act of God and the life of creation, such that creaturely destiny can be taken up and achieved. The Logos, as the productive principle of difference is the generative act of creative formation, through which He is active as the origin the individual creatures and of the order in relationships between creatures. Through these two aspects – perceived through the united cooperation of Son and Spirit in the work of creation – the description of the world as creation is decisively determined, insofar as the reality of the world is first made transparent through the idea if its own variety in the work of the Logos and then the dynamic work of the Spirit. Before the Son and the Spirit can be viewed as principles of the cosmic order and dynamic (through the lens of their world-immanent work), the Trinitarian act of God in creation must be examined again directly under the aspect the internal differentiation of *creation, preservation, and divine government.*

To the first topic: creation is not an action within time, rather, an eternal act of the eternal God, in which the finite reality of creatures along with time and their temporality is constituted. As the timeless origin of all time, the divine act of creation thus "cannot be restricted to the beginning of the world. It is contemporary with all created time." (ST II, 37) Indeed, the act of creation is related to the beginning of the existence of said creation. "It does not follow, however, that the act of creation relates only to the beginning of the world and is thus restricted to this time of the beginning. If it were, it would be an act in time, not an eternal act of God. Time would not then be posited with the existence of creatures. The transition from eternity to time would take place already with God's moving out of the immanence of his essence to the act of creation. If the act of creation were itself already an act in time, we would unavoidably have to inquire into the time preceding it. We would also have to face the notion of a change in God with the transition to creation." (ST II, 38) Despite a few reservations regarding certain metaphysical presuppositions regarding a timeless eternity, Pannenberg shares Augustine's thesis decidedly; the world has not been created in time, but with time (*non in tempore, sed cum tempore*). The profit and relevance of such a thesis is double: "First, this view avoids the appearance that the world's origin rests on an arbitrary resolve of God. A constitutive factor in understanding the act of creation is that it is an act of divine freedom. But it is not the result of chance, of a capricious whim with no basis in the inner life of God. Second, and above all, Augustine's thesis opposes any restriction of the divine action in creation to the beginning of the world. The eternity of the act of creation offers a presupposition for the understanding of God's preserving activity as continued or continuous creation." (ST II, 39 – 40)[6]

To the second: the term "preservation" presupposes the prior existence of creatures, and thus the preceding act of creation; it is thus temporally structured. What is preserved in its existence must already exist. "Preservation also implies that what is to be preserved does not owe its existence to itself. It would need no preservation if it had the cause of its existence in itself. Insofar as God's creative act establishes the existence of creatures, they are referred primarily to God for their preservation in existence." (ST II, 35) Pannenberg judges that God's action of preservation, without which all creation would return to the nothingness from which it came, can be understood as continued creation due to the fact that the existence of individual creatures is not depended upon God's creative action in its beginning, but also in every moment. The objection that the assumption of a continual creation and a full contingence of creation itself raises questions about the independence of the creatures and their actions, or at least about their identity and continuity, is rejected by Pannenberg as a non-starter, as God is faithful to Himself in his creative action. "The faithfulness of God guarantees as well as makes possible the emergence and persistence of continuously existing forms of creaturely reality and their ongoing identity and independence." (ST II, 40) In order to express the preservation faithfulness of the Creator in His support of creation, one need not suppose a definitively finished creation, immune to the new in the actual sense. It is the contrary that is the case, that the creative preservation of creation by God takes place with, in, and among the action of divine production.

Pannenberg makes this aspect valid in particular in the face of an understanding of the physical principle of inertia which abstracts from all change as well as against a concept of self-preservation which, in contradiction to his own thought, fails to notice that self-preservation is only necessary in relation to the contingency of one's own being, and thus can be aligned only to a changing identity. Pannenberg argues in contrast to the modern independence movement of the creaturely world against the dependence on the continual intervention of God, which has reached its high point with Spinoza's interpretation of the physical principle of inertia as self-preservation. Instead, Pannenberg offers a picture concordant with the natural sciences using the

---

6 *Creatio continuata* or *creatio continua*.

idea of field theory, which is much more compatible with the concept of God's creative act pervading all phases of the world-process. With these conditions, the criticism of the idea of miracles is also easier to meet. Miracles occur, as Augustine and Samuel Clarke (with recourse to the Christian Aristotelianism of the High Scholastics) have said, not against nature in the sense of an external interference in an objective world order. They break at the most the limited human knowledge of nature, which also allows the insight that "the existence of the world and humanity is a much greater miracle than all the spectacular events that astonish us because they are unusual." (ST II, 45)

To the third: just as the creative act of God, so the contingency of the created is not only something at the beginning, but rather indicative of creaturely existence in its entire extension. Creatures are thus not merely initially dependant on God's creative preservation, but throughout their own duration as well. Thus one may assume, in the sense of the biblical witness and in trust in the faithfulness of God, that God desires to preserve that which he has created precisely through opening a new future in a productive, active manner. "Far from being in opposition to the persistence and self-preservation of finite things, the preserving work of God makes possible the independence of creatures that finds expression in the possibility and fact of their self-preservation. God for his part reaches the goal of his creative action only with the producing of creatures that persist and that exist independently insofar as by its very nature this goal had as its object the producing of that which is distinct from the Creator and can exist independently. God's work of preservation is in the service of the independent existence of creatures, and his cooperation with their development is in the service of their independence in action." (ST II, 52) The doctrine of divine concurrence with the actions of creatures serves a double theological role. On one hand, it makes clear "that creatures are not left to themselves in their activities. On the other side, we are not to see in God's working an omnicausality that excludes the autonomy of creatures and their possible deviation from God's purpose. Such deviation might be out of keeping with God's own creative ends, but this risk goes hand in hand with the independence that is given the creature and without which God's creative action could not come to fulfillment in his work." (ST II, 48)

The doctrine of divine concurrence with creaturely action is essentially connected to the idea of preservation in this sense, a move which connects the temporal existence of creatures with their origin in the creative act of God, even in the case of the occurrence of sin. Concurrence finds its *telos* in the doctrine of divine government, that is, the doctrine of providence. The doctrine of providence is orientated on the end and future completion of creation. The central theme of divine government is "God's supremacy over the misuse of creaturely independence." (ST II, 58) This shall prove advantageous for the true and creation-appropriate independence of each creature. God's government of the world thus does not refer solely to the steadfastness and consistence of creation in the order created with it, rather it also contains the care of God for each individual creature, presciently for the integral whole of that creaturely existence. Not so, that God would use an individual creature merely as a means to an end; rather, each is an end in itself. Pannenberg does not hesitate to say, "the idea that God, not creatures, is the final end of his world government has a harsh sound and leaves the impression that his rule is one of oppression." (ST II, 53, fn. 135) Opposite this, Pannenberg makes the point that God's creative action, as confirmation and expression of His free love, is entirely devoted to the creatures. "They are both the object and the goal of creation. Herein is his glory as Creator, the glory of the Father, who is glorified by the Son and by the Spirit in creatures." (ST II, 57)

4. The World of Creatures

The doctrine of the creation of the world through the free creative act of God can be differentiated from the doctrine of the world of creatures, but not separated from it, at least not when the world is to be understood as God's created world and the creatures in it as God's creatures. The knowledge of God in creation theology is connected with that of the world in a differentiated and yet inseparable manner. This does not, according to Pannenberg, allow the world-referential obligation for faith to give an account of faith in God the creator to retreat with the idea of creation into mere subjectivity, as this would have as a consequence a position that opposed world-awareness, and would thus necessarily reduce the plausibility of the belief in creation. Instead of indulging in subjective immunization strategies, one must take action and enter the conversation between theology and the formation of theory in natural science. This is not to occur at the level of such theory-formation, but at the level of philosophical reflection about such formation. "[Theology] cannot ignore what the sciences have to say about the world. Naturally, the tasks that are proposed can hardly be discharged in a summary fashion. The deliberations that follow may at least point the way, even if several things remain open to questions, as in other parts of dogmatics. In distinction from other discussions of the objects of the act of creation, i.e., of the creaturely world, we shall not turn at once to the variety of creaturely forms. We shall first look again at the work of the Son and the Spirit in creation, this time from the standpoint of their immanent working, the principles of cosmic order and dynamics. On the one hand this will make more concrete our trinitarian handling of the doctrine of creation, while on the other hand it will clarify the relation to basic aspects of the scientific description of the world." (ST II, 60–61)[7]

The world as creation is interweaved with *the principles of designed order and living dynamics*. The cosmic order of created reality is understood

---

7 Cf. "Toward a Theology of Nature. Essays on Science and Faith" 1993 (Ted Peters, ed.).

primarily as the work of the Logos, the cosmic dynamic of the same is primarily understood as the work of the Spirit. One must not abstract from the cooperation of Son and Spirit in the work of creation; the working of the Logos in creation is communicated through the Spirit as much as the dynamic of the spirit is not graspable without the organizing activity of the Logos. One notes merely that Pannenberg sees the control center of this cooperation between Logos and Spirit as marked by the idea of information.

Regarding the *creation mediation of the Logos*, which finds its manifested fulfillment in the incarnation of the eternal Son in Jesus, this completes itself through the particularizing of each creaturely gestalt through differentiation from God as Creator and from all other creatures. The determination for each creature, given by the Logos, is decisive. Each creature is to arrange itself in self-differentiation from God as a creature next to other creatures, in a commonly given world and according to a created order. Difference from God and difference from others among creatures cannot be separated from one another. As created entities, creatures are finite. "A finite being is limited by other beings, not merely by what is infinite, but also by other finite things. It has its distinctiveness only vis-à-vis other finite things. Only in this distinction does it exist. Hence the finite exists as a plurality of what is finite." (ST II, 61) This is not to say, that creation has existed directly as a multiplicity from its temporal beginning. However, creation is arranged according to the mediation of the Logos to an essential component of irreducible creaturely gestalts in the world. These are governed through creaturely order, whose foundation and epitome is the Logos, as different to be united as one world. The order of creation from the Logos is, of course, not to be simply identified with the order present in the natural laws of phenomena: the natural-law order of the phenomena "is indeed the epitome of the rules for the emergence of phenomena in the process of time, but as such it is abstract, detached from the plurality of creatures in their concreteness." (ST II, 62) However, the Logos is "not the abstract order of the world but its *concrete* order. It is so because in the concept of the divine Logos we cannot separate the eternal dynamic of self-distinction (the *logos asarkos*) from its actualization in Jesus Christ (the *logos ensarkos*). The universal Logos is active in the world only as he brings forth the particular *logoi* of specific creatures." (ST II, 63)

In the light of the definitive unification of the Logos with Jesus of Nazareth as a single creature different from all others, one may see that the entrance of the Logos into an individual gestalt is essential to His effect in creation. As a generic, providential, and conductive principle of concrete individuality, the Logos does not cease to remain the universal guarantee of the general. He is manifest as the differentiated unity of generality and particularity, which He is in Himself and who in that single human, the "new man", unites humanity and through humanity the multiplicity of creatures to an integrated whole. It is confirmed: "The incarnation is the integrating center of the world's historical order, which is grounded in the Logos and will find its perfect form only in the eschatological future of the world's consummation and transformation into the kingdom of God in his creation. Therefore, the incarnation cannot be an external appendix to creation nor a mere reaction of the Creator to Adam's sin. From the very first it is the crown of God's world order, the supreme concretion of the active presence of the Logos in creation." (ST II, 64)

The insight drawn from the incarnation regarding the creative function of the Logos revealed in Jesus Christ, that is, that individual particularity and ordered generality are equally ensured, is not merely maintained with reference to history. The historical context is not under the abstraction of the contingent, singular, individual, new, never-yet-there, chain of events, rather, it is constituted through these. Equally, the creative function is maintained with respect to the event-context of nature ,as this is event-contingence is considered today to be the foundational character of all occurrence, the historical as well as the physical. After all, the irreversibility of the direction of time is valid not only for historical contexts, but also those of natural occurrences. "Hence the regulated order of nature does not conflict with the contingent working of God in the producing of creaturely forms but is, in fact, an important means to this end. The uniformity of natural occurrence is on the one hand an expression of God's faithfulness and constancy in his activity as Creator and Sustainer, while on the other hand it is the indispensable basis for the development of ever new and more complex forms in the world of creatures." (ST II, 72) Pannenberg judges the human to have taken a foundationally unsurpassable leading position among the gestalts which continually become more complex in the irreversible path of time. The entire history of the universe can be seen as a pre-history for the appearance of humans, in accordance with the anthropic principle. Whether and to what extent this thesis – suggested by the Christian doctrine of incarnation – is plausible in the natural sciences is to be examined in the context of the explanation regarding the series of gestalts in the construction of the creaturely world. Prior to this Pannenberg ponders over the *dynamic effect of the Creator Spirit*, which corresponds to the work of the Logos as the arranging principle of cosmic order.

The divine gestalt is the life-giving and moving principle of creation. Such is the witness of Holy Scripture (cf. ST II, 76 ff.). Even if there was in it "no general conception of cosmic movement to denote the various movements and activities of creatures [developed]", the is an initial point in the concept of the creative dynamic of the Spirit of God which Pannenberg takes up in order to connect the effects of the Creator Spirit with the modern idea of a field[8] in physics. This connection is suggested both by the terminological history as

---

8 Decisive for Pannenberg's theological understanding of the dynamic of natural occurrence is the connection of the modern concept of the field in physics with the Spirit-concept of the Old Testament and the *pneuma* doctrine of antique Greek thought. Cf. "Toward a Theology of Nature" (1993) (above, fn. 65).

well as the history of ideas, as well as from factual considerations – despite the principle difference between the theological and physical point of view when attempting to describe the reality of the world, which Pannenberg explicitly grants. The reason for using the idea of a field in natural science taken back to the pre-physical, philosophically influenced state as a theological device is found in Pannenberg's own theological method and subject – namely, that the specific biblical speech of God as Spirit is appropriately expressed. This has traditionally been expressed as rational subjectivity, as *nous*, which Pannenberg finds unfitting for the idea of God as Spirit. It is more in accordance with the biblical witness to speak of the Spirit of God (or God as Spirit, respectively) "as a dynamic field that is structured in trinitarian fashion, so that the person of the Holy Spirit is one of the personal concretions of the essence of God as Spirit in distinction from the Father and Son.

The person of the Holy Spirit is not himself to be understood as the field but as a unique manifestation (singularity) of the field of the divine essentiality. But because the personal being of the Holy Spirit is manifest only in distinction from the Son (and therefore also from the Father), his working in creation has more of the character of dynamic field operations. Even in the mediatorship of the Son in creation the personal relation to the Father takes full shape only in the incarnation, in the distinction for the man Jesus from the Father, though all creaturely distinction from God and from other creatures is to be understood as deriving from the Son's self-distinction from the Father and its manifestation.

The same applies to the Spirit's work in creation. In distinction from the Son's mediatorship in creation and its significance for the distinction and otherness of every creature, it relates to the link and movement that connects the creatures to one another and to God." (ST II, 83–84) The relationship of creatures to one another, differentiated from God and in that differentiation differentiated from one another in accordance with the divine Logos, is only possible when space and time is given them through the dynamic work of the divine Spirit. Space and time are in this sense central aspects of the creative work of the Spirit.

As the infinite God calls the finite into being as that which is different from Him, He gives it *space*[9] next to Himself in such a differentiated manner that the difference from the eternal God to the finite and the difference of the finite entities and their location are set within this space. "In God's own immeasurability itself distinctions are posited and permitted that go with the existence of creaturely finitude. As regards the concept of space, this means that the plurality of places, and therefore of limited spaces, comes into being with the making of creatures. Presupposed is the plurality in God himself, namely, that of his Trinitarian life. The eternal contemporaneity of the

---

9 For the controversy regarding the relation of God to space in Newton and Clarke on one hand and Leibniz on the other, cf. "Toward a Theology of Nature" (above, fn. 65).

three persons in their natural relations might suggest the idea of spatial distinctions and relations in God himself. The Trinitarian distinctions, however, are not fixed divisions. In the act of self-distinction each of the persons is one with the other from whom it is distinguishing itself." (ST II, 86 – 87) Other than the Trinitarian differences within God, the difference from God present in creation "take the form of division, of divided existence, thought not to the exclusion of relations between things divided. The space of creatures is constituted by the fact that they are related precisely by their finitude and limitation. From this standpoint space is the epitome of relations between divided spaces, between points of space." (ST II, 87)

Thus it is that space is the epitome of relations, partial space, and locations respectively, and one says farewell to the idea of infinite space as an empty container for the reception of objects (*receptaculum rerum*). One retains, however, the assumption that a unity of space is given for all separation and the relationships between the separated. The relational definition of the idea of space presupposes the unity of space as, to echo Kant, an "infinite given quality" (ST II, 88, with reference to Kant's *Critique of Pure Reason* § B 39), and understands this as a condition of its possibility. Pannenberg connects he unity of space presupposed by every concept of a relation between partial space or locations with the immeasurability of God which constitutes the created world. The *immensitas Dei*, which is essentially one and inseparable, is not to be directly equated with the limitless separable space of geometry. Otherwise, "we arrive either at the pantheism of Spinoza or at the idea of empty space as a container for things yet to be created. Geometric space may well be unlimited and therefore potentially infinite in the sense that it can be expanded without limit, but it is not really infinite. Its potential infinity is only a broken reflection of the infinity of God in the human spirit. By his infinity God is present to all things, constituting the omnipresence of the space of creation. His infinity is also a presupposition of every human view of spatial relations in which things are both distinct and related. The perception of space, which according to Kant is, with that of time, at the basis of all human experience, is a way of intuiting the Infinite. According to Descartes, this intuition is a presupposition of the defining and distinguishing of all knowledge and all ideas. Time and space as forms of perception are thereby also without limit, and they thus precede all the finite contents of experience. But every concept of space suggested by geometry differs from the concept of the space of perception as an infinite totality, for it reconstructs the perception of space either for conception or purely conceptually." (ST II. 89 – 90) As the idea of space is constituted through the simultaneity of the different, it has the idea of *time* at its foundation. In the same manner, the approach to the idea of space as that which encloses everything which is simultaneously present can be brought up into the idea of time. The starting point here is an interpretation of simultaneity. Under the conditions of physical measurement, the thought of absolute simultaneity and the aggregation of space and time into space-time as a four-dimensional continuum has become problematic, at least since the theory of relativity has demonstrated the locative relativity and observational system reference in all measurements. The thought of simultaneity is, however, not completely eliminated. Instead, it shows itself empirically as relative simultaneity. "Relative simultaneity is simply that of what is not simultaneous in itself. In the case of our sense of time it is made possible by the phenomenon of the present that bridges time" (ST II, 91), which is at its most complex in the experience of duration. This is made evident in detail in Augustine's famous treatment of time in the eleventh book of his "*Confessiones*". While the human experience of a temporally extended present, which contains the past as remembered and the future as expected, is limited, the eternity of God is "the undivided present of life in its totality" (ST II, 92). "We are not to think of this as a present separated from the past on the one hand or as the future on the other. Unlike our human experience of time, it is a present that comprehends all time, that has no future outside itself. The present that has a future outside itself is limited. A present can be eternal only if it is not separate from the future and if noting sinks for it into the past." (*Ibid.*) Describing the idea of eternity in this manner is, according to Pannenberg, not an abstract idea, but rather "constitutive for the experience and concept of time. Only if time is basically a unity, i.e., as eternity, can we understand the nexus of that which is separated in its course." (ST II, 93)

This is explicated using Plotinus' foundation of the idea of time out of the thought of eternity in its opposition to the Aristotelian tradition of understanding time as well as Kant's assumption of an original unity of time present as presupposed in the concept of various times. In this context Pannenberg first opposes the theory that time is to be derived from the movement of specific physical phenomena as an abstraction. This one-sided orientation on the measurement of time and the amount of movement fails to recognize, along with the pre-physical character of time, the unique nature of the modes of future, present, and past. The differences between these tend to fade out in the face of the thesis of the foundation uniformity of moments. Secondly, when regarding Kant's attempt to ground the unity of time on the subjectivity of the human Pannenberg notes: "[T]he subject as a finite entity cannot be the basis of something infinite, of something that for Kant, too, is an infinite totality. At all events, however, it can be the principle of duration without end and therefore of potential infinity. We can understand this only in terms of the constitution of subjectivity itself by intuition of the Infinite as the condition of all the finite contents of the consciousness, including the thought of the ego itself. Fichte came back to this insight of Descartes at the end of his discussion of the constitution of the self-consciousness in terms of a positing of the ego. We cannot conclude, then, that Kant solved the problem definitively by substituting subjectivity for eternity as the constitutive basis of time. Nor did the early Heidegger fare any better when he developed this idea." (ST II, 94)

If eternity is the ground for the unity of time as well as the condition for the connection between the modes (respectively, that which is separated by moments of time), then time cannot be derived from the idea of eternity in the sense that eternity is seen as the origin of time or that time is the consequence of eternity: "Any attempt to conceive of time's origin presupposes time." (*Ibid.*) Pannenberg thus echoes Augustine in teaching that God created time along with creatures. As creation is basically good, so is the temporal nature of creaturely being. The temporal nature of creaturely being as such will not find its end in the eschaton, however, the separation of future and past from the present will, as this marks the old eon. The differences created by the finitude of the finite and the process of time will certainly remain; they cease to be separating differences. Thus, though the divergence of life-moments within time cannot be one of the conditions of finitude, Pannenberg notes that it still "has something to do with the finitude of creaturely existence, if only as a transitional feature on the way to consummation." (ST II, 95) The most important line of thought for the complete concept is as follows: "Succession in the sequence of time is obviously a condition of the attainment of independence by creatures as essential entities, their independence in relation both to one another and to God. Only in the process of time can a finite being act and thus manifest itself as the center of its own activity. After it has won independence, such a being can be preserved or renewed as it participates in the eternity of God, a point we cannot develop further here. To win it and thus to achieve its individuality, a being needs the conditions of becoming and perishing in time. In saying this, we see in what sense cosmic time is to be regarded as the subject of God's creative action. Because the Creator's action aims at the independent existence of his creatures as finite beings, he willed time as the form of their existence.

The independent existence of creatures has the form of duration as an overarching present, by which they are simultaneous to one another and relate to one another in the distinction of space. Since they do not have their existence of themselves, their present is distinct from their derivation as their past. They have, however, another relation to eternity which constitutes their origin. For their existence as duration they are referred to eternity as the future of the good that gives duration and identity to creatures. But since as creatures they are distinguished by their independence from their origin in eternity, in the same way they also have their future outside themselves, although in the duration of their existence they already exist as an anticipation of the future of their total being." (ST II, 95 – 96)[10]

According to the temporality of creaturely existence, and from the development of the awareness of this temporality, the *future* receives the greatest importance among the modes of time. The future, which creatures approach throughout the duration of their existence, appears ambivalent. On one hand, it threatens to dissolve the creaturely gestalt and to make its

---

10 The first line of this quote should read "as finite entities" (*endliche Wesenheiten*). – Trans.

transience definitive. On the other hand, the future is "the field of the possible. It is thus the basis of the openness of creation to a higher consummation and the source of what is new, i.e., of contingency in each new event." (ST II, 97 – 98) The latter aspect is that in which in Christian faith the ambivalence of creaturely expectations for the future is brought up into the promise. This is Pannenberg's thesis, that the creative power of the future as the field of the possible expresses the dynamic of the Spirit of God, which appears in the light of the eschatological completion in the offing through its power over the future. In the light of this Spirit-promised eschatological completion of creation, it is not merely the evil of transience that can be accepted as the price for the coming into being of independent creaturely gestalts. This light shines also into the frame of the natural knowledge today, which it can understand better than it understands itself, under the presumption of the dynamic which opens future possibilities from the divine Creator-Spirit. Thoughts on the idea of "field" should show "that the theologically based idea of a dynamic of the divine spirit working creatively in all events as the power of the future is by no means alien to a philosophy of nature. It stands in a demonstrable relation to the basic data of science. Indeed, it can set scientific descriptions in a new light by putting them on a different plane of argumentation. Confusion with scientifically possible statements is excluded, but there may well be convergence in philosophical reflection on them." (ST II, 101) The power of the future manifested in the creative dynamic of the spirit is, according to Pannenberg, not only the origin of the contingency of individual events, but also the origin of durative existences and the consistent order in the course of natural events, without which there could be no durative existences. Beyond this, the effectiveness of the Spirit in His power over the future represents the unity of life, which merely partially appears in the course of temporal moments. This prevents the de-integration and estrangement of the individual moments in a life, that it be lead to an integrated whole – that integrated whole which is its eschatological purpose.

The understating of the eschatological work of the Creator-Spirit, as well as the description of this Spirit as a field of force that creates creaturely space and brings about independent communal existence in His creative action, offers Pannenberg (among other things) the opportunity to reform the Christian *doctrine of angels*. Angels are, as Pannenberg reads from the biblical witness, not primarily personal gestalts or spiritual beings, but rather powers and cosmic functions whose effects can be the object of perception by the natural sciences in another perspective. Here as well it is the idea of "field" which offers the perspectival mediation. Angels represent particular fields of gravitation within the whole of the field, which is ensured in its unity by the divine Spirit. As good powers, they stand in the service of God's rule over creation. Opposite to this, the "fallen" angels build satanic and demonic centers of power, which in the undertow of their anti-God separations are eager to shatter the continuation and preservation of creation. One should note, that Pannenberg finds an aspect of the effectiveness of a virtually creation-destroying corruptive power in the principle of entropy within the world-process; the fact of the temporal inversion as the condition of the continuity of natural events, however, is primarily an expression of the faithfulness of the Creator in His desire to bring forth independent creaturely gestalts and can only be negatively seen from the perspective of the danger of a threatened self-conclusion of existing reality. "At any rate, no destructive power is the only determinative ground of the creaturely reality in which it holds sway. Through all other powers and fields of force may be seen also the working of the divine Spirit as the origin of life in the creatures. In the working of the Spirit, as in that of the divine Logos, the future of the consummation in the kingdom of God predominates. Theological talk about the dynamic of the Spirit of God in creation differs in this regard from the field theories of physics that work in terms of natural laws. The resultant problem arises also, however, in discussions of scientific theory. Here it takes the form of the question how a field theory relates to the evolution of life and whether it calls for a fresh formulation of physical cosmology. We find approaches to such issues in attempts to arrive at a thermodynamic description of conditions for the rise and evolution of life." (ST II, 109)

The world of creatures, which is administrated by the Logos as the principle of cosmic order and filled with the dynamic work of the Creator-Spirit, is structured as living through the *series of creaturely gestalts*. There is commonality despite the historical conditions of individual statements between the presentation of the divine work of creation, as the Old Testament in the 6th century before Christ in the priestly document reports, and the modern natural sciences – in the foundational idea of a phased sequence of gestalts in the building up of the creaturely world. "The sequence may be different at some points from that of modern science, but science today has also arrived at its own idea of a sequence in its understanding of the world." (ST II, 118) In contrast to this, the priestly report of creation far from the thought of a creaturely reality through the evolution of gestalts, as it has the view that "the initial creation established an order for all time so that each of the works for creation would have lasting duration." (ST II, 118–119) In Pannenberg's judgment this view is neither for the totality of the biblical witness representative, nor it is as itself convincing, as God's activity as Creator is not to be restricted to the beginning stage of the world, rather, it is to be seen as continuing. "If it is to do justice to the full biblical witness, then, the doctrine of creation has the task of uniting the interest of this account in the constancy of the order that God has established once and for all with the concept of ongoing creative activity. In the context of modern science the idea of a fixed and constant order no longer need imply an immutability of the divinely created forms in their different genres and species. Though the story does not mention these, the idea of unbreakable natural laws does sufficient justice to that concern. The theory of evolution has given theology an opportunity to see God's ongoing creative activity not merely in the preservation of a fixed order but in the constant bringing forth of things that are new." (ST II, 119) Apart from certain exceptions, this has not been recognized by theology over a long time, much to its own detriment.[11]

The essential theological advantage of the theory of "emergent evolution", which rejects a reductionistic understanding of evolution and allows for the new which cannot be derived from the old to come into being in the process of the genesis of creaturely gestalts, is founded for Pannenberg, against a theory of the constancy of all creaturely types since the beginning of the world, that one may speak plausibly about the historicity of nature from a scientific perspective. This was not the case with classical physics. As the analogies to historical processes have already become apparent in the context of the macro- and micro-cosmic framework of the biosphere, the history of nature in its development becomes a manifest event, such that humans can achieve their purpose as the highest developed beings. Indeed, the possibility of another form of intelligent life beyond that of humans (or a further evolution of those humans into a higher form) cannot be rejected on purely biological observation, although there are no empirical indications of such. Yet it is scientifically judged (though not evident, as implausible) when Christian theology, in the certainty of the incarnation of the divine Creator-Logos in the human Jesus takes the step to the assertion that "the rise and development of life and the appearance of humanity bring fully to light for the first time the meaning of all creaturely reality." (ST II, 133)

In this perspective, one may describe the cosmic process (increasing with the expansion of the universe) as an irreversible and goal-oriented development which integrates all partial moments to the universality of the entire world. The evolutionary process within this development gives rise to creatures that are continually more independent. Though the independence of entities in the inorganic realm is comparatively small, it "reaches a higher stage with living creatures, i.e., independence as self-organization of the forms of existence. With living creatures we have for the first time self-directed activity that is not merely an effect of external causes. This type of activity is aimed at something outside, at the environment in and by which these creatures live. In plants independent activity is limited by the fact that they are spatially fixed. Animals, in contrast, can move about freely. In relating to their environment, therefore, animals also relate to themselves, to the future of their

---

11 Next to theories of physical cosmology, creation theology must also deal with the problem of the place of man in the natural scientific description of organic life. Cf. "Toward a Theology of Nature" (above fn. 65). For the nearer definition of the connection between the particularity of human life and the pre-human evolution, Pannenberg gives importance to the idea of emergent evolution, which he sees in the context of the field-activity of the Spirit. – Theological possibilities of a positive acceptance of the theory of evolution (in contrast to the so-called creationists) are given in "Human life: Creation versus Evolution?" in: T. Peters (ed.), Science and theology. The New Consonance, 1998, 137 – 148.

own lives, as we see very clearly in their search for food. The reality around them, and with it the conditions of their own survival, is no longer simply external to them. Nevertheless, an express self-relation is still lacking prior to the stage of the human form of life, except perhaps in the case of chimpanzees. There is not yet any consistent distinguishing of other things in objective reality as really other. Correspondingly there is no distinguishing of the future as future from the immediate present." (ST II, 133–134) This ability to differentiate is first present with humans, whose developed self-relation is connected with the explicit referentiality to God perceived in the religiosity of man on one hand and with the relation to other humans and the world of objects on the other hand as that which is different from the "I". Yet the human is what he is not in an unmediated, direct manner, but rather through mediation. "It is not by direct divine creation, but by the detour of the expansion and cooling of the universe, the formation of atoms, molecules, and stars, and the development of planet earth with its atmospheric conditions that the independence of creaturely existence became possible that took shape in plant and animal and finally human life." (ST II, 134–135) With this orientation of the series of creaturely gestalts on humanity, it is not to be understood that all pre- and extra-human forms of creaturely existence are merely means for the achievement of an objective outside of themselves. Rather, they have their sense in themselves, something that the human is aware of precisely when he recognizes "that our origin in the evolution of life is a condition of the independence of our existence as creatures. This being so, it is hard to see the point of the struggle against the evolutionary theory." (ST II, 135)

5. Creation and Eschatology

The differentiated relationship between the doctrine of creation and eschatology is grounded in the Trinitarian units of the act of creation. The unity of the eternal creative act of the Trinitarian God is, on one hand, a presupposition for time and the differentiation between beginning and end in order to, on the other hand and at the same time, free the temporal existence of creation from the temporal irreversibility characteristic for all creatures which gives the difference between beginning and end. The divine act of creation would thus be falsely defined, if it were identified with its own unity with the beginning of creation. The creative work of God is not exhausted in a beginning of the world abstracted from the process of temporal development; God's starting encloses the world as a whole, in its entire temporal extension. This means at the same time, that the being and actions of creatures are not set in definitive finality from a simply initial (and in its initiality bygone) creation, as this would exclude true event contingence and creaturely freedom for the present and the future.

In contrast to the idea of creation finished in the beginning of the world-time, as the priestly account of creation and the creation myths of the peoples presuppose, as well as in contrast to the connected assumption of an original-beginning divine presence, Pannenberg undertakes an attempt to "think of the eschaton as the creative beginning of the cosmic process" (ST II, 145) by linking up with apocalyptic tradition and especially Jesus' announcement of the eschatological coming of the Kingdom of God: "The universe and its history are thus set in a different light from that of the first creation story. The issue there, too, was the totality of world occurrence and not just the beginning. But the totality was seen to be grounded in the beginning. Such a view is characteristic of mythical conceptions, which trace back a normative order of the world to a basic primal time that is both the beginning and the model of all that follows." (ST II, 145 – 146) if then it is the eschatological future of God in the coming of His Kingdom which determines the perspective for understanding the world as a whole, the beginning of the world loses its function as a unchangingly valid founding of its unity in the whole of its processes and is "merely the beginning of that which will achieve its full form and true individuality only at the end." (ST II, 146)

Against the assumption of universe without beginning and without limitation in duration, Pannenberg calculates with its beginning and end. The *thought of a temporal beginning and end of the world* is demanded by the thesis of its finitude in the doctrine of creation, whereas a lack of beginning or unlimited duration would imply infinitude. If a temporal beginning is a necessary part of the finite, and thus of the world as the epitome of all finite things as a whole, then a beginning to time itself is claimed, in a certain manner. Indeed, with Pannenberg one cannot think of the origin of time out of God's eternal creative action simply as timeless. Rather, he teaches along with Augustine that time is not without beginning as a creaturely unit, even when this beginning cannot be described in a temporal sense. A presupposition of this argument is that the idea of the world as a whole is indispensable and inevitable as well as empirically logical, rather different than Kant claimed. The latter aspect of empirical sense-making is confirmed for Pannenberg by modern physics and the retreat from an infinite universe to a big-bang theory. A temporal beginning to the world is elementally connected with this standard model of cosmological genesis. This remains true when this temporal beginning which we think of as the beginning of time cannot be precisely described physically. Despite this, the finitude of each event (or process) in time means that each has a beginning. "Insofar as we think of the universe in toto as a finite process, to that extent we must assume that as such it had a temporal beginning, notwithstanding the relativity of temporal processes and measures. Modern ideas of a universe that is unlimited in space and time (not just in one direction but in every direction) see the parts o the world as finite but do not see the world in toto as a finite process. In contrast, physical cosmology with its standard model of an expanding universe suggests finitude at least as regards the beginning." (ST II, 156) Indeed, the beginning of the finite world-process in the irreversibility of its course does not deal with "a beginning 'in' time as though empty time preceded it, but a beginning of time itself, yet a beginning that for its part is already temporally defined as the beginning of a sequence of moments in time. The theory suggests itself that in such a beginning phase time itself takes shape as a sequence of events and a measurable flow. Subjective or imaginary time may thus extend itself to infinity close to the beginning. But objectively, i. e., relative to the total process of the universe, the beginning fixes a boundary separating it not from some preceding time but from eternity." (ST II 157)

It is not only it its beginning, but also in the end to which it strives through the irreversible course of time that the world comes on the borders of the eternity of God. It is valid "that the finitude of the world, insofar as its [sic] has a temporal structure, includes its end." (Ibid.) Physics has first gotten a concept of an end to the world through the second law of thermodynamics, in the sense of thermodynamic equilibrium. As limited and theologically problematic this perspective may be, it is clear that a temporal end to the universe corresponding to its temporal beginning is physically thinkable.[12] To define this end as the location from which the entire process of the world is grounded since its beginning remains the task of the eschatology at the close of the theological system.

Without an eschatological perspective, the *theodicy question* which arises in the doctrine of creation must remain open: "An answer is possible only when we see that creation is linked to the divine work of the reconciling and redeeming of the world. If creation comes to completion only with the world's reconciliation and redemption, then the Creator is allied to us in the battle to overcome evil and to reduce and heal suffering in the world. Only the eschatological consummation of the world can definitively demonstrate the righteousness of God, and therefore his deity, in the world of creation." (ST II, 173)[13] The question of theodicy is called forth by the fact of wickedness and evil in the world, a fact which seems to falsify the goodness of creation. Although this question, as we have noted, drives one to an eschatological answer, it is connected with the protological topic insofar as it remains problematic even in light of reconciliation and completion, why it is that the Creator did not create a world without suffering and guilt originally. To derive both from the freedom of the creature to decide and act does not offer a theological way out, as suffering and pain are common in the pre-human world of living things and cannot be explained as general consequences of the sinful self-centeredness of humans. However, the indication that evil has its origin in the freedom to decide and act of creatures is not able "to absolve the Creator of

---

12 For the treatment of Frank Tiplers "Physics of Immortality" (1994) cf. "Eine modern Kosmo-
     logie: Gott und die Auferstehung der Toten" (1997), in BSTh 2, 93–98.
13 Cf. also "Die christliche Deutung des Leidens" in BSTh 2, 246–253.

responsibility of this creation of his. Although creatures may be free, even in their freedom they are still God's creatures. Concern to absolve the Creator has been a mistake in Christian theodicy. The attempt cannot succeed, nor does it accord the NT testimony, for in and with the crucifixion of his Son God accepted and bore responsibility for the world he created." (ST II, 166)

If the path to answering the theodicy question, which crops up often in the Christian tradition, remains blocked, then one can connect the possibility and actuality of wickedness and sin with risk – a risk which is not externally added to the creative action of God, but one which is inherent to the determined completion of the act of creation, a risk which is taken for the sake of creation. This risk is, along with the creaturely independence intended in the creative act of God which belongs necessarily to the good of the creature, the condition of the possibility for free community with God and creatures, necessarily and inseparably. As the condition for the achievement of this goal, the communal relationship between creature and Creator, God accepts the risk of sin and wickedness when carrying out His creative activity. "God did not will wickedness and evil as such. He could not take pleasure in them. They are not an object of his will. Nevertheless, they are in fact accompanying phenomena. As such they are conditions of the realizing of his purpose for the creatures, and they come under his world government, which can bring good out of evil, being oriented to the reconciliation and redemption of the world through Jesus Christ." (ST II, 167) Though the independence for which the creature was created builds the ground for the possibility of evil and wickedness, the facticity is not connected to the divine desire for creaturely independence, nor with the finitude and limitations of the creatures. It is first with the move towards independence of the finite from its infinite ground and the connected self-perverting limitation which brings forth factual evil. The root of evil is thus not in the finitude of the creature as such, which is a unit that is good and aimed to a good purpose, but much rather "[w]e are to seek the root of veil…in revolt against the limit of finitude, in the refusal to accept one's own finitude, and in the related illusion of being like God (cf. Gen. 3:5)." (ST II, 171) Differently said: "The source of suffering and evil lies in the transion from God-given independace to self-independence. Here also is the source of the further sufferings that creatures bring on themselves beyond the measure of their finitude." (ST II, 172) The move for independence from control of creatures from one another, which is necessarily connected with their rejection of divine control, "[w]e see this on the ascending line of forms of life, and it comes to a climax in human sin, for among us the relation to God has become thematic." (*Ibid.*) The inscrutability of human sin is negatively reciprocal to the height of the *imago Dei* in human created purpose. The doctrine of man deals with both.

§4 Anthropology (ST II, Chapter 8)

1. The Human as Personal Unity of Body and Soul

With the phrase "The Dignity and Misery of Humanity", which serves as the subtitle of the chapter on anthropology in the Systematic Theology, Pannenberg refers to the two traditional main aspects of the Christian doctrine of man: the image of God and sin. "Together the two basic anthropological statements in Christian theology – the statements about our creation in the divine image and about our sin – are the presupposition of God's redeeming work for us through Jesus Christ. We need redemption because of sin, which is the root of our alienation from God and the self. But we can speak of redemption only in relation to an event that creates freedom for the redeemed. The fellowship with God helps us to self-identity, and this in turn presupposes that we are destined by nature for fellowship with God." (ST II, 180) The latter can be seen as the first and foundational thesis of Pannenberg's theological anthropology. The humanity of the human is, according to his creaturely determination, structured for God. The human is created in the image of God. This is the basis of humanity's special status within creation. It is not under evolution-historical aspects, but rather "[o]nly from the standpoint of the religiously and biblically grounded awareness of their destiny of fellowship with God, the author of the universe, can we say assuredly, however, that all creation culminates in humanity." (ST II, 175) This requires, of course, "we must (1) be able to look at the world of as a whole, notwithstanding the openness of nature; (2) show that humans stand in a unique relation to the origin of the universe; and (3) assume that in them the purpose of finite life is both comprehended and fulfilled." (*Ibid.*) The first condition, to capture the entirety of the world, is fulfilled in the recognition of the world as the creation of God and in the recognition of God as the Creator of the world, respectively. The special status of humanity among the other creatures in its role as the second condition has its ground in the third, that is, in "the definitive actualizing of the relation to the Creator, which is meant for all creatures as such, in the human relation to God." (*Ibid.*)

The highest and most final realization of the human's relationship to God, which is the goal of all creation according to its creaturely determination, is, according to Pannenberg, found in Jesus Christ as the incarnate Son of the omnipotent Father. It is first from Him and to Him that one can definitively claim that the creaturely disposition common to all creatures finds its completion and fulfillment in the human relationship with God. Thus the connection between Christology and anthropology is not first from a Christological perspective (cf. ST II Ch 9), but also from a anthropological perspective a differentiated and yet inseparable one. The destiny of humans as made definitively real in Jesus Christ, to be in communion with God, builds the inviolable dignity of the person. This dignity raises the person above the natural world as well as above the contexts of social power. For each human is made in the image of God and thus is, as an individual, of infinite value.[1] Traditionally, a Christian anthropology expresses this in the "doctrine of our buman nature as spiritual and not just psychosomatic" (ST II, 180). Pannenberg follows this course by beginning his examination of the creaturely destiny of humans with a section on the human as personal unity of body and soul (ST II, 181–202). This is the general framework of interpretation for his *doctrine of the image of God*.

The living body of the human is animated and in the carrying out of life organized for awareness and self-awareness; the human soul is embodied and should not be thought of in a disembodied manner. "Prevailing trends in modern anthropology see the soul and body as constitutive elements of the unity of human life that belong together and cannot be reduced to one another." (ST II, 182) Pannenberg's judgment is that "[w]e may view this modern understanding as in line with the intentions of the earliest Christian anthropology." (*Ibid.*) Essentially, the early patristic writers defended the body-soul unity of man as the foundation of Christian anthropology against a Platonism which rose up to become the leading philosophy of the antique world in the middle of the 2nd century. They did this under the following aspects: 1. The soul is indeed the life-principle of the body, but it is not a self-moved divine substance, rather, just as the body, different from God, even in the case of its immortality (which was argued even among Christians). 2. The idea of a pre-existence of the soul and a possible reincarnation was rejected from church doctrine with the indication "that the soul is created with the body." (ST II, 184) The so-called traducianism understands the creation of souls as something that occurs in concert with the body in begetting; creationism understands this as something directly undertaken by God.

Despite this foundational criticism against platonic anthropology, the biblical view of the body-soul unity of humans is only in certain respects brought forth in patristic writings, as the reigning model to explain the relationship between body and soul was that in the sense of two substantial partial principles. This was not sufficiently secured against dualistic tendencies. The Aristotelianisim of the high scholastic period (as paradig-

---

1 That and to what extent the insight in the value of eternity "of the individual and the individual life has been one of the most important contributions of christendom to the experience of the structure of human existence, as to the development of humanity" is shown in "Die Bedeutung des Individuums in der christlichen Lehre vom Menschen" in: Die Bestimmung des Menschen. Menschsein, Erwählung und Geschichte, 1978, 7–22, here: 8.

matically represented by Thomas Aquinas and confirmed as church doctrine in the council of Vienne in 1312 [DH 902]) brought unarguable progress, insofar as it thought of the soul as the form of the human body (*humani corporis forma*): "On this view the soul is not just a partial principle but that which makes us human in our bodily reality. Conversely, the body is the concrete form in which our humanity, the soul, finds appropriate expression." (*Ibid.*)

The Aristotelian understanding of the human body-soul relationship does find itself comparatively much closer to the biblical understanding of humanity than does the platonic-influenced anthropology. Nonetheless, Pannenberg sees the remaining difference in the *Spirit-reference of the embodied soul.* Spirit is, after all, according to the biblical tradition not a soul-power in the sense of the Thomistic *anima intellectiva,* but rather "as the power of God that generates and sustains the life of both soul and body and is thus at work in it." (ST II, 186) Through the action of the creative life-energy of the Spirit of God in the created human, the former does not become a part of the being of the latter. "Rather, it means that creaturely life has an eccentric character, that it is referred to the divine power of the Spirit that works upon it." (*Ibid.*) This is confirmed explicitly by the Old Testament word *ruah.* It was first with Hellenism that Judeo-Christian thought was invaded by the idea that an understanding of spirit as an essential part of the being of the human soul in the sense of a soul-power independent from the Spirit of God. "The pneuma that works in us could then be regarded either as an essential creaturely element or as an essential divine part of the creaturely soul." (ST II, 187) Both concepts are not compatible with the biblical understanding of Spirit, according to Pannenberg, especially the equation of the human spirit-soul with reason – not even with the presupposition that Christian theology has retreated into agnosticism regarding the presumption of the divinity of the rational spirit-soul.

An identification of sprit and reason is out of the question according to the biblical witness first due to the fact that the actions of God affect all living beings; this is not to be limited to humans. Secondly, the specific Sprit-referentiality which marks the embodied human soul and makes up the precedence of humans before other creatures can only be secondarily associated with intellectual ability. Primary is the association with the destiny of community with God, as grounded in the image of God in humans. The rationality of humans is thus to be derived from the destiny of humans to the image of God, and not the other way around. Human reason does indeed require, as do all other life-functions of creatures, the sustaining work of the Creator-Spirit in order to appropriately make real its creaturely ability to know – this matches the creaturely disposition of humans to the image of God. This does not exclude the idea that reason is "the dominant function of the human soul, in the relation of the whole person to the Spirit." (ST II, 190) However, reason is not spirit, but is reliant on Spirit; it can only accord to the idea of reason when reason is not equated with Spirit, but "eccentrically" grounded in Sprit.

As aware and self-aware life is only known as embodied life, the bodily life of humans is disposed to be carried out as aware and self-aware.[2] The relationship of a human as an embodied soul determined to aware and self-aware life with the Sprit as the creative original reason of life is, according to Pannenberg, in an elemental manner "in the sense of life that in adult experience grasps the distinction between the self and the world, while in the symbiotic sphere of early childhood no clear distinction is yet made between the objective and the subjective aspects of the relation to the world." (ST II, 192) With such a "sense of life", an implicit self-reference is present, based on the quality of desire or lack thereof. This reference is that which the human shares "with animal life and perhaps with all living things, for all living things, as autocatalysts, are processes of self-organization that are characterized as such by a relation to the totality of their own existence." (ST II, 193) An explicit self-awareness comes from a self-familiarity prior to all reflection which comes as a consequence of the "experience of the encounter with others" (Ibid.). This process comes to the conclusion of not merely the differentiation of objects from one another, but also the differentiation of the actual "I" of one's own life from other objects. As a consequence of the awareness of the egocentricity of one's own world of awareness, a differentiation between body and soul can be built in the context of experienced intersubjectivity: "Over against the soul as the inner world of the consciousness stands the body, which, like the things of the world and in distinction form the inner world of my consciousness, is there for others as well as myself." (ST II, 194) The apparently obvious consequence, "to regard the inner world of the conscious-ness as the true I in distinction from the body" (Ibid.), is not an option for Pannenberg, as this would inappropriately limit the idea of the soul as well as that of the ego. Just as the idea of the souls contains more than the interior world of awareness, so does the index word "I", by referring to the speaker, refer to bodily individuality. This does not imply a restriction to the function of "I think", as the philosophy of the transcendental ego in the Kantian tradition suggests. Thus, Pannenberg rejects the idea to declare the instance of "I" to the precondition of every form of objective awareness, as well as to declare it to the ground of the unity of experience. "Not the I but the divine Spirit is the ultimate basis of the interrelatedness of that which is distinct in the consciousness, of the interrelatedness also of the I and the things of the world, especially similar living creatures." (ST II, 196) The Spirit is the one who works each in-one-another of ecstatic and inwardness that interpenetrates all that

---

2 Under particular reference to the discussion between Karl Popper and John C. Eccles regarding the placement of human awareness in evolution, Pannenberg explicates the differences and relations between awareness and spirit in "Bewußtsein und Geist" in ZThK 80 (1983), 332–351; reprinted in BSTh 2, 123–140.

exists. This is in order to build the highest step (in our knowledge) of human self-awareness, without becoming one with one with it; the self-awareness of humans is itself finite and only takes part in the infinite, insofar it is grasped by the infinite and taken past the limits of its own finitude, as well as insofar it is made capable of that self-transcendence to which it is destined.

According to the famous definition of Boethius, "person" is the term for a rational individual: *"Persona es naturae rationis individua substantia"* (MPL 64, 1343). In contrast to this idea of personhood, Pannenberg's concept orients itself on the *persona*-understanding of the tradition of Trinitarian and Christological theology. In both cases, this is made up by constitutive relations. In Christology, the idea of person refers to the relation to God which is constitutive for the human existence of Jesus. It is in this manner that human personhood should be understood, that is, through the reference to God and through the existence in destiny to community with Him. "Without the works of the divine spirit in use there could be no personality in the deeper sense of the term. For personality has to do with the manifestation of the truth and totality of individual life in the moment of its existence. We are not persons simply because we have self-consciousness and can distinguish and maintain our own ego apart from others. We do not cease to be persons where we no longer have this identity in the self-consciousness, nor are we without personality where it is not present. Personality is grounded in the destiny that transcends our empirical reality." (ST II, 198) Personality is closely connected to eccentricity, self-transcendence, to the world- and God-openness of human existence. Even when it is not yet certain, who we actually are, nonetheless we exist as persons: "This is possible only in anticipation of the truth of our existence, which is mediated to us now through the Spirit by means of our feeling for life.

We can attain to the totality of our own lives, notwithstanding its fragmentary form at each moment, only in relation to our Creator. But we achieve our particularity in our encounter with others. Both types of relation are in their own ways constitutive for our individual personhood." (ST II, 200)

2. Transcendence of Personal Existence

The *concept of a person* has had a long history of meaning in the Christian tradition. This is especially connected to the fact that the translations of the Greek word *hypostasis* in a Trinitarian-theological context made use of the Latin word *persona*. *Hypostasis* achieved a central place in philosophy and metaphysics based on the Platonic tradition, and with Plotinus and Porphyry it gained the formal meaning of a manifestation of the divine One. The term received its own Christian sense through Athanasius. Although he, like Origin, originals used *ousia* and *hypostasis* without making any difference between the two, it was Athanasius who made their differentiation possible, as well as making it possible to think of being and hypostasis as a differentiated unity. This was very close to the Neo-Platonic terminology, with the decisive distinction that hypostases of the One do not index steps after it; the three hypostases of the Godhead are coordinated but not subordinated: Father, Son, and Holy Spirit are hypostatically different and one in being at the same time.

To express the Trinitarian differentiation of the single divine being through the concept of hypostases suggested itself not least due to the fact that this often referred to the concrete realization of being in the antique world. In the technical language of the Peripatetics, for example, the term refers to the being of an entity *in concreto*, the particular realization of being in the individual thing. While it is in every other case that each singular thing is the realization of a particular being, in the mystery of the Trinity the divine being has three hypostases. A comparable mystery can be established in a Christological context, insofar as the divine and human natures are unified in Jesus Christ, as according to the Chalcedonian formula. When one assumes as a consequence the enhypostasis of the human nature of Jesus Christ in the Logos, one can avoid the idea of a human nature robbed of its individual being, when its anhypostasis is grounded in a referentiality such that the being of the human Jesus is thought from His complete participation in the Logos, that is, from His relation to God. The person-ness of Jesus Christ would then be the epitome of being grounded in God, and is to be thought of in the manner of a constitutive relationality. This constitutive relationality is, grounded in another manner, to be taken into account for the other but nonetheless one in being divine hypostases.

Without being able to go into the further history of this term in Christian thought, with its relationship to the idea of substance, subsistence, and the individual person, it is desired here to establish that Pannenberg takes this complex terminological history as an opportunity to revise the usual famous definition from Boethius of a person as an rational individuality, so that he might define personhood from the human destiny of communion with God. This is the object of the expression "transcendence of personal existence". This is taken from the anthropological monograph[3] of Pannenberg, which will be examined more precisely in what follows. The human is a person according to the destiny present in human nature – to be grounded eccentrically and self-transcendentally in God, that one achieve find human fulfillment and completion in communion with God. Said differently: the destiny of being the image of God is that which allows the human to be a person.

Because he thinks of personhood from the context of the relationship between God and human, Pannenberg is, as mentioned, not only skeptical but downright critical of the common equation of personhood with *self-awareness, ego, and subject*. An extensive grounding for this criticism is

---

3 Anthropology in Theological Perspective, Philadelphia, The Westminster Press, 1985 (= Anth.).

delivered in the fourth and fifth chapters of "Anthropology in Theological Perspective" and builds the common thread of the examinations, which are given in an exceptionally perspective-rich manner. To sketch the major points of the argument: the connection to the considerations regarding the world-open nature of humans, which grounds the special status of humans in creation, offers the insight that the eccentric foundational form of the human as one being among others as to another "implies the distinction of this (material or personal) other not only from still other objects but also from my 'self.' In a further step, the question then arises of the relation between my being present to the other and my being in myself." (Anth., 159) As the concrete development of these references takes place in the social context which is implicit in the human structure of behavior, Pannenberg removes the preliminary abstraction away from the social dimension of human life-processes of the first section of the anthropology in order to develop the process of the development of the ego, subjectivity, and self-awareness under the title "the human person as a social being", which titles the entire second section of the anthropology.

First, the historical path towards independence for the individual in community is examined first, along with the possible antagonistic conse-quences, such as those from an abstract individual who removes himself solipsistically from social relations, or from a totalitarianism which reduces the individual to a mere function of the social. The systematic foundation thesis is the assumption of an irreducible common origin of individuality and sociality. Just as the individual "I" constitutes itself in the relationship to the social "Thou", so does the social "Thou" only function as itself in the essential openness for the individual and his significance. Pannenberg takes the co-called dialogical personalism as an indication for a possible alternative to an anthropology which things of the ego as sovereign subject. This alternative is profiled further in the context of G.H. Mead's theory of the social self. Pannenberg judges that the achievement of Mead lies in "that he went beyond the broad personalist thesis that the ego is constituted by its relation to the Thou and undertook a concrete and nuanced description of this dependence." (Anth., 190) The insight is central, that the self that we are aware of in our self-awareness rest on the picture which others have of us. "It follows from this theory of the genesis of self-consciousness that the human being as a self-conscious ego is not grounded in itself and independently of others. Rather, self-consciousness and the self-conscious ego are constituted though relation to the other. This is not to say that the ego is a creation of the Thou; the point is, rather, that individuals comprehend themselves by putting themselves in the place of others over against themselves." (Anth., 187) Pannenberg finds a remaining difficulty for Mead's theory in the idea that "only a self that is detached from the ego porved to embody the dependence of the individual self consciousness on the process of social life", where he fails to see "the social conditionaing even of the ego" (Anth., 190). Also, Mead failed to answer the "question (which cannot be raised until that first problem is solved) of the unity of ego and self." (*Ibid.*)

The *problem of identity* referred to here is the topic of the fifth chapter of Pannenberg's anthropological work, first from the perspective of the analytic ego psychology, whose advantage over Mead's theory of the self is found in the insight "that the ego undergoes a process of development or formation that is marked in a decisive way by a processing of the social environment in which the individual develops." (Anth., 199) The unity of the ego and the self remains an unsolved problem. With this in mind, Pannenberg turns to the classical attempt of J.G. Fichte, to think of the unity of the ego and the self and thus of the unity of the self-awareness. He writes: "For two reasons this attempt has lost none of its relevance for the contemporary discussion of the origin and development of the ego, a discussion that derives its character chiefly from psychology.

The first reason is that the unity of ego and self...continues to be neglected even today. This unity is all to easily taken for granted and presupposed, even though ego and self are for the rest described in completely different ways: the self as a product of society and the ego as preceding any social relations, or the self as object of a development and the ego as productive source of this development. Thinkers see no need of reconciling these differences and showing that ego and self are in fact unified in the self-conscious ego.

There is a second reason for the continued relevance of Fichte's philosophy of the ego. Just as contemporary psychologists take for granted the unity of ego and self, so too they assume almost as readily that this unity originates in the activity of the ego; they assume it even while they also strongly insist that this activity must assimilate and integrate the social relations within which the process of identity formation takes place. Now such an explanation of the unity of ego and self as due to the activity of the ego is also found in Fichte's first model for the unity of self-consciousness as proposed in the first edition of his *Wissenschaftslehre* in 1794. Consequently when present-day thinkers trace the unity of ego and self back to the activity of the ego, they are still accepting the gramework of Fichte's first *Wissenschaftslehre*. It is all the more significant, then, that Fichte found it impossible to stay with this model of self-consciousness." (Anth., 201) The reason for this is developed on the basis of Dieter Heinrich's 1967 study "*Fichte's ursprüngliche Einsicht*"[4]. The result is that the theory of the "I that sets itself" must be considered to have failed, due the the inability to derive the unity of the ego and the self from the ego itself.

Whether the presupposition of transcendental philosophy which Fichte shared with Kant, that is, that "the unity of 'I think' underlies all experience and therefore cannot be derived from any experiential data" (Anth., 203), is done for, is another question entirely. Pannenberg does not give an immediate answer, though he does establish that throughout the 19th century and in the

---

4 Fichte's original insight.

following time the tendency was to understand self-awareness not merely as mediated by the experience of objects, but from as derived and derivable from the context of object-reality. Pannenberg warns toward caution, however, with reference to Mead, reminding us "how easy it is to fall short of the stage of awareness for the problem that was reached even in the idealist thematization of self-consciousness, even at the very time when we believe we have passed beyond it by transcending the tarting point of the philosophy of consciousness." (Anth., 206) A similar thing can be said "for many of the current attempts to use the tools of linguistic analysis to move beyond the idealist theory of the subject" (*Ibid.*). For these too often lead back to "the question asked in transcendental philosophy regarding the constitution of self-consciousness." (Anth., 209) One must particularly in the context of Kant-reception take care to retain a differentiated view of things.

With reference to Kant's doctrine of the transcendental ego, which makes the unity of the self-awareness to condition of possibility for the connections in the awareness of objects, one should first "[bear] in mind that this is a transcendental assertion and does not mean that a unitary ego must be present antecedently to any and every consciousness of objects. A view like the last-named has already fallen victim to a confusion between transcendental and metaphysical statements." (Anth., 219) Pannenberg judges certain things among Kant's teachings to be questionable and misleading, such as his "description of the transcendental presupposition as a 'unity of consciousness'...[f]or it suggests that such a unity must explicitly underlie each moment of consciousness – as asserted in fact in the metaphysical idea of an 'archego' as the basis for the stream of consciousness. By speaking this way, Kant himself fostered the confusion between his transcendental apperception and that king of metaphysical notion." (Anth., 220) Pannenberg's criticism of the assumption of a continual and previously available ego is aimed against this confusion. To what extent this impacts the "idealist representation of the ego in transcendental philosophy or, at any rate, a widespread interpretation of the idea of transcendental subject" (Anth., 212) can be left unexamined here. It is decisive, that the idea of an existing and remaining real-ego as the condition for the unity of self-awareness is not plausible. The Kantian assumption of a synthetic function of the transcendental ego becomes untenable where it is connected with the claim of an unchanging subject actually at the foundation of the stream of consciousness. In this context, on should note the comment that the differentiating of the transcendental and empirical ego "cannot render the first completely independent and separate from the second, without at the same time causing the loss of the very starting point of transcendental reflection: the consciousness that intuits, represents, and judges." (Anth., 213) In connection with the insight of Heidegger and others regarding the temporality of the condition of being, this should "give pause, above all, to those who much too quickly judge the attempts of psychology and social psychology at a theory of the genesis of the ego to be purely empirical in value and without relevance to philosophy – especially to the philosophy of subjectivity of transcendental idealism, which asserts the ego and its identity to be the ultimate transcendental basis of all achievements of consciousness." (Anth., 213)

To contradict this claim, Pannenberg refers to the possibility of an egoless identity of the awareness which is has not yet proceeded to explicit self-awareness, in connection with Dieter Heinrich. This is that which occurs in dream-awareness, and is presupposed in the awareness in early childhood. "The possibility of reaching an explicit self-consciousness on this basis does indeed presuppose an original, although unthematic, familiarity of the consciousness with itself that is subsequently differentiated and articulated in explicit self consciousness." (Anth., 220) To what is this original familiarity related? By answering this question, Pannenberg sees a turnaround in the normal relationship between ego and self: "the ego does not establish itself through its action by positing itself. The ego is not the continuously existing subject of my individual development, a subject that is always present behind all changes in consciousness and gives ever new definitions of itself in the process of its identity formation, but is not itself changed thereby. Rather, the ego is primarily tied to the moment and receives its continuity and identity only in the mirror of the individual's developing consciousness of itself as the totality of its 'states, qualities, and actions.' In the initial stages of development the individual's own self must first of all achieve distinction from that of the mother. This distinction comes through the development of object perception and is completed only be the acquisition of speech. Only then can there be the coordination and distinction that are attained through use of the indexical word 'I' for the presentation of the person's own self." (Anth., 221)

With this turnaround of the traditional relationship between ego and self, and with the insight that identity and continuity ground the ego in the self, the presuppositions which lie at the foundation of Pannenberg's theory of the *personhood of humans* and their religious dimension are pulled in. the connection between foundational trust and self-identification takes a decisive mediating function between the subjectivity-theoretical analysis and the doctrine of human personhood. The foundational trust, which is set up in the early phase of personality development through the symbiotic connection with the mother, but which requires dissolution when it should remain, is aimed for Pannenberg "in its proper sense…to that agency which is able to protect and promote the self in its *wholeness*." (Anth., 234) The idea of a person refers to this entirety of the self, and this reference gives it a central position in Pannenberg's anthropology: "The wholeness of the self, which infinitely transcends the limitations of life at any given moment, finds its present manifestation as personality." (Anth., 235) This is the anticipatory presence of the self in its entirety in the ego. "The word 'person' establishes a relation between the mystery – which transcends the present of the ego – of the still incomplete individual life history that is on the way to its special destiny and the present moment of the ego. Person is the presence of the self in the moment of the ego, in the claim laid upon the ego by our true self, and in the anticipatory consciousness of our identity.

This is why we connect the concept of freedom with the person, since freedom means more than the capacity, which is always given with openness to the world, to distance oneself from impressions and objects and therefore also to dwell in them and attend to them. In its deeper sense, freedom is the real possibility of being myself – which is also the true meaning of autonomy in Kant's sense, where autonomy is the expression of my identity as a rational being. In this sense, freedom and personhood belong together, to the extent that personality describes the presence of the self in the ego." (Anth., 240)

In order to make this initial explication of the topic of identity with the unthematic intimacy of the awareness with itself, Pannenberg begins the sixth chapter of his anthropology ("Identity and Nonidentity as a Theme of the Affective Life") with the thesis that the entirety of being in the life of a human manifests in the unthematic intimacy, rather than being primarily a knowledge of fact of an identical self-awareness. It is *feeling* in which the personal life of subjects is carried out. The term "feeling", along with the term "mood", refers to the "presence of the always as yet incomplete whole of life" (Anth., 244) prior to each thematic self-reflection in the form of that inexpressible self-relation that is characteristic for the original familiarity of the awareness with itself. Its genuine self-reference does not have the gestalt of an explicit self-awareness, but is rather of a pre-reflective nature, in order to appear as in the positive and negative modes of self familiarity as desire or reluctance, respectively. Thus it is "that in 'elevated' moods and positive affects, in which human beings are most at one with themselves, they are not preoccupied with themselves but are 'ecstatically' open and surrendered to the reality of their life-world and of the ground which sustains it. In 'depressed' moods, on the other hand, and in negative affects they prove to be thrown back upon themselves." (Anth., 266) The tension between eccentricity and centrality, which determines as the foundational character of human existence the entire experience of the human, influences as a result the life of emotions and affective moods in a particularly elemental manner.

Rather than discussing the wide framework in the history of theory which forms Pannenberg's understanding of the topic of feelings, a breadth that reaches from David Hume to the present, here the distance and nearness to Schleiermacher is noted. While the thought of the presence of the entire, undivided being in feeling, formulated in connection with Steffen, is judged as relevant and not outmoded, the description of the idea of feeling with the turn of phrase "direct self-awareness" is vehemently criticized. "Feeling renders us familiar with ourselves in the whole of our being, without our as yet having or needing an *idea* of our self. The reference to the self signals its presence only in the pleasure or displeasure that marks feeling. This familiarity with self may well be the condition for the understanding and use of the worlds 'I', 'self', and 'my' and thus provide the basis for the development of self-consciousness in the proper sense of this term. Self-consciousness in this proper sense comes into being only in connection with the *cognitive* development of the child.

Schleiermacher was wrong, therefore, in opposing feeling as 'immediate self-consciousness' to the idealist philosophy of consciousness and at the same time making it the point of departure for something like a transcendental deduction of religious experience. Some decades later, R. H. Lotze more correctly described the relation between feeling and self-consciousness when, on the one hand, he made feeling the source of the evidence of the unity of thinker and object of thought in self-consciousness and, on te other, made the cognitive, not the affective, structure of the self-consciousness consist in the distinction and unity of ego and self. This shows in an exemplary way that every understanding, including every understanding of the self, must move beyond feeling into the medium of thought. This entails very extensive corrections in Schleiermacher's conception of the relation between thought and religion, philosophy and theology.

The fact remains, however, that in its reaching out to the totality of life, feeling anticipates the distinction and correlation effected by the intellect, even though because of its vagueness feeling depends on thinking for definition. Thought, on the other hand, can never exhaustively transfer to its own sphere what is present in feeling. This is true not only of self-consciousness but of the whole spectrum of experience; it is also, of course, very significant for the relation between religious experience and philosophical or theological reflection as well as for the relation between religious consciousness itself and the objective character of its representations." (Anth., 251 – 252)

3. The Image of God as the Destiny of Humans

As a person, the human is referred an open destiny beyond his own reality and the reality present in the world, and thus is the human also referred to God. "The bible uses the concept of image of God to describe this human destiny; in the belongingness to God, which sets human beings apart, it sees that special dignity which makes human beings inviolable and grounds the prohibition against taking their lives (Gen. 9:6). The invocation of God's rights as the divine Majesty makes the inviolability of human dignity immune against human caprice." (Anth., 242)[5] In regard to the biblical witness, the already

---

5 Cf. "Der Mensch – ein Ebenbild Gottes?" in: Zeitwende 39 (1968), 812 – 821; reprinted in BSTh 2, 141 – 149. Cf. also Gottebenbildlichkeit als Bestimmung des Menschen in der neueren Theologiegeschichte, 1979 (Bavarian Academy of Sciences, Philosophical-Historical Class. Report 1979, Volume 8). Further: "Der Mensch als Person" in: H. Heimann/ H.J. Gaertner (eds.), Das Verhältnis der Psychiatrie zu ihren Nachbardisziplinen, 1986, 3 – 9; reprinted in BSTh 2, 162 – 169. Cf.

established fact of a close connection between anthropology and Christology is confirmed in the context of the doctrine of the *imago Dei:* "In Paul's sayings about Christ as the image of God into which all others must be transformed, the Christian doctrine of the divine likeness must see an elucidation of our general destiny of divine likeness. But in so doing it may not expunge the differences between the fulfilling of our divine likeness in and by Jesus Christ on the one hand, and the OT statements about Adam's divine likeness on the other. To do this is to miss the point that our destiny as creatures is brought to fulfillment by Jesus Christ." (ST II, 210) It is first from the message of the New Testament, which witnesses to Jesus Christ as the image of God (2 Cor. 4:4; Col. 1:15; cf. Hebr. 1:3) and promises the transformation of the believer in this image (Rom. 8:29; 1 Cor. 15:49; 2 Cor. 3:18) is it shown "finally clear[ly]" (ST II, 202) that the Image of God as the destiny to communion with God is the creaturely destiny of each human in their personhood. The *imago Dei* of the human, which according to Genesis 1:26 ff. is the measure and prerequisite for the human reigning function in creation, consists for Pannenberg essentially in the fact that the human, according to the creaturely disposition, is destined for personal communion with God. Symbolized by walking erect, this applies to the whole human, and cannot be reduced to the spirit, soul, or reason (respectively), as it has been often done in the tradition. It is also not, as Karl Barth and others have claimed, to be restricted to the relationship between husband and wife as the reflection of the divine Father-Son relationship. It is not merely in one respect, but in the differentiated unity of body and soul, of individuality and society, that the human is in personal entirety destined to communion with God, as it is revealed as completed in Jesus Christ. As communion with God in person, Jesus Christ is the epitome of the *imago Dei*, which has been expressed in the tradition (among other ways) that one differentiated with regard to the idea of image between Christ as original image and Adam as a reflection, and connecting the two thoughts through the idea image of the reflection being recapitulated through the original.

The traditional understandings of the *imago Dei* in humans, despite all their differences, are judged by Pannenberg to have one commonality, "that this likeness to God was present at the beginning of human history, namely, in the perfection of the original estate of the first human being before the fall." (Anth., 50) The differences are in the distinction and relation of *eikon* and *homoiosis* or *imago* and *similitudo*, words that are used to translate the Hebrew expressions *zelem* and *demut*. While the reformers saw the image of God consisted in the actual relation to God, which as a result of sin would lead

also "Christliche Wurzeln des Gedankens der Menschenwürde" in: W. Kerber, Menschenrechte und kulturelle Identität, 1991, 61 – 76; reprinted in BSTh2, 191 – 201. "Person is…neither the self in its difference to the ego, nor the ego in its difference to the self. Person is the presence of the self in the ego in the claiming of our ego through our true self and in anticipatory awareness of our identity." (Christliche Anthropologie und Personalität (1975), in: BSTh 2, 150 – 161, here: 160).

to a perversion and loss or original righteousness entirely, the medieval-catholic view divides between the formal structural nature of human beings and the current relation to God. Thus this latter can also speech under postlapsarian conditions of a remaining rest-*imago*. Despite these differences, both of these confessional concepts are oriented to the *concept of a perfect original estate.*

The traditional concept of Adam having a perfect original stat as well as that of a loss of the image of God through the Fall fails to stand up to Pannenberg's exegetical and systematic trial. Thus, he departs from this concept in favor of the idea of an evolutionary image. Pannenberg finds this thought pronounced in the thought of Herder, who takes it as the "point of departure for modern philosophical anthropology" (Anth., 43, bold subtitle). The assumption of a developing image of God is already to be found in the context of a differentiation of degrees of intensity in similarity to God, as one finds in Irenaeus, as well as in the circles of the renaissance philosophy. It remained for Herder to take up these beginnings and to connect them to the foundational insights of modern anthropology, that is, regarding the human as an unfinished being. It should be added, that Pannenberg's criticism of the original estate, oriented on Herder, is also defended against theories which do not refer to this as an historical beginning state, but as a transhistorical status. For speech about an original estate, lost through sin, in which one was connected with God, is only tenable "if that state may also be claimed to have been the initial state of humankind at the beginning of human history. Talk of a loss presupposes a state prior to the loss, and then the question cannot be avoided of whether or not such a state ever existed. A refusal to allow this question, even though one continues to tell of a loss through sin of an original human state of union with God, can only be regarded as a trick to gain immunity, an effort to use obfuscation as a way of avoiding the logical implications of one's claims and their weaknesses. There can be non loss of something that never existed. As a historical claim about the beginnings of human history, the idea htat there was an original union of humankind with God which was lost through a fall into sin is incompatible with our currently available scientific knowledge about the historical beginnings of the race. This being the case, we should renounce artificial attempts to rescue traditional theological formulas; one such attempt is the idea of an origin that is supposedly nonhistorical." (Anth., 57). However, by such a relinquishment, Pannenberg need not give up the interest which determines such a postulate. This interest orients on the fact that one experiences being human as a state with duty, as well as the insight, that one always fails in this duty. This is much better reflected in the thought of a yet-to-be-achieved destiny than in any type of mythical orientation on primeval time. The idea of an original estate is thus to be diligently transferred into the idea of an evolving image of God, as it has been pre-formulated by Herder. If, then, one cannot associate the image of God with a legendary original estate, but must understand it as a "becoming" that can only be appropriately understood in becoming, then the term coincides with that of the *destiny of humans*. The term "destiny", which Pannenberg attributes to K.G. Bretschneider (cf. Anth 54), refers to the goal of eschatological completion to which the human is oriented in the process of his history. This goal of completion is not only, and not primarily the rule of humans over the rest of creation, but rather also and primarily the human communion with God and participation in His wisdom, justice, and abiding being. Pannenberg accents this later aspect emphatically, insofar as for him not merely the virtue of a wise and just life, but also the eschatological destiny of the human to participation in the eternal life of God belongs constitutively to the idea of communion with God.

If, then, the purpose of the image of God of the human is fulfilled in the completed connection with God, because the "relatedness to God has its inner *telos* in fellowship with him" (ST II, 224), then one must assign the image of God of Christ and that of Adam to one another such that Christ is the revealed realization of that which Adam is designed for as creature. As the unifying of God and human in Jesus Christ is a matter of the communion between God and human in an unsurpassable form, one can say "that our creation in God's image was related from the very outset to this fulfillment that has come, or broken in, in the history of Jesus of Nazareth." (ST II, 225) The human is, in this sense, designed from the beginning of his history for the communion with God manifested in Jesus Christ. This disposition is not external to the being and real life-actions of the human, but rather it belongs to the human in the most inherent manner possible. It is thus also not at human disposal. Of course, that goal to which the human is aimed is from his own nature to him "not even present…as a goal but only in an indefinite trust that opens up the horizon of world experience and intersubjectivity, and also in a restless trust toward overcoming the finite." (ST II, 228) The human foundational trust comes to determination only in the Spirit of Jesus Christ, though whose inspiriting work the human knows himself eccentrically grounded in God, that he might find rest in Him.

The examination of the doctrine of the image of God of the human in the first part of "Anthropology in Theological Perspective" is – one should remember, here at the close – marked out in the context of a detailed analysis of the human in nature and the nature of the human. The particular status of humans in nature, which makes up *the peculiar nature of humans*, is characterized in debate with behaviorism and behavior research and in connection with the so-called philosophical anthropology through the use of terms such as "world-openness", "eccentricity", and "self-transcendence". Pannenberg shares with this latter direction of thought the foundational principle, that the special status of humans among animal can no longer be grounded by the arguments of the old soul-metaphysics, but rather only through the bodily nature of humans. These indicated terms refer, thus, not at all to the soul-mind dimensions of humanity but to the psychosomatic unity that he is in a differentiated, but unseparated manner. Methodically, it is the case that "speaking very generally, experience of the world is the way by which human beings reach experience and themselves." (Anth., 72) The effort of Pannenberg's anthropology is thus decidedly more empirical, and yet, he believes that nonetheless it is precisely in this manner and without unindicated borrowings from soul-metaphysics that one can prove the religious theme as inherently belonging to the being of humans. The world-open, eccentric, self-transcending human is essentially structured for God. Pannenberg does not make the claim, that he gives an anthropological proof for God's existence. That God exists, and what the divinity of God is, can only be experienced from God in revelation. However, the search for God, however unspecific it may be in its questioning, belongs to the humanity of humans. Religion may then be seen as an anthropological universal. For as well as in his relation to the world as well as in his relation to himself, the human is structured for relation with God. This is only realized according to destiny when this disposition in the diligent process of human self-differentiation from God, the consequence of which the human is a human among humans in a common world. This self-differentiation from God is itself only possible there, "where we are already lifted above ourselves by the Spirit of God and are thus enabled to accept our own finitude." (ST II, 230)

4. Centrality and Sin

The human is the eccentric, self-transcendent and world-open being. however, it is also egocentric, self-centered, and reflected into itself. This ambivalence creates a general "ambiguity in human behaviour" (Anth., 80). In the chapter on anthropology in the Systematic Theology, this ambivalence is described with the terms dignity and wretchedness. While the dignity of the human, as grounded in the destiny of communion with God, cannot be dissolved through any external evil and injustice, it is sin, with its God-adverse pervertedness, that estranges the human from his creaturely destine and leaves him wretched and without dignity.[6] "Misery...is the lot of those who are deprived of the fellowship with God that is the destiny of human life. Alienation from this destiny does not abolish it. Its continued presence is the basis of our misery, for in alienation from God we are robbed of our true identity." (ST II, 178–179) The sinful human becomes in a certain manner the law court for himself, for the dignity of his destiny turns against him in his undignified behavior. This makes up the actual *wretchedness of the sinner*. According to Pannenberg,

---

6 Individual aspects of hamartiology are handled in "Die Maßlosigkeit des Menschen" in BSTh 2, 215–219 and "Aggression und die theologische Lehre von der Sünde" in: ZEE 21 (1977), 161–173; reprinted in BSTh 2, 220–234.

the idea of wretchedness describes the lost situation of the God-adverse human correctly due to the fact that it allows one to see the connection between sin and its consequences more clearly than the simple reference of sin. A similar breadth of meaning is founded in the *idea of alienation* as the second leading idea of the Pannenbergian hamartiology. In the original German, there is an etymological connection between wretchedness (*Elend*) and alienation (*Entfremdung*) through the association with the idea of a distance from the homeland.[7] Additionally, there is a hamartiological advantage in that it expresses the "two sides, both an action we can take and a situation we can find ourselves in" (ST II, 179): "We can alienate ourselves from someone, and we can also be in a state of alienation." (*Ibid.*)

To be added to this is the fact hat Pannenberg dedicated an entire section to the idea of alienation and the hamartiological meaning of this idea in his "Anthropology in Theological Perspective" (Anthr. 265–285). First, he refers to the right of Christian theology on account of the terminological-historical result to treat "the concepts of alienation and self-alienation as part of their heritage." (Anth., 269) It is not as Paul Tillich, who brought this idea in particular degree into the interpretation of the idea of sin in modern theology, assumed. Not first from Hegel and Marx in connection with Hegel, rather, it has "much older roots" (Anth., 267) which include the biblical witness. From the content, the idea of alienation is to be precisely differentiated from that of self-expression, as well as "connected less with reification than with the question of whether in the course of their identity formation individuals have found or missed the structures of meaning that are constitutive for selfhood. In other words, the concept of alienation must be connected with that of identity." (Anth., 278) As the separation of the sinner from God, the idea of alienation refers to "separation from their own destiny, which is communion with God." (Anth., 271) The human alienated from God is alienated at the same time from himself and his world. When "the real destiny of human beings refers them to God, then the alienation from God that results from their self-love is the source of their alienation from themselves." (Anth., 279) A surmounting of alienation is thus only from the carrying ground of sense in God possible, as God surrounds the self and the world in a rescuing manner, in order to convert the human out of his perversion.

Pannenberg's interpretation of the ambiguity of human behavior and the ultimate brokenness and perversion of the identity of the human identity through egoism and concupiscence begins with the tension between the *centeredness and eccentricity*. This tension is not in itself a manifested perversion already, but merely an indicator of ambivalence and equivocity inherent to the human structure of existence. However, it marks in its unspecificity the background horizon of a possible and factual conflict

---

7 This can be also mirrored in English with the use of the term "estrangement" as a synonym for alienation. – Trans.

between the central form of organization and the eccentricity of the human, which is the epitome of all sinful discord. This conflict is, in Pannenberg's judgment, in no case to be equated with the difference between body and soul. The realized perversion of human centeredness cannot be restricted to the body of the human, nor can it be ascribed primarily to it. For it affects the body-soul connection as a whole and thus the psychosomatic unity of the human as such in its entirety. Sin is not only a carnal issue, but rather one that addresses the whole human: it is in this that not only the difference between soul and body, subjectivity and embodiedness, between the knowing ego and carnal existence takes gestalt. It is much more present in the self-awareness as an opposite of the ego to itself.

That some light might be cast upon this thought, Pannenberg notes, "the fact that exocentricity by its nature means a being present to the other; it is then from the vantage point of the other that the ego approaches its own body and, in its body, the embodiment of its impulses and its striving fro pleasure." (Anth., 85) Connected to this observation is the following analysis, decisive for the foundation of Pannenberg's hamartiology: "In its exocentric self-transcendence the ego is originally present to what is other than its body, but it is in knowing the otherness of the other, which is identical with its body, as distinct from all else, that it knows itself to be distinct form itself. Being present to the other *as* other opens up the dimension of self-consciousness with its distinction from self and unity with self; this dimension remains nonetheless full of contradiction because the ego makes its appearance on both sides of the distinction, being both different from and identical with its body, while in this contradiction which the ego is, its unity too remains an open question.

This exocentric self-transcendence, this being present to what is other than the self (i. e., originally what is other than the body) constitutes the ego or person. At the same time, however, the ego, in its identity with 'itself', also places itself over against the other. This is the root of the break in the ego, the root of its conflict with its own exocentric destiny. Initially, of course, there is question only of a tension. Even the act by which the ego sets itself against the other is made possible by the exocentric constitution of the ego, and the act can therefore remain integrated into the process of exocentric experience as one phase of that process. As a matter of fact, however, the ego's setting of itself against the other – and therefore also against its own exocentricity – becomes the organizing principle of the unity of the individual's experience. The ego continues to be constituted as exocentric, but its presence to the other now becomes a means for it to assert itself in its difference form the other. Presence to the other becomes a means by which the ego can dominate the other and assert itself by way of this domination.

Even this domination is still ambivalent. It can be at the service of the exocentric destination of the ego. Only when the setting of the ego against the other becomes total and *everything* must be made a means to the self-assertion of the ego, only then does the break of the ego from itself and its still constitutive exocentricity become acute. It is only the locking up of the ego in its opposition to everything else that fixes it in a contradiction of its exocentric destination. When the ego becomes certain that it is itself the truth of the contents of its consciousness and that therefore 'it is all reality,' when it becomes certain that it possesses within itself the truth of all reality, and when it endeavors to implement this arrogant claim in its relation to the world, then the ego distorts its own makeup, inasmuch as it subordinates its consciousness of objects, that presence to the other by which it is natively constituted, to itself as distinct from everything else, instead of finding its unity in the exercise of its exocentric destiny and allowing its particularity to be canceled out and rediscovered at a higher level in the process. To be sure, the attempt of self-consciousness to implement its arrogant claim in its relation to the world has in fact the ironic consequence that the ego wears itself out in the effort to integrate its world and thus becomes something different, contrary to the intention behind its self-assertion; this happens no matter how doggedly the ego holds to this intention." (Anth., 85 – 86)

This sketched out analysis of the *perversion in the constitution of the human ego* is seen by Pannenberg as essentially confirmed already in the classic doctrine of sin espoused by Augustine. This has, in its fundamentals, lost nothing still today from its enlightening power, and retains the superiority over other forms of Christian hamartiology through two advantages: "The first advantage is the empirical orientation of Augustine's psychological description. The other advantage also depends on this psychological approach and has to do with the relevance of sin to the relation of human beings to themselves." (Anth., 81) This first advantage prevents that the reference to the self-referentiality of the human in his brokenness becomes hamartiologically trivial and that the recognition of sin becomes a pure matter of faith. Indeed, according to Augustine the full perception of the radical nature of sin is first possible in the light of grace. Despite this, the phenomenon of concupiscence, which Augustine sees as the method by which sin plies its dreadful trade, proves itself to be an appearance of empirical-psychological evidence. The empirical alignment of Augustinian hamartiology makes it possible, so Pannenberg, to reduce the sinful perversion in the constitution of the human ego to a merely moral perversion, but rather to attribute it to the more general fact of a perversion of the human relationship to the world. The concupiscence, whose core proves to be egoism and hubris, *amor sui* and *superbia*, which themselves imply a turning away from God, come to light in the experienced situation of humans in the twisting of means and end in the worldly relation. The relevance of sin for the relation of the human to himself, the psychologically evident identification of which is the second advantage of Augustinian hamartiology, is thus in a recognizable relation to the situation of the perversion of the human relation to the world.

In the Systematic Theology, the "classical significance of Augustine for the Christian doctrine of sin" (ST II, 241) is renewedly emphasized with the intention, that the reasons for this importance be "more clearly" (ST II, 242 fn. 224) demonstrated than in "Anthropology in Theological Perspective." In the Old Testament, speech about sin in all its fashions deals with the transgression of norms for action; first with Paul sin is described "as something which precedes commands" (ST II, 239). "The OT view of the corruption of the heart as the root of transgressions prepared the ground for this teaching, yet in principle that detaching of the concept of sin from that of the law was a step toward a new idea of sin as an anthropological condition." (*Ibid.*) This is the point at which Augustine's hamartiology is put into position: the paramount importance of the Bishop of Hippo for the Christian doctrine of sin is, according to Pannenberg, essentially "consists in the fact that he viewed and analyzed the Pauline link between sin and desire more deeply than Christian theology had hitherto managed to do. The many aspects of his teaching that call for criticism should not blind us to this extraordinary achievement, we certainly cannot accept unquestioningly his idea of an inheriting of Adam's sin by succeeding generations, his resultant tendency to see the sinfulness of desire exclusively in sexual terms, and his much too undifferentiated interpretation of the responsibility for decisions of the will (which is necessary to any concept of sin), an interpretation that sometimes prevented him, at the const of linguistic consistency, from describing desire itself as sin rather than the acts to which it gives rise. Rightly have these aspects of his teachings come under attack. Nevertheless, theology must grasp the important basic thought that lies behind them and assert it apart from the dubious aspects." (ST II, 241–242)

"Thou shalt not covet" is, according to Romans 7:7, the sentence which summarizes all the prohibitions of the Law. The dreadful existence of sin is thus exposed as false desire. With this, Paul's sense, *epitymia* (*cupiditas* or *concupiscentia*) is not merely the consequence of sin, that is, a punishment, but rather as such already an expression and manifestation of sin. The term concupiscence does not "fully define sin." (ST II, 241) As a manifestation of sin, however, "concupiscence is in fact sin, though the core and root of its perverted nature may still be hidden." (*Ibid.*) In agreement with the Pauline use of language, Pannenberg sees Augustine as tending to identify concupiscence with sin and to identify the false desire as the structural deformation of the will as the foundational form of human sin. "According to Augustine, the perversion of sinful desire rests on on a perversion of the will. In assessing priorities, the will sets lesser (worldly) good above the supreme good (God) and even uses the latter as a means to attain the former. This is where we see the immoderate nature of the sinful will, for the result is a corruption of the order of nature, which Augustine viewed as a hierarchy of values in which the lesser serves the greater. Since we no longer accept this hierarchical view of the cosmos in a Platonic sense, it might seem that Augustine's thesis that sinful desire has perverted the order is now obsolete. Yet Augustine's analysis culminated in a thought that was independent of the

Platonic hierarchy and that would outlast its rejection. In the nonobservance of the orders of nature Augustine found an autonomy of the will that puts the self in the center and uses everything else as a means to the self as an end. This is pride, which makes the self the principle of all things and thus sets itself in the place of God.

For Augustine, pride is the core of perverted desire. Those who desire seek everything that hey desire on their own behalf, and this functions implicitly as the final goal of desiring. The self-relation in the structure of desire that comes to expression in the term 'concupiscence,' even thought formally the reference might seem to be to something else (i. e., God as the supreme good), is usually implied rather than stated in Augustine's use of the term. Because the excessive self-affirmation of pride is for the most part only implicitly present and active in desire, the sinful will that is active in the desire for external things does not initially or universally attain to the deepest depth and consistency of a sinful will, namely, hatred of God as a result of pride that sets itself in the place of God and that will inevitably fail in the attempt. In this regard Augustine thought that the situation of human sinners differs from that of fallen angels, who, as purely spiritual beings, do not sin by way of concupiscence but directly through pride. In the last resort, however, sin drives even us humans to hatred of God. In the kingdom of the world, then, lover of self finally means hatred of God, while in the kingdom of God love of God puts the self in its proper place." (ST II, 243 – 244)

By grounding the sinful opposition of the human to God not solely in the reluctance to follow the demands of the divine Law, but also with the general structure of being of human desire, Augustine went formally beyond the Pauline thought of Rom. 7:7. Despite this, he gave the doctrine of sin a fundamental-anthropological basis which accords to the content and the deeper sense of the Pauline thought. "Opposition to the commands of a positive divine law became rejection of the position that belongs to God by right in relation to his creatures, including his human creatures. In this way Augustine translated the core of Paul's statements from the narrative form of Rom. 7:7 ff. into a more general conceptual form, a structural statement regarding universal conduct relative to the reality of God. The universal extent of sin that Paul could maintain in view of the universality of death as its effect (Rom. 5:12) became for Augustine a conclusion that he drew from his anthropological analysis of sin itself." (ST II, 245)

Augustine saw the perversion of humans first in a *perversion of the order of the cosmos*. Under modern conditions, the location of the problem is shifted insofar as the primary hamartiological attention is not to the human world-but to the human self-relation. This is a view, rather than to that of the cosmos, the *perversion of the inner order of human nature* itself. Just as Augustine had seen the failure to be oneself primarily as a consequence of sin, and had described the nature of sin as a perversion of the order in the universe, so did the medieval doctrine remain primarily hamartiologically oriented on the world-relation of the human. "Only when the idea that human beings are integral parts of a universe hierarchically ordered to God has lost its power and when modern interpretations of the human person as self-conscious being had made their appearance could the opposition of human beings to themselves become the central theme in the anthropologically structured concept of sin." (Anth., 96) An excellent example for this is offered by Kant's doctrine of radical evil. This is comparable to Augustine's hamartiology in that it attempts to explain the generality of sin and its radical nature from a general structure of behavior that roots in the nature of humans. The difference from Augustine is essentially the fact that Kant defines sin in a theory of subjectivity, a concentration which leads to being the failure to be oneself, and it is first in consequence of that that he sees it as a perversion of the human world-relation. If this itself cannot be described as a wrong turn from the beginning, the actual lack of the Kantian doctrine of sin in comparison to an Augustinian hamartiology lies in the following: "A serious weakness as compared to the Augustinian description, however, is that in Kant the perversion of a proper human relation to god was no longer constitutive for sin as it is for Augustine with his phenomenon of concupiscence. For the relation to God Kant substituted the relation to the voice of the moral law that speaks to us. The switch in the ranking of religion and morality, of God and moral law – although Kant seriously tried to base religion on morality – is something that Christian theology cannot accept." (ST II, 246)

Because he rejected a moral functionalization of religion, and because he expanded the subjective-theory initial stages of the description of evil through reflection on the general nature of self-awareness to the relation of the finite self-awareness to the Absolute, Hegel earned, in Pannenberg's opinion, a distinct advantage over Kant as well in a hamartiological aspect. "Hegel's concept of desire brings further differentiation into Augustine's doctrine by ascribing to human desire, as an expression of the self-consciousness, a thrust toward the Infinite, which helps us to see why the I can put itself in the place of the true Infinite and Absolute. Desire is not bad in itself. What is bad is the will that identifies itself with it instead of raising itself above mere self-seeking. It ought to be motivated in this direction by the thought of the Absolute that the theoretical consciousness develops. But is not elevation to the concept of the Absolute always riveted to finite subjectivity as its basis?

It was here that Kierkegaard developed and deepened Hegel's description of sin." (ST II, 247–248) Despite the great importance which Pannenberg attributes to the Kierkegaardian analysis of the phenomenon of fear, he also rejects the move to give the *idea of fear* the status of in-betweenness which would replace the freedom of indifference between innocence and sin. Fear and fearful worry about oneself are not neutral foundational structures of human existence in the world, but are already themselves expressions of sin. Indeed, worry and care about oneself and about one's own self-preservation is in no case perverted in itself, but rather God-commanded and according to creation. However, it is only appropriate when it occurs in "trust in the source that is constitutive of one's existence and selfhood while at the same time it transcends these" (Anth., 103), and not in the manner of fear or fearful anxiety which is determined by false striving after security and the desire to control the conditions of human life. Such a perverted striving is characteristic for a self-perverted fixation on the own ego, which lies at the foundation not only of "the thirst for confirmation…by those around us" but also of the diverse forms of aggression (cf. in detail Anth., 142 – 153), and which is delivered up and fallen victim equally to the extremes of self-idolization and despairing self-hate. The ego-fixation consequently does not let itself "be derived from anxiety, since it is already contained in it. But in the situation of temporality anxiety constantly reproduces the fixation. The uncertainty of the future and the incomplete nature of our identity feed the anxiety. By anxiety, then, we are caught fast in the self. The alternative is confidence in the future and a present life based on such confidence. But if this were not constantly given to us, we would not be capable of it. We also continually close off ourselves against it in anxiety about ourselves.

Thus far Reformation theology was right to call *unbelief the root of sin.* In anxiety about themselves we either refuse, or are unable to accept our own lives as a gift, to be thankful, and to move on confidently to the future. Trust in this sense, of course, is not yet faith in the sense of turning to the God of the Bible. Faith in this express sense is possible only on the basis of the historical revelation of God." (ST II, 251) It is first in the light of the divine self-revelation in Jesus Christ that the being of believing trust and the un-being of a lack of faith (as it destroys itself in the hubris of a human wanting to be as God) are recognized for what they are: salvation versus damnation.

Sin is, according to Pannenberg's anthropology, closely connected with the natural conditions of human existence. The ambiguity and the ultimate brokenness of human identity deals in an elemental manner with the central form of organization of the human and the tension which rules between human centrality and eccentricity. The structural nature of human existence does not yet include the case of sin (which thus cannot be imagined as necessary and predetermined), but only the fallibility. However, there where it is factually and in general the case, the tension between centrality and eccentricity is dissolved to the advantage of the central form of human organization and the central instance of the ego, instead of including the ego in the process of eccentric self-transcendence, there it is that human destiny is missed and in a sinful manner perverted. In order prevent a misunderstanding of this claimed close connection between sin and the natural conditions of human existence, one should take note of the following: "It is precisely the natural conditions of their existence, and therefore that which they are by nature, that human beings must overcome and cancel out if they are to live their lives in a way befitting their 'nature' as human beings." (Anth., 108) it is the destiny of the human, which is contained within the nature of his being, that he transcend the natural conditions of his existence. That is precisely his uniqueness in contrast to the extra-human creatures which grounds his special place in the cosmos. One can derive from the destiny inherent in the nature of human existence, to transcend the natural conditions of existence and to bring in the centrality of the organizational form, an indication how the problem of responsibility with the idea of sin as guilt and yet closely connected to the natural conditions of human existence. "If *sin* is anchored in the natural conditions of human existence, then is not human nature as such already 'sinful'? But how is it possible to speak here of 'sin,' since sin consists in the perversity of the will?" (Anth., 107) The answer to this question is depends decisively on the understanding of the idea of responsibility. "[I]f I am responsible only for what my free choice has preferred when the opposite was just as possible, then nothing can be sinful that is part of the natural conditions in which I find myself from the outset." (Anth., 110) The situation presents itself differently, however, when the idea of responsibly is not develop from the formal idea of neutral freedom, but from the thought of material freedom, which is which is aimed at the concordance of human conduct with the destiny of the human.[8]

Although the *idea of responsibility* has been connected with that of "the concept of freedom of choice, this…being understood as a decision-making power that stands apart from the alternatives between which a choice must be made" (*Ibid.*) through the ages, Pannenberg sees the thought of arbitrary freedom greatly limited and unfit, both in its general anthropological meaning as well as in its hamartiological, to appropriately ground human responsibility and the attribution of human sin as guilt. Only the thought of material freedom can do this, when referenced to the image of God destiny of the human. This is not "to be understood as an indifference that is neutral in the face of possible objects of choice" (Anth., 115), but rather "has to do with personal existence as a single whole which manifests itself in individual actions and decisions, with the result that human beings claim their present life situation as their own in light of their human destiny. Therefore in keeping with their consciousness of their own destination they know themselves to be responsible for their own condition and activity and for turning the natural and social givens of their own life situation into a fulfillment of their destiny. Since, moreover, the destiny of individuals as human beings links them with others in the common life of a community, these individual accept responsibility not only for their separate actions and destinies but also for spheres of responsibility that extend beyond these to embrace the life situations and behaviors of other

---

8 Cf. the debate between Thomas Pröpper and Wolfhart Pannenberg in 1990in the *Theologischen Quartalschrift* (Th. Pröpper, Das Faktum der Sünde und die Konstitution menschlicher Identität. Ein Beitrag zur kritischen Aneignung der Anthropologie Wolfhart Pannenbergs, in: ThQ 170 [1990], 267–289; W. Pannenberg , Sünde, Freiheit, Identität. Eine Antwort an Thomas Pröpper, in: ThQ 170 [1990], 289–298; reprinted in BSTh 2, 235–245).

human beings." (Anth., 115–116) Comparable is the situation for the natural conditions of human existence along with the human body as their epitome, which indeed, no human chooses, but for which each human has an inherent and peculiar responsibility.

If, then, it is the material freedom which grounds responsibility, then it is ultimately this freedom alone which decides over the status of the formal freedom, in itself indifferent and ambivalent, and in its unspecifictiy tending towards ambiguity and ambivalence. Formal freedom of choice only gains a relative sense under the condition, that one assume an own destiny in the process of material freedom. Set alone, or insisting upon itself alone, this formal freedom is not only ambivalent, but manifestly perverted: the idea of a freedom of choice against God and the Good undermines itself. It is for itself and taken in its formal indifference an indication of the alienation from that which is truly good for the self and the world. This can be learned, according to Pannenberg, from Luther's thesis regarding the captivity of the human in a *servum arbitrium* as well as from the renewal of subjective theory in Kierkegaard's description of the despairing situation of the own identity in the infinite striving for self-realization in the face of the constitution of the self from God. "Though we have a formal ability to choose, on the basis of our finite subjectivity and by our own action we cannot be righteous before God. As Kierkegaard puts it, on our own we cannot achieve our own identity." (ST II, 249) This clears up, as Pannenberg contrasts against J. Müller's doctrine of formal freedom, "that a will that can choose differently when face to face with the norm of the good cannot be in fact a good will. It is more than weak because it is not firmly set upon the good. To the extent that it can choose differently face to face with the given norm of the good, it is already sinful because it is emancipated from commitment to the good." (ST II, 258)

The alienation, which stands for the idea of formal freedom apart from its material destiny, is perceived first not in the form of a developed awareness of guilt but rather in the undetermined manner of feeling. In *the feeling of self-alienation*, which is characterized by indetermination, the feeling of one's own non-identity comes into the light, in order to become more specific with the growing clarity of the identity and eventually to take on the gestalt of an explicit awareness of guilt. In contrast to the simple feeling of self-alienation, the developed awareness of guilt is in the normal case always "related to a quite determinate objective situation, a determinate transgression of a norm. This implies that, to this degree at least, there is a clear knowledge not only of personal identity and the demands this identity makes on personal behavior but also of the person's own failure and the nonidentity this creates. The relation to personal identity and nonidentity as a whole is the special characteristic of the feeling of guilt that accompanies a concrete consciousness of guilt and that is rightly regarded as the normal form of guilt feeling in the psychically healthy individual." (Anth., 286) According to Pannenberg, the awareness of guilt and the feeling of guilt which always accompanies the concrete awareness of guilt "The Greek very *synoida* means first of all a cognizance (a co-knowing)." (Anth., 295) With an extensive terminological history, Pannenberg shows to what extent the appearance of the idea of conscience, which for is of characteristic importance for the phenomenon itself, is connected with the origin of explicit self-awareness. In the manner of conscience the subject is in the condition to understand itself and to become aware of itself. "The feeling of shame was already a germ from which conscience could emerge." (Anth., 294) The human is his own accomplice in knowledge. This comes primarily to light with reference to injustice and guilt. Because and insofar the human in himself is his own knowledge accomplice for his own behavior, he develops an internal awareness of injustice and of guilt. The understandable and fitting consequence of this development is "intelligible and proper that although the concept of conscience had its origin in the experience of guilt, it should not have been limited to this sphere but should have acquired the general meaning of consciousness in the sense of an awareness of ones own behavior and being and thus be able to become as well the preconscious conscience and thereby a normative authority for the way one lives one's life." (Anth., 296)

Theologically, this results in the necessity that one does not moralistically underdetermine *the idea of conscience*, but rather to connect it according to the original meaning of *syneidesis* and *conscientia* closely with the themes of the identity and self-awareness of the human. In contrast to the "moral phenomenon of conscience...made independent of the general problematic, including the theoretical, of self-consciousness" (Anth., 299), one must regain the original breadth of the horizon connected to the idea of conscience. The conscience does not represent an opaque measurement of "soul" isolated to the moral awareness of norms and their representation; is is much more a matter of the identity-giving and –preserving perception of the destiny of the human, which is oriented to the entirety of the personal life as well as the entirety of the world. With this, the conscience in the group of self-feelings takes "a special place because in it not only is the whole of life vaguely present in the form of a positive or a depressed mood, but at the same time the individual's own ego becomes an object of consciousness as a subject of deeds or omissions in regard to which the judgment of conscience declares it to be blameworthy. In this negative judgment there is at the same time a positive reference to the identity that is forfeited by the action and to the social order that is injured by it.

By its negative content, conscience thus forms a bridge from the feeling of the self to self-consciousness in the narrower sense of an explicit apprehension and knowledge of the self. But at the same time, as a feeling it precedes the always incomplete retrieval by rational reflection of the meaningful inter-relationships that ground the judgment of conscience. The reason is that, for feeling, the whole is not incomplete but is present as a whole. It is this which gives feeling its immediacy and ground the certainty that is peculiar to feeling.

Yet conscience is not to be opposed to reason (and theoretical self-consciousness), since if such an opposition is erected, the connectedness of this world, which as a context of meaning grounds the structure of conscience, is disrupted or at least rendered opaque, and conscience succumbs either to an irrational subjectivism or to heteronomy." (Anth., 308) First through the reflective reference to the world and the understanding acceptance of its sense-foundations (as they are revealed religious behavior and in reference to God) does the conscience become an independent quantity, superior to the alternatives of subjectivism and foreign control.

5. The Radicality and Universality of Sin, and the Deadly Implications

In order to make more explicit the radical and universal nature of sin, Christian hamartiology could not restrict itself to a doctrine of current sins, but was forced to develop a doctrine of *peccatum originale* as original, inherited sin. This means that humans do not first become sinners through their actions. They are instead already sinners before all individual action, and in a radical manner, due to the fact that the root of sin lies deeper than any single sinful action. This understanding is one which Pannenberg decidedly wishes to retain, even under the conditions of the completed dissolution of the traditional concept of original sin. For Pannenberg, a "[reduction] to the individual act" (ST II, 234) is out of the question. For such a reduction would do justice to neither the radical nature of sin, the idea of which encompasses much more than the appearances of the manifest evil, nor the generality of sin. "The universality of sin forbids the moralism that will not accept solidarity with those who become the instruments of the destructive power of evil. Sin's universality shows such a moralistic attitude to be hypocrisy. The Christian doctrine of the universality of sin has the specific function, for all the need to check manifest evil and its consequences, of helping to preserve solidarity with evildoers, in whose conduct the sin that is latently at work in all of us finds expression. This antimoralistic function of the doctrine has often been underrated. In the modern world it has fallen victim to the dissolution of the doctrine of original sin when a different doctrine of sin's universality has not replaced it. If such views for their part are based on the idea of actual sin, moralism can be advocated only in part and at the cost of enhanced guilt feelings. Weakening of the conviction that a universality of sin precedes all individual acts has opened the door to the moralism that either seeks evil in others or be inward aggression procures self-destructive guilt feelings." (ST II, 238)

After the concept of an original, radical sin against God of all humans in

Adam could no longer fulfill the function for which it was developed (because not only the idea of monogenesis, but also that of a physical inheritance of sin by Adam's descendants and that of the theory of imputation had lost all plausibility), theology attempted to fill the position of the doctrine of *peccatum originale* with the thought of a kingdom of sin. This kingdom of sin attempted to settle the foundational sin in its human universality not only from the context of natural origins, but from the social interwovenness and connections of individuals and generations. "In the place of the natural transmission of sin from generation to generation we have the concept of its mediation through social relations between individuals." (ST II, 255) Pannenberg illustrates this with the examples of Kant, Schleiermacher, and Ritschl, and up to Piet Schoonenberg and Karl Rahner. He does not find that the foundational radical nature of the falsity which lies at the ground of all actions was sufficiently preserved in the thesis of an original sinfulness grounded in the social situatedness of humanity. For "the social context into which [individuals] grow as being a world that is alien to them and that estranges themselves from their real selves; they [can distinguish] this even though it does not remove them from that world. Only if sinfulness in the sense of a distortion of the subjectivity that underlies all action is linked from the outset to the ego in its becoming will there be no longer any right to such a distancing. If this distortion must be regarded as a 'natural biological datum', it is also a datum essential to the concept of original sin." (Anth., 128) In contrast, the biblical sense of speech about sin is missed, when this is not considered as a thirst for evil inherent in each individual, but merely as a structural situation external to the individual. Indeed, the individual cannot dissolve the situation of social situatedness and thus social involvement in sin, neither for himself or others. "Yet even if the individual cannot escape the influence of society, it may still be regarded as an alien power from which to hold aloof. In this case the individual will not regard the self as intrinsically evil." (ST II, 256)

This, if the fact of the situatedness of the individual in the social context of life cannot give a sufficient replacement for the concerns of the traditional doctrine of original sin, then the essential matter of this doctrine as well as that of the Augustinian hamartiology in contrast to Pelegiansim "only if we recognize in sin a basis state of the natural constitution of the perverted life in the individual. Only thus do individuals have to identify themselves with sin as part of themselves, since their own existence in the body is the basic form of the self that identifies them as individuals, the basic form on which all the other aspects of selfhood build." (ST II, 257–258) The reformulation of the doctrine of original sin, which has become obsolete in the form we have received it, must take its beginning with the natural conditions of human existence. It must do that even more than the thought of a super-historical fall into sin, which on occasion is the suggested replacement of for the idea of a primeval fall in modern hamartiology, as this presents a mythological fact which is as untenable as an idea of original sin which retains the natural transfer of sin through the course of generations. The tightly interwoven nature of sin with the natural conditions of human existence comes, according to Pannenberg, clearly from the context of the centeredness of life in itself, as it shows itself in the self-centeredness of humans. This centeredness of life and the human ability to be an ego are not in themselves sinful. The fact of centeredness does not "stand in simple opposition to our distinct destiny of elevation above everything finite, including our own finitude, for this movement of life is constitutive for the I itself.

Nevertheless, the perversion of the relation of the finitude of the self to the Infinite and Absolute is so close that except in the case of express distinction of the self in its finitude from God, the self does in fact become the infinite basis and reference point for all objects, thus usurping the place of God. Usually this does not take place in the form of revolt against the God of religion but in that of the anxiety of the self about itself, in that of the excessive nature of its desires. At work here is the implicit form of the absolute self-willing that alienates us from God by putting the self in the place that is God's alone, even though the relation to God is not an object of decision." (ST II, 260 – 261)

It remains to be asked how it is under the conditions of the good creation of God that sins could have been possible at all, and how they can be at all possible. The foundational correctness of this question and the theological attempts to answer it are defended by Pannenberg explicitly. That lies in the diligence of his refusal, to allow factual sins to become a pure matter of faith. "Those who declare that the fact of sin is simply a matter of the knowledge of faith that does not need support in the human reality that is accessible to universal experience fail to see that Christian faith does not create the fact of sin but presupposes it, even though awareness of its depth comes only in the light of the knowledge of God mediated through Jesus Christ. Hence those who have not yet attained to faith in Jesus Christ are not thereby freed from the tie to the corruption in the structure of their conduct to which the word 'sin' refers. If this matter were not independent of the knowledge of faith (even if its nature as unbelief and disregard for God comes to light only in that knowledge), then what Christians say about sin would in fact fall victim to the complaint of Nietzsche and his followers that we have here a calumniating of life. What Christians say about human beings as sinners is true to life only if it relates to something that characterizes the whole phenomenon of human life and that may be known even without the premise of God's revelation, even if this revelation is necessary to bring its true significance to light." (ST II, 236)

If this is true, then, as said, neither the *question about the possibility of sin* nor the attempt at an answer can be in principle avoided. In this aspect, Pannenberg also joins his voice to Augustine's, who made explicit "that God did not force us to sin, had he done so, it would not be our own sin, and the very concept of sin would be shattered. What Augustine plainly had in view was that in creation God took our foreseen sin into account but was looking ahead to his own future redemption and consummation. Schleiermacher ventured to think along similar lines in the 19th century.

If we ignore here the danger of a deterministic misunderstanding and the absurdities to which it leads, we can see in such thoughts a worthier expression of faith in an omnipotent Creator God than in the approach that views the entry of sin and evil into creation as an event that takes the Creator by surprise, that is inexplicable in terms of faith in God, that cannot be regarded as divinely possible, but that in its supposed isolation seems to be a real counterforce to the Creator in the experience of his creatures. Instead of cherishing this kind of dualism, Christian theology ought to find in the permission of sin the cost of the creaturely independence at which God's creative action aims. As creatures that have attained to full independence, we humans must develop and become what we are and ought to be. In the process we can all too easily give our independence the form of an autonomy in which we put ourselves in the place of God and his dominion over creation. But without creaturely independence the relation of the Son to the Father cannot manifest itself in the medium of creaturely existence." (ST II, 264 – 265)

The radical nature and generality of sin is in the false desire of humans empirically provable. This is definitively recognized in the light of the destiny of humans as revealed in Jesus Christ. Desire, when perverted, has the virtually deadly implication which make understandable the *connection between sin and death* in the Christian tradition. Pannenberg, too, puts emphasis on the foundational plausibility of the reference between the general fate of death and the universality of sin, which one encounters in Paul and which has been received throughout the Christian tradition. The general reign of death contains an indication that the fact of sin shows a general root of evil prior to all action, which is set by the central form of organization of human existence and its penchant to isolate itself – a penchant which leads to the relationless domination of dead centrality over living eccentricity. "The inner logic of the link between sin and death as Pail stated it arises on the presupposition that all life comes from God. Since sin is turning from God, sinners separate themselves not only from the commanding will of God but also from the source of their own lives. Death, then, is not just a penalty that an external authority imposes on them but lies in the nature of sin as its consequence. Paul was undoubtedly thinking of physical death. Certainly the death that comes as a result of sin is not just a natural process. Its severity lies in separation from God. This is in line with the OT view that death separates from God (PS. 88:5; cf. 6:5; 115:17; also Isa. 38:18). The explanation that it results from sin simply offers the reason for this separation. It does not mean that natural mortality has nothing at all to do with death in this sense. In separation from God in death, we see the deeper nature of physical death, which is posited already in the nature of sin as separation from god. Only on this premise could Paul in Rom. 5:12 adduce the universality of the fate of death in proof of the universal propagation of sin in the human race." (ST II, 266)

The fact that the bodily death of humans is a consequence of sin was held by Christian theology in the antique world and the middle ages despite all differentiation between physical and spiritual death. With the 18th century, especially within Protestant theology, the opinion arose that death as such belongs to the nature of the human as a finite living being. Only to the sinner is it that death appears as blameworthy, whereas it is otherwise fully appropriate to the creaturely destiny of the human creature. The distinction which one encounters between natural death and death as judgment in the writings of Althaus, Brunner, Barth, Jüngel, and others matches this opinion. This is criticized heftily by Pannenberg, because it fails to recognize (and allows a failure of recognition) that it is a matter of life and death in the truest sense of the word for humans in relation to God, and not merely a matter of the forms of the subjective experience of death. The perverting of the relation with God which occurs in sin is death implicitly. To call death a penalty for sin is problematic, according to Pannenberg due to the idea of sanction connected with the idea of punishment. This does not do justice to the biblical connection of an action and its consequence, as Paul claims for the connection between sin and death. "Death is the result of the break with God, who is the source of life. It is to be seen in concert with the other results of sin. Being in opposition to the Creator, we are also in opposition to our fellow creatures, to the earth, to animals, and to other people (cf. Gen. 3:14–19). These are not penalties imposed from without and having no connection with the nature of sin. The conflict of sinners with creation, with other people, and even with themselves follows from the nature of sin as a breaking of the relationship to God. There is an inner logic here. The law of nature that leads from sin to death takes place without any special divine intervention." (ST II, 270) The objection which claims that the concept of death as a consequence of sin has the necessary consequence that death is not first implied by factual and guilty wrongdoing, but rather as the creaturely finitude as such is met by Pannenberg with the following argument: "Christian hope expects a life without death (1 Cor. 15:52 ff.). this life in fellowship with God cannot involve a total absorption of creaturely existence in God but expects its renewal and definitive establishment. The finitude that is part of creaturely life will not be set aside by participation in the divine life. It follows, however, that finitude does not always have to include mortality. The eschatological hope of Christians knows a finitude of creaturely existence without death. Hence death cannot be necessarily a part of the finitude of creaturely existence. Only of existence in time is it true that the finitude of life and mortality go together." (ST II, 269–270)

The factual coincidence of finitude and mortality in reference to the existence in time is, according to Pannenberg, decidedly determined thought the fact that the entirety of existence which completes the finitude is not available to the creatures which are subject to the process of time. As temporal creatures which become aware of their temporality through the differentiation of the present from the past and future, we are prevented from "definitively achieving the totality of our finite existence. We can certainly anticipate this totality. Only thus can we have any duration and identity of existence in the process of time. But even with our anticipations we are tied to the standpoint of the present moment, which in the process of time is succeeded constantly by new moments as we move into an open future." (ST II, 272) Pannenberg continues: "The temporality of creaturely existence is a condition of the independence that we have yet to achieve (cf. ST II, 95 f.). Only as a result of becoming in time can finite existence, on the condition of its link to the eternal God, stand independently before God in the totality of its temporal span. In passing through temporality, the creature with the finite future of its life that is yet before it also has an end outside itself. But the end of our existence, as the externally appointed limit of our duration, is death. Death is not itself external to our existence. The end that has yet to come casts a shadow in advance and defines the whole path of life as a being for death in the sense that our end is not integrated into our existence but threatens each moment of our living self-affirmation with nothingness. We thus lead our temporal lives under the shadow of death (Luke 1:70; cf. Matt. 4:16).

At the same time in each moment of our present our self-affirmation of life is marked by the antithesis to our end in death. Death is the last enemy of all living things (1 Cor. 15:26). Fear of death pierces deep into life. On the one hand it motivates us to unrestricted self-affirmation, regardless of our own finitude; on the other hand, it robs us of the power to accept life. Either way we see a close link between sin and death. The link is rooted in sin to the extent that only the nonacceptance of our own finitude is so hard for us who know ourselves to be living beings and affirm ourselves as such is connected with the structure of temporality in which our end, and with it our wholeness, is still ahead of us. That the end and totality of finite existence in time are still ahead of us characterizes the situation in which sin actually arises, that is, the unrestricted self-affirmation that with apostasy from God implies death as the end of our existence." (ST II, 272–273)

This is to say that it is not already with outstanding nature of the end and whole given in the temporality of human existence that death is there. The outstanding nature o the whole of existence is an instance of finitude, but not an indication that death belongs to the creaturely destiny of the human as creature. Pannenberg can indeed agree with Paul when he says that the subjugation of creatures to the power of transience goes back to the Creator-God (cf. ST II, 97–98); nonetheless he remains at the thesis that death, in contrast to finitude and the temporal transience of creaturely existence, is only part of God's creation in connection with sin.[9] Presupposed with this is the

9 To the hamartiological dimension of the problem of time and to the (if one can call it such) postlapsarian temporality of our existence cf. "Tod und Auferstehung in der Sicht christlicher Dogmatik" in: KuD 20 (1974), 167–180; reprinted in GSTh 2, 146–159, here: 154: "Our expe-

insight, decisive for the entire dogmatics, that creation is for humans understood in becoming, and can only be understood in becoming, towards an eschatological hope of fulfillment. With the presupposition, which is emphasized by the indication of the continual creative action of God which always brings forth good from evil in the context of His rule over the world, one can ultimately integrate the aspect that the connection between sin and death has a previous history in the pre-human evolution of life. "In this history a demonic dynamic seems to have developed that culminates in human sin and the dominion of sin and death over humanity." (ST II, 274)

rience of time is determined through the fact that we define the present and future each in relation to the present of our ego. The temporality of our existence is thus not...simply an expression of our creaturliness. In its particular form, influenced by ego-referentiality, it is determined also by the sin of man. For this ego, however, which falls together with the central form of organization for our embodiedness, which builds the highest peak of this our bodily existence – for this ego, the end of our life process means death. This did not have to be so. If we could exist as ourselves, as the finite whole of our existence, then the end would be integrated as a moment in the identity of our existence, and it would then set no end for that existence. The ego, however, in its selfishness, which structures its self-awareness, always has its end outside of itself. Insofar the saying is correct, that as long as we are, death is not, and when death comes in, we are no longer. Indeed, as humans we know about death, but, as Freud said, we don't believe in our own death. The ego has its end outside of itself, and precisely for this reason is it a being unto death. In reference to this, the Pauline word about death as the wages of sin retains its evidence for death as such, and not for a particular aspect of death, as if one could distinguish the death of the curse from a 'natural death.' The life which goes towards death in the process of time is always already the life under the sign of the difference between the ego and the self, that life which is characterized in its biological structure by selfishness, that is, by *amor sui*, the life of sin that also founds the temporality of our life history.

§5 Christology (ST II, Chapters 9–11)

1. Theory of the Christological Tradition

In the afterword of the fifth edition of "Jesus: God and Man",[1] Pannenberg described the method which he followed summarily as a "method of questioning the processes of tradition through history regarding their systematic form".[2] Characteristic for this process is the phrase "Christology from below" which goes back to Albrecht Ritschl. In contrast to a "Christology from above", which directly presupposes the premises of the doctrine of the trinity and the idea of the Logos and argues from there, a Christology from below attempts to ground Christological statements in a mediated manner, from the historical Jesus. Pannenberg expands this method of grounding, stretching it out to the entire process of the history of tradition – from the appearance of the historical Jesus, through His death and the message of resurrection of the disciples, and to the formation of Christological dogma and the modern Christological discussion in the context of theology entire. The goal of his method is to develop the fundamental statements of Christology from the effective functional logic of the tradition. With this, he does not claim to have reached a dogmatically final result, but rather to have given scientific hypotheses, whose preliminary nature accords to the unfinished nature of the process of history and to the proleptic character of all knowledge.

At the beginning of the first edition of "Jesus: God and Man" this starting point is developed in detail beyond the shorter characterizing. In contrast to conceptions which develop Christology from the unmediated self-awareness of faith or the unquestioned authority of the community *kerygma*, Pannenberg defines the Christological task as such: "to establish the true understanding of Jesus' significance from his history, which can be described comprehensively by saying that in this man God is revealed." (JGM, 30) The consequence of this task is that one cannot declare Christology to be a function of soteriology, but rather the opposite, that soteriology is a function of Christology. The emanation of the factually founded meaning of Jesus must take its point of departure from His history and the soteriological relevance implicit in that history, and not from a meaning for us, as it appears in subjective perception or is made present in ecclesial proclamation. It is only in

---

1 Jesus: God and Man. Translated from the 2nd edited edition. SCM Press 1968 (=JGM).
2 The *Nachwort zum 5. Auflage*, as the English translation was prior to this, is only available in German. The quote comes from page 415 in the German version. Further quotes from this section are translated, and marked „Nachwort", with the German page number given. – Trans.

this manner, according to Pannenberg, that the revealed divinity of Jesus can be demonstrated as the foundation of His salvific meaning and differentiated from religious projections of diverse types.

Analogous to the diligent rejection of a soteriological functionalization of Christology, the determination of its task with the method of a "Christology from below" in contrast to a "Christology from above" results in: "for a Christology that begins 'from above,' from the divinity of Jeuss, the concept of the incarnation stands in the center. A Christology 'from below,' rising from the historical man Jesus to the recognition of his divinity, is concerned first of all with Jesus' message and fate and arrives only at the end at the concept of the incarnation." (JGM, 33)[3] Despite this strict emphasis on the distinction between a "Christology from below" and a "Christology from above" Pannenberg had already made known in the first edition of this work that the difference in method is not a matter of alternatives, or even of contradictory opposites. A relative right is given to the formulation of questions from a "Christology from above" as well as the incarnation-theology beginning connected with it. This tendency grows stronger in later years, and certain modifications of the overall concept can be seen.[4]

Although one cannot speak of an abstract methical conflict in a critical

---

3 For the event of the incarnation as the dogmatic core of the Christian Christmas-festival, cf. „Mythos und Dogma im Weihnachtsfest", in: W. Haug/R. Warning (eds.), Das Fest, 1989, 53–63.

4 For this, the most important article is „Christologie und Theologie" from 1975 (KuD 21, 159–175, in addition to the already quoted afterword to the fifth edition of the monograph and the Christological considerations of the second volume of the Systematic theology. Already in the article (GSTh 2, 129–145) Pannenberg pointed out the danger of seeing the methods as opposed to one another in abstraction. If an incarnation-Christology „from above" threatens to fail to recognize that the Godhood of God as the direct presupposition of the argument is first revealed as such in the historical person of Jesus Christ, so does a Christology „from below" fall prey to the danger of beginning with the thought of a humanity or humanness of Jesus isolated from God, apart from his connection with God (cf. GSTh 2, 136 f.), instead of thinking of the humanity of the human and that of Jesus as already always determined by God. From this it follows, that Christology can only fulfill its theanthropological task of thinking of the differentiated unity of God and man when it leaves an abstract opposition of theology and anthropology behind. Methodically, Pannenberg finds the „perhaps surprising result" (GSTh 2, 132) that the classic incarnation-Christology „from above" and the modern Christology „from below" have the same fault – they must both presuppose a reality of God and man which was to be won from Christology in the first place, in order to begin their Christological work. „This means, however, that neither the one nor the other is able to think of God as revealed through Jesus of Nazareth and thus the unity of God and man in Jesus." (ibid.) – As is the relative context of Christology and anthropology is, so is that between Christology and theology a mutual one, though the mutuality of the founding relationships and the relation requires an inclusive grounding in a theology of the Trinity. „The God Jesus is only accessible through the man Jesus, but also the man is only accessible through the God. The unity of God and man in the person of Jesus can only be interpreted when one could break into this circle, in which the man Jesus and the God present in and through him determine one another, such that Jesus himself in person belongs to the Godhood of God. In this circle of divine life, however, one cannot come unless one is already in…without the Spirit of the communion of the Father and the Son there is no knowledge of God and no knowledge of Christ." (GSTh 2, 134)

sense in "Jesus: God and Man", Pannenberg nonetheless referred to it as a "limitation"[5] of his original concept, which merely handled the reality of God as a presupposition of Christology and did not thematize this reality appropriately in the Christology. It is not sufficient, "to think of God as a *presupposition* of Christology. Much more the statements to which Christology comes require that one thinks of God as revealing Himself in Jesus."[6] Then, however, it is necessary that one understand the constitution of the person of Jesus Christ from the divinity of God, something that is only possible in a Trinitarian manner. Indeed, such an undertaking goes beyond the limits of a monograph on Christology, but it is nonetheless indispensable to the task of Christology, and achievable in the systematic context of theology as a whole. The form of this achievement is sketched out in the afterword: "precisely when the 'Christology from below' has successfully shown that the thought of incarnation expresses the structure of meaning in the history of Jesus, this result gives us the task of thinking of the history of Jesus as well as the actions of God. This means that they are to be thought of as expressions of the sovereignty of God, and thus from the divinity of God."[7] A leading function in the argument is given to the assumption "[that] the unity of Jesus with God is must not be thought of as simple identity,"[8] but that the structure has a unity mediated by difference. Foundational to this is the insight that Jesus is not and does claim to be immediately one with God, but rather is revealed as the Son of God, and thus as one essentially belonging to the divinity of God precisely in the manner of diligently maintained self-differentiation from the divine Father. The "thesis of the indirectness of the sonship of Jesus, according to which the relationship of the human Jesus to the Logos must always be thought of as mediated by His relationship to the Father,"[9] receives a key role in the argumentation for Pannenberg as it leads to a new formation of traditional Logos-Christology through the means of the meaning of the human Jesus, found in the relationship to the divine Father. This allows one to think of the relation of God to the self and the world in the person of Jesus Christ. The renewal of Logos-Christology, which Pannenberg in 1964 had "judged as rather unpromising"[10], is characteristic not only for the design of the Systematic Theology in general, but also in particular for the explicitly Christological sections in the second volume. The idea of the Logos has become, differently than in "Jesus: God and Man", the "topic of Trinitarian theological reflection in reference to the incarnated constitution of the person of Christ."[11] Though Pannenberg had referred the idea of incarnation in 1964

---

5 *Nachwort* page 421.
6 *Nachwort* page 422.
7 *Nachwort* page 422.
8 *Nachwort* page 423, syntax modified.
9 *Nachwort* page 424.
10 *Nachwort* page 424.
11 *Nachwort* page 426.

to "exclusively…the beginning of the earthly course of Jesus as the basis of his individual life" and concluded "that Christology should not begin with the concept of the incarnation" because this is first mediated through traditions which go out from the earthly appearance of Jesus Christ, now Pannenberg takes the internal logic of the eternal son as the founding, effective ground of the earthly existence of Jesus and thus thinks of the incarnation as constitutive for Jesus. "But we cannot do this without prejudice to the creaturely independence of Jesus in his history if this history is predetermined by an event of incarnation at the very outset. Precisely the creaturely independence of the human history of Jesus has to be thought of as the medium of the incarnation, but in such a way that the constitution of the person of Jesus takes place in the whole process of this history. Otherwise Jesus would first be a mere man and would then later become the Son of God by union with this human person." (ST II, 384–385, fn. 173)

Regarding the Christological process, this means that "we cannot regard a christology from below as ruling out completely the classical christology of the incarnation. It is simply reconstructing the revelatory historical basis that classical christology has always in fact presupposed, thought never properly explained. Only methodologically do we give precedence to arguing from below, presupposing, of course, that this procedure leads to the conclusion that the concept of incarnation is not a falsification but a pertinent development of the meaning implicit in the coming and history of Jesus. In truth, material primacy belongs to the eternal Son, who has become man by his incarnation in Jesus of Nazareth." (ST II, 288–289) As the methodological quintessence for the histological method practiced in the second volume of the Systematic Theology, the result is that "rightly understood…the two lines of argument from above and from below are complementary." (*Ibid.*) In the task of a "theory of the christological tradition" (ST II, 282) which, as historical presentation already begins with a systematic character, as it should explicate the meaning of the factually appearance of Jesus Christ, comes also that "we must think of [Jesus'] history as the action of God that has its basis in God" (ST II, 288). To be added, is that at the crossing of the two movements, Christology from above and from below, is the event of the resurrection. Pannenberg allocates the resurrection of Jesus to the historical basis of a "Christology from below" (cf ST II, 293), because the grounding function of the resurrection for faith cannot be separated from the real facticity and thus the historicity of this event. On the other hand, the fact that Pannenberg sees the occurring of the end of all history proleptically-anticipatorally in the Easter event results in the decided "from above" character of this event, as coming from God alone, made real by God and God making real. Precisely in this doubly-one meaning is Easter the original date of a theanthropologically explained and to be explained Christology.

2. Jesus, Human Before God

The Christological topic of the humanness of Jesus contains more problems than one sees at first. If, as according to Pannenberg, it is the case "there can hardly be any doubt about the fact with regard to Jesus' earthly life that one has to do with a man whose behavior is more or less to be understood in analogy to what we know as human behavior in ourselves and others" (JGM. 189), one may "perhaps with regard to the Jesus who has been raised and transformed into a new life…ask whether he can be called a man in the full sense of the word." (*Ibid.*) Regardless of this question, Pannenberg takes it as a part of "Christology from below" to begin the second section, titled "Jesus the Man Before God" with a self evident presupposition: "In the contemporary scene it no longer seems particularly remarkable that Jesus was a real man. This is rather the self-evident presupposition of all statements about Jesus, both inside and outside the church." (*Ibid.*) At most in theology itself with this presupposition examined as a problem after the fact, namely, from the knowledge of the divinity of Jesus.

In order to avoid premature conclusions from these general comments, which certainly need further precision, on must keep the following in mind: 1. In "Jesus: God and Man", Pannenberg deals with Jesus as a human before God first in the second part, and with the presupposition of the treatment of the knowledge of the divinity of Jesus, which was examine din the first section. The fact that the knowledge of the divinity of Jesus is mediated by the perception of the characteristic humanity of Jesus, and further through the proleptic character of his earthly claim to authority, is true. Nonetheless, this is to be brought into harmony with the larger organization of the work. 2. Regarding the conceptual construction of "Jesus: God and Man", one must consider that (as said in the afterword to the 5th edition) the presentation of the divinity of Christ, and the development of the thought of the unit of Jesus with God mediated indirectly and through self-differentiation, which the first section leads to, does not already have its end in this, but rather in the third section – this should be understood as the "overall topic of the whole book".[12] Pannenberg adds: "with this comes to the treatment of the humanity of Jesus in the second section the function of a working-out of that difference between Jesus and the Father, which then is made valid as the condition of His unity with God. That this implicit Trinitarian-theological sense of Jesus as man before God is not explicitly handled in the second section, is a weakness of this second section, which should be rectified in a reworking of this book."[13]

The constitution of this noted difference of Jesus to the father, which, according to Pannenberg, makes up the condition of His unity with God as the

---

12 *Nachwort* page 424.
13 *Nachwort* page 424.

Son and which is examined exhaustively in the second section of the
monograph, is already present in the first section, when it is structurally
described as the *proleptic movement in the claim to authority by Jesus prior to
Easter.* in contrast to the common Christological proceeds at the time of the
publication of the monograph, Pannenberg desires to ground the unity of
Jesus with God indirectly from the mediated context, and decidedly not with
direct reference to the claim of authority by Jesus on earth. This is a context
given, as with the proleptic, with the character of the earthly life of Jesus as
structured towards the future eschatological confirmation. "There is no
reason for the assumption that Jesus' claim to authority taken by itself justified
faith in him, on the contrary, the pre-Easter Jesus' claim to authority stands
from the beginning in relationship to the question of the future verification of
his message through the occurrence of the future judgment of the Son of Man
according to the attitude taken by men toward Jesus. Thus has been shown the
proleptic structure of Jesus' claim to authority, which is analogous to that of
the Old Testament prophetic sayings. This means, however, that Jesus' claim to
authority by itself cannot be made the basis of a Christology, as thought his
only involved the 'decision' in relation to him. Such a Christology – and the
preaching based upon it – would remain an empty assertion. Rather,
everything depends on the connection between Jesus' claim and its
confirmation by God." (JGM, 66)

The proleptic character of Jesus' claim to authority lies structurally at the
foundation of the self-differentiation of Jesus from God, and is verified in real
history by the apocalyptic understanding of history that He had. This is the
condition of His divine sonship, and is worked out in the second section of the
Christology with detailed reference to Jesus' actions and fate, which is seen as
the revelation of the destiny of humanity because, but only because, of the
divine confirmation occurring on Easter and upon which the claim of Jesus to
authority was based, making it dependant on this confirmation. As the
eschatological confirmation of the Jesus' proleptic claim to authority by virtue
of his resurrection by God is to be seen as factually having occurred, as worked
out in the relevant part of the first section, Pannenberg can begin the second
section with the sentence (with the assumed position of the first section on the
knowledge of the divinity of Jesus): "As God's revelation, Jesus is at the same
time the revelation of the human nature and the destiny of man." (JGM, 191,
italics in Pannenberg)[14] However, this foundational sentence should be
understood according to the proleptic constitution of the historically
appearing gestalt of Jesus, as has been mentioned, and not as a direct
presupposition. Thus, it requires a backwards connection with Jesus actions

---

14 That we cannot isolate the term „Son of God" christologically and that much more the filial
relation of Jesus is to be understood as the definitive realization of the destiny of man already
proclaimed in the Old Testament Scriptures has been demonstrated in „Die Bedeutung des Alten
Testaments für den christlichen Glauben" in: BSTh 1, 255–265, in particular 258 f.

and fate, without whose peculiarity one can neither unity of Jesus with God and therewith His divinity nor His true humanity, which reveals the destiny-appropriate nature of humanity, as these are manifest in the diligently maintained self-differentiation of Jesus from the Father in His actions and suffering. The structure of the second section of "Jesus: God and Man" is according to this insight.

Jesus is the *revealer of the true nature of humanity* due to the fact that he makes human destiny in an exemplary and universally valid manner through his actions and fate. The humanity of Jesus is, however, not exhausted in the function of an example to be imitated. Much more it effects at the same time that which it demonstrates as example, such that it opens up the fulfillment of creaturely destiny for all humans, which have part in Him in the power of the Holy Spirit through faith. This is the actual salvific meaning of the humanity of Jesus. In this sense, the doctrine of the humanity of Jesus marks the soteriological component of Christology. Insofar it is a matter of "the soteriological power of Jesus' humanity, not only the fact that Jesus simply was a human being." (JGM, 190) This is according to the "formal law" (JGM, 205), that it is not first dogmatic, but rather biblical Christology which takes the peculiarity of the human Jesus in its unity of generality and peculiarity instead of removing the peculiarity from the universal meaning. "Certainly it involves the unique, the individual in Jesus – not merely the universal human characteristics which Jesus of course shared. However, Christology involves Jesus' uniqueness only under a certain perspective, namely, to the extent that it has universal significance, to the extent that this particularity possesses saving significance for all other men." (JGM, 189)

Instead of exhaustively covering the manners in which Pannenberg identifies the salvific meaning of Jesus for the humanity of humans, in this context it is merely maintained that Jesus is the representative of humanity before God in His actions as well as His fate, as the Easter glorification as divine Son demonstrate to universal and perpetual effect. The thought of *vicariousness*, which is inherent to speech of Jesus as the new Adam, does "not involve only – and not primarily – Jesus' death. It is already contained in Jesus' realization of man's destiny as such, in his simply becoming the representative of true humanity" (JGM, 197). In the particularity of the work of Jesus, to be understood in the complex entirety of His historical individuality, the anthropological universal meaning of Jesus as the new Adam to light – He is the realized *imago Dei*, the human in full possession of the Logos, the truly faithful one, and so forth. This comes to light primarily through the fact that His devotion to the coming Kingdom of God is determinative for His entire earthly history. Pannenberg refers His office as the epitome of His action, without desiring to renew the traditional doctrine of three offices in the sense of *munus propheticum, munus sacerdotale* and *munus regale*. From the three named offices, the prophetic characterizes the earthly existence of Jesus "to some extent properly" (JGM, 221), where the other two find no purchase. The foundational sentence with which Pannenberg describes the task which Jesus knew Himself to have is: "The office of Jesus was to call men into the Kingdom of God, which had appeared with him." (JGM, 212, italics in Pannenberg) The universal validity of this message, whose composure coincides with the proleptic character of Jesus' claim to authority in the same manner as His office and person coincide, consists in (structurally seen) the fact that he self-differentiation of Jesus from God and His coming Kingdom presents not only the condition of the divine message revealed at Easter, but is representative for the destiny of the humanity of humans as such. The human is destined to be a child of God, as a creature, and this can only be realized under the condition of an inequality with God. After all, the human unity with God is not a direct unity, but one which is absolutely mediated by difference.

This difference is worked out individually in reference to Jesus' call to the Kingdom of God under the following aspects: 1. Jesus' imminent expectation 2. The presence of salvation 3. The fatherhood of God and 4. The life in love. The sequence of these aspects gives a systematic context, insofar as the nearness of the kingdom of God contains salvation within the speech and action of Jesus because it is the trustful nearness of God the Father Himself, whose commandment fulfills itself in the community of the love of the children of God. To be added is, that Pannenberg judges the historical Jesus to have expected the coming of the Kingdom unequivocally and in concert with the apocalyptic tradition as temporally near: "[T]he contrast between eschatology and history cannot be maintained either for the apocalyptic or for Jesus. Without the conviction of the temporal imminence of the transformation of the world with the coming of the Kingdom of God, that openness toward the future which is so characteristic for Jesus' message would never have arisen. Cut loose from every reference to a temporally concrete future, the attitude of unworldly openness in the framework of a noneschatological understanding of the world could hardly endure, apart from the fact that it would mean something other than the conduct to which Jesus calls." (JGM, 242) Nonetheless, Pannenberg sees the time problem as relativized under the conditions of Easter with the consequence, that neither the chronically unfulfilled imminent expectations nor the (in regard to this to establish) error of the historical Jesus must make the Christian awareness more difficult. Even when we as Christians can no longer share the imminent expectation of Jesus, we are able to "live and think in continuity with it and thus with Jesus' activity if we recognize Jesus' imminent expectation…as having been fulfilled in Jesus' own resurrection. We experience this continuity as long as we retain the expectation and hope for its universal consequence that has not happened yet, namely, the universal resurrection of the dead as entrance into the Kingdom of God." (Ibid.). In this sense, that imminent expectation of Jesus can be described as "superfluous for all who come after him through Jesus' resurrection. The nearness of God, his salvation and his judgment, is eternally guaranteed by Jesus, since his imminent expectation has been fulfilled in Him.

Therefore, since Jesus, mankind has been freed from the question of when the end will come." (JGM, 243)

3. The Unity of Jesus with God as the Problem of His Life and Death

Analogous to §6:II and §3:I of "Jesus: God and Man", Pannenberg speaks[15] again in the second volume of the Systematic Theology of the nearness of the Kingdom of God as the central content of the proclamation of Jesus. This is done under the aspect of clearing up the foundations for the claim for the unity of the human Jesus with God. 1 He emphasizes again, that Jesus' awareness of authority "was not the basis of the content of his proclamation. On the contrary, it was its consequence or accompaniment." (ST II, 327) The particularity of Jesus among the other humans which consist exactly in the peculiarity of his connection with His divine Father is not at all based on a direct claim to divine authority, but rather finds is ground in the full devotion to the coming Kingdom of God, as is characteristic for the message of the Kingdom as the epitome of Jesus' relation to God. The thought confirms itself again, that the unity of Jesus with God is not a direct, but an indirect unity mediated through radically maintained difference – the decisive principle of Pannenbergian Christology. The theoretical formal structure of unity mediated through difference, as it is characteristic for the relation of Jesus with God, takes a real-historical gestalt in the idea of the future coming. This is not in the manner of direct presence, but in the manner of the *future nature of the presently effective Kingdom of God.* To speak with Pannenberg: "We must not see statements about the presence of the kingdom as alternatives to the idea of its future coming. The reference is to the inbreaking of the future of God, but we must understand this future itself as the dynamic basis of its becoming present." (ST II, 329) One must add that a relation of correspondence exists between the ides of unity mediated through difference and the real-historical concept of a present developed from the future forbids one to neglect

15 The insight won by Johannes Weiß and Albert Schweizer into the eschatological character of the message of Jesus and the early Christian faith contains, for Pannenberg, implications which require a reformulation of the entire understanding of reality and which must decide on its rightness in problems of ontology, epistemology, anthropology, and the philosophy of history. The conception of theology itself can, of course, also not remain untouched. „To say that the revelation of God is not a supernatural event which breaks into history perpendicularly from above but rather that it is the theme of history itself, the power that moves it in its deepest dimension, is to say something about God and his relation to the world. Furthermore, if it is true that only with reference to the *totality* of reality can one speak meaningfully about a revelation of God as the world's creator and lord and that reality (understood as historical) is first constituted as the totality of a single history by the end of all occurrences, then eschatology acquires constitutive significance not only for the question of knowledge, but also for that of reality, of God." (BQiTh, xv)

one of the two aspects. Both aspects condition one another mutually, just as the human reality of Jesus in space and time stands in a mutual relation of conditionality with the eternality of His divine sonship. This makes the following valid: "If the human history of Jesus is the revelation of his eternal sonship, we must be able to perceive the latter in the reality of the human life. The deity is not an addition to this reality. It is the reflection that the human relation of Jesus to God the Father casts on his existence, even as it also illumines the eternal being of God. Conversely, the assuming of human existence by the eternal Son is not to be seen as the adding of a nature that is alien to his deity. It is the self-created medium of his extreme self-actualization in consequence of his free self-distinction from the Father, i.e., a way of fulfilling his eternal sonship. It is this precisely because in it he has left the sphere of deity in order that in the medium of creaturely existence, he might be bound to the Father as the one God in his self-distinction from him, and that he thus might fulfill our human destiny as creatures and deliver us from the confusion of sin." (ST II, 325)

If, then, the Kingdom of God which Jesus proclaims in accordance with his personal relation to God presents itself in correspondence to the characteristic form of unity mediated through difference in the mode of the future, then it is decisive for the salvific character of the approaching Kingdom of God as in the message of Jesus that this coming is the arrival of God the almighty Creator as Father. The message of the fatherhood of God is not only so inseparably connected with the preaching of Jesus about the Kingdom of God that it is to be evaluated as the essential content, but it is at the same time the proclamation of the fatherhood of God the Lord, a fact included in the relation of Jesus to God to such an extent that this is the authentic expression of inner nature of Jesus. God the approaching Lord of Creation will prove himself to be the Father of his creatures – indeed, He is already perceivable as present in His fatherhood in faithful trust in His future coming, which determines the message of and is spoken out in Jesus' proclamation of the Kingdom of God. The true nature of creation will be revealed by this coming, and the possibility will be opened up that it can accord to the constitutive order in thankful obedience, as it is documented in the commands of divine law. To quote "Jesus: God and Man" once more: "[I]n Jesus' proclamation the true nature of creation is revealed for the first time in the light of the approaching end. This has fundamental significance also for the understanding of creation itself. Creation is not to be understood as an act that happened one time, ages ago, the results of which involve us in the present. Rather, the creation of all things, even including things that belong to the past, takes place out of the ultimate future, from the *eschaton*, insofar as only from the perspective of the end are all things what they truly are. For their real significance becomes clear only when it becomes apparent what ultimately will become of them. Therefore, the nearness of the imminent Kingdom of God puts all things into that relation to God which belonged to them as God's creatures from the very beginning. It is just this that demonstrates the universal truth of Jesus' eschatological message: it reveals the 'natural' essence of men and things with an urgency nowhere achieved outside of this eschatological light. Therefore, Jesus' preaching can use every day examples in its parables. Even the structure of the parable presupposes the correspondence of creation and *eschaton*." (JGM, 230–231)

The sign-works of Jesus can be taken as evidence for this, along with the parables in the speech of the wisdom tradition about the coming of the Kingdom of God and especially the Our Father, with its request of the coming of the Kingdom that includes everything else. In the witness of Jesus of the initiation of the coming Kingdom of God, creation is seen as the kingdom of the fatherhood of the almighty Creator-God and as the kingdom of the children of God, human creatures, in one world that has been proven in the area of God's rule. It is thus also at the same time that the way to the fulfillment of the commandments in the protological sense of the constitution-order of creation is eschatologically made open. The manner in which this is to be thought of concretely is developed in the second volume of the Systematic Theology with a particular richness of perspective. To name only a few aspects: the essential connection in the message of Jesus between the absolute priority of the approaching Kingdom of God prior to all other duties and situations of humans and the uniqueness of God, whom one is to trust entirely and alone, is strongly emphasized. The fact is also brought out that faith, through trusting devotion to the all-one God, gains a share of God's Creator-goodness and on eschatological salvation – faith is also drawn into "the movement of the love of God as it aims beyond individual recipients to the world as a whole." (ST II, 332) Jesus' message of the coming Kingdom of the fatherhood of God destines the believer in, with, and through faith thankfully to lead a life of obedient love to oneself and to one's neighbor in a given, common world, for which Jesus' is a prototypical example.

If the earthly Jesus can be seen as the proclaimer and representative of the coming Kingdom of God at the same time the representative and mediator of divine will and in the differentiated unity of His eschatological-protological historicity as the representative human before God, then his connection with the fatherly Creator-God has become the *"point of contention in his history"* (ST II, 334). The occasion for this is "the ambivalence that surrounds his coming" (ST II, 335). This is, according to the measure of the pertinent passages of the second volume of the Systematic theology, grounded primarily in the fact that the authority with which Jesus proclaimed the nearness of the kingdom of God exposed him to the appearance of godless, even anti-God arrogation. Through this, His person and office fall into twilight: "Could any mere man make himself out to be the place of the presence of God? Did not this claim lack the humility due the God of Israel? The appearance of Jesus necessarily raised the suspicion that he was arrogating to himself the authority and power that in truth came to him only in reflection of his proclamation of God." (*Ibid.*) It is precisely in the context of these questions, as Pannenberg adds, that it is demonstrated "how much depends o beginning with the content of the message rather than a supposed claim to authority if we are to understand the proclamation of Jesus. Those who regard his sense of authority as the root of his message and appearing share at bottom the view that caused his opponents to reject him." (*Ibid.*) After all, the opponents of Jesus did not judge relation to God under the visage of unity mediated trough difference, but rather under that of a direct self-identification with God. As a consequence of this judgment, Jesus must have appeared to them as the diabolical spawn of the first Adam, a bodily *peccatum originale.* The conviction and ultimate execution of Jesus is thus in the understanding of his opponents not an act of caprice, but one of extreme consequential correctness. Pannenberg attributes significant meaning to the perception of this fact: the Passion loses "the appearance of being accidental" only in virtue of "the inner connection between the offence taken at the appearance of Jesus and the ambivalence of the claim to personal authority." (ST II, 338) This is however a presupposition that one recognize the Passion of Jesus as "an essential part of his divine mission" (*Ibid.*) and to recognize the salvific meaning in His death on the cross.

Pannenberg underlined the conceptual importance of this perspective in the afterword to the 5th edition of "Jesus: God and Man" with the comment, that in this, as far as he knew, was "for the first time in the history of Christology the vicarious sense of Jesus' death on the cross not only claimed but grounded from the history of Jesus as well."[16] Decisive for this grounding is the previously mentioned visage, that the implicit structure of meaning in the history of the earthly Jesus is ambiguous is a (so to speak) "pre-Easter" observation insofar as it contains both possibilities in itself, namely, to judge the person of Jesus as God-sent or as God-blaspheming. Jesus' claim to authority, as outspoken in the proclamation of the approaching Kingdom of God, is also not only due to its inner constitution, but also for the sake of the clarity of external judgment structured on the basis of divine confirmation. Without this confirmation, Jesus would not only not be that which His from the beginning under Easter conditions, but must also appear as the exact opposite of Himself: not as the true human manifested in his unity with God, but as a envoy of Evil.

Already in "Jesus: God and Man" is the relation which "cannot be overlooked" (JGM, 251) of Jesus fate of death in Jerusalem identified with His prior behavior – in particular, Jesus' relation with the torah and thus primarily in reference to his relation to the lawless and sinners. In choir with the so-called antitheses of the Sermon on the Mount it is Jesus' love and care for the despisers of the Torah and the claim of the authoritative proclamation of forgiveness of sins which offered the internal reason (when not the external) for the arrest, conviction, and ultimate execution of Jesus. Throughout the

16 *Nachwort* page 420.

trial of Jesus might possibly have been incited through acute events such as the conflict in the Temple and the accusation, that here is a revolutionary pretender to the office of Messiah at work: "[T]he deeper basis of the conflict that led to the indictment is certainly to be sought in the whole of Jesus' activity, especially in the way in which he placed himself above the law and claimed the authority of God himself for his activity." (JGM, 252)[17]

With this, Pannenberg notes explicitly that the accusation of blasphemy against Jesus "was not merely a malevolent slander without any basis. Had Jesus' claim to authority not proved itself to be legitimate, if one did not believe with the disciple in its future confirmation but judged it only in the light of what was presently at hand, then Jesus could very easily appear to be a blasphemer, one who placed himself on a par with God. If Jesus' claim to authority did not find the future confirmation for which his disciples waited, it must be understood as the most frightful pretention possible." (JGM, 253) According with this, at a later place: "The depth of Jesus' conflict with the Jewish tradition, the real, profound ambiguity of the situation in which Jesus had involved himself, and thereby the depths of meaning of his passion itself are obscured when, motivated by rash zeal for the image of Jesus' purity and sinlessness, we see only ill will on the side of his opponents. Jesus was not undone by a few inadequate individuals, but by the Jewish law itself, whose traditional authority was called into question by the mode of his activity. To that extent Paul is right when he says that Jesus came under the cure of the law (Gal. 3:13). This does not involve just the superficial sense that according to Deut. 21:23 every person hanged is cursed by God. Even Paul himself probably did not intend such a superficial meaning, but had in view that the curse expressed the exclusion of the transgressor from the community of God's

---

17 In „Judentum und Christentum: Das Besondere des Christentums" (in P. Lapide and W. Pan-
     nenberg [eds.], Judentum und Christentum. Einheit und Unterschied. Ein Gespräch, 1981, 39 –
     31; reprinted in BSTh 1, 278 – 286) Pannenberg has emphasized that one cannot understand the
     events in Jerusalem in the context of the execution of Jesus without the context of the previous
     history of the conflict. This affects Jesus' practice of the forgiveness of sins, his activity as an
     exorcist, and his negligence of the strict rules of Sabbath healing and other rabbinic instruc-
     tions. „It appears to me", writes Pannenberg, „extremely important for a true understanding
     between Jews and Christians today that one does not trivialize these conflicts, which were
     connected with the actions of Jesus, and which were surrounded by the unique ambiguity of the
     situation, and that one does not put it down to the apologetic tendency of the Gospels to take the
     blame off the Romans. Sure, there were such tendencies, but one cannot explain everything
     through recourse to them. One must find the ground of these conflicts, to the ground, which is to
     be sought in the message of Jesus himself, in the apparent arrogant blasphemy in his person, in
     the way he forgave sins, but also in other aspects of his appearance and in the unique ambi-
     valence of his position regarding the tradition of the Law. This ambivalence is also, by the way,
     found in Paul. On one hand the Apostle says that the Law is spiritual, and it belongs on the side of
     the Spirit of God. Its command is holy, righteous, and good. On the other hand, however, he
     declares the freedom of faith from the orders of the law. In both aspects, the structure of the
     Pauline argument can be understood as a continuation of Jesus' message." (BSTH 1, 282) Cf.
     however the foreword to „The Apostle's Creed in Light of Today's Questions" (1972).

people. Jesus could come under the curse of the law only if and to the extent that he stood as a transgressor against the law and thereby against God himself who had given the law. That, however, was in fact the case, since he had set himself above the traditional authority of the law through his claim to authority. This action appeared at the same time to question God himself as the one how had made known his will in the law." (JGM, 254) Pannenberg continues "Only from the perspective of Jesus resurrection is all this seen in a new light. If Jesus' resurrection from the dead could only be understood as an act of God himself upon Jesus and thus as the confirmation of Jesus' pre-Easter activity, the judgment of the Jews is upset. If and only if Jesus has really been raised from the dead, not he but the one who rejected him in the name of the law was the blasphemer, even more, if the same Jesus who was rejected in the name of the law afterward has been raised by God, then the traditional law itself is revealed to be at least an inadequate expression of God's will." (*Ibid.*)

The interpretation of this passage, quoted at such length due to its importance for the concept as a whole, requires particular care. It is that which determines, with its understanding of the relation between the death and resurrection of Jesus, also the relation between – traditionally said – Law and Gospel. This can be summarized in the foundational problem which Pannenberg himself notes: the question, whether Jesus' conflict with the law, which lead to His death on the cross, is primarily a conflict with a human perception of the divine will, which is to be further developed in human history, or if it is primarily to be seen as a conflict with the will of God and thus with Jesus divinity itself. In order to answer this, one must clear up first what, precisely, the "justification of Jesus by the Father in his resurrection" (ST II, 343, italics in Pannenberg) is. What does it mean, when it is said: "What previously was blasphemy is not the expression of the highest authority, or true unity with God himself; what previously seemed to be demanded for the sake of the divine law is not revealed to be blasphemous outrage. Jesus' resurrection cleared away the ambiguity that hung over Jesus' pre-Easter activity. Therefore, the message of freedom from the law results from the perspective of the resurrection." (JGM, 255) Before this is examined in detail, it must be quickly noted that the sketched examinations in "Jesus: God and Man" regarding Jesus' self-understanding and the disastrous character of his conviction are confirmed in the pertinent passages of the Systematic Theology regarding the trail of Jesus. That it is theologically by no means "the fixing of Jewish guilt for the death of Jesus" (*Ibid.*) but rather a matter of the appropriate theological understanding of the action of God in the passion of Jesus has been made clear by Pannenberg unequivocally.

4. The Easter Confirmation of the Unity of Jesus with God

As Jesus' proleptic claim to authority and life witness appears not merely ambiguous, but as disproved in the face of the events of the cross, one cannot speak of the Christological and soteriological meaning of the Earthly One without the Easter event. It is first in virtue of the Easter confirmation of the earthly Jesus as the Son of God that one can recognize that his Humanity is revealed to us as God's being. The idea of a resurrection from the dead, which is connected in an elementary manner to the Easter event, is something which Pannenberg tries to shed light on in a first step in "Jesus: God and Man" in that he sketches out the role of this thought in the history of tradition and in the context of an apocalyptic expectation for the future, as it was impressed into the horizon of understanding in early Christianity. Significant is primarily the connection between resurrection and the end of time: "If Jesus has been raised, then the end of the world has begun." (JGM, 67, italics in Pannenberg) At the same time, the Crucified is manifested as the glorified son of Man under the eschatological conditions of His earthly life, and in this God is conclusively revealed as He Himself. In the words of the Resurrected, as transmitted by the early Christian tradition, it is this and thus the resurrection of the Crucified One itself that is explicated. According to Pannenberg, this includes the motif of the transition across the limits of Israel to the mission to the Gentiles and the universalization of Christianity.

The speech about the *resurrection of the dead* is, according to its nature, parabolic and to be spoken of only metaphorically.[18] This it to say, it is not a situation which can be identified by sense-experience. Much more, the everyday process of waking from sleep and getting up served as a picture of the event that is hidden from empirical observation this side of the veil. To speak with Pannenberg: "[t]he intended reality and the mode in which it is expressed in language are essentially different. The intended reality is beyond the experience of the man who lives on this side of death. Thus the only possible mode of speaking about it is metaphorical, using images of this-worldly occurrences. Anyone who has become conscious of this structure involved in speaking about the resurrection of the dead can no longer fancy that he knows what is thus expressed in the same way that one knows an occurrence that has been investigated scientifically. Rather, this is a metaphorical way of speaking about an event that is still hidden to us in its true essence." (JGM, 75)

---

18 The stance that Pannenberg took in 1964 regarding the metaphorical character of all speech about the resurrection was limited in „Dogmatischen Erwägungen zur Auferstehung Jesu" in KuD 14 (1968), 105–118; reprinted in GSTh 2, 160–173. This limitation was connected to the insights of the religious origin of the concept of person (cf. „Person und Subjekt", reprinted in GSTh 2, 80–95) as the starting point for an attempt for new efforts regarding. the uniqueness of religious speech as such. Cf. also „Gottebenbildlichkeit und Bildung des Menschen" in ThPr 12 (1977), 259–273; reprinted in GSTh 2, 207–225.

In order not to come to a false conclusion form the analogy of sleeping and waking, Pannenberg makes especially clear that the Easter event is to be strictly held apart from the simple revivification of a corpse as known in antique miracle literature as "a reality of an entirely different sort" (JGM, 77)-it is not a matter of "the *temporary* return of a dead person into this life" (*Ibid.*) in the resurrection of Jesus, but rather of His eschatological completion in and through God. The end-times character of the resurrection of the dead in the world of apocalyptic concepts is in this aspect of particular relevance, as it is true in general, that the negligence of apocalyptic, the foundations of Christian faith would be at one's disposal: "Why the man Jesus can be the ultimate revelation of God, why in him and only in him God is supposed to have appeared, remains incomprehensible apart from the horizon of apocalyptic explanation...the basis of the knowledge of Jesus' significance remains bound to the original apocalyptic horizon of Jesus' history, which at the same time has also been modified by this history. If this horizon is eliminated, the basis of faith is lost; then Christology becomes mythology and no longer has true continuity with Jesus himself and with the witness of the apostles." (JGM, 83) The current importance of the apocalyptic horizon of meaning is, so Pannenberg, grounded in the time-invariant result of the future- world- and God-openness of the human, demonstrable as anthropological universal, which makes up the eccentricity of the human nature. From this anthropological result, Pannenberg draws the superiority of the hope of resurrection as opposed to the thought of immortality, insofar as the former is relative to the trans-finalization of the whole human in the differentiated unity of body and soul.

These argumentations occur slightly shortened in the relevant passages of the Systematic Theology, although Pannenberg makes an effort to respond to misunderstandings which had developed from the thoughts developed in "Jesus: God and Man" (cf. ST II, 346, fn. 61). Among other things, one should note the remark that the resurrection of Jesus is the reason for Christian faith "not as an isolated event, but in its reference back to the earthly sending of Jesus and his death on the cross" (ST II, 344), which is not externally added to the Easter event, but rather belongs essentially to it. Thus, the Easter event does not uncover or reveal merely the meaning "that the crucifixion and the earthly history of Jesus already had in themselves. Only the Easter event determines what the meaning was of the pre-Easter history of Jesus and who he was in his relation to God. To do this the event had to be an event with its own weight and content, namely, the resurrection of Jesus from the dead to a new life with God. This event dispelled and removed the ambiguity that had earlier clung to the person and history of Jesus and did not simply disclose a meaning that had previously been hidden, but still present, quite apart from the event of his resurrection." (ST II, 345 – 346) To be added is the fact that Pannenberg opposed the false assumption in the afterword to the 5th edition of "Jesus God and Man" that he had made the so-called apocalyptic "dogmatically to the significant horizon for the meaning of the person and history of Jesus, but in particular of His resurrection"[19] in an isolated manner. Opposed to this is that the statements about the importance of the apocalyptic expectation of the future for Christology did not aim at a dogmatic pre-decision, but rather merely had the methodological intention of viewing the historical context of the proclamation of Jesus and His history as well as the early Christian perception of the Easter event.

Next to the controversy regarding the Christological meaning of apoc-alyptic concepts, the object of hefty controversy is also Pannenberg's assumption of the *historicity of the resurrection*, which was seen as the main thesis of his Christology. Commonly, as it is not difficult to see, these controversies were and are "influenced by terminological establishment".[20] Regarding Pannenberg's own idea of historicity, it coincides by and large with the expression "has actually taken place (ST II, 361)", every event, which is claimed to have really happened, is factually claimed as historical, even when the historical proof of its facticity is arguable and remains so until further notice. For the sake of the reality of the Easter event which one wishes to claim reality for, one may not relinquish the idea of historicity in resurrection-theology. For "the thesis that Jesus rose again, that the dead Jesus of Nazareth came to a new life, implies already a claims to historicity." (ST II, 359, italics in Pannenberg, cf. ST II, 360–363)[21] Decisive for this historical belief in the reality of the Easter event are primarily the appurtenances of the Resurrected One, secondarily the empty tomb of Jesus in Jerusalem. The factual relation of both traditions, which in Pannenberg's judgment "came into existence independently" (JGM, 105) can be referred to in that the latter first in connection with the former, and not for itself, "takes on significance for the whole subject" (ST II, 353). In this case, however, it is from significant importance, insofar as it makes the suspicion difficult "that the appearances of the risen Lord might have been mere hallucinations. It also resists any superficial spiritualizing of the Easter message, though leaving room for the thought of a changing of the earthly corporeality of Jesus into the eschatological reality of a new life. We thus cannot explain the finding of the empty tomb as a product of Easter faith and must recognize that it happened independently of the appearances. Accordingly, even if this tradition developed in the light of Easter faith, we must still assign to the report the function of confirming the identity of the reality of Jesus encountered In the appearances with his resurrection from the dead." (ST II, 359)

This summarizes neatly what is said in "Jesus: God and Man" (cf. JGM 88–106) regarding the *tradition of the appearances of Jesus and the tradition of the*

---

19 *Nachwort* page 416.
20 *Nachwort* page 417.
21 Cf. „History and the Reality of the Resurrection" in G. D'Costa (ed.), Resurrection Reconsidered, 1996, 6272; reprinted in BSTh 1, 319–326.

empty tomb. With reference to the manner and nature of the Easter appearances, one must keep in mind "it may have involved an extraordinary vision, not an event that was visible to everyone." (JGM, 93) At the same time, one must in no case judge the Easter visions as necessarily imaginary. One should count on the possibility of visionary experiences which do not arise from subjective projections not just generally, but especially in the case of Jesus' resurrection due to the fact that the majority of the appearances and their temporal distance block a hypothesis of subjective visions as well as does the "improbability of the assumption that people who came from the Jewish tradition would have conceived of the beginning of the events connected with the end of history for Jesus alone without compelling reasons. The primitive Christian news about the eschatological resurrection of Jesus – with a temporal interval separating it from the universal resurrection of the dead – is, considered from the point of view of the history of religions, something new, precisely also in the framework of the apocalyptic tradition. Primitive Christianity required a long time to learn that with Jesus' resurrection the end had not yet begun in general, and still would not arrive for an indefinite time. One observes how the Easter message as an account of an event that happened to Jesus alone only gradually took shape in the horizon of apocalyptic tradition. Something like this did not arise as the mental reaction to Jesus' catastrophe." (JGM, 96) With these premises, the resurrection of Jesus can be claimed as a historical event with a high degree of probability. This must be theologically claimed, when it is to be claimed as really having occurred. "There is no justification for affirming Jesus' resurrection as an event that really happened, if it is not to be affirmed as a historical event as such. Whether or not a particular even happened two thousand years ago is not made certain by faith but only by historical research, to the extent that certainty can be attained at all about questions of this kind." (JGM, 99) If one grants this, the last thing to be asked is to what extent an event, in which in Pannenberg's estimation the end of history occurs, can validly be seen as historical. This question returns to the aforementioned terminological establishment. Pannenberg answers as follows: "Because the life of the resurrected Lord involves the reality of a new creation, the resurrected Lord is in fact not perceptible as one object among others in this world; therefore, he could only be experienced and designated by an extraordinary mode of experience, the vision, and only in metaphorical language. In this way, however, he made himself known in the midst of our reality at a very definite time, in a limited number of events, and to men who are particularly designated. Consequently these events are to be affirmed or denied also as historical events, as occurrences that actually happened at a definite time in the past." (*Ibid.*)

5. Jesus' Unity of Being with God as Personal Unity

Christology in general, and the Christological dogma as it is defined in the councils of Nicaea-Constantinople (325/381) and Chalcedon (451) serves the task of the explication of the unity of Jesus with God as it is manifested in the Easter event. The Easter-revealed unity of Jesus with God is, to repeat once again, not a direct identity or an indifference, but rather a unity mediated though difference. Precisely in the fact that Jesus radically and diligently differentiates Himself from the Father is Jesus one with the Father and proves Himself the eternal Son of God. Seen the other way around, the Father would not be what He is if He were not inseparably connected and one with Jesus as His Easter-revealed Son. If, namely, "the Father is form all eternity the One he is shown historically to be in relation to Jesus his Son, and through him, then we cannot think of the Father apart from the Son." (ST II, 367) The assumption of the preexistence of the Son of God, with which Jesus is personally one mediated through His difference, results "inescapabl[ly] not only if we assert the fellowship of Jesus with the eternal God but also if we maintain the link between the eternal identity of the Father God whom Jesus proclaimed and the relation to Jesus as his Son." (ST II, 370) If, then, the statements about the preexistence (and in accord with this) about the incarnation are non-negotiable, they nonetheless would remain abstract and external to the reality of Jesus Himself, if they were to not find their grounding through His historical relation to God as the Father working in creative omnipotence.

The historical relation of Jesus to God is, according to Pannenberg, essentially characterized through *self-differentiation*. This self-differentiation, as it is completely characterizing for Jesus' person and work, must be seen as the internal reason for his divine Sonship. Said a different way: "Rejection of any supracreaturely dignity before God shows itself to be a condition of his sonship. It is mediated by his self-humbling (Phil. 2:8). This constitutes the indirectness of the identity of Jesus with the son of God." (ST II, 373) Pannenberg refers once again in this context to the afterword to the 5th edition of "Jesus: God and Man", where it is said "that the doctrine of the deity of Jesus Christ is rounded off only with these statements concerning the indirectness of his deity by way of his relation as man to his heavenly Father, and not with the portion of the book devoted to knowledge of his deity. This means that we must view part II…as part of the doctrine of his deity precisely because the humanity of Jesus in his difference from the Father, as well as his relation to him, is the revelation of his deity" (ST II, 373, fn. 140, cf. the Afterword of the German edition of JGM, pg. 423 f.). to be added that in Pannenberg's own words, the third section of "Jesus: God and Man" severs the presentation of the divinity of Jesus, insofar as is explicates the implicit Trinity-theological sense of the unity of Jesus with God mediates through self-differentiation. This occurs with particular emphasis in the Systematic Theology, for example when

Pannenberg refers to the relationship of correspondence between the self-differentiation of the eternal Son from the father, as it is effective in the self-relinquishing which leads to the incarnation, and the self-abasement of Jesus in obedience to his sending by the Father that the connection of the divine Son with the Father, in difference that of one being, has found its perfect expression in the self-differentiation of Jesus from God.

The self-differentiation of the earthly Jesus from God finds its peak in his death on the cross, which Pannenberg refers to (in agreement with E. Jüngel) as "integral to his earthly existence" (ST II, 375). This occurs in its most extreme form, insofar as Jesus was devoted to the father entirely on the cross, even to the separation of dereliction and abandonment by God. If He had insisted on His finitude – making this independent from God as an opposite – he would have been disloyal to his sending and with it the sonship connected to the Father in unity. The death of Jesus is, though fate, at the same time the consequence of his filial obedience to the divine mission. He could not, as it is said, "be the Son of God by an unlimited duration of his finite existence. No finite being can be one with God in infinite reality." (*Ibid.*) By not making His humanity independent from God, in contrast to the fist Adam and the adamitic human race, God's infinitude was revealed in Him, in order to bring humanity and the world into the power of the life-giving divine Spirit in the Trinitarian context of divine love, which itself is the instance in which the Godhood of God fulfill itself.

Pannenberg's thesis of the extreme peak of self-differentiation from the Father in the death on the cross would not be sufficiently measured, if it were not brought into connection with the assumption which claims that the suffering and death of Jesus represent a debilitating crisis of his claim to authority as well as His relation to God in connection with this claim, that is, the basis and the epitome of His own self. In a certain manner, the idea of self-differentiate which serves as a structural idea of Pannenberg's Christology, has a part in this crisis, insofar as the self of Jesus perishes and disappears in the execution of this differentiation which makes up the mode of his unity with God. This does not leave the unity mediated by self-differentiation untouched, but affects it in its innermost. However, one can also discover an additional parallel to this in the crisis of the self-differentiation of Jesus from God, as it is a consequence of His self-differentiation that at the end everything must be such that it is only God who matters and not the self which knows itself as differentiated from God.

From this perspective, it can be understood that Pannenberg calculates not only with Jesus' lack of knowledge regarding the day of eschatological judgment, but also with the lack of knowledge which can be called uncertainty regarding the eschatological confirmation of his sending in the character of the being of Jesus and His self-awareness, diligently self-differentiated from the Father. "This lack of knowledge is actually the condition of Jesus' unity with this God." (JGM, 334) That this lack of knowledge takes on not merely the gestalt of manifest uncertainty on the cross, but rather the gestalt of despair in the self, the world, and God cannot be excluded. however this may be: the fact that the glory of Christ cannot be derived without gaps and in historical continuity from the self-awareness of the earthly Jesus is clear. The crisis of the cross, which appears not to indicate the decline of the self-awareness of Jesus and His unity with God mediated through self-differentiation, can only be solved through and with the assumption of that very divine act which is Easter. Only under the presumption of Easter is the crucified Jesus manifested as the one who belongs to the Godhood of God in unity of being and as the one who is identical with the Son of God in His self-differentiation from God and His connection with God the Father in community of persons.

The Easter unity of being between Jesus and God is a personal unity with the father, and the reverse is true, says Pannenberg. The ideas *unity of being and unity of person* are thus inseparable, without ending up in unallowable abstractions. Despite this, if one wishes to differentiate between them for a moment, one must see that the manner in which Pannenberg uses unity of being finds its end in the idea of personhood which it grounds. This is true insofar as the internal character of the unity of being of Jesus with God is the personal communion with the Father. The expectation of the unity of being between Jesus and God, as it is implicit in the Easter event, is served in "Jesus: God and Man" by §4, whereas the personal unity of Jesus with God is developed in §9. Regarding the unity of being of Jesus with God it is not sufficiently described when it understands the manner of the presence of God in Jesus merely in the sense of an increased Spirit-inspiration ("Jesus was not a divine person, but only a man filled with the Spirit of God" JGM, 121) or simply phenomenal presence. The mode of the presence of God in Jesus is much more that of strict revelatory presence, and this is such that God is revealed as Himself in Jesus. The idea of self-revelation includes the idea of unity of being just as that of certainty includes the uniqueness, individuality, and eschatological finality of the revelation. At the same time, it sheds light that the idea of self-revelation, which contains the idea of unity of being without defining this as substantial indifference, by virtue of the differentiation unity of revealer and revealed carries with it already the foundational structure of the doctrine of the Trinity, though this may not be thus directly presupposed for the Christological argumentation.

Jesus did not become the revealer who belongs in unity of being to the Godhood of God through a particular single event, but rather through the entirety of His life which ended on the cross, as it is carried out in the Easter event. With this, he did not become first in the Easter event something which He was not before, although He would neither have been nor would be what He is without His resurrection. Easter is thus the integrating factor of the historically differentiated life of the Jesus who died on the cross, who by virtue of this is connected in unity of being to the eternal life of God. A further consequence of this is that Jesus the revealer *is* not first since an individual event nor through a single event, but from eternity to eternity. This truth is the object of reflection for the thought of incarnation and preexistence, which both have their correctness in the idea of Jesus as the revealer of God from eternity. However, to conceive of an incarnation of the preexisting one would be inappropriate if it were to merely regard the beginning of the earthly existence of Jesus as if it were presupposed directly for His historical appearance, without being mediated through both of these.

As the revealer who belongs to the godhood of God in unity of being Jesus is, as has been said many times, not one with God without difference or in the manner of indifference, but in the manner of the identity of identity and difference. This is the thought of the doctrine of the Trinity, as it identifies the intra-divine difference and unity of Father and Son as the reason and truth of the revelatory reality of Jesus. "God's essence as it is revealed in the Christ event thus contains within itself the twofoldness, the tension, and the relation of Father and Son. The deity of Jesus Christ cannot therefore have the sense of undifferentiated identity with the divine nature, as if in Jesus, God the Father himself had appeared in human form and had suffered on the cross. This was the opinion of modalism concerning Jesus' divine identity. The modalists thought they could save God's unity only be identifying Jesus with God without differentiation…In contrast to the modalists' position, the differentiation of Father and Son in God himself must be maintained, because this differentiation, which is characteristic of the relation of the historical Jesus to God, must be characteristic of the essence of God himself if Jesus as a person is God's revelation." (JGM, 159–160) To have demonstrated the intra-divine difference between Father and Son is, according to Pannenberg, the essential accomplishment of classical logos-Christology. The renewal of this method is, however, only promising when it is undertaken with a view to the historical revelation of God in Jesus of Nazareth rather than speculatively looking away from it. This is also true for the current attempt to reformulate the traditional thought of the Jesus Christ as mediator of creation.

The sixth paragraph of "Jesus: God and Man" ends with considerations regarding the doxological structure of statements about the godhood of Jesus as well as with reflections to the pneumatologically developed doctrine of the Trinity and to the problem of the personhood of the Holy Spirit. In another perspective the problem of personhood is thematic in the final paragraph of the introduction before the excursus (JGM, 30), insofar as this should define the unity of being between Jesus and God as a personal communion of Father and Son. Decisive is, once again, what Pannenberg calls (also in this context) the dialectic of the sonship of Jesus. He also describes it as the indirectness of the identity of Jesus with the son of God. One cannot, it is said again, "properly understand Jesus' sonship without taking his relation to God the Father as the point of departure. The question of the unity of the man Jesus with the eternal Son of God cannot be put and answered directly." (JGM, 334) It is first the personal relationship to the God of Israel perceived as Father, as it comes to light in His life and fate, does Jesus prove Himself to be identical with the Son of this Father, wherewith, to speak with Pannenberg, the retroactive effect of Easter makes up the *conditio sine qua non* of this unity. Jesus is "one with God through his dedication to the Father that is confirmed as a true dedication by the Father's acknowledgement of him through Jesus' resurrection." (JGM, 336) In the execution of personal devotion, Jesus is the Son of the Father, who for His part is totally devoted to the Son, that He have personal communion in unity of being and that He might prove Him the incarnate Logos in the integrated entirety of His life process. This thought builds a differentiated but inseparable connection of mutual referentiality, and this is also valid for the relation between the order of understanding and being implicit in it. "Thus the perception of Jesus' eternal sonship as dialectically identical with his humanity is based noetically upon the particularity of just this human being in his relation to the divine father; ontologically, the relation is inverted, for the divine Sonship designates the ontological root in which Jesus' human existence, connected with the Father and nevertheless distinguished from him, has the ground of its unity and of its meaning." (JGM, 337)

It is to the latter aspect that the doctrine of the enhypostasis of the humanity of Jesus refers. One must keep the misunderstanding at a distance, as if the humanity of Jesus were grounded directly from the Logos and not mediated by his personal communion with the Father. In the context of the doctrine en- and anhypostasis the dialectic of the identity of Jesus with the eternal Son of God is also confirmed: "[T]he understanding of this man, in his humanity changed into its opposite, leads to the confession of his eternal divinity. Conversely, anything said about an eternal Son of God an be sufficiently established only be recourse to the particularity of this man, to his unity with God. The synthesis of this dialectic, the unity of God and man in Christ, emerges fully only in the history of his existence. This happens not just in the history of his historical, earthly existence in his isolated individuality, but in the history of his existence to the extent that it embraces all reality from the perspective of his historical particularity." (JGM, 342–343) To develop this in detail is the task of the final section, §10 of "Jesus: God and Man", which is titled "The Lordship of Jesus Christ" and connected to the introductory sentence "Shown to be the Son of God by his dedication to the Father, Jesus is the eschatological ruler toward whom all things are, so that all things are also through him." (JGM, 365, italics in Pannenberg)

Instead of looking more closely at this foundation which, as has been mentioned, fulfills itself in the reformulation of the doctrine of Jesus as mediator of creation, we will instead quote a longer passage. From this longer passage, one can see the decisive insights with reference to the entire argumentative process of Pannenberg's Christology, precisely due to the fact that is marks out the borders of the argument individually: "The ineradicable difference between God and man in Jesus Christ can...be understood only when one pays attention to the fact that this difference certainly was integrated into a whole in Jesus' personal community with the Father (by which it constantly appears anew accompanying the personal distinction), but this integration cannot be said to belong to his own individual vital unity. A preferable description of the historical reality of Jesus' historical life is that the particular elements of human life in Jesus' existence were integrated in this way to a whole by his person, that the integrating person realized itself precisely thereby as the person of the Son belonging eternally to the divinity of God. One must observe, however, that because of its relational character the person of Jesus in his historical life must be understood as much passively as actively. It should be clear that we have here a degree of complexity in the matter to be expressed that brings us to the limit of what can be expressed at all and which, therefore, even in a systematically coherent succession of statements, can no longer be described with a sufficient degree of concreteness (i. e., in all its aspects).

With this reservation, we can move a step farther. If the history of a person is accomplished in the give-and-take of acting and receiving, the existence of Jesus is integrated into the person of the eternal Son of God precisely through the history of his earthly way in its reference to the Father. In this sense, the person of Jesus is the locus in which God's essence (in which Jesus participates as a person of the Trinity) and the essence of man, integrated through just this person, is united, as is apparent from Jesus' resurrection. This is the case first in the particularity of Jesus' historical life and then extending to all human reality." (JGM, 344)

6. The Reality of Redemption in the God-Man

The cross of Jesus[22] is the consequence of the ambiguity of His message and His claim to authority. The relation of His message about the Kingdom of God to the divine commandments and His practice of the forgiveness of sins, as well as His communion with sinners, must have appeared particularly unclear. This ambivalence is not swept aside by the events of the cross as such. It is rather the contrary, that the crucifixion appears not only to confirm the ambiguity of Jesus' sending, but to make its failure definitive. Thus a fully new event was requires, in order to connect that life of Jesus ending on the cross and the death on the cross itself with a salvific sense. This new event occurred with the resurrection of the crucified one. While the Easter event has "an immediately clear and unavoidable meaning within its own context" (JGM, 246), this is quite different with the crucifixion of Jesus. "Precisely because of Jesus' resurrection, the question had to arise as to why Jesus had to go the way

---

22 Cf. „Theology of the Cross" in: Word and World 8 (1988), 162–172; reprinted in BSTh 1, 296–307.

of suffering to the cross if God was subsequently to acknowledge in the resurrection the unheard-of claim with which Jesus appeared." (*Ibid.*) The oldest interpretations of Jesus' death answer this question in various manners, but always such that the necessity of the events of the cross and the soteriological relevance, whatever it might be, was emphasized. One comes to a closer definition when one thinks of the cross of Jesus in the context of his conflict with the divine commandments, a conflict which makes up the deep ambiguity of His earthly reality.

Pannenberg interprets the death on the Cross as *vicarious penal suffering*, presupposing the connection between the Jerusalem catastrophe with the earthly conduct of Christ – the former is a reflex to the latter. Regarding the thought of vicariousness, the general horizon of understanding is determined by the insight that there is no replacement in personal life, but much more a social connection of responsibility. "It is grounded in the social character of human existence that every person continually deals in responsibilities that include other people to some degree. Every person is involved in the society in which he lives by what he does and b his share in the deeds of others." (JGM, 268) If then, one can consequentially speak of a action-consequence connection which affects the whole community in contrast to an idea of guilty which ignores the social context of responsibility to an extreme, and in this sense from a transfer of the consequence of sins (as large portions of the history of religion presuppose, and as does, in its own manner, the Old Testament tradition)in an anthropologically plausible manner, then the vicarious sense of the death of Jesus consists in the decisive manner of the fact that the death of the blasphemer condemned to death by the Law, which He suffered on the cross, is manifested from as the judgment of death for His judges, in them Israel and all of humanity, from the Easter sense-reversal. The death of Jesus can be understood thus as vicarious for Israel, and for the sake of the connection of the Jewish Law-thematic with the universal anthropo-logical problem of sin and death, as vicarious not only for Israel, but for all humanity. With this, Pannenberg gives "vicarious" an inclusive rather than exclusive interpretation, although it does include an exclusive moment in it. The latter is the case, as only Jesus "died completely forsaken, while the death of all other men can find safety in community with him." (JGM, 264) "Jesus' death meant his exclusion from community with the God whose coming Kingship he had proclaimed. He died as one expelled, expelled by the entire weight of the legitimate authority of the divine law, excluded from the nearness of the God in whose nearness he had known himself to be in a unique way the messenger of the imminent Kingdom o God. No one else must die this death of eternal damnation, to the extent that he has community with Jesus. Whoever is bound up with Jesus no longer dies alone, excluded from all community, above all no longer as one who is divorced from community with God and his future salvation." (JGM, 263)

From the latter quote, it is already apparent that Pannenberg connects the vicarious sense of Jesus' death primarily with the punishment suffered on the cross. Accordingly, he gives precedence to a theory of penal substitution among the other theories of the salvific meaning of the death of Jesus. In contrast to the concept, common primarily in the ancient church, of a ransom for the devil brought on the cross, and in contrast to an anselmian satisfaction theory, the thought of penal substitution retains the fateful character of the death on the cross, as well as the context of the conflict with the Torah which the earthly Jesus had, which made up the ambiguity of His claim to authority and the source of his ultimate trial. The thought of penal substation is thus the most fit to express the vicarious salvific meaning of Jesus' death on the cross. To have recognized this, following Paul, is considered the decisive achievement of Luther's soteriology, which remains untouched by justified individual objections. "Luther was probably the first since Paul and his school to have seen with full clarity that Jesus' death in its genuine sense is to be understood as vicarious penal suffering." (JGM, 279)

The foundation of the staurology developed in §7 of "Jesus: God and Man", according to which Jesus' death on the cross is revealed from His resurrection as the suffered punishment in our stead for the blasphemous existence of humans is taken up in the second volume of the Systematic Theology and unfolded in three aspects. These three aspects are the subsections of the 11th chapter, "The Reconciliation of the World",[23] and he characterizes them, looking back, as follows: "In the first section of this chapter I tried to clarify the systematic function of the Pauline concept of reconciliation. We saw that what is at issue is the way to the salvation of the world through overcoming the opposition to God into which sin and death have plunged us. My aim in the second section was then to show that the world must be reconciled to God, not God to the world, and that God's act in reconciling the world certainly took place in Christ's passion. The concept covers not merely the past history of Jesus, however, but also the present apostolic ministry of reconciliation. In the third section I then reached a similar conclusion, namely, that we cannot restrict the significance of the death of Christ as vicarious expiation to the crucifixion of Jesus as a past event but that there is also a dimension of implicit representation that is actualized only with the bringing in of those 'for whom' Christ died." (ST II, 437)[24]

How it is that this inclusion of humans in the events of reconciliation is to be thought such that the subject position of God in the human is not removed but confirmed is the topic of the fourth section, in which the doctrine of the triune God as the redeemer of the world is developed. The Trinitarian constitution of the events of the reconciliation of God with the world brings first in view that

23 The original German has here the addition „through Jesus Christ", which, while not present in Pannenberg's title, captures Pannenberg's thought appropriately. Cf. above, the foreword to the German edition. – Trans.
24 Note that Pannenberg's German text lacks all first-person phrasing. – Trans.

"[c]learly the Father does not act alone in the offering up of Jesus to death. Jesus himself is not simply passive in this action, for the Son is also acting subject in the event." (ST II, 441) This insight forces Pannenberg, as he notes, "to correct the position that I took up in 1964" (ST II, 446),[25] insofar the standard of the Trinitarian constitution of the event of reconciliation must speak of an action of the son of God not only in, with, and under the human activity of Jesus but also in a manner which includes and integrates the difference of His action and suffering. This fact, and the implicit consequence are made evident through the following sentences: "Naturally the Son of God incarnate in Jesus acts through his human activity, but his action embraces the distinction between the human activity and the fate of Jesus. The earthly activities thus have contexts other than those that appear on a purely historical approach." (*Ibid.*) From this it follows, among other insights, a modification or constructive further developing of the criticism present in "Jesus: God and Man" of the rational *idea of the office of Christ:* "If the human and historical level of the history of Jesus is transparent to the presence of the incarnate son of God concealed in it, as became clear in the light of the exaltation of the Crucified, then not only is the messianic dignity of Jesus Christ in virtue of his kingly office perceived to be present in hidden form in his earthly appearance, but the fate of execution that overtakes Jesus is also seen to be an act of self-offering on the part of the incarnate Son of God, who is at work in this history. This is the content of the activity of the exalted Lord, who rules the world by the word of the gospel and the power of the Spirit, creating faith in the gospel, putting all opposition to it to shame, assembling believers, and in this way preparing the way for the kingdom of the Father in the world, as he had already in his earthly work made the coming rule of God present to believers." (ST II, 448)

If, then the reconciliatory office of Christ combines passion and action into a differentiated unity, it is not that the atoning effect of the resurrected crucified One becomes real itself directly and exclusively, but rather mediated by the Holy Spirit and in an inclusive manner, such that humans are brought by the Holy Spirit into the effective reality of reconciliation revealed in Jesus Christ: "Through the Spirit reconciliation with God no longer comes upon us solely from outside. We ourselves enter into it." (ST II, 450) Being unified with Christ and the reality of reconciliation with God manifest in Him, which faith takes into itself in the power of the divine Spirit, does not remove the eccentricity of faith and the difference of the believer from his foundation, but much more it confirms this: [F]or the Spirit himself differentiates himself from the Son by not openly glorifying himself but glorifying Jesus as the Son of the Father and the Father in the Son. The Spirit, who is himself God, brings with him fellowship with God, but only as he distinguishes himself from the

<hr/>

25 Again, in the original German, this is in passive voice without first-person, „to correct the position taken in 1964". – Trans.

Father and the Son, and with himself all those whose hearts he fills and lifts up to God. Even the 'ecstatic' working of the Spirit does not mean that self-distinction from God is no longer a condition of fellowship with him. It makes it possible for us to rejoice in this distinction in peace with God." (ST II, 453) If then, it is the personal being of the Spirit not to be in itself but in others with itself, then the faith corresponds to the Spirit in which it grounds through the fact that it relies on the witness of the Spirit as it is spoken out in the Good News of Jesus Christ. With this, Pannenberg does not wish to tighten the idea of the Good News to the forgiveness of sin, as forgiveness of sin "is one essential element of [the Good News], but only one." (ST II, 462) Instead of limiting the Good News in the perspective of medieval penance piety to the word of absolution, it is the epitome of the Kingdom of God as not only proclaimed but brought in anticipatory fulfillment by Jesus Christ. "Where the salvation of God's lordship is present, all separation from God is overcome. For believers, then, participating in God's reign means the forgiveness of sins and the new commandment of love." (*Ibid.*)

§6 Pneumatology and Ecclesiology
(ST III, Chapters 12 and 13)

1. The Pneumatological Process
and the Coming of the Kingdom of God

The topic of the church is at the center of the third volume of the Systematic Theology.[1] Under the title "The Messianic Community and Individuals", the 13th is "by far" (ST III, xiii) the most extensive chapter, dealing with the internal structure and external constitution of the church. The communion of the individual with Jesus Christ and the community of the faithful with one another are understood in a differentiated but inseparable context. Following an explication of faith, hope and love as the fundamental salvific effects of the Spirit in the individual Christians in the aspect of the justified state of a child of God, Baptism and Holy Communion come into view as the elemental signifying gestalts of the salvific presence of Christ in the life of the church. Following this, the idea of Sacrament and the office of leadership are connected to this as the signifier and tool of the unity of the church. The chapter on ecclesiology closes with explanations of the church and the people of God, which find their continuation in the 14th chapter with its considerations of election and history. The "context of the church's existence and of the specific form of the presence of God's Spirit within it" (ST III, 97) marks the Kingdom of God, in which the salvation economy of God is completed and in which the process of the pouring out of the Spirit as pneumatological finds its fulfillment. Correspondingly, prior to the chapter on the eschatological completion of creation (15th chapter), which itself is mediated through the doctrine of election and the chapter on ecclesiology, is the twelfth chapter, entitled "The Outpouring of the Spirit, the Kingdom of God, and the Church". Insofar as the pneumatically determined thought of the

---

1 For Pannenberg's analyses of the modern situation of the church, and in particular of Protestantism, cf. the following: 1. Pluralismus als Herausforderung und Chance der Kirche (BSTh 3, 22–33) 2. Angst um die Kirche. Zwischen Wahrheit und Pluralismus (reprint BSTh 3, 34–42) 3. Zwischen Skepsis und Hoffnung: Zur Lage der Kirchen in Deutschland (BSTh 3, 45–53) 4. Christianity and the West: Ambiguous Past, Uncertain Future (reprint BSTh 3, 54–64). Pannenberg expects essential impulses from a renewal of the alliance between faith and reason, so important in the history of Christendom, which leaves behind the irrationalities of fundamentalism as well as secularism. Secularism is principally criticized for a pluralism that does not enable freedom, but rather destroys it: in any case, principal pluralism is a contradictory idea, as "Pluralism presents itself as a dogma which demands general acceptance and which threatens those who think differently with sanctions." (BSTh 3, 24)

Kingdom of God functions as "the framework of reference for [the church's] relation to the political economy and its constitutional order" (ST III, 97), it is within the horizon of the Kingdom of God that the relationship between the church and the political order is negotiated. According to the Christian view, both have a merely preliminary meaning, which reflects in the distinction between Law and Gospel, a fact to which the final section of the 12th chapter is dedicated. The "doctrine of the Spirit as an eschatological gift that aims at the eschatological consummation of salvation, that guarantees this, and that thus gives assurance of salvation in all the earthly fragility of Christian existence" (ST III, xiii) begins with the remark that pneumatology is a matter of "much more than just cognitive divine help in understanding an event of revelation that would otherwise be unintelligible. The work of the Spirit of God in his church and in believers serves the consummating of his work in the world of creation." (ST III, 2) instead of restricting the reality of the Spirit to a supernatural principle of knowledge, one must consider the connection between the bestowal of the Spirit and eschatology. One must also order both to the pneumatological process aimed at the completion of creation in the Kingdom of God as the final ground of the history of the world, the arrival of which the communion of the faithful is elected by their Lord to expectantly serve. The latter remark suggests that the work of the Spirit, whose eschatological gift opens to the faithful the participation in the eternal life of God and His Kingdom for the salvation of creation, occurs continually and omnipresently in close connection with the actions of Jesus Christ as the Son of God. However, the Spirit is not merely a mode of Jesus Christ or a manner of His presence, rather a distinct Trinitarian person, without whose witness Jesus Christ would not be recognized as who He is, nor would He be who He is: the eternal Son of His divine Father. Also in the context of the determination of the particularity of the soteriological form of the work of the Spirit one must carefully think about the being of the Trinitarian God as interwoven by personal self-differentiation. It is first from this perspective that one is able to recognize what the soteriological meaning of the fact that the Spirit, in giving the believer a part in the Filial relation of Jesus Christ to the Father at the same time gives a share in the Godhood of the Trinitarian God. In doing so, the eschatological gift of the Spirit of God is not so to the individual believer, but rather the communion of saints in the parity of common origins between individuality and sociality. In the Lucan story of Pentecost as the original date of the church, this situation has found "an expression which became authoritative for the time following".[2] As a creature of the Spirit of the communion of the Father and the Son, the church is a communion of the Spirit in which individual connection with Christ cannot be separated from the

---

2 This part is missing from ST III, 13, where it merely refers to giving expression. The entire phrase is ...*das hat einen für die Folgezeit maßgeblichen gewordenen Ausdruck gefunden in der luka-nischen Pfingstgeschichte (Apg. 2,1 ff.).* – Trans.

communicative unity of His Body. As the spirit-filled Body of Christ, the church is in all her appearances structured essentially towards the unification of individuality and sociality. Under this aspect, the already emphasized ecclesiological connection between Christology and pneumatology is confirmed once again. The church is "the creation of both the Spirit and the Son" (ST III, 18). A one-sided Christological grounding of the church, as has not always been avoided in the western tradition, must thus be equally judged as false as a spiritualizing interpretation which abstracts from the constitutive referentiality to Christ of the Spirit. In a nutshell: *Church is the pneumatic presence of the Future of Christ.*[3]

The advancement of the pneumatological process is one with the coming of the Kingdom of God, the future of which was made anticipatorily present in Jesus Christ. With the founding connection of pneumatology and Christology for ecclesiology, one sees the context of its realization. The church is what she is for the sake of the completion of creation in the Kingdom of God. "The consequence of this for the doctrine of the church is that its relation to the kingdom of God, as an anticipation of the future fellowship of the humanity renewed in this kingdom, must form the context for an understanding of the church as the fellowship of believers that is grounded on the participation of each in the one Jesus Christ." (ST III, 20) Pannenberg's ecclesiology develops the idea of church initially from the aspect of the coming Kingdom of God, "as

---

3 For the topic of the church as the present form of the future of Christ, cf. "die Auferstehung Jesus und die Zukunft des Menschen", in KuD 24 (1978), 104–117; reprinted in GSTh 2, 174–187. Foundational for the argument is the following passage: "If the tradition of appearances in the gospels are such that the Resurrected One is there in His individual body, then there is a one-sidedness in this which requires the correction through the Pauline thought of the church as the body of Christ. At the same time, one can say in the other sense that the reality of the Resurrected One does not exhaust itself in the fact of the church. This reality has revealed itself as grounded in itself, or much more, in the creative power of God, prior to the formation of the church and next to the community of the disciples. But this reality of the Resurrected One is not competed in itself apart from the communion of the saints. It grounds, includes, and transcends this communion. In the Pauline scriptures this fact is expressed through the differentiation and allocation of head and body." (GSTh 2, 184 f.) Pannenberg also expresses himself regarding the consequences" which come from the unity of the resurrection body of Jesus Christ with the church for the hope of resurrection of the faithful, and beyond this, for the relation of the resurrection and the Kingdom of God. When the resurrection of Jesus does not mean the reconstitution of the separate reality of an individual, separate-from-others embodiedness, then also for the resurrection of the faithful it will be valid that the separation of individuals from one another in their bodily existence is one of those moments which will be fundamentally, deeply changed in the eschatological metamorphosis of this mortal life into the new bodilyness of the resurrection of the dead. This must not remove all individual difference, as indeed the resurrected Christ is not only one with the church as His body, but also remains distinguished from her in this unity. One cannot get around that fact that one is reminded by this interpenetration of unity and difference of the difference of the Trinitarian person in the unity of the divine life. The new life from the resurrection of the dead will be more tightly connected with the Trinitarian life of God than our life now, without a removal of the difference between God and creature." (GSTh 2, 185 f.)

the provisional representation of which it has its existence." (*Ibid.*)[4] Along with this it is made clear, among other things, that the formation of the post-Easter congregation is connected with Jesus and His earthly work only through the relation to the dawning Kingdom of God. A church which wishes to hold tightly to her connection to the earthly reality of Jesus will thus not be able to turn away from her destiny in the service of the Kingdom of God. However, otherwise the eschatological referentiality, as it finds its prototypical expression in Jesus' calling of the Twelve, is ecclesiologically absolutely constitutive. "The kingdom and the church are not herewith simply identical." (ST III, 30) It is in contrast so, that the church must firmly differentiate herself from the future communion of humanity in the Kingdom of God, "in order that it may be seen to be a sign of the kingdom by which its saving future is already present for people in their own day." (ST III, 32) The category of self-differentiation has also fundamental importance in ecclesiology. Just as her Lord, in whom she grounds herself by the power of the divine Spirit, is unified with the Godhood of God through self-differentiation, the church is the present signifier of the Kingdom of God not through a self-equating, but though the resolute differentiation of her own presence from the future of the coming Kingdom.[5]

The orientation of the church to the coming Kingdom of God, without the taking into account of which one cannot grasp the ecclesiological topic appropriately, connects her at the same time in a different manner with the topic of the *political order of society*. The topic of political order also stands in a constitutive relation to the Kingdom of God. With this, the service of the church in society consists primarily in the function, that she prevents a self-absolutizing move in the political order through her existence and the execution of her life of worship, and in "a challenging of the claims of every political and judicial order, whether monarchical, oligarchical, or democratic,

---

4 Already in the "Thesen zur Theologie der Kirche", which were published in 1970, Pannenberg covers the ecclesiological horizon of the connection of the kingdom of God and the Chrich. Through this connection, the church is in its nature referred to the whole of human society, whose eschatological destiny she is to bring to light. Cf. also "Christlicher Glaube und Gesellschaft" in: U. Hommes (eg.), Gesellschaft ohne Christentum?, 1974, 109–123; reprinted in EuE, 115–128. "The symbolic representation of the future Kingdom of God in the life of the church must be understood as the central idea of the history of Christendom." (Erwählung und Geschichte, in: Die Bestimung des Menschen. Menschsein, Erwählung und Geschichte, 1978, 85–113, here: 105)

5 The ecclesiological attempt to connect the ecclesial symbolic nature with the concept of sacrament and to define the church as a sacramental sign of God's reign is not one which Pannenberg encounters in fundamental rejection, but indeed with points of difference. This is, as will be spoken of later, in the idea of the sacrament in general and the relation to the mysterium of Jesus Christ in particular. In this it is clear that the eschatological sign-function and instrumentality of the church is not a direct one, but is mediated through the spiritual participation in the mysterium of Jesus Christ as the foundation and epitome of sacramentality. This is a confirmation of the fact that the church as a sign and effect of the coming Kingdom of God does not have its purpose in itself, but finds its goal "in the future of a humanity that is reconciled to God and united by common praise of God in his kingdom." (ST III, 45)

to embody the form of social life that is ultimately in keeping with human destiny." (ST III, 52) As a consequence of better or worse perception of this function, the difference between state and church has become characteristic for the cultural traditions influenced by Christendom. "By its difference from the state the church not least of all helps to humanize the political order itself in its relation to individual citizens, because the church's existence unceasingly reminds the state of the difference between its own order and the definitive actualizing of our social destiny, thereby limiting its claims on individuals." (ST III, 56) This service is, in Pannenberg's judgment, even under the conditions of modern secularism not at all obsolete, as the societal understanding tends toward ideological self-absolutization, much like totalitarian systems in contrast to the tradition Christian understanding of the secularity of political order. Also and precisely for secularism with its tendency towards a general leveling-out, the ecclesial service of differentiation between the preliminary and the final is indispensable. In opposition to the ideology of neutrality which wishes to immunize itself from religion, one must particularly call to mind the fact "that the distinction [of spiritual and worldly power] had developed only on the soil of Christianity and was linked to specific Christian presuppositions, namely, to the eschatological awareness of Christians and its constitutive significance for the concept of the church." (ST III, 57)

The pneumatological process and the coming of the Kingdom of God build, in Pannenberg's concept, not only the constitutive horizon of ecclesiology and the relation of the church to the political order in general. They also mark the context of a critical reception of the theme of *Law and Gospel*, which became primarily characteristic and influential in the theory-traditions of the reformers.[6] The thematic connection is created by the premise that the

---

6 The Lordship of God, upon the final implementation of which the Christian expectation of the Kingdom is referred, has the specific character of a government of right. Its living being cannot be appropriately expressed in the concept of law, as this sets the behavior of humans to a normative possibility, against which the freedom of the body opens a principally unlimited multiplicity of possibilities of creative situation-handling, which can reach to the breaking of the law, which in some cases is necessary so that the justice of the intention is fulfilled (cf. Gesetz und Evangelium, München, 1986 [Bavarian Academy of Sciences. Philosophical-historical class 1986, volume 2], 5 – 24). Pannenberg's interpretation through the theology of history of the turn from law to the Gospel of Christ understands itself from here, though one should add, that the gospel power of love lies at the root of all human-assisting justice formations as the power of mutual acceptance. "Insofar as love always brings about new forms of human community, connection of the separate, it brings forth positive right. The right, which comes from love, is not an ideal order with the claim of timeless validity (thus, not in this sense natural right), but rather concrete solutions for concrete emergencies, until further notice, namely, until a new situation requires new solutions. A theological grounding of right, which orients itself on the revelation of the love of God in Jesus Christ, thus has to do with the making possible of positive justice through the love which creates community, not with the planning of ideal, once and for all revealed orders of justice. Thus, the grounding of justice from love cannot start with the *commandment* of love; this has only the task

differentiation and differentiated reference between Law and Gospel are essentially a matter of the complex relationship between religion and the legal order. More precisely, they are a matter of the detachment of Christian awareness from that gestalt of a close connection between law and religion, as was definitive for the Jewish Torah-piety. Despite the foundational superiority over against temporally invariant cosmological manners of grounding political order, the historical legal tradition petrified, in Pannenberg's judgment, in the course of a traditionalistic consolidation "became in the form of the torah a special feature in the national tradition of the people of Israel instead of representing a universal expression of the righteous will of the one God for all people." (ST III, 59) With this particularistic petrifaction came a formalizing of the Mosaic Law. The message of the Kingdom of God through Jesus and His suffering, death and resurrection mediate the conviction of Christianity, which is referential to both tendencies, in that the authority of the Jewish Torah is dissolved by the Good News. What this dissolution actually means, and how the relationship between Law and Gospel was to be determined was, however, not yet clear, and it remained not only problematic in the course of further history of Christendom, but also notoriously contended. In order to make one aware of the complexity of the topic, Pannenberg sketches out first "the main phases in the history of the exposition of the relation between law and gospel in Christian thought", namely, "the Pauline view, the patristic and medieval interpretation of the gospel as new law (*nova lex*) and the Reformation doctrine of law and gospel." (ST III, 60) While in the theology of the reformation traditions the Law was set as an expression of the demands of God opposite to the Gospel as the promise and proclamation of the forgiveness of sin, Pannenberg reads Paul's use of Law and Gospel as referring to "tow realities in salvation history that belong to two different epochs in what God does in history." (ST III, 61) According to this, the Law in the Pauline sense is not an eternal form of the divine will, but rather limited form the beginning in its duration of validity. The Law is not final, but has an end. This end is not merely applicable to parts of the Law, such as the ritual laws, but rather the entire Law, including the moral commandments. In the place of the Law delivered through the Torah comes the Gospel of Jesus Christ, as the sublation of Law in *heilsgeschichte*. How one should think precisely of this sublation in the differentiated unity of ending, fulfilled preservation ,and completion is at least partially unclear in Paul's thought, which makes it easy to understand the disparate understandings of the relation between Law and Gospel in the time thereafter.

While the interpretation of Gospel as *nova lex* in the sense of a developing doctrine of natural law was characteristic for the early church and medieval theology, the theology of the reformers has taken Law and Gospel no longer

of teaching man how to love in the first place." (Zur Theologie des Rechts, in: ZEE 7 [1963], 1 – 23; reprinted in EuE, 11 – 40, here: 38 f.)

primarily in the manner of *heilsgeschichte*, but "this view does not primarily contrast and relate law and gospel structurally" (ST III, 72)- a consequence of this structural-typological view that the Law cannot be merely identified with the Jewish Torah as a specific form of positive law, but must be identified with the *lex naturae*, that is law in general, or better, in its temporally invariant generality. This was, according to Luther, that with which the Decalogue was one in any case, as the core of the Mosaic Law. If then, the temporally transcendent general validity of the Law cannot be dissolved through the Gospel as a matter of *heilsgeschichte*, then the differentiated connection between Law and Gospel is essentially determined in the differentiation and allocation of the divine claims, which has as its consequence the verdict of guilt and the *mortificatio* of the sinner, and the divine pronouncement, which grounds the salvation and *vivificatio* of the one condemned by the Law in unconditional grace.

Indeed, Pannenberg acknowledges that the persevering achievement of the relevant reformation-based doctrinal statements in "plainly working out the structural difference between the liberating work of the gospel and the functions of the law. Yet the way of defining the distinction was still tied to the penitential mentality of the late Middle Ages and the contemporary discussion of the sacrament of penance. They differed profoundly from what Paul said about faith's freedom from the law as the basic determination of Christian life in general. As an application of Paul's teaching to a situation and to problems different from those that faced the apostle, they stand in need of material criticism in the light of the biblical witness." (ST III, 82) This material criticism refers only to, though in particular wise, the fact that Luther's structure-typological view of the relation between Law and Gospel does not eliminate the final character of the change begun in Jesus Christ, but it has perhaps dissolved it into a series of repeatable changes. (cf. STIII, 84) This established trend is encountered by Pannenberg as he confronts Luther with his own original insight, according to which the singular and once-for-all-time Baptism accords to a sacramental effect as a turn in the life of the human to the eschatological turn of world history in Jesus Christ, in reference to which all that is old is literally and once-and-for-all bygone and all is genuinely made new. "By baptism, which links the baptized to Jesus Christ, there takes place in their lives as a sight – but really – the same eschatological turn that came into human history through Jesus Christ. In the case of baptism, too, this turn is a past event, but it does not slip away from us into the past, for our baptism already anticipates the future of our individual lives as it anticipates the uniting of our future death to the death of Christ and thereby opens up for us also the hope of participation in his resurrection." (ST III, 85)

If then, one can define the relation between Law and Gospel, given this perspective of the reality set in Baptism, as merely (in an actualistic sense) a lifelong series of legal *mortificatio* and Gospel *vivificatio,* as Luther made evident through the late medieval penance tradition as the reference frame and

Sitz im Leben of his doctrine in both critique and construction, then the formality of the structure typology of demand and pronouncement, as characterizes the Lutheran Law-Gospel dialectic, is to be overcome in its content that the Law is *materialiter* and not directly to be equated with the eternal will of God, as was the case in the Reformation, analogous to the ancient and medieval church. The eternal will of God cannot be thought of, in a Christian sense, as *lex aterna*, in the manner that it is manifest as *lex naturae*. For the eternal will of God is revealed in Jesus Christ as love. "The law binds one to a specific from of conduct. Love has the power to give new life to what is right by developing in extraordinary circumstances, and without disrupting the nexus of social life, new solutions and modes of action that do better justice to the situation." (ST III, 76) Thus, it is misleading to refer to the apostolic instruction and Christian paranesis (or better, paraclesis [cf. ST III, 89 fn. 270]) as Law. As exegeses of the Christian being in Christ they are not of a legalistic nature, but rather of the nature of love, which knows itself bound in and through freedom.

This result is concludingly attributed "to the difference but also to the mutual relation between the gospel and the legal order (including the political) as the root of the distinction between church and state that characterizes Christianity in its history." (ST III, 60) A decisive function comes within this reference to the thesis that the idea of Law is not only to be differentiated from the love-Gospel of Jesus Christ, but also for the idea of right as such. Legal regulations and the *righteous will of God* which aims at the making possible of human community are not identical with the form of the Law, including the natural law. Otherwise, the freedom of Christians spoken in the Gospel from the Law would have to be necessarily against divine justice. This is only not the case, when the divine righteous will and the Law can be differentiated, and the Law has no constitutive function for right and justice, but merely a helping function. This is the precise starting point of Pannenberg's argument, in which the idea of right is a middle term "between love, the motivation for acceptance of others, for the recognition that establishes and preserves fellowship between persons, and law, which serves to preserve right fellowship as an intrinsically universal norm." (ST III, 93)

In the form of generality, in which the Law serves right, there lies, according to Pannenberg, the weakness and limitation, as this hinders the taking into account of the individual case. As it is, in its general form, not open for the individual case in its incomparable particularity, the Law is not able to ensure right and justice completely. It requires the expansion of the critical-constructive connection with love, indeed, sublation into love. For love alone completes righteousness. Thus love alone is the eschatological manifestation of the righteous will of God, whose being is love and nothing other than love. To bring this to awareness, and keep it in mind, is a decisive task of the church. By fulfilling this task, the church makes clear the difference between the preliminary and the final, as she does for the political order of the culture and for the legal structure of a community in a determining manner, in order to avoid every type of totalitarianism.

2. The Communion of the Spirit and the Fundamental Work of the Spirit in the Individual Christian

The differentiated unity of individuality and sociality is foundational for the inner structure of the church, which must take into account her external constitution.[7] Pannenberg does plead for an integrated expansion of ecclesiology in an informative excursus (cf. STIII, 21–27) regarding the place of ecclesiology in the construction of dogmatics opposed to the rule coming from the 19th and 20th centuries that the presentation of the individual appropriation of salvation has precedence over a treatment of the idea of church. After all, the communion of the individual with Christ is always already mediated through the ecclesial proclamation and the administration of Sacraments. Nonetheless, it does not follow that the individual should be subordinated to the church in the form of its representative authorities. For the ecclesial mediation of salvation accords to its purpose only insofar as she frees up the immediacy of the individual to Jesus Christ. So little as this directness of the individual is to be understood as unmediated and tending to solipsism, so little also is the individual believer a simple function of a ecclesial whole set over him.

The foundation of the chapter on ecclesiology (13th chapter) "The Messianic Community and Individuals" confirms this situation: the communion of the individual with Jesus Christ and the communion of the believers build a differentiated connection. As a creature of the Spirit of the communion of the Father and the Son, the Spiritual community of the church is that of a *communio* which allows the participation in Christ to reveal the individual and the universal as a living unity rather than opposites. Using the ecclesiological formulae *communio* and *congregatio sanctorum*, as is characteristic for the idea of church in reformation theology, Pannenberg examines and explains this in detail. With this, the primary point which one should note is the observation that the church, as communion of saints, finds its primary gestalt of realization in the worship celebration of a collected local congregation. "It is

---

7 It is the – not least ecclesiologically important – sense of the eschatological symbolism of the Judeo-Christian tradition and the connection of the idea of the Kingdom of God with the idea of the resurrection of the dead that is characteristic for it to make apparent the future unity of humanity in the common origin of individuality and society. For the final overcoming of all alienation presupposes the consummation of the human destiny of the individual as much as that of society, and it demands that all individuals have a place in the completed common nature (cf. "Zukunft und Einheit der Menschheit", in: EvTh 32 [1972], 384–402; reprinted in EuE, 166–186).

not in the first instance...a universal institution with a central leadership. The reality of the church is manifested in local communities that are gathered around the Word and sacrament and that also form a fellowship among themselves." (ST III, 103) As true as it is that each local congregation is church entire, so truly is she in her being inalienably connected with a reference to the Church Universal. This connection, which finds its expression in the mutual acknowledgement of the representative office holders in the individual local congregations and in particular in the conciliar assembly, is mediated through the common confession of faith in the one Lord upon whom the unity of the church is grounded. "Only by the common content of faith are individuals aware of belonging to the fellowship of believers over and above mere external church membership." (ST III, 110) At the same time, it is the agreement in common confession and its content which connects the individual church congregations through the universal church to one another and allows the own church. Instead of going into detail, here we emphasize that the claim "to be stating the church's faith definitively and comprehensively for all Christendom" (ST III, 120) was raised for the first time in the ecumenical symbol of Nicaea and Constantinople 381. This is the source of the "claim...unique to" (*Ibid.*) this confession of the awareness of faith of the Church, as it was acknowledged by the Reformation and has been brought to awareness by the ecumenical movement of the present.

In homology, one cannot separate the confessional action of the individual and the confession of the Church in which the individual joins.[8] Prior to

---

8 To the idea of confession as well as the judgment of the confessional situation of the present, cf. "Konfessionen und Einheit der Christen", in ÖR 22 (1973), 297–308; reprinted in EuE 241–253, here 252 f.: "The different and in part opposite doctrinal formations of the Lutheran and reformed churches in the 16th and 17th centuries are present today only as elements of tradition in a changed context of ecclesial life and theological problems. Thus one can say in one perspective, which acknowledges the intention on both sides to confess Jesus Christ, that the opposites of that time have lost their church-separating meaning within the whole of today's situation." To what extent Pannenberg sees this as valid also for the relation between Reformation churches and the Roman Catholic Church, cf. among others "Reformation and Einheit der Kirche", in: EvKom 1975, 587–593; reprinted in EuE, 254–267. "The one Church of Christ can only come forth today in the separated churches to the extent that they are able to acknowledge both theoretically and practically the fact that also the other Christian churches and traditions belong to Christ. In this, each of the confessional traditions has its contribution to make to the greater catholicity of a future form of Christian churches which unites all Christians – but also already for a greater catholic breadth within the churches separated today." (EuE, 258) – Regarding the problem of the lack of success of the constitution or reconstitution of the doctrinal consensus of the 16th century in the Lutheran churches, cf. "Bleiben in der Wahrheit als Thema reformatorischer Theologie" (in: W. Pannenberg and Th. Schneider [eds.], Verbindliches Zeugniss II. Schriftauslegung – Lehramt – Rezeption, 1995, 122–134; reprinted in BSTh 3, 342–354) as well as "Überlegungen zum Problem der Bekenntnishermeneutik in den evangelischen Kirchen" (in: KuD 41 [1995], 292–302; reprinted in BSTH 3, 355–365). "Luther's thought that the remaining of the church in the doctrine of the Gospel wins concrete form precisely in the critical mutual relationship between the office of proclamation in the church (on all levels of its perception) and the reception of its activity of teaching could also have lasting importance as an impulse to the formation of new

Pannenberg's treatment of the fundamental work of salvation by the Spirit in the individual Christian, he takes up the *problem of the relationship between being an individual Christian and the Church*, "now in the sharpened form of the question how the church's mediation of an individual relation to Jesus is connected with the immediacy of individuals to Jesus Christ in the act of faith and confession." (ST III, 122) To give away the result (cf. ST III, 134 f.): the holy Spirit is the medium of the God-immediacy of every individual as well as the means by which the individual believers are connected to the communion of the Body of Christ, such that each individual Christian and all Christians together find their common ground in Jesus Christ and come to themselves as well as to one another through Him ecstatically. "Where the spirit of Christ rules, we cannot play off the freedom of faith against the fellowship of believers and the duty of maintaining it. Nor, under the lordship of the Spirit of Christ, can the communication of the gospel take the form of clerical domination that does not let believers attain to the true freedom of immediacy to God but keeps them dependent." (ST III, 130) This results in the thesis "that the work of the spirit releases and reconciles the tension between the fellowship and the individual in the concept of the church, and with it the underlying anthropological tension between society and individual freedom in that sign at least is meant to be experienced as overcome in the church in anticipation of the future of God's kingdom. Along these lines", continues Pannenberg, "the next section will deal with the general basic form of the works of the Spirit in individual Christians by faith, hope, and love, but in such a way that in the event we will also see the place of individuals in the life of the church. The work of the Holy Spirit lifts individuals ecstatically above their own particularity not only to participation in the sonship of Christ but at the same time also to experience of the fellowship in the body of Christ that unites individual Christians to all other Christians. This is not just a matter of lifting up the individuality of Christians into the social union of the church. What will come to light is that the raising up to existence outside the self in Christ (*extra se in Christo*) does not simply assure individuals of their freedom in Christ but in so doing brings them to the place of believers' fellowship. Not just the individual but the church, too, in its liturgical life has its existence outside itself in Christ. In this way it shows itself to be a fellowship of the Spirit." (*Ibid.*)

The being of the communion of the Spirit is ecstasy in the most literal sense:

---

forms of a representative perception of binding doctrine in the church." (BSTh 3, 353). One must follow this hermeneutic rule: "The modern recognition of the truth of Christian faith is the interpretive instance for the ecclesially binding content of earlier confessional statements, however, not in the sense that new doctrine may be proclaimed in the name of modern scriptural interpretation. It must be proven, that it is a matter of a new recognition and formulation of the truth of Christian faith as of the content of the one confession of the church through time. In this sense the earlier confessional texts received as doctrinally correct and as giving the measure for the church reman the controlling instance for church doctrine of later times and also the instance of interpretation for their statements." (BSTh 3, 358).

it has its being, in which it grounds, outside of itself. This is valid for the whole of the community of the Spirit as well as for each individual member. Each believer is grounded *extra se*. Only by virtue is the ecstatic effect of the Spirit in Christ is the believer, and only by virtue of this does he come to himself and his own destiny. As the ecstatic effect of the Sprit, which leads the individual beyond himself in order to bring him to his eccentric-self-transcendental fate and to connect him to others in the community of faith, it is in particular *faith, hope and love* which are considered. *Faith* takes in this a primary place, as it (as precisely defined by Luther's reference to the biblical idea) is nothing else and claims to be nothing else then a trusting reliance, that is, a being-in-another.[9]

The fact that faith has a "fiducial" nature cannot hinder one to think of faith as an eccentric leaving of oneself – which unites own with the ground of trust – along with the moment of attention and agreement. If, then, *fides* is a "for of the way we relate to truth" (ST III, 136) of God in Jesus Christ, then *notitia* and *assensus* belong inalienably to it. Indeed, faith, speaking primarily of *notitia*, is not merely historical knowledge and understanding. However, the facticity of the salvific reality which grounds faith and thus the historicity is presupposed; this must be so, in order for faith to be certain of its foundation and not merely fall into depraved subjectivism. Under modern conditions, this means for Pannenberg that dogmatics cannot be lukewarm towards the results of historical-critical exegesis – at least, not if it wishes to avoid losing the touchstone of the historical self-revelation of God, through which faith is mediates and without which the predetermined nature of the ground of faith must be forfeited along with the eccentric character of a trusting leaving of the self. The correctness of this insight is not changed by the fact that faith, due to the non-abolishable character of probability inherent to all historical knowledge, has continually only a preliminary-hypothetical knowledge of its object. It is in contrast so, that the awareness of truth in faith must itself make a place for the relativity of its knowledge of its own object. "In contrast to the dogmatism of absolute truth claims that dominated the history of Christian thought for so long, recognition that historical knowledge is limited and provisional can be for Christian faith an occasion for deeper reflection on its own nature in its own provisional situation this side of Gods definitive future. As concerns the object of faith itself, Christian trust in God can be the basis of quiet confidence that no historical criticism can destroy the truth of God's revelation but that this truth will constantly emerge even from the results of critical exegesis and reconstruction of the history of Jesus if revelation really did take place in that history. In the process, however, it is always necessary to distinguish in the faith tradition of the churches, and

---

9 For the idea of faith in detail, cf. "Wahrheit, Gewishehit und Glaube" in GSTh 2, 226–264, in particular 236 ff, for the specific find in Luther, cf. Der "Vater im Glauben" – Luthers ökumenische Aktualität, in: U. Hahn and M. Mügge (eds.), Martin Luther – Vorbild im Glauben, 1996, 76–86; reprinted in BSTh3, 260–267.

already in the biblical texts themselves, the content of God's revelation that is basic for faith and the time-bound forms of its presentation." (ST III, 154–155)

The difference between the faith-founding content of the divine revelation and the time-conditions formulations thereof of cannot be determined in the sense of a separation between the ground of faith and the thoughts of faith (cf. W. Herrmann), as if the ground of faith would be comprehensible without the thoughts of faith, that is directly and without mediation through its exegetical gestalts. "Only critical reflection on the expositions present can separate the object (as basis) and the criticized forms of its exposition, and even then, over against the old interpretations that now seem to be inadequate, the basis stands only in the form of a new exposition." (ST III, 157–158) Analogous to the relation from fact and meaning is the relation between the ground of faith and the thoughts of faith, as a differentiated context of relationship, that indeed allows difference, but not disconnection. One must, with this, presuppose in the sense of factual logic: as the meaning suits the fact itself and is not conceived first in interpretation, so does the foundation of faith come to light as itself through the course of the history of interpretation. This internal logic as well as the insight in the fact that all attempts to interpret the foundation of faith as in its factual nature are themselves interpretations, accords in Pannenberg's judgment exactly to the Christian event of revelation itself, which grounds faith, and through whose eschatological character the awareness of the difference of the present of human life and the ultimate future of God, which is in the history of Jesus Christ proleptically anticipated (and thus itself belongs to the difference from foundation and thought of faith as a part of the identity of the foundation of faith) is set. With this complex situation, Pannenberg finds the fact immediately connected that "the history of Jesus has in its specific material structure the form of the promise" (ST III, 161)- a fact which only faith in the execution of *notitia* and *assensus* can accord to in (and only in!) the manner of trust in God. It is able to do this regardless of the preliminary nature of all knowledge and all specific thoughts of faith, due to the believing trust, which, determining one to eccentric self-transcendence through the knowledge of Jesus, whose history by anticipating and making present the eschatological future of the Kingdom of God in the power of the Spirit that opens this very fact up to believing trust, by relying on God the Father alone. The structural accordance between *promissio* and *fides* can, then, ground the thesis – as it already has in the theology of faith of the reformers – that "only *fiducia* does justice to the history of Jesus understood as promise, for only *fiducia* accepts the promise as promise. It is always presupposed here that seeing the history of Jesus as promise is in fact apt, and that we have here the promise of God himself, the promise that is for all of us in Jesus Christ. Only herein do we have a basis for assurance of faith." (*Ibid.*)

The certainty of faith is in reference to the integrity of the selfness of the believer. It is thus not a mere matter of certainty in reference to objects of experience, but rather also of self-certainty, despite the extent to which this is mediated through the experience of objects in its experienced immediacy. To deny the mediation through the experience of objects would, according to Pannenberg, end up in a self-independence movement of the ego and its certainty in opposition to he experience of the world and thus implicitly against every constitution of human subjectivity from God mediated through *heilsgeschichte*. This is neither anthropologically nor theologically tenable. The constitution of the ego-certainty present in the certainty of faith man thus not be removed from the mediating context of world-experience as the framework-context of *heilsgeschichte*. As a consequence, the certainty of faith cannot have a character of unmediated immediacy, but – as with the recognition of the truth – requires a process of experience and reflection. It is a consequence of experience and reflection because it does not seek and find is reason and foundation immediately in itself, "in tension with the ongoing process of experience and is always exposed to assault, whether in relation to its object, the reality of God and its own historical basis of faith, or as regards its own subjectivity in relation to the object of faith." (ST III, 170) With this it is once again confirmed, what was said in the context of *fides* and *promissio*. The certainty of faith cannot remain in itself in the process of experiencing the world and the self, but is oriented to and spread out to the completed entirety of the own life and the reality of the world, as it can only be brought about by God and the eschatological coming of His Kingdom. Without trust in God and an anticipatory self-leaving towards the coming of the divine Kingdom there is no certainty of faith; it is on the contrary so, that the certainty of faith essentially has a proleptic and fiducial character.

As a trusting and anticipatory inclusion of the eschatologically completed whole of the self and the world, the certainty of faith is elementarily determined by feeling, without ceasing to be reflexive and referred to experience. For "[i]n feeling we relate originally to the whole of our life and our world" (ST III, 169),[10] as it is proleptically anticipated in all reflection and execution of experience. In this sense, Pannenberg can say: "After the manner of feeling we have to confess that the consummation of the world and our own lives has dawned in the history of Jesus and that it is present to faith even if still provisionally, refracted by suffering and death. Without this affirmation in feeling of the implications that the concept of God and statements about his action in the history of Jesus contain, we cannot make the act of faith. But if the gospel speaks in this way to our feelings, we can accept it as the promise of God

10 Analogous is true for the relation of *certitudo* and *conscientia*: "Certainty and conscience belong together, because in both it is a matter of the whole of reality and thus of us ourselves. Certainty is a matter of the placement of individual experiential contents in the whole of our experience, conscience is a matter of the formation of one's own self, the whole of our being, in the details of our behavior. Both are, on account of the incompleteness of our experience and our own lives, only possible as an anticipation of the consummation of the world grounded in the future of God" (Wahrheit, Gewißheit und Glaube, in: GSTh 2, 226–264, here: 262).

himself, and when that happens it is plain also that faith in it, trust in Jesus Christ, is God's own command, and thus in faith we can be sure of the truth of God in Christ notwithstanding the assaults to which this faith is still exposed." (ST III, 172)

He who believes, hopes. "The faith that has its basis in the promise of God and understands itself as trust in God and his promise is never apart from hope." (ST III, 173) This is grounded in the promise-character of faith and its fiducial being. The self-reference implied in faithful trust in God's promise is thematic in *hope*. As faith relies on God, it expects from the God-relation also always something for itself – and it is correct to do so: for a promise that contains no *pro me* or *pro nobis*, or which had no such "for" reference would not be a promise at all. The promise of God relativizes and criticizes those fully shortsighted human goals of hope which hinder the eternal salvation of the individual and the completion of humanity in the coming Kingdom of God. God does not, however, ruin hope as such. Much more, faith can be certain of the eschatological fulfillment of its hope for the salvation of the world and the self. The hope of salvation, which is essential to faith (which itself, as faith, is certain of the fulfillment), is thus first certain hope and categorically distinct from the coincidental expectation of luck. Secondly, it is "essentially eschatological hope that reaches beyond this earthly life and the present state of the world" (ST III, 181); and thirdly it is a hope for the self and the world, that is, for the salvation of the individual and the entirety of creatures. Thus to the perspective of hope belong individual and general eschatology together. It is valid, that the hope of faith does not hope for anything which does not serve love. The other way round, the being of love expresses itself in a central manner in common hope.

Love, which in its Christian sense is united with faith and hope, is according to Pannenberg essential love of God and love of neighbor, a loving reference to God and a loving reference to other humans and the world. "In both relations we are drawn into the movement of divine love, but in different respects. In love of God, as a response that the Holy Spirit makes possible to the love received from God, we have a part in the intratrinitarian life of God, in the mutuality of fellowship between Father, Son, and Spirit. By love of neighbor we take part in the movement of the trinitarian God toward the creation, reconciliation, and consummation of the world, as the works of the economic Trinity proceed from the life of the immanent Trinity, so love of neighbor issues from love of God, and thus also from faith, which preceded the works of neighborly love. Yet in love of God and love of neighbor we do not have two wholly different realities but two aspects of human participation in one and the same love of God that according to Rom. 5:5 the Holy Spirit has poured into believers' hearts." (ST III, 193) The unity of the love of God and the love of neighbor is indeed a differentiated unity, but nonetheless an unseparated singular unity, because it is a matter in both manners of love of different forms of the participation of humans in the dynamic of the love of the triune God.

The aspect of Spirit-opened participation of the human in the divine love is that which leads Pannenberg to a more precise definition in the relation of faith and love of God. With this firstly, the idea of the love of God requires a closer determination, as it can refer to God's love for humans (with all creatures) as well as the humans' love for God. One should start with the exegetical facts, that the katabaitc love of God for humanity and the word, as it proves effective in the sending of the Son, determines the New Testament statements about the love of God decisively. On the other hand, in the New Testament, the anabatic love of humans for God, when it is mentioned at all, recedes in comparison. This tendency also comes to light in a certain manner with the biblical understanding of *agape* in distinction from *eros* and *philia*. Nonetheless Pannenberg holds that the conclusion that, more or less, the thematic of the love of the human to God is either directly to be brought into line with the thematic of faith or differentially to be identified with the thematic of the love of the neighbor for an error. Regarding the relation between faith and human love for God, it is the case that faith and the hope connected to it find their completion in the love of the human for God, and without this would not be what they are. "For by love believers have a share in God's own nature and are united with him." (ST III, 182) With this, though, the faith of the believer is not immediately identical with his love for God, insofar as "love for God is more than the act of faith" (ST III, 192, f. 282). For, taken for itself, the act of trust in faith "does not contain all aspects of love, for love does not just link up with the object of trust as trust itself does, but is also the power of recognizing what is different. In this way it makes fellowship possible, and it is thus the presupposition and condition and setting of a life in faith rather than identical with faith. Nor is it just the presupposition of faith, for trust also gives access to the riches of the mutuality of love and is itself already an element in this mutuality." (ST III, 191 – 192) In this, the love of the human for God is a constitutive implication of faith. In its execution, faith achieves the fulfillment of its own destiny.

According to Pannenberg, the fact that faith includes human love for God as a constitutive implication is a matter of "great systematic significance" (ST III, 192): "For by it our elevation to participation into Jesus' filial relation to the Father is taken up into the thought of the downward movement of God's *agape* to us, and our understanding of the divine loive itself is modified also by making room for an element of mutuality, and hence also for Aristotle's friendship love. The step is thus taken from a monotheistic to a trinitarian understanding of the divine *agape*. Precisely in relation to the mutuality of relations between the trinitarian persons, each of which seeks the glorifying of the other, the Trinity shows itself to be the expression and form of the divine love that constitutes the divine life. If there were not this mutuality in the relation between God and us, if in faith we stood before God merely as recipients of the divine love, how could it be said that the love of God is poured into our hearts (Rom. 5:5)? There is an element of mutuality here. If we love

God, we can understand this only as the work of love, which God himself is, in his creatures. But this creative and reconciling love of God also makes it possible that creatures should freely love the Creator by relating to him as Father. We love God by letting him be God to us as Jesus let the Father be God to him, by letting him be *our* God, *our* Father, and thus by putting our trust and confidence in him." (ST III, 192 – 193)

The Trinitarian understanding of divine love, according to which the love of God for humans, in which faith trusts hopefully, sets free human responsive love for God and thus a moment of mutuality, is that which allows, according to Pannenberg, not only that one can think of the katabatic love of God with the anabatic love as connected. This itself allows space next to the idea of Christian *agape* and next to Aristotelian *philia* for the Platonic *eros* striving after the good and the beautiful. Also, it makes possible a corresponding understanding of the love for the neighbor, which is differentiated from but inseparably connected to the love for God. This is to be understood as a participation in the dynamic of the love of God for the world, as it is grounded in the participation in Jesus' filial relationship to the Father through the power of the divine Spirit in the love for God of the believer. The interest, caused by reformation theology, to differentiate love and faith in an analogous sense to faith and works, is thus in Pannenberg's opinion preserved, without endangering the inner unity of faith and love. This also avoids reserving the idea of love for the inter-human relationship of humans and referring to the human relation to God exclusively with the idea of faith, not bringing this into connection with the idea of love. The loving participation in divine love, to which the faith which trusts in God is freed, is the condition of possibility for a neighbor-love which loves the neighbor for his or her own sake. For self-acknowledgement as well as the acknowledgment of the neighbor as one to be loved for his or her own sake find their steady ground only in God.

That God's love for humans is the presupposition for the human's love for God, himself, others, and the world, is handled again in an individual section on love and grace. With this, in detailed analysis of the traditional gestalts of the doctrine of grace, it is made clear that the gift of grace given by the Spirit of God is that very sharing gift in the filial relationship of Jesus to the Father, which allows the believers to be in Christ and the divine love and allows the divine love and Christ to be in the believer. "The Spirit by whom believers are 'in Christ' and by whom, therefore, Christ also lives in us, is the same Spirit by whom the love of God fills our hearts. Grace is not a quality or power that is different from Jesus Christ and that is imparted to us; it is Jesus Christ himself…as the gift of divine love (Rom. 8:32) to whom believers are conformed by the Spirit (8:29) as they are drawn into his filial relation to the Father and thus reconciled to God and freed to participate in God's love for the world." (ST III, 202)

Faith, hope, and love are what they are in the execution of ecstatic self-transcendence, as the Spirit achieves. In a Spirit-caused ecstatic manner, the most concentrated mode of which is Christian *prayer* (the treatment of which Pannenberg thus deliberately assigns to pneumatology [cf. ST III, 202–210]), faith, hope, and love have a real share in the filial relationship of Jesus Christ to the Father. Being a child of God is thus the comprehensive idea which unites faith, hope, and love in a differentiated manner. *How does the fact that the Christian is a child of God relate to justification?* In answering this question, Pannenberg closes his examination of the fundamental salvific effects of the Spirit in the individual Christian.[11] First, it is made explicit, that the doctrine of justification is neither in Paul nor in the remaining New Testament the only form of expressing the salvation given in Jesus Christ, but rather is one form among others in the explication of this topic. Also, the Pauline doctrine of justification has only in western Christendom central importance for the understanding of salvation, under the influence particularly of Augustine. Regarding that student of Augustine named Luther, the foundation for his understanding of justification is built by the ecstatic communion of faith with Christ, which preserves the real participation in His righteousness and thus on the righteousness of God, and which grounds the freedom of the children of God.[12] "Righteousness here is one of the blessings of salvation in which believers share by their relation to Christ. Other blessings are wisdom, sanctification, life, and salvation itself. The whole life of Christians in faith might be described as being in Christ. Always basic in this regard is our Christian being 'outside ourselves,' and with this also the distinction between Christ and believers. Only because as believers we live beyond ourselves in Chrsit in recognition of this distinction, and in the self-transcendence of the act of faith, does Christ also live in us." (ST III, 217)

The real participation of the believer in the reality of Jesus Christ rests in its unity with Christ beyond oneself, and in this reality it is to be called ontic. This raises the question, "how this matter relates to the empirical reality of believers 'in themselves.' What we read of here are only initial effects of faith fellowship with Christ and his righteousness in the lives of believers. In their empirical existence, then, believers share in the righteousness that is theirs in

---

11 Cf. in this context also Pannenberg's position on the common declaration on the doctrine of justification from October 31, 1999: 1. Die Gemeinsame Erklärung zur Rechtfertigungslehre aus evangelischer Sicht, in: J.B. Hilberath and W. Pannenberg (eds.), Zur Zukunft der Ökumene. Die "Gemeinsame Erklärung zur Rechtfertigungslehre", 1999, 70–78; reprinted in BSTh 3, 289–294. 2. Neue Konsense, entschärfte Gegensätze und protestantische Ängste, in: IDEA 5.2.1998; reprinted in BSTh 3, 295–299. 3. Thesen zur "Gemeinsamen Erklärung zur Rechtfertigungslehre", in: Evangelisches Gemeindeblatt für Württemberg 93 (1998) Nr. 6, S. 4; reprinted in BSTh 3, 300–302.

12 The most important inheritance of the Reformation is, according to Pannenberg, the thought of Christian freedom. "…the doctrine of justification is only the theological formulation and grounding of this freedom." (Reformation und Einheit der Kirche, in: EvKom 1975, 587–593; reprinted in EuE, 254–267, here 260. Cf. also BSTh 3, 173–185). For the systematic explication of this inheritance, cf. among others the contributions in the collection "Gottesgedanke und menschliche Freiheit", 1972, in particular: Anthropologie und Gottesfrage, op.cit. 9–28.

Christ outside themselves only inasmuch as there is imputed to them, as regards their empirical constitution, that which they are in Christ." (ST III, 217 – 218) From this context, to which among other things Luther's difficult-to-understand phrase *"simul iustus et peccator"* belongs, is the place which Pannenberg finds it can be made clear why the thought of eccentric communion with Christ in theology of justification can connect to the concept of forensic imputation of the righteousness of Christ. As the being of the Christian in Christ is, despite all possible and commanded advancement, continually in a state of becoming as at the beginning in the empirical life of the Christian, God counts the righteousness of Christ to the benefit of the Christian, respectively faith to righteousness. In the thought of Melanchthon and broad sections of the Protestant Orthodoxy the theory of imputation became independent in a manner different from the theory of Luther, although the forensic justification definitely included an effective making-righteous in one manner or another.[13] The latter fact shows, according to Pannenberg, "that the purely forensic interpretation of the act of justification, if understood as the basis of our righteousness before God, goes hand in hand with supplementation by ideas of a real renewal, for otherwise the divine verdict on us would remain external. Luther's description of justification as an expression of fellowship in faith with Christ is not affected, however, by that kind of objection because in the act of faith we are wholly in Christ and are thus renewed in ourselves. Luther's statements do raise the question how the two aspects, our being *extra nos* in Christ and our being in ourselves, are to be understood as related aspects of one and the same person." (ST III, 219)

After the examination of the decree on justification of Trent leads to the result, that "the central difference that remains between the council's teaching and the various forms of the Reformation doctrine is the different evaluation of the significance of faith on one side, and the sacramental mediation of incorporation into Christ on the other," (ST III, 221 – 222) Pannenberg returns to the "difficult question" (ST III, 219) under the aspect of the righteousness of faith and in particular the connection between Baptism and faith.

Regarding the role of faith in justification, it is doubtless from the Pauline witness that faith itself is righteousness that is valid before God. To justify means accordingly for Paul, to declare the believer righteous for the sake of his faith in Jesus Christ. "[I]f we follow Paul the *declaring* righteous cannot be regarded as the basis of the righteousness of believers but already presupposes this. In Rom. 3;26 God *declares* righteous those who are so on the basis of faith." (ST III, 223 – 224) Not so, as if faith were the instance of acceptance of the divine judgment of righteousness, but much more that the judgment of

---

13 To the relation between the acceptation-doctrine of Duns Scotus and the Reformation doctrine of justification, cf. the contribution in C. Bérubé (ed.), Regnum hominis et regnum Dei. Acta quarti congressus scotistici internationalis, Volume I, 1978, 213 – 218; reprinted in BSTh 3, 268 – 274.

righteousness has faith as its object. The decree of righteousness is thus not a creative judgment and "not a 'synthetic' judgment that links the predicate of righteousness to a subject that has no righteousness. Instead, believers are righteous before God in virtue of their faith and for this reason they are declared righteous. This verdict is wholly analytical. It corresponds to the fact to which it refers, not in the sense of anticipating an initiated making righteous of sinners in themselves as the3ir moral renewal, but as a verdict on them as believers." (ST III, 224 f.)[14]

With this, though, the problem of the unity of the newly constituted ego *extra se* and the empirical ego in the temporal course of life in the believer becomes virulent again. Pannenberg takes up this problem with renewed reliance on Paul, that the judgment of God which declares the faithful to be righteous must be an end-times judgment "which in virtue of their relationship with Jesus Christ has been passed already for believers, although…the resultant waiting for eschatological salvation will end only at Christ's return." (ST III, 223) The divine decree of righteousness thus has an anticipatory character and corresponds with Baptism as its constitutive sign of effectiveness. In connection with Paul Althaus, Pannenberg can call the doctrine of Baptism "a doctrine of justification in concrete form" (ST III, 233) and at the same time astoundingly note "the link between baptism and justification has played hardly any role at all in the development of the doctrine of justification in Reformation churches." (*Ibid.*) As a Spirit effected sign of the communion with Christ, Baptism give the believer a real share in the filial relationship of Jesus to His divine Father and lets the believer in this manner participate in the eschatological life of God Himself, so that the believer might live in his temporal existence under empirical conditions as a child of God by grace.

In this sense, Baptism is the foundational execution of justification, although it must be added, that the event of justification (at least in the gestalt of the forgiveness of sins) is only one moment in the occasion of Baptism and does not exhaust the fullness that surrounds the entirety of human existence. The statement of justification in the sense that God declares the believer to be righteous retains the particular function, to allow the baptized Christian as a believer and not yet completed individual the certainty now already of participation in eschatological salvation. "This assurance is also related to the participation of the baptized in Christ's filial relation. But the statement about justification, which expressly calls faith the form of righteousness before God, also delimits faith from every human attempt to get right with God and the self

---

14 To repeat the decisive sentence, it is valid "that the factual righteousness is the foundation of the declaration of righteousness, not the other way around" (Die Rechtfertigungslehre im ökumenischen Gespräch, in: ZThK 88 [1991], 232–246; reprinted in BSTh 3, 275–288, here: 288). However, the factual righteousness of the Christian does not consist of his own works, but in faith in Jesus Christ and in the righteousness of God revealed in Him. The believer is righteous, because he has in faith a share in Christ and thus in the righteousness of God. Due to this participation, he is declared righteous by God.

by human power or action, or even to get right with self alone in this way...The formula of the righteousness of faith clings to the fact that the Christian life as a whole is a life in faith, the faith that lifts us up above ourselves to fellowship with Jesus Christ and therein also to hope and love, but always in such a way that participation in the life of divine love is sustained by ecstatic faith and only thus protected against corruption into human self-relatedness." (ST III, 236)

3. The Sign-Nature of the Salvific Presence of Christ in the Life of the Church

The Spirit-effected communion of the individual with Jesus Christ in faith, hope, and love and his participation on the relation of the Son with the Father, which is allowed him through the individual status of a child of God, is not an unmediated direct communion, but one which is mediated through the church, specifically, through the worship life determined by the execution of signifying actions. In this the ecclesial mediation of the directness of the status of child of God in faith, hope, and love does not make its directness impossible; it is in contrast so that it allows the individual Christian to reach a direct relationship to Jesus Christ and His divine Father by the power of the Holy Spirit. The God-immediacy of the individual, however, due to its mediated character cannot be understood in the sense of a solipsistic individualism. Instead, it must be seen as a belonging to the Spirit and the people of God as well as being a member of the Church as the body of Christ in the sense of ecclesiological parity and the common origin of individuality and sociality.

The individuality of the individual Christian in his singularity and incomparable particularity does not go without saying. It is grounded in the ecclesial execution of *Baptism*,[15] which, as an effective sign of faith, hope, and love, mediates the directness of the state of being a child of God and thus the absolutely singular, because God-grounded, individuality of the individual. Baptism is "an act that constitutes the new existence of Christians as these individuals" (ST III, 237), which includes this individual in the community of the church in the confirmation and preservation of singular individuality. While the sinfully perverted being of the old Adam is determined by the

---

15 "The rebirth of the human in baptism grounds an eschatologically final new determination of the indentity as a person, which at the same time must be caught up to by the process of the formation of identity in the course of human life." (BSTh 2, 8). This thesis is developed in detail in "Identität und Wiedergeburt", in: O. Marquard and K. Stierle (eds.), Identität (Poetik und Hermeneutik VIII), 1979, 607–611; reprinted in BSTh 2, 170–174. Cf. further: Christsein und Taufe, in: Christliche Spiritualität. Theologische Aspekte, 1986, 48–58.

opposites of self-being and otherness and through destructive antagonisms that are necessarily connected with these opposites, Baptism frees one from this perverted wrongdoing in which the *peccatum originale* lurks and constitutes a new, Christian identity. Baptism does this through granting to the baptized in a significatorily effective manner and through faith, hope and love the participation in the filial relationship of Jesus to His divine Father and thus in the Trinitarian life of God. As the baptized gains through Baptism a personal share in the filial relationship of Jesus to the Father as the constitutive ground of his identity, he has a real share in the whole context of relation, in particular the reality of cross and resurrection. Baptism occurs in the manner of a *mortificatio* of the old Adam into Jesus Christ's suffering and death, that it might in the power of the Spirit of the Easter glory of the resurrected crucified One bring about a *vivificatio* to take part in the new human existence. By connecting one to the death on the cross of the resurrected one, Baptism anticipates the death of the baptized in a significantly effective manner and identifies the eschatological whole of one's temporally extended life history proleptically. Baptism is thus not something for the mere beginning of a life, throughout the course of which it slides into ever-greater historical distance, but rather it encloses the entire earthly course of life for the baptized.

The meaning-content of Baptism, which effects the entire earthly course of life for the baptized, and in which the essential uniqueness and unrepeatability is founded, offers Pannenberg the opportunity to examine the relationship of *repentance* to Baptism, and in this context also that to *confirmation* and *the anointing of the sick*, which he interprets as concentrated forms of Christian Baptism remembrance. The relationship between Baptism and repentance is examined in its historical development, including the traditional controversy regarding the problem of post-Baptismal concupiscence. Systematically, it is judged that this relationship is one of differentiated unity, insofar as contrition and conversion to God exist in Baptism in a one-and-for-all manner, yet at the same time must be practiced in daily remorse and repentance, that the reality of Baptism is made real in the temporal course of the life of the baptized. Repentance is the daily appropriation of the unique conversion undertaken in Baptism. The uniqueness of the act of Baptism and the relation of it to the entire path of the Christian life present a connection. For, with the *perfectum praesens* of Baptism "our baptismally based new identity as Christians is set 'outside' the old humanity but is lived out physically in it, so that our lives are destined to be absorbed by the new identity and transformed into it." (ST III, 253) This essentially paraphrases the idea of Christian repentance, and, at the same time, give the foundation for the critical and constructive judgment of the traditional ecclesial institute of repentance, and, if necessary, to reform this latter.[16]

16 For the topic of Protestant repentance piety, cf. "Protestantische Bußfrömmigkeit" in: Christliche Spiritualität, 1986, 5 – 25. Pannenberg contrasts the one-sided orientation of penetential

Repentance is, in all possible forms, a remembrance of Baptism.[17] This is valid, *mutatis mutandis* for the possible practice of the anointing of the sick as well as to the *conformatio* which originally belonged to the rite of Baptism. The ritual separation of confirmation from Baptism is a historical consequence of the general spread of paedobaptism and an indication of the unity of Baptism and confirmation, which is to be preserved even under changed circumstances. Pannenberg stresses the unity: "In all circumstances the appropriation by the baptized is part of baptism." (ST III, 265)[18] accordingly differentiated is the judgment regarding the ecclesial practice of paedobaptism, which, if one wished to declare it the only possible form of Baptism would have to declare a large portion of the practice of the early church as discredited. The foundational admissibility of paedobaptism is, in Pannenberg's opinion, nonetheless given, as Baptism by nature does aim at the faith of the receiver, but does not necessarily presuppose said faith, "because in any case faith can only *receive* baptism" (ST III, 262).

As gift and reception, so do Baptism "as the reconstitution of the person and…faith as the appropriating of baptism in its outworking" (ST III, 275) belong inseparably together. With this, Baptism is "the actual reconstitution of the person in the form of the sacramental sign. As an anticipatory sign of the whole life history of the baptized in terms of its end it is referred to its outworking by appropriation of its content in faith. But this outworking is itself possible only in the light of baptism, and at each moment is knows that it is a work of the Spirit who is given by baptism. In other words, the appropriation and outworking of baptism are done *by Christians*, i.e., by subjects newly constituted in the act of baptism, not subjects that are supposedly present already behind all experience and that remain the same as its contents change. For by baptism believers come into relation to the death and resurrection of Jesus Christ, and as Christ's Spirit reminds Christians of Jesus (John 14:26; 16:13 ff.) he also assures them of their own identity on the basis of baptism. In this regard their new subjectivity does not have the form of a self-identity that in virtue of self-familiarity stands opposed to all that is not the self. Participation in the relation of the Son to the Father by the Spirit changes the structure of self-identity itself." (ST III, 274–275)

The developed understating of the relation between Baptism and faith rests on the presupposition that Baptism, which promises to lead the human to his destiny of eschatological completion as a creature set up for this, is, as God's

---

piety on the problem of the guild of sin and its removal with his forms of Eucharistic piety, as they have become alive in the course of the ecumenical movement and in the evangelical churches (Eucharistische Frömmigkeit – eine neue Erfahrung der Gemeinschaft der Christen, in: op.cit., 26–47.

17 To the form of Christian repentance as remembrance of Baptism, cf. among other "Christsein und Taufe" in: Die eine Kirche. Evangelische Katholizität (*festschrift* for H.-J. Mund), 1984, 58–65; reprinted in BSTh 3, 65–73 (cf. Christliche Spiritualität, Göttingen 1986, 48–58).

18 Pannenberg's original German refers to the appropriation of faith, *Glaubensaneignung*. – Trans.

gift, donated by God Himself. "Can we justify this premise?" (ST III, 275) Pannenberg answers this question positively, though he would rather derive the practice of Baptism from the Baptism of Jesus by John than from the commandment in Matt. 29:19 or the word of promise in Mark 16:16 due to the historical-critical problems. This Baptism, as is demonstrated by early church tradition, the foundation and origin of Christian Baptism. As the historical Jesus saw a connection between the martyrdom that stood before Him and His disciples and the water Baptism of John, it produces the meaning which was taken up again in the early church, that Baptism is a dying with Jesus, through which the baptized is connected anticipatorily in faith with the holiness of the resurrected crucified One.

The sociality of the Christian life, which is a necessary part of its individuality, also does not go without saying, just as the God-grounded singularity of the individual Christian. The sociality is grounded in the *effective sign of the Lord's Supper,* in the execution of which the church sees its ground of constitution as a community of faith, hope, and love in the gestalts of bread and wine. This is given to each individual Christian, so that the communion of the body and blood of Christ is grounded and received. As the function of Baptism was to be understood already implicitly as the constitution of the church communion through the completed integration into the body of Christ, this situation becomes explicit in the Lord's Supper. Conversely, the Lord's Supper as the functional sign of the body of Christ refers back to Baptism, which grants each individual communion with Christ. Baptism and Holy Communion are thus in a mutual relationship of implication and explication. "By baptism we become members of Christ and his body, and the celebration of the Lord's Supper renews the church's fellowship by representing and repeating its grounding in the supper of the Lord." (ST III, 292)[19]

As in the case of Baptism, Pannenberg sees it as necessary for the founding of the celebration of the Lord's Supper that one refer to the entirety of the Jesus tradition, and not limit the definition to the tradition of the Last Supper in the night of Jesus' betrayal.[20] One must think especially of the celebrated meals which the earthly Jesus held as a central, symbolic act, in order to give

---

19 The importance of Baptism and the Lord's Supper for Christian spirituality has been worked out in "Baptism as remembered 'ecstatic' identity", in: D. Brown /A. Loades: Christ. The Sacramental Word. Incarnation, Sacrament and Poetry, London (SPCK) 1996, 77 – 88. Cf. also BSTh 3, 74 – 85.

20 "Dogmatics would do well to make the thought of the initiation of the Lord's Supper as so broadly that the unsolved historical questions regarding the course of events of the last meal of Jesus are not prejudiced, but remain open. One cannot, however, relinquish a continuity of the meal celebration of the early church with Jesus such that this is the historical development of the core inaugurated by Jesus himself, so long as one is not prepared to give upt the claim of an initiation of the Lord's Supper by Jesus." (Die Problematik der Abendmahlslehre aus evangelischer Sicht. Ein Beitrag zum ökumenischen Gespräch über das Abendmahl, in: Evangelisch-katholische Abendmahlsgemeinschaft?, 1971, 9 – 45; reprinted in EuE, 293 – 317, here: 297)

symbolic presentation to His message of the proximity of the Kingdom of God. The meal-practice of the earthly One gives us not only a framework for the Last Supper of Jesus in its referentiality to the coming death for the sake of the Kingdom of God, but also gives the example for the post-Easter meal celebrations of the early church, in which was celebrated the living salvific presence of the One crucified and resurrected for the eschatological salvation of humanity and the world.

How the living salvific presence of the resurrected crucified One is to be grasped precisely in the worship celebration of the Lord's Supper, which shows the church the ground of her own being, is explained by Pannenberg in a detailed treatment of the doctrine of transubstantiation and its theoretical forms of refutation. In this, he defines the mode of Eucharistic presence of Jesus Christ as a whole and unseparated personal presence, regardless of the command *communion sub utraque specie*, that belongs to the completeness of a sacramental sign also according to Vatican II, and in contrast to an objective understanding of the presence of body and blood in the elements of bread and wine. This is explained through an examination of the signifying character of the meal-actions of Jesus in connection with an appropriation of theories of the so-called transsignification or transfinalization. In the change in meaning of bread and wine, as it is in the Eucharistic celebration, it is, as was said, a matter of a genuine change in being, insofar as the change in meaning which occurs is not merely in the intentions of the celebrants, but in the situation itself. Accordingly, it is a matter in the liturgical gestalt of the celebration of the Lord's Supper (that of Anamnesis) not merely an act of human remembrance, but rather a matter of Jesus Christ making Himself present through His Spirit, to which the liturgical Epiclesis refers and is laid out as the correlate of Anamnesis. By the means of His making Himself present, through which He shows Himself as the living subject of His remembrance by the power of the Holy Spirit, the Lord of the Meal is genuinely present in the reality of His earthly life history as elated through the Easter participation in the eternal life of God. The presence of Jesus Christ in Communion is thus to be thought of as in the differentiated unity of His glorified Person and the life history given to the coming of the Kingdom of God and leading to the cross – not as an immediate descent of the ascended One in the elements. With this, there is not only a constructive relation between the celebration of the Meal and the Kingdom of God, but also one with the sacrifice on the cross, the reality of which in the Lord's Supper is neither repeated nor added to, but very much made present in the gestalt of the resurrected crucified One as once-and-for-all having occurred. "Inasmuch as part of this is that the death of Jesus has the character of an expiatory offering, the community shares in this as it recalls it at celebrations of the Supper." (ST III, 315) This, of course, does not occur such that the sufficiency of the reconciliatory death of Jesus is limited or relativized. Much more, those who receive the Meal of the Lord in faith receive the real communion with the resurrected crucified One and are thus brought in to His filial relationship with the Father. To this belongs inseparably the obedient giving of the self, as it was done on the cross, and the recipient is completely embraced by the Father-love of God.

In the Lord's Supper, the ground of her being is present to the church. Through the reception of the Holy Meal and the gaining of a share in the body of Christ, the faithful are connected to one another and united as the body of Christ, which the church is destined to be. The Lord's Supper and church congregation belong in "close material connection" (ST III, 325). This is confirmed through the fact that the Last Supper of Jesus was, according to New Testament tradition, not held as an open congregatory meal, but was a meal for the circle of disciples. Thus Pannenberg rejects the occasionally demanded and practiced lack of limitation in admission to Communion, and reserves it for baptized Christians. Just as the circle of disciples of Jesus, the church membership and the Lord's Supper are principally open to all humans, as all humans are called to be disciples of Jesus. However, "being a disciple" (*Jüngerschaft*) without discipleship (*Nachfolge*), and with this, without the readiness to accept the gift of Baptism, is unthinkable. If, thus, only the baptized are invited to the Lord's Supper, then this invitation is valid – insofar as there are no grave issues of church discipline which speak against it – for all baptized, with all possible inclusion of children. No church can and may of itself take the invitation of Christ to His Meal and "restrict [it] to its own historically particular fellowship"[21] (ST III, 329). With this is presupposed, that the Eucharistic communion with God, as the prototypical gestalt of church, has an inalienable connection to the Church Universal, just as the Church Universal conversely, in its catholicity transcending the limits of time and space, is unable to exist without the concrete local congregations of worship. To be added is that the donatory nature of the Lord's Supper never occurs speechlessly, but that the words of institution belong to it constitutively. As the epitome of the Gospel, these can only be understood when they are connected with the word-proclamation of the sermon, which explicates their meaning. Of course, the proclamation of the Gospel is not limited to the Eucharistic worship service. At the same time, proclamation is organized towards it in all its forms, insofar it unfolds through proclamation of the eschatological future of the arrived One the sense of exactly that event which is celebrated in the Meal of the resurrected crucified One in Anamnesis and Epiclesis.[22]

---

21 The Eucharist is "not only expression and sign of already existing ecclesial unity, but also the source and root from which the unity of Christians lives and will always be renewed. This speaks for the opinion, that the Eucharistic communion need not stand first at the goal of the process of ecclesial unification, but rather can also be the present power of Christ for the way to this goal." (Das Abendmahl – Sakrament der Einheit, in: Christen wollen das eine Abendmahl, 1971, 29–39; reprinted in EuE, 286–292, here: 287)

22 Cf. as a whole "Die Problematik der Abendmahlslehre aus evangelischer Sicht. Ein Beitrag zum

Baptism and the Lord's Supper have long, when not from the beginning, been called *Sacraments*. The Greek term *mysterion*, which is translated as *sacramentum* in the old Latin Bible translation, is encountered only in Eph. 5:32 in connection with something later called a "Sacrament", namely, marriage. The central content of meaning of the term *mysterion* in the New Testament is in its eschatological importance, which is connected to a Christological importance insofar as the history of Jesus, especially His passion, is conceived of in the light of Easter as an anticipation of the eschaton. It is within this frame of reference that the transition of the idea of mystery or Sacrament at the turn of the second to the third century to referring to Baptism and the Lord's Supper can be understandable. "By them the eschatological salvation that Christ's passion effected is now accessible." (ST III, 347 – 348) With this, it should be noted, "that baptism and the Lord's Supper are not called 'sacraments' on their own but only with reference to the passion of Christ that by them is present for our salvation." (ST III, 348) The sacraments find their unity in the salvific mystery of Jesus Christ, and not in a preconceived general notion of the sacramental. A general idea of the sacramental, such as in the normal manner since Augustine, of a genus for symbolic action, stands in danger of at least loosening the connection of the so-called Sacraments with the divine mystery of salvation. Pannenberg pleads according, that we use the term Sacrament merely as "a matter of actions or states of life that are there independently of what they are later called comprehensively" (ST III, 338). The controversial theological weight of the confessionally argued number of the Sacraments is thus "a much less important [issue]" (*Ibid.*). This is all the more valid, as in the evangelical churches next to Baptism and Lord's Supper, which were already in the scholastic period referred to as *sacramenta maiora* or *principiala*, the practice of anointing of the sick is practiced, although merely in a facultative manner, which means that a ritual action is performed which is referred to as a Sacrament beyond the Orthodox and Roman Catholic theology.

Regarding the question about institution, Pannenberg holds, in contrast to a theory of outsourcing the individual Sacraments from a "root Sacrament" of the church, and despite the existing historical-critical problems, the "proof of a special institution of each sacrament by Jesus Christ himself" (ST III, 341) to be essential, "since sacraments impart grace and Christians cannot think that any other than Jesus Christ can do this. So long as we hold fast to this function of the sacraments, we have to insist that only God himself in Jesus Christ can institute a sacrament of the new covenant. In his function as the source of grace and reconciliation, Jesus Christ stands inviolably over against the church as the Head of his body." (*Ibid.*) Regardless of and taking explicitly into account his own demand for a special initiatory proof for the individual

ökumenischen Gespräch über das Abendmahl, in: Evangelisch-katholische Abendmahlsgemeinschaft?, 1971, 9 – 45; reprinted in EuE, 293 – 317.

Sacraments, Pannenberg holds it as for inevitable and factually commanded, due to the given exegetical problems, to grasp the *idea of institution* as wider than was traditionally the case. In the course of his expansion, the idea of initiation no longer needs "an express saying of Jesus along the lines of the command to baptize or the command to repeat the Supper. Instead, we simply have to show that the Supper and baptism go back to Jesus inasmuch as their early Christian origins may be understood as a result of data in the history and practices of Jesus in the light of the Easter event." (ST III, 344) This is the case with the Lord's Supper as well as with Baptism. Analogous to the canon of the New Testament, which the church "imposed" upon itself in the second century through the obligatory evidence of its content as an original witness of Christ, "the Lord's Supper and baptism imposed themselves on the disciples of Jesus in virtue of their experience of the history of the Lord. In this sense we may say that God instituted baptism and the Lord 's Supper by Jesus Christ and in the power of his Spirit. Along these lines we give a Trinitarian formulation for the institution instead of basing it exclusively on the historical Jesus. Nevertheless, we also maintain the link to the person of Jesus and above all the thought of a divine institution. Baptism and the Lord's Supper are not creations of the primitive church, they are not purely human inventions. God himself has established them in connection with his saving revelation in Jesus Christ." (ST III, 344)

If then the demonstrable belonging to the salvific mystery of Jesus Christ, whose presence for the faithful is opened in a signifying effective manner by the Holy Spirit, is the criterion for the sacramentatilty of Baptism and the Lord's Supper, which themselves in a different but united manner connect with Christ, then the question is raised, whether along with them the Christ mystery finds presentation in the life of the church in other ritual under-takings. Pannenberg's answer is necessarily differentiated, as the possible use of a general idea of Sacrament, as has been said, does not allow one to overlook the difference which prevail between Baptism and the Lord's Supper as well as (greater) between these and the actions referred to as Sacraments in parts of the Christian tradition beyond these. However, Pannenberg – induced in particular by the relationship in Eph. 5:32 of marriage and the Christ mystery (cf. ST III, 358 – 364) – is not fundamentally opposed to an expansion of the understanding of Sacrament which would stretch it out to include confirma-tion, penance, and anointing of the sick on one side and ordination and marriage on the other. Confirmation, penance, and the anointing of the sick participate, as concrete forms of the baptismal event, "as it were, in the sacramentality of baptism as they articulate and communicate its relevance for life at important points – independent acceptance of the baptismal confession, renewed forgiveness of sins, and relationship with Christ in suffering and death." (ST III, 357) In a comparable mediated manner can *marriage* and *ordination* be brought into connection with the idea of Sacrament, which is not immediate to them. In this, the Lord's Supper – the Sacrament of the Christ-communion of all faithful – functions as the decisive point of reference, insofar as marriage and ordination each in their own way can be sights of that which is signified in the Eucharist: "In every case the criterion for calling a church action sacramental is whether the content of the action, if not necessarily the action itself, has its origin in Jesus Christ, and whether it has the function of a sign that expresses the mystery of Christ that unites Jesus Christ and his church." (ST III, 367 – 368) Otherwise, one should note the specific character-istic individuality of each situation and symbolic action respectively, from which the argumentation takes its starting point. This is analogously valid for the differentiated relationship of sacramental implementation to the imple-mentation of the proclamation of the Word, which itself is variously differentiated. So much as Word and Sacrament belong inseparably together and as much as a Sacrament without the word could never be a Sacrament, so little are Sacraments "simply...illustrations and embodiments of the salvation already pronounced to us by the Word of promise" (ST III, 351). The proper noun "Sacrament" is thus for many reasons to be preserved.

4. The Office of Leadership as Sign and Tool of the Unity of the Church

To serve the unity of the many in the ecclesial community of faith is the task of those offices in the church connected with ordination. With this, one must assume the task "to proclaim the gospel and to lead in praise of God at liturgical recollection of the event of salvation that is its basis" (ST III, 371), which is given as the plumb line for the ecclesial leadership and the church as a whole. All of the faithful have the common calling to give witness through their speech and actions to the eschatological sending of Jesus Christ and the coming Kingdom of God to which they are elected. "The common task of all Christians to confess their faith and to pass on the gospel message, bearing witness to it with their lives, involves also a common responsibility that this should take place in keeping with the unity of believers in Jesus Christ and therefore in common. Christians would not fulfill the common task if they were to bear witness to Jesus Christ in isolation and even in contradiction with others. The task incumbent on all Christians demands that it be carried out in concert. Common fulfillment has to be observed at celebration of the Eucharist as well as in witness to the faith. But it does not arise spontaneously, nor is it any kind of common fulfillment. It has its basis in the gospel of Jesus Christ. It is always a given for the plurality of church members, but it has also to be posited for the plurality of their individual contributions to the life of the community in order to integrate these into the unity of witness to Christ. An authority that has this function is referred on the one hand to the common faith consciousness of church members but represents to them on the other hand the unity of the commission of Jesus Christ in which that consciousness is itself grounded and from which it must be constantly renewed." (ST III, 375)

The specific difference between the ecclesial office of leadership, which is grounded in ordination, and the commission in which all of the baptized faithful participate commonly in the participation of the priesthood of Christ, consists essentially of the ordered service to the "unity of the community in the faith of the gospel in spite of all the differences among members and among the gifts conferred on them by the Spirit." (ST III, 387 – 388).[23] This official service is ordered by God Himself and not merely a function of the individual will of the congregation. Although the ecclesial office of service, as it found prototypical expression in the local congregation Episcopal office of early Christendom, does not lead back directly to "an order that the apostles set up to appoint successors" (ST III 378) and cannot factually be compared to the apostolic office, it does have in its own manner a share in the apostolic task to serve the unity of the congregation in the Gospel through doctrine and leadership, with which the postapostolic office holders are given the norm of the apostolic Gospel for their service. The functions of teaching and leadership build a differentiated unity, insofar the assignment of official teaching of the Gospel is connected to an assignment of leadership, which in its case it perceived primarily in the form of the *doctrina evangelii*. The particularity of the ecclesial office of teaching and leadership is, to come back to the starting point of the argumentation, in the reformation tradition well known to be characterized by the mark of publicity.[24] Pannenberg takes up this

---

23 For Pannenberg's ecumenical understanding of the office, there are significant indications in "Ökumenisches Amtsverständnis", in: Catholica 28 [1974], 140 – 156; reprinted in EuE, 268 – 285. In the center of this examination stands the question of the uniqueness of the office connected to ordination in relation to the priesthood in which all baptized believers participate. "That it is a matter not only of a gradual difference to other functions, but rather of a qualitative and essential uniqueness, on the protestant side no indignation need arise when such an essential difference remains comprised of the life-context of the communion of the faithful." (EuE, 272) in this sense, the specific difference of the ordained office is determined by its leadership service to the unity, away it is characterized by the public perception of the common cause of all Christendom. The uniqueness of the service of leadership in relation to the participation in the sending of Christ that is open to all believers is accordingly characterized by the concept of the public. This idea can integrate that of "*repraesentatio Christi*". "Questionable is only if the thought of the *representatio Christi* already is able to refer to the *uniqueness* of the ordained office. When it is correct, that all Christians have part in the office and sending of Christ through the communion with Christ in faith, then the consequence is, as Luther once wrote, that each is a Christ to the other (unusquisque alteri Chistus quidam fieri). With this is thus no particularity of the ordained office. If the representation of Christ to the faithful were to be exclusively the prerogative of the ordained office, then one would deny the participation of every believer in the mission of Christ, in contrast also to the second Vatican council." (EuE, 279 with reference to WA 7, 66, 3 ff.). cf. further "Die ordination zum kirchlichen Amt" (1988), in BSTh 3, 96 – 99.

24 With its interpretation of the uniqueness of the ordained office of the church, in which the mark of publicness (CA XIV: publice docere) is connected with the necessity of a service to the unity of

aspect and inspects it: the difference between the office of teaching and leadership and the assignment to serves which all baptized Christians participate in does not consist of a special status of grace for the inhabitant of the office of teaching and leadership. Though ordination into this office, the status of parity in grace among all baptized is not dissolved. Also, ordination does not ground any exclusive claim to representation of Christ. It is much more the service of the Gospel *publice* practiced through teaching and leadership to the unity of all that have participation in the priesthood of Christ that grounds the particularity of the ecclesial offices connected to ordination in distinction to the universal priesthood. "The public nature of the church's ministry of preaching and leadership that relates to the unity of the whole church, and that represents it at the level of the local worshiping community, means that ministers do not act in their own name but on the authority of the commission to teach the gospel that is given to the Christian world as a whole, and therefore on the commission of Jesus Christ himself. In this specific sense the church's public ministers act *in persona Christi* and also in the name of Christianity as a whole and of the commission that it was given with the sending out of the apostles." (ST III, 389)

The particular office of the church, into which, according to Pannenberg, men and women can be equally called, is mediated through *ordination*. Referring to this as a Sacrament is, as a rule, in the reformation tradition rejected. This rejection, however, does not succeed (as not only the example of Melanchthon proves) uniformly or for fundamental reasons. If there is agreement regarding the office to which ordination is connected, then the sacramentality of the symbolic act of ordination in evangelical doctrine, carried out through the laying on of hands and prayer, need not be challenged. For in its own way, ordination can be seen as a concretization of the salvific mystery which connects Christ and His church, "even if, unlike baptism, it does not impart justifying grace to the recipients or their institution as children of God, but presupposes already the relationship to Christ and his church that has its basis in baptism." (ST III, 397) That the symbolic action of ordination has effect and communicates a gift of grace is taught explicitly by the reformers, even when this is not referred to as *character* in the sense of an

---

the various levels of ecclesial life, the Lutheran church has, according to Pannenberg, "achieved its most important contribution to the ecumenical understanding of the office" (Das kirchliche Amt in der Sicht der lutherischen Lehre, in: W. Pannenberg (ed.), Lehrverurteilungen – kirchentrennend?, III. Materialien zur Lehre von den Sakramenten und vom kirchlichen Amt, 1990, 286–305; reprinted in BSTh 3, 100–118). For Luther himself the following argument is decisive: "On one hand the task and the power (*potestas*) of proclaiming the Word and administering the sacraments given to all Christians. On the other hand, an individual may, because this power is *common* to all, not make use of it without the agreement of the whole. From this thought, the internal connection of the various, otherwise easily seen as contradictory, statements of Luther regarding the ecclesial office and the universal priesthood of the faithful and the baptized...is opened." (BSTh 3, 109)

impression into the soul of the receiver, but is described as a charisma to service."Thus the gift conferred on ministers by their ordination relates to their function, not to their personal standing in grace." (ST III, 398) However, this has nothing to say against the preservative nature of the acceptance into service of the ordained, but rather for it, as the fact that the churches of the reformation hold fast to the unrepeatability of ordination proves: "As the baptized are baptized once and for all, so the ordained are permanently called to the church's public ministry even though they may cease to exercise their ministry or be inhibited from its exercise." (ST III, 399)

Regarding the authority of ordination as competence and ability to give valid ordination, the reformers, despite the initiation of non-episcopal ordination (which, on the Roman Catholic side, yet today is evaluated as the essential cause of *defectus ordinis* in the interruption of apostolic succession), valued the canonical practice of ordination as a sight for the unity of the church. In deviation from it, one saw merely an exception to the rule in exceptional circumstances, for the sake of the Gospel necessary and legitimate. This found its confirmation not last in the fact that the so-called "'presbyterial' ordination of pastors by pastors as a form, if not the regular form, of Episcopal succession on the ground that the ministries of bishops and presbyters were originally one and the same." (ST III, 401) This fact was valid for the reformers "in agreement with a main line of medieval thinking about ministry in both theology and canon law." (ST III, 402) Pannenberg holds it for unjustified, given these presuppositions, to speak of a lack of or in the *ordo* of the office in the reformation tradition, especially as the latest discussions regarding apostolic succession have been dominated by the insight "that the primary issue is succession in the teaching and faith of the apostles and only secondarily is it a matter of succession in office." (ST III, 403)[25]

In the service of the ecclesial unity the homogenous idea and thus the identity of being for the ecclesial office is grounded. The unity of the church, which is a matter of attributes of the ecclesial being; "it is no accident that unity comes first" (ST III, 405), because the holiness, apostolicity, and catholicity of the church can be understood as implications of their Unity (cf.

---

25 If one proceeds from the roots of the office of bishop in the ancient and early church, then a bishop's function is to be defined as the service to the unity of the local congregation in the teaching of the Gospel. Cf. "Das kirchliche Amt und die Einheit der Kirche", in C. Krieg (ed., among others), Die Theologie auf dem Weg in das dritte Jahrtausend (*festschrift* for J. Moltmann), 1995, 271 – 283; reprinted in BSTh 3, 138 – 149. For the importance of the office of bishop in Lutheran doctrine, cf. further "Lutherans and Episcopacy", in C. Podmore (ed.), Community – Unity – Communion. Essays in Honour of Mary Tanner, 1998, 183 – 188; reprinted in BSTh 3, 150 – 155 as well as "Gospel and Church: The Proposed Concordat between Lutherans and Episcopal Churches in the USA" , in: E. Radner and R. R. Reno, Inhabiting Unity. Theological Perspectives in the Proposed Lutheran-Episcopal Concordat, 1995, 71 – 75; reprinted in BSTh 3, 155 – 159, where Pannenberg deals more precisely with the modern Lutheran-Anglican efforts towards church communion.

in detail ST III, 405 – 415)[26], is in Jesus Christ "both a given fact and a task for the churches of the Christian world. It is a given fact as the fellowship of the body of Christ in faith and the sacraments. It is a task in the sense of being a unity, grounded in Christ, that has to be preserved and renewed." (ST III, 405) The latter is that to which the unified service of the ecclesial office refers, the identity of which is grounded in its task of service. Regardless of the ordination-connected office in one being, the particular structural forms have not developed coincidentally. As the tradition of the reformation recognized the local congregation as the foundational gestalt of the church, the local pastor was seen as the prototype of the ecclesial office holder. However, the legitimacy of the historical development of regional and supra-regional leadership offices was not challenged; these were, in contrast, valued as functionally commanded. In the history of the church, the task of regional and supra-regional ecclesial leadership is given "especially from the 4th century onward…to the bishops. At the same time presbyters had the task at the local level, with a consequent far-reaching change in their ministry. The difference between the ministry of bishops and that of presbyters (acting as local pastors) became the difference between local and regional leadership." (ST III, 416) Opposite this, in early Christendom it was a matter such that "both bishops and presbyters ministers to local churches….the distinction derived from the different roots of the Christian ministry of church leadership in the Jewish and Jewish Christian office of elders on the one hand and in the Pauline churches on the other, where the episcopate and diaconate (Phil. 1:1) arose that related originally to house churches." (ST III, 417) If one acknowledges the historical complexity of the development of ecclesial office structure and the fact that the factually connected office functions given traditional office titles (namely, that of bishop) have changed significantly in the course of history, Pannenberg notes that the goal should be agreement on the fact "that both the modern form of regional episcopacy and the ministry of the presbyter-priest or pastor today have an episcopal character." (ST III, 418 – 419) The distinction between the two offices would then not be a sacramental one, but rather one of episcopal jurisdiction and competence and its range.

---

26 The importance of eschatology for the essential attributes of the church is emphasized by the following, among others: Einheit der Kirche als Glaubenswirklichekit und als ökumenisches Ziel, in: US 30 (1975), 216 – 222; reprinted in EuE 200 – 210; Was bedeutet es für die getrennten Kirchen, sich auf eine gemeinsame Vergangenheit zu beziehen?, in EuE 211 – 218; Die Bedeu-tung der Eschatologie für das Verständnis der Apostolizität und Katholizität der kirche, in: KuD Beiheft 2 (1971), 92 – 109; reprinted in EuE 219 – 240. Both the unity of the church as well as ist apostolicity and catholicity can only be properly understood with reference to the future of the Lord of the church.

While Pannenberg judges the recommendation of a renewal in all Christian churches of the *threefold structure of the ecclesial office* in the sense of the Ignatian scheme of diaconate, presbyteriate and episcopate, as "not very helpful" (ST III, 418), he holds the institutional distinction of an episcopal pastor on the local level and an episcopal bishop on the supra-local level as functionally necessary. This is valid in a comparable manner for the *office of service to the unity of the Church Universal*, though one is not to challenge the special position of the Bishop of Rome. "It is a fact of Christian history that with the end of the primitive Jerusalem church the church of Rome became the historical center of Christianity. If any Christian bishop can speak for the whole church in situations when this may be needed, it will be primarily the bishop of Rome. In spite of all the bitter controversies resulting from chronic misuse of the authority of Rome in power politics, there is here no realistic alternative. The general public no less than most of the churches of the Christian world are aware of this today. We ought freely to admit the fact of the primacy of the Roman Church and its bishop on Christianity. Not the fact itself so much as the way of describing it is the point at issue, along with the question of the implied rights." (ST III, 421)

In taking up the demand of theological reinterpretation and practical reconstitution of the papal office of the Bishop of Rome Pannenberg examines exhaustively the *dogma of infallibility and the primacy of jurisdiction for the Church Universal*, as well as the claim that the primacy of the Bishop of Rome in the church entire exists by the power of Jesus' installment of Peter as the head and rock of the Church in Matt. 16:16 – 18 and John 21:15 – 17 *iure divino*. Due to the exegetical and historical issues, Pannenberg judges this claim as critically as he does the idea of an infallible teaching office. The promise given to the Church as a whole that causes it to remain in truth can never be connected directly with a representative organ for the Church as a whole. Even papal decisions *ex cathedra* are thus necessarily dependant on the reception of the Church as a whole, that they might practically when not necessarily in a formal-juridical manner be seen as definitively valid. "If there is no reception in the long run, then unavoidably the claim of the teaching office that in a given statement it was expressing the faith awareness of the whole church is a dubious one. Nor does the whole church include only the totality of those believers who at a specific time are in communion with Rome. In includes the Christian world as a whole. Given our present fragmented state, it is doubtful, then, whether, in these conditions, any utterances of a supreme teaching office can be recognized as infallible in virtue of an appeal to the representative function of this office vis-à-vis the whole church." (ST III, 428) Regarding ultimately the jurisdiction of the authority for a universal leading office of the Church, this should be essentially constituted by the legal role for the highest unity in inter-church relations. "This is less a function of power (*potestas*) than of the ability to persuade (*auctoritas*). The weight of the pope's authority will grow in the Christian world as a whole the more he advocates reconciliation

both by word and deed in the divided churches and the more he brings the
special needs of suppressed and persecuted portions of the Christian world to
the attention of the whole church." (ST III, 429)[27]

27 Protestant considerations on the Petrine service of the bishop of Rome can be taken from
   "evangelische Überlegungen zum Petrusdienst des römischen Bischofs" in: P. Hünermann
   (ed.), Papsttum und Ökumene. Zum Petrusdienst an der Einheit aller Getauften, 1997, 43–60;
   reprinted in BSTh 3,366–377. Cf. further: Die lutherische Tradition und die Frage eines Petrusdienstes an der Einheit der Christen, in: Il Primato del Sucessore di Pietro. Atti'del Simposio
   teologico Roma diciembre 1996, 1998,472–475; reprinted in BSTh 3,386–388. The latter article
   was, as Pannenberg notes in the foreword to BSTh 3 "Delivered in a consultation organized by
   the Roman congregation of the faith regarding the practicing of the papal primacy in 1996 in
   Rome. I have introduced this text with thought to my position regarding the rejection of the
   concluding report of the Anglican and Roman Catholic commission on the papal office." (BSTh
   3,10. Cf. Der Schlussbericht der anglikanisch-römisch-katholischen Internationalen Kommis-
   sion und seine Beurteilung durch die römsiche Glaubenskongregation in: KuD 29 (1983), 166–
   173; reprinted in BSTh 3,378–385, here; 384 f.: In reading this position, the Christians of the
   churches which are separated from Rome cannot reject the conclusion that the old concept of the
   goal of Christian reunification through a simple return to Rome is still not overcome.") – That
   the universal ecclesial premacy in the context of a communio-ecclesiology can be called in
   connection with LG18 and 23 "Principium et fundamentum of the unity of the church" is
   rejected by Pannenberg (cf. "Kirche als Gemeinschaft der Glaubenden", in BSTh 3,11–22, here:
   17).

§7 The Doctrine of Election and Eschatology (ST III, Chapters 14 and 15)

1. The People of God and the History of Humanity

As the community of those who are brought together[1] through Word and Sacrament to the *communio sanctorum* and the body of Christ as He effectively is presented in the Lord's Supper, the church is at the same time the people of God to which people of all nations despite their ethnic or other social differences belong by virtue of their faithful share in the status as children of God mediated by the filial relationship of Jesus to the Father. The idea of the people of God functions in Pannenberg's concept as a mediating idea between ecclesiology and the doctrine of election, as it belongs to both sections of doctrine and can connect both factually.[2] In its conveyance, the doctrine of election is assigned the function to "supplement that of the church. It will do so from the standpoint of the concrete historical form that the essential being of the church takes in the world. For election involves sending, and sending directs the elect into the world and into its history, which is moving toward the future of the reign of God." (ST III, 434)[3]

---

1 To the communio-ecclesiology concept of the church "as a community in which the faithful are unified among each other through the Eucharistic participation of each one in the body of Christ" cf. "Kirche als Gemeinschaft der Glaubenden" (1996) in BSTh 3,11 – 22, here: 13. The event of Eucharistic celebration functions, according to Pannenberg, at the same time as the key for the understanding of the connection between local congregations and the Church Universal: "As all participants of the worship service receive the one body of Christ along with the bread, they are, according to Paul, also connected among one another in the unity of the body of Christ. That, however, occurs not only in the individual local congregations, rather everywhere, where the Eucharist is celebrated. The body of Christ which is present in the worship of the local congregation unites the participants with all others who believe in the same Jesus Christ and who are connected with His body through Baptism and Lord's Supper." (BSTh 3,15)

2 "With the topic of the people of God a concrete historical conception of election has remained effective in the Christian tradition, which is deeply different from the individual perspective of the classic doctrine of election." (Erwählung und Volk Gottes, in: Die Bestimmung des Menschen. Menschsein, Erwählung und Geschichte, 1978, 41 – 60, here: 58)

3 To the ecclesiological, religio-political, and theological-historical implications of the thought of election cf. the three concluding chapters of the book "Die Bestimmung des Menschen. Menschsein, Erwählung und Geschichte", 1978, 41 – 113: 1. Erwählung und Volk Gottes. 2. Das christliche Imperium und das Phänomen einer Religion im Christentum. 3. Erwählung und Geschichte. The most important function of the concept of election and the concept of judgement which depens upon it consists of the fact that "an interpretation of historical experience in the sense of devine action within the series of events" (op.cit. 1997) is made possible. With this: "The intention of the devine action of election in history is not limited to a community separated from

Just like Pannenberg's doctrine of the church, his doctrine of election is determined by the insight in the essential unity of individuality and sociality. The election of the individual is thus, against the operative individualistic tendency in thought of election in the tradition, continually connected to the community. This is not last thus the case, because the revealed eschatological destiny of all humanity revealed in Jesus Christ is anticipatively manifested in the event of the call to share in God's eternal election. As each of the elect is called that in him the destiny of humanity as a whole becomes an event, a historical call without which the idea of his eternal election cannot be appropriately thought, he is as an individual called and chosen to the communion of the church and in connection with this to take up a productive world- and human-history share in the sending of the Son dedicated to the coming of the Kingdom of God.

With this view of things, the doctrine of election is freed from a series of abstractions which have accompanied it since the time of Origen and Augustine. This affects for one thing the often-encountered detachment of "individuals as the objects of relation from all relations to society" (ST III, 442), against which Pannenberg holds that the elect, through their selection to salvation, in no case are preserved alone and in opposition to others, but in the realization of that universal salvific will of God in which the individual election is grounded. Thus the static and oppositional state of humans before God, as a claimed divorce between the elect and the damned, is proved inappropriate. This is connected in the eschatological judgment of God in its anticipatory prematureness with two further, tightly connected aporias of the traditional doctrine of election, namely, on one hand to confuse the action of election of the eternal God in abstraction from His concrete historicity witnessed to in the Bible, and on the other hand to limit the divine intention of election to future participation in salvation with the dissolution from every historical function of the elect. If these abstractions, which contradict both the Old Testament as well as the New Testament idea of election, are removed, then a series of false alternatives is taken care of, which weighed down the medieval and the reformation doctrine of predestination, to their detriment. "*Either* from the beginning God assigned eternal salvation to only some of his creatures and passed over the rest, abandoning them from the outset to the final destiny of eternal damnation; *or* the universality of this divine will to save was preserved in principle, but in individual cases its efficacy was made to depend on the creaturely reaction and thus on the response of faith to the divine offer of

the remainder of humanity, however, most certainly not to individuals taken out of their social context of life. The love of God is aimed at humanity, which presents itself in individuals, and at individual humans, who at the same time embody the destiny of all humanity in their lives. For this reason, God has elected individual men and women, but not as isolated atoms of salvation. Thus, in Christendom there is no place for sectarian encapsulation of the supposedly true elect. Such elitist exclusivity could only have the effect that the electing love of God presents itself preferentially to those who are excluded." (op.cit 116)

grace, a response that has been calculated already in the divine foreknowledge and that is thus responsible for some being foreordained from the very first to eternal salvation, while others are left to eternal perdition." (ST III, 444) This aporia of a self-destructive dialectic between determinism and tendential Pelagianism or semi-Pelagianism, which pulls the doctrine of predestination back and forth, can only be overcome through the insight "that we are to seek God's eternal election in Jesus Christ, not behind him in a hidden decree of God that is quite different from his historical turning toward us in Jesus Christ." (ST III, 446)

It remains to be cleared up how it is that the *historical calling and eternal election* of humans relate to one another, while avoiding separation. The appropriate answer to this question depends apparently on the correct Christological definition of the relation between time and eternity, where it is valid: as time and eternity, in Jesus Christ the temporal calling and eternal election of the human stand in a differentiated but inseparable relation, the structure of which one can only experienced when protology and eschatology are put into connection in the relevant Christological manner. The thought-execution of this connection results in the quintessence of Pannenberg's doctrine of election, Christological concentrated and Trinity-theologically developed: "The Son is the ordering as well as the consummator of creation. We find an echo of this truth in the statement that believers are elect 'in him' before the foundation of the world. Assurance of their election is anchored in the creative principle that is from the very first the basis of the world's existence. But the Son is not the origin of the world in the same yaw as he will be its consummator. He is at its origin as his self-distinction from the Father becomes the generative principle of all the reality that is distinct from God, both in that distinction from God and in relation to other creatures. Here is the basis of the particularity and independence of creaturely existence. The Son is the consummator, however, inasmuch as all things will be gathered up into one in him. Independent existence is a premise of this. The difference between the work of the Son in the creation and the eschatological consummation of all things leaves them room, then, for their independent life. Yet in spite of this difference protology and eschatology are always related already in the eternal fellowship of the Son with the father by the spirit. The independent ongoing existence of creatures always needs fellowship with God by the Spirit. And as by the Spirit the Son lives in eternal fellowship with the Father, so it is only by the Spirit's work that a filial relation takes shape in creatures, and again only in such a way that the Sprit glorifies the Son and the Father in them, enabling them, like the Son, to accept their distinction from the Father, and therewith their finitude and creaturehood. As the Spirit is the origin of all life, so by his work there emerges the spontaneity of the filial relation to the Father in creatures. This is mediated by the work of reconciliation by which the Son leaves space for the independence of creatures alongside himself, independence for their relation to the Father that the Spirit will actualize as participation in the filial relation of Jesus Christ to the Father. Thus the Spirit will consummate creation by summing up all things in the filial relation of Jesus to the Father.

All those who are elect in Christ who participate in his filial relation to the Father and who are thus related to him. Those who receive and accept calling to faith in Jesus Christ can thus be certain already of their eternal election. Yet election is not a possession only of those who are now called. It does mean participation in the consummation of the eschatological destiny of humanity and all creation." (ST III; 454 – 455)

The relation of the individual human to the destiny of humanity and the world is, according to Pannenberg, mediated concretely "by the relation of elect individuals to human destiny by the fellowship to which the elect belong and which is for its part the object of divine election." (ST III, 455) The Christian church has understood itself from the beginning as the chosen *communion of the elect.* The eschatological idea of the people of God brings this to expression. It would, however, be falsely defined, when it would be associated with the immediate identity of the church and the Kingdom of God. For the coming of the Kingdom of God, which it is to serve, is only useful to the people of God when it knows itself united with the eschaton through self-differentiation and knows itself connected with the awareness of symbolically preliminary nature of its own constitution and the relation to the universality of humanity which transcends its own particularity, as is the aim of the salvific intention of God. If, then, the content of the idea of the Kingdom of God is developed in the context of ecclesiology and a theology of election, then the historical dynamic which points beyond its internality will become apparent, that which is characteristic for the self-transcendent nature of the church and its eschatological mission. Through this one is also led to an understanding of the relationship between Israel and the Church, so often characterized from suffering and guilt, which overcomes the old-fashioned thesis of substitution: undoubtedly the church must understand itself as the people of the new covenant that was concluded in the blood of Jesus Christ and that is renewed at every celebration of the Lord's Supper. But it should not on this account contrast itself as the 'new' people of God with the old Jewish people of God as though the latter had been set aside with the old covenant." (ST III, 477)[4]

The internal dynamic which points outside of the internality, with which the idea of the church as the people of God is connected, has not least effects on the shape of the relation between *Christendom and public order.* Opposed to a principal separation of the idea of church from the political order of society and its tasks, which has led to the tendencial dissolution of worldly power form all spiritual conditions[5] (decisively conditioned by the modern

---

4 Pannenberg writes in German that the church *may* understand itself as such, not that she *must* (...*darf sich die Kirche als Volk*... pg. 516 of the German version). – Trans.
5 The introductory text of BSTh 1 deals with the situation of religions and Christendom in the

secularism of the western political world as well as the antagonism of the confessional era), Pannenberg strongly supports the assertion for the right and duty of Christian faith "to claim recognition and influence as a normative basis on which to shape every sphere of human life, not just individual conduct, but life in society as well, including matters of law and politics. But in the process the influence of Christianity on the shaping of the political and social order will always have to be related to a distinction between what is provisional and what is definitive, between what is secular and what is spiritual.

It is one thing, however, if this distinction is made as a basic differentiation *within* a conception of social order that has a full Christian basis, and another when a secular state that sees itself as absolute practices the principle of separation from religion and thus gives Christianity only a marginal role in social life." (ST III, 482)[6] to this comes that the tendency towards marginalizing religion and Christendom in the modern age has not seldom been accompanied[7] by a secular belief in election of particularly nationalistic

secularized culture of modern Western society, as well as with the internal limits of the development of the secular culture of modernity (11 – 26, Das Heilige in der modernen Kultur [1986]). Cf. further: Christentum in einer säkularisierten Welt, 1988, as well as: Die Erfahrung der Abwesenheit Gottes in der modernen Kultur, 1984, 9 – 24. Among the diverse analytical aspects it is primarily the following which earns attention:"The cult of the sphere of privacy is only the flipside of the coin of the tendential limitation of the objective foundations of our society to the economical interest. But the striving after a sense of human life, which connects the individual with the rest of humanity, can neither be reduced to economic interest nor to private caprice." (Zukunft und Einheit der Menschheit, in: EvZh 32 [1972], 384 – 402; reprinted in EuE 166 – 186, here: 184)

6 To this context belongs Pannenberg's judgment of Luther's so-called Doctrine of the Two Kingdoms: "Luther's differentiation between the spiritual and worldly regiment of the framework of his treatment of the Augustinian topic of the two kingdoms has brought the spiritual nature of the church to new validity as it excludes all forms of political reign. It has also correctly emphasized her difference to the preliminary nature of the political order of societal life. However, Luther lost sight of the Christian universalism present in the idea of empire in the ancient and medieval church, as he oriented his understanding of the worldly regiment upon the particularism of territorial reign in his own time. Thus, on the ground of his doctrine the arrogation of reasons of state (of the territorial states and later of the national states), could only be criticized in the light of natural law or divine law respectively, but not from specific Christian principles, and in particular not from the Christian thought of love. The thought of love is that which, according to Luther, motivates the participation of the Christian in the worldly regiment, but does not change its form of justice. Through this, Luther unintentionally advanced the cause of the progressing independence of political institutions and ideas from Christendom." (Thesen zur Theologie der Kirche, 1970, These 23. Cf. further: Luthers Lehre von den zwei Reichen, in: Gottesreich und Menschenreich, 1972, 73 – 96; reprinted in EuE 97 – 114)

7 The universal direction is characteristic for the Christian thought of election. "The thought of a chosen people means from now on a return prior to the Christian turn to the whole of humanity. The nationalistic secularization of this thought must thus be judged to be anti-Christian." (Nation und Menschheit, in: Monatsschrift für Pastoraltheologie 54 [1965], 333 – 347; reprinted in EuE 129 – 145, here: 140) To the problematic connection of the thought of election and the awareness of nationality cf. further the studies "Erwählung und Volk Gottes", "Das christliche

character (cf. ST III, 518–521), the destructive consequences of which are historically evident, and additionally prove that the political order, when removed from its religious foundation of legitimacy, will such another quasi-religious or perverted-religious ground of self-justification. "The thesis that the state is totally free as regards religion is thus an illusion." (ST III, 482) For precisely governmental freedom of religion has a religiously mediated culture to thank, which finds its principle in the thought of tolerance. "The church did not itself formulate this principle, thought it would have been natural for it to do so. It reached it only by way of a detour via a world that was alienating itself from the church, and to this day divisions among Christians in the church are making it take the lesson to heart even to the transforming of its relation to other religions." (ST III, 525–526)[8]

2. The Common World of Humans

With the relation of the Christian churches to the societal common existence and to governmental order[9] we have already spoken to by example the topic of the human world of culture and its constitution. Pannenberg develops this in the perspective offered by the doctrine of election in multiple aspects. With this, he can connect to the third section of his anthropological monograph of 1983, which handles the common world of humans and begins with an examination of the foundations of culture. "The world that human beings share has never been a natural world. It is nature as they have interpreted and shaped it and subjected it to their own service, but also as it limits and, in many instances, frustrates their efforts. It is, above all, the world of human relations. Moreover, when we speak of the shared world of human beings we are not referring simply to human beings as gathered in society within a natural environment. A social way of life and the formation of groups are not

Imperium und das Phänomen einer politischen Religion im Christentum" as well as "Erwählung und Geschichte", in: Die Bestimmung des Menschen, Menschsein, Erwählung und Geschichte, 1978, 41–113.

8 Cf. "Einheit der Kirche und Einheit der Menschheit" in: J. R. Nelson and W. Pannenberg (eds.), Um Einheit und Heil der Menschheit, 1973, 7–21; reprinted in EuE 318–333, here: 332 f.: "The primary desire of the ecumenical movement of the churches must remain the unification of Christianity, because church is nowhere fully realized when she does not exist as one general Church, which appears in the local and regional churches. But the Christian ecumenical movement cannot solve this its own task without at the same time creating a model for the combinability of unity and plurality. This is true also in relation to other religions and in the area of the political world. Not only through a Christian taking of positions to the current problems of the secular culture but rather much more and decisively through the overcoming of its own problems of ecclesial unification can the ecumenical movement be a factor for the unification of humanity."

9 Cf. in addition the study "Die gesellschaftliche Bestimmung des Menschen und die Kirche" in: Die Bestimmung des Menschen. Menschsein, Erwählung und Geschichte, 1978, 23–40.

specifically human realities but are widespread among the higher animals. The specifically human form of common life is constituted by the concept of a shared world, which we call 'culture.'" (Anth., 315)

With these culture-theoretical approaches, which seek to ground the *nature and constitution of culture* as a common world of humans, two typical groups can be made out: the first understands culture essentially in the symbol-creative action of the individuals; the other understands it from the formation of societal organization. In order to avoid these two aporias, which are caused by opposing abstractions, and to get to a factually correct understanding of culture, Pannenberg notes that it requires "a third level which is distinct from individual and society and on which the symbolizing activity of the individual is related to the foundations of social life." (Anth., 319) This level is thematized in religion and myth in the self-understanding of most cultures, and these form the reality which grounds the cultural order. Despite the indispensable nature of culture-theoretical perception for this situation, myth and religion cannot be declared to be the factors that constitute the unity of culture unproblematically. "Rather, it is the tension between the claims of the mythical and religious tradition, on the one side, and the changing life experience of individuals and community, on the other, that provides the field in which the life-style of a culture is formed and renewed- here even religion and myth undergo change, since reality itself, the fundamental order of which is described and actualized by myth and religion, presents itself in ever new ways to the experience of society." (Anth., 321) The nature and unity of a culture cannot be founded on either the mythic and religious legitimating-founding or in exempting this, rather, only so, that the cultural process is understood as a differentiated mediation connection of traditional sense-holdings, as myth and religion hide within themselves. With this, the creation of sense is understood as human subjectivity, which is presupposed by as well as further developed by myth and religion.

The highly complex demand of a theory of culture appropriate to its object makes, under the common theories today, the interpretation of culture from the *phenomena of the game* as the most likely to be correct, in Pannenberg's judgment. "Playing together, in its various forms, is to be seen in all modes of communal life, including even cult. On the other hand, playing also forms the biological basis of all the free and creative activity of individuals." (Anth., 321 – 322) A game, therefore, is fit for these reasons particularly in order to open the understanding of culture as a world of humanity that mediates to individuals and society the nature of humans and transforms their environment. In this, Pannenberg relies in his treatment of various positions on the examination of Johann Huizinga, who developed the thesis in his book "Homo ludens" (1938) that "all forms of cultural life can be traced back to the main types of communal play: to representational playing, on the one hand, and to contests according to rules, on the other. But Huizinga himself conceded that the two types of game may interact with each other in the forms of cultural life.

Representational playing comes first genetically and objectively, but in all playing with others an element of competition is always present." (Anth., 326) The cultural importance of the representational function of a game is especially explicit in the cultic game as that, when one wishes, which is the foundational liturgy of human life in a common world. In *cultus* humans make themselves certain of the foundations of their culture, in order to immerse themselves in it at the same time. This is valid for pre-biblical religions and culture, but the general foundational structure means that it is, despite the reflexive awareness of mythos-breaking historicity, also valid for the Judeo-Christian tradition. "Even the Christian liturgy is still a sacred play at the center of which is the supper that sums up the ministry and destiny of Jesus and links the created reality of human beings and their social life with their eschatological destiny. For the community that remembers Jesus and awaits his future, that supper becomes here and now a meal shared with him; by means of it, Christians' lives and their world are made part of the history of Jesus Christ. For this reason the celebration of the supper of Jesus includes the praise of the community. In this they anticipate the song of the angels who praise and glorify God and the song of the eschatological community of those who have reached the goal. Undismayed by present appearances, they also glorify God's righteousness as manifested in his conquest – still incomplete here on hearth – of sin and death." (Anth., 337 – 338)[10] In the presenting game, which takes its fullest form in *cultus* as the organizing centre of the common world of humans, the human makes real "that being-outside-themselves to which their exocentricity destines them" (Anth., 338, in order to find a cultural order in the differentiated unity of individuality and sociality, without which human life could not be led humanely. This process is not executed speech- or thought-lessly; much more the acting developing of human culture is conformed to the learning of thought and speech. "This means that in its function as a basis for culture, play is closely connected with specifically human intelligence and language. Together these lay the foundations of the shared human world." (Anth., 339)

Regarding the much-discussed relationship between *speech and thought*, Pannenberg holds fast to the priority of thought to the verbal, in opposition to the so-called speech-relativism. Pannenberg holds this for empirically proven, calling especially on the research of J. Piaget. Just as the development of intelligence precedes in development the learning of language, it remains the long-term function of reason to differentiate the meaning content of the real brought to expression in speech and the coincidental nature of linguistic forms of expression. Nonetheless, thought is in itself in an elemental sense dependant on speech, at least when it wishes to come to a differentiated self-perception and self-presentation. The result of the relation between speech and thought,

---

10 Pannenberg actually makes no reference here to present appearances, but merely notes that this action is counterfactual (*kontrafaktisch*). – Trans.

according to which language, though a differentiated formation organ of thought, can only be understood through a prior development of thought, is what Pannenberg sees as implying "not automatically…that language is a product of the thinking subject and that speech is therefore an action." (Anth., 362) In contrast to the modern tendency of anthropological generalization and radicalization of the idea of action, as can be observed paradigmatically in A. Gehlen, it is absurd in a language-theoretical sense to expand the discovery of the active character of perfomative expressions to a universal speech-act theory with the help of the idea of an illocutionary act. The successful conversation could never be grounded as the activity of an actor-subject, but only from the entire horizon of meaning in which the individual grasps beyond himself and is communicatively connected with the interlocutor(s) in a common movedness by the factual context in speech, which one cannot refer to in a merely end-rationalistic manner. If, then, a merely instrumental use of reason stands in danger of robbing speech of its meaning, then its perception requires an inspired (*inspirierte*) attention in which creative action and inspirations (*Eingebungen*) mutually interpenetrate imagination (*Phantasie*). "The inspirations of the imagination set in motion the constructive imaginative activity that is connected with reflection…as a result of this activity, the objective thematic horizon that is anticipated by the attention acquires concrete form or, as the case may be, is enriched by this or that particular trait. In the light of the role of attention, it becomes understandable that, on the one hand, we cannot force the inspirations of the imagination to appear and that, on the other, such inspirations do not exclude human activity but, rather, energize it to a productive concretization, in the medium of the objective theme on which attention is focused, of that totality of the person's own life which has been anticipated in feeling. The power of imagination is thus in fact the vital element at work in freedom as the latter takes concrete form. At the same time it can manifest itself to the eyes of the theologian as a paradigm of the relation between grace and freedom." (Anth., 381) The task of theology is accordingly to identify the religious implications of speech, and to identify them. How this should occur is given in the detailed examination at the end of the seventh chapter as an example (cf. Anth., 384–396).

The eighth chapter of Pannenberg's "Anthropology in Theological Perspective" is dedicated to the *cultural meaning of social institutions.* The idea of a social institution, which gives durative order to human coexistence, is, according to Pannenberg, to be understood neither one-sidedly in the sense of a priority of the whole of society over the individual nor one-sidedly in the sense of a priority of individual actions, but rather from the mutuality of the relationships between individuals. The regulation of mutual individual relationships is the topic of all institution formation as well as the occasion for the development of their different foundational forms. "Reciprocity (correspondence) in the behavior of individuals (a phenomenon rendered permanent by being institutionalized) binds together the formal structural elements of particularism and mutuality that are found in this behavior. For, on the one hand, individuals seek to assert themselves against others. This is the element of particularism; it cannot bys itself be the basis of a lasting relationship. Permanence only arises when to particularism is added the element of mutuality, which motivates individuals to adapt themselves to others." (Anth., 412) If, then, particularity and commonality build the structural moments of all institutionalism in their reciprocity, then the forms of institutionalization can be ordered under the aspect, whether in account of each moment the particularity of commonality predominates. The latter is given in a prototypical manner the case of the family, the former is such in the case of the institution of property and the economy as production and exchange of property. "All other institutions can, without prejudice to the thematic peculiar to each, be seen as variants, further developments, or combinations of the two basic formal types that find their purest and most original embodiments in the institutions of property and family. One of these types takes the form of a social association,. In addition to the family, this type includes tribe, people, and state, but also other forms of community, such as religious communities. The second basic type of institution comprises forms of communication in which individuals relate to one another as they assert their independence. This type includes, above all, the institutions of economic life as well as the broad area of the juridical sphere; the juridical order, however, especially when it develops into civil law that is authorized and enforced by the state, also embodies a concern for those interests which the community insists on in opposition to individual interests." (Anth., 413 – 414)

Without going into detail[11] regarding the treatment of property, work,[12] and

---

11 The lecture regarding eschatology and sense experience, held in 1972 at a congress on the future of religion in Nijmwegen, and published as "Eschatologie und Sinnerfahrung", in: KuD 19 (1973), 39 – 52 (reprinted in GSTh 2, 66 – 79) refers the judeo-Christian connection of the religious theme with eschatology to the religious state of the present at that time. His predicted renewal of interest in religion has "in the course of the following years come about, but unfortunately, along with it came the feared tendency to flee from the world, which unlike Christian eschatology does not unify with religious renewal through the affirmation of the world and the responsible administration of the same by humans. Much more, these two moments have come apart from one another, because the social-critical impulse of the late 60's used religion as a motivating power, but held the religious as such for passé, while for the reaction of the religious renewal, the critique of society has faded into the background. The alliance of religious feeling with the natural world against the dynamic of technology and industrial society merely appears to lead beyond this dilemma. The present environmental euphoria, with its romantic visions of a sacred unity of man and nature, is blind to the political ends which it actually serves. Due to its economical and political naïveté, it can offer in the long run no replacement for solutions in the relation of religion and society. Upon this field, however, a new awareness of the relevance of religion for the whole of society has been formed through the sociological work in religion of the last two decades. This has effect on the general theory of religions. The ideas of the lecture in this direction have been in critical dialogue with such work since 1972, however, there is also a continuation of the reflection of the differentiated whole of church and state as an expression of the eschatological awareness of Christendom." (GSTh 2,9)

economy (cf. Anth., 416–427) on one hand and regarding seyuality, marriage and family (cf. Anth., 427–443) on the other, as well as those to political order, right, and religion (cf. Anth., 444–484), we merely note here that Pannenberg sees the critical and constructive description of the connection of particularity and community in the process of institutionalization, which is connected back to the fundamental-anthropological categories of centrality and eccentricity in human behavior, replaces the traditional theological doctrines of the order of creation and the order of providence. The institutional orders need not longer, in the light of this change in perspective, appear as time-invariant givens, without thusly making their meaning into a historical disposition. Religion is constitutive for the genesis of this meaning, and thus from the legitimation of institutional order as a whole. In the Christian sense, the religious legitimation of institutional order cannot, however, succeed in the manner of an original myth, but can only succeed such that the institutions (and in particular, the institution of the nation, the totalization of which in the 20th century has produced[13] immeasurable suffering) must be consequently ordered towards the historical coming of the Kingdom of God, the future of which allows the present establishments of political rule and human culture to appear in that preliminary manner, which to match makes up their destiny. Their structuring towards the future Kingdom of God removes from the institutions the burden of the unfulfillable expectations and demands of their individual members. "If individuals seek to achieve their identity directly through their social life, they will consistently overtax the capacities of the institution of communal life. This is true of marriage, family life, and the state as well as of work and property. Then the individual will either be consumed by these institutions or estranged from the life they provide, or else the institutions themselves will break down because too much is demanded of them. The communal life of individuals can be successful only if they avoid this overtaxing of institutions and of institutionally organized personal relations, and if those who play social roles keep a certain distance from them in dealing both with others and with themselves. Only then can social institutions and the role behavior of individuals in them become a medium for *representing* or bodying forth persons and their more deeply grounded relationships with one another in the light of their religious vocation to union with God.

---

12 The phenomenon of human work from a theological perspective is treated in "Fluch und Segen der Arbeit. Das Phänomen menschlicher Arbeit aus theologischer Sicht", in V. Schubert, Der Mensch und seine Arbeit. Eine Ringvorlesung der Universität München, 1986, 23–46; reprinted in BSTh 2, 202–214.

13 On account of a quickly progressing globalization, there is world-political relevance to the foundational sentence "that precisely the pluralism of powers that restrict one another can be the human correlation to the unity of the Kingdom of God, while the unlimited power of a single instance too easily takes on anti-Christian characteristics" (Der Friede Gottes und der Welt-friede, in: Frieden. Vorlesungen auf dem 13. Deutschen Evangelischen Kirchentag Hannover 1967, 1967, 45–62; reprinted in EuE 146–165, here: 164.

Any institution of the shared human world will reveal its true nature only to the extent that it is understood and lived as representational, that is, as representing or manifesting that destiny of human beings and their community which transcends the limitations of our earthly condition." (Anth., 480–481)

The destiny of humans and their community, which transcends the limitations of earthly conditions, is the topic of Pannenberg's ninth and final chapter of his anthropology, titled "Human Beings and History." History builds not only the element of the concrete life process of each individual human, in it the order of the common world of culture is caught up. Pannenberg underscores the fact that the theme of history is fit to integrate all individual anthropological aspects into a unified horizon, against the – in modern times, not seldom appearing – attempt to ground anthropology on a supposed "always-same nature" of humans in opposition to the theme of history. It is also not sufficient, to reduce the anthropological importance of history to an existential of being human that one calls "historicity", as the human awareness of historicity and thus the historicity of the human itself are never independent from the experience of history. As all other anthropological structures, human historicity and the awareness of this have first formed in the process of historical experience, and lie under the changeability. The historical genesis of the historicity of humans is then inseparably connected with the Judaeo-Christian tradition, which loosed the religious awareness from being chained to a primordially grounded time-invariant cosmic order, and opened it up for temporality and the historical arrival of the new.[14] As it expanded beyond the Jewish people to the history of humanity and the human as such, the Christian thought of the historicity of humans has given eschatology that universal-anthropological importance which gave the presupposition for the overcoming of the orientation on primeval time of myth and mythos, as well as for the transcendence of the fixation of antique philosophical thinking on that which always is. This occurred with the assumption, that the human finds to himself and his destiny first in the communion with Jesus Christ and His history, in which the eschaton occurs proleptically and the end of history, of each individual, and of humanity, had been anticipated. If Christian theology has disguised the revolutionary aspect of this insight through a doctrine of the original estate which remained

---

14 To the specific temporality in Judeo-Christian tradition cf. "Zeit und Ewigkeit in der religiösen Erfahrung Israels und des Christentums" (1975), in: GSTh 2, 188–206. "In the history of Christendom, the system of society has not been understood as a representation of the original order of the cosmos, but also not solely on the foundation of a positive order of right which has been transmitted by those proceeding, but rather as a preliminary reflection of the eschatological Kingdom of God, the coming of which will form this present world anew. For this reason, the history of Christianity, in distinction to other 'cultures' is characterized by the distinguishing of political and religious institutions." (Erwählung und Geschichte, in: Die Bestimmung des Menschen. Menschsein, Erwählung und Geschichte, 1978, 85–113, here: 108)

connected to mythos for a great deal of time, it has come into its own effectively in Herder's doctrine of the becoming of the image of God in humans.

This is the connection point for Pannenberg's anthropology, in order to end its concept in an understanding of *history as the formation process of the subject*. Histories describe the formation process of the identity of their object. This is valid for the history of individuals, but also for the history of institutions and groups as well as ultimately for the history of humanity overall, which encompasses all other histories within it. The singular of the history of humanity and its unity cannot, however, be understood, analogously to the history of the individual human, immediately from itself and its individual aspects, but only by the means of an anticipation of its ultimate end, in which the context of the whole is completed and integrated into a entirety of meaning. The asserted unity and uniqueness of history has, accordingly, the character of anticipation, which is at the mercy of the evaluation by the further process of history. Having this in awareness, is in Pannenberg's judgment is not as the opposite of the orientation of the primeval-always-existing a deficient mode of the humane, but rather a form of human which accords to the finitude of earthly humanness. The anticipatory awareness of the truly existing in its historicity forms, as it is said, "a higher stage of the general consciousness that the true and abiding are present in human life." (Anth., 516) This is the case, because it does not seek the unity and totality of self and world in itself, but expects it from God and His Coming, as it is mediated by the historical arrival of the future One. That which appears in feeling in a pre-reflective manner, to step out of its indeterminacy in the historical course of human experience and take on a preliminary-hypothetical reflection-form, that will be revealed as itself at the end of history: the whole of meaning, in which all that is individual is in good hands, brought to the integrated unity and fullness of its being. "History as a formative process is the way to the future to which the individual is destined. As long as the journey is incomplete, it can only be described in terms anticipatory of its end and goal. It is in the light of that end and goal that human beings grasp the meaning of their lives and the task life sets them. Way and goal must, of course, be so related to each other that the way thus far traveled can be interpreted as a way to that goal, just as the actual life history of a person must be capable of being integrated into the identity he or she projects. For the human person as historical being is not only the goal but also the movement of the history that leads to the goal. This movement, however, derives its unity from the future by whit it will be competed. Therefore only through anticipation of this future can human beings presently exist as themselves." (Anth., 527)

The idea of the person is the most concise expression of this fundamental-anthropological fact. As a subject, and precisely as a subject, the human is under presuppositions which cannot (principally not!) be described as products of human action. These are not merely natural or social presuppositions, but rather ones of such nature that they can only be adequately perceived in religious relations, because they are a matter of the condition of possibility of that which lies at the foundation of every self- and world-relationship, namely, subjectivity. The subject among other subjects who is aware of itself and its finitude in a common, given world is only possible for the human as a person, which – instead of dying off in empty circles of useless self-constitution – is certain of itself as given in the divine Spirit. It is in this sense that the conditions of constitution for human subjectivity can be stated as the following formula by Pannenberg: "the human being as person is a creation of the spirit." (Anth., 528) The Spirit is at the same time the one whose particular work is in the present-ness of the eschatological future in the life of the individual and the Christian community. Personality and Spirit-present future-openness belong thus inseparably together.

Revelation, obligation to the Covenant, the task of missions, and the experience of preservation and judgment – these are the key words which make up the topic of *God's action in the history of Israel and the Christian church*. This occurs while taking into account the biblical story and its witness, but not at all by limiting itself to this, rather, beyond as well into the history of humanity in general and the particular history of Church and Christendom. The theological interpretation of this, in the light of the doctrine of election, which itself includes the aspects of calling and sending but also that of judgment, is seen by Pannenberg as an extremely important but mostly neglected task. The method in which this is managed can be described with the following sentence: "A presentation of church history that is true to its theme may neither overlook the truth claim of the Christian belief in God nor simply presuppose it dogmatically." (ST III, 507) In a material sense, we point merely once more to the fact which comes in Pannenberg's historical concept in theology of election, the "category of judgment" (ST III, 516): "We are also to see as an expression of God's judgment in history the alienation of the modern world of Western culture from Christianity inasmuch as its secularism is ultimately derivable from the results of the church's 16th-century divisions and the Wars of Religion that they occasioned in the late 16th and 17th centuries. The shattering of social peace by the intolerance associated with confessional differences, as more recent historical investigations of 17th-century history tell us, was the decisive reason for the abandoning of what had hitherto been the prevailing view that the unity of religion is an essential basis of the unity of society. The emancipating of society with its political, economic, and finally its cultural forms of life from all ties to religion has produced the secularism of the modern world of Western culture. But the results of the schism in the Western church were the starting point." (*Ibid.*) God's historical judgment action requires repentance and new beginning, and gives Christianity and its separated churches the occasion for working through their own history and tradition in a self-critical manner – without which the new beginning of ecumenism in the 20th century will have no blessing, and long-term success will be modest.

To be added and mentioned for itself is something that actually results itself from the examination of the people of God and history as well as of the common world of humans: the context of "Ethik und Ekklesiologie" is not only characteristic for the collection of articles which carries this name, but also for Pannenberg's theology as a whole. Foundational is the assumption "that the institutionalization of the religious topic of church may claim an important place in the context of the general problems of ethics. However, this implies also the other way round, that a factually appropriate explication of presentation of the doctrine of the church should take its place in the wider context of the ethical questions in society, state, and justice." (EuE, 5)[15]

15 Pannenberg's ethics is oriented on the thought of the future of the Kingdom of God as the highest good as is decisive for the message of Jesus. From this orientation, a consequence is the rejection of the thesis of a direct "evidence of the ethical" as diligently as the assumption that ethics requires a foundation in a prior understanding of reality. The "relativity of ethical content is not able to be overcome upon the ground of the ethical itself" (Die Krise des Ethischen und die Theologie, in: ThLZ 87 [1967], 7–16; reprinted in EuE 41–54, here: 51). "First from the individual understandings of reality as a whole result the basic principles of an ethical behavior." (EuE, 52) Pannenberg handles the problem of grounding ethics and the Kingdom of God in "Theology and the Kingdom of God", 1971, as well as in the volume dedicated to Trutz Rendtorff "Grundlagen der Ethik. Philosophisch-theologische Perspektiven", 1996. After analyses and diagnoses to the situation of morality and ethics in the secular culture of modernity, and examinations of the original situation of ethics and the most important paths of its traditional grounding, Pannenberg groups his own ethical concept into the context of Christian assumption of the Platonic question of the Good. While the deontological ethic of Kant becomes depraved without a lasting validity of the principles of natural law and becomes an abstract formalism, the natural law including the Christian command ethic which connects to it requires an anthropological foundation, in order to be recognized and acknowledged as a binding expression of the common nature of being of humans. At this point, the Socratic-Platonic manner of grounding ethics proves itself, as before, the best travelled, in so far as it takes its initial point as the human striving for that which is not yet realized, but which is indispensable for the realization of the being of man. The orientation of ethics on the thought of the sought-after Good can be connected easily to the Christian thought of the Kingdom of God, whose ethical relevance, according to Pannenberg, is not limited to a specific Christian ethic. "This results from the connection of the concept of the Good, which is constitutive for ethics, with the idea of God. The concept of the Kingdom of God as the place of communion of man with God makes the thought that God is the highest Good for man and the ground of every other form of the Good in its precedence to all striving of humans for that which is good *for them*, more precise. To that extent, the thought of the Kingdom of God receives a universal ethical relevance, even for a purely philosophical ethical reflection." (op.cit 73) If the future of the Kingdom of God is prior to all human action, such that this priority functions as a mediating instance of the difference between individuals and community, then light is shed on the fact that the thought of God and His Kingdom does not only have a motivating function, but also a grounding function for the content of ethical statements. This is made clear in detail in Jesus' interpretation of the law as a consequence of his eschatological message, within which the examination of the relation of the biblical thought of neighbor-love to the phenomenon of well-wishing (cf. op.cit. 77–80) earns particular attention. Following this are examinations of the anthropological presuppositions of Christian ethics as well as of their universal human relevance. To conclude, a few paradigmatic

3. The Completion of Creation in the Kingdom of God

The people of God, which the church and its individual members have been elected to be, is called and sent through God's action of election to be "a model of his kingdom" (ST III, 524) in the middle of the antagonisms of world history. This appears already, as it is in the case in a sacramental manner in the Eucharistic celebration of worship. With this, the people of God is the church in her worship celebration and all that belongs to it, essentially structured towards the community of a renewed humanity, which is the target of God's action of election. The election of the Christian people of God thus has the character "of dynamic inclusiveness, i. e., of a movement toward the inclusion of all" (ST III, 523), which is to say, "[T]he election of individuals, and also of the people of God to which individuals belong as members, is *open* to the participation of all people in Jesus' relation to God." (*Ibid.*) This openness corresponds to the opening of the whole history of the world to the completion of creation in the coming Kingdom of God.

The future of the Kingdom of God as the epitome of Christian hope is the central topic of the doctrine of last things. This has been referred to as *eschatologica*, eschatology, since A. Calov. All of the individual topics, such as the resurrection of the dead and the last judgment, are contained within the theme of the Kingdom of God. This determines, beyond the locus "*De novissimis*", the entire dogmatic context of doctrine in a decisive manner, although this has not often been recognized by Christian theology. In the modern age, it has been first brought to memory by the rediscovery of the apocalyptic character of Jesus' end-times preaching though Johannes Weiß. "Because god and his lordship form the central content of eschatological salvation, eschatology is not just the subject of a single chapter in dogmatics; it determines the perspective of Christian doctrine as a whole." (ST III, 531) All of its individual aspects are eschatologically determined and structured towards the theme of the Kingdom of God, the coming of which Jesus proclaimed and the future of which the resurrection of the crucified One revealed in anticipation.[16]

Pannenberg begins his way of grounding eschatological statements with a

---

aspects are developed for the working out of the profile of a specifically Christian style of life within the context of today's secular society: 1. Self-realization and service; 2. Self-control; 3. Marriage and family; 4. Christian action in the secular state (cf. op.cit. 108 – 142).

16 The eschatological nature Pannenberg's thought is developed in the aspects to the doctrine of God, ecclesiology and ethics in: Theology and the Kingdom of God (1971). This determines all other aspects of Pannenberg's doctrine, including ontology: "The nature of things may not be understood as timeless, but rather is dependent on the process in time and will first be decided by the result of time, although it may well be a matter of the identity, of the quiddity of things that have long past." (Zukunft und Einheit der Menschheit, in: EvTh 32[1972], 284 – 402; reprinted in EuE 166 – 186, here: 180).

tour of the demise of eschatology in the newer history of theology, and an examination of the insights which enable the renewal of eschatology. These also re-establish eschatology in theological against the tendency to temporalize the futuristic sense of biblical eschatology. Following this, the place of the eschatological text in the pneumatological context of dogmatics and the relation between individual and general eschatology is examined. The end-times work of the Spirit, which grounds the specific connection between pneumatology and eschatology, can only be understood in Trinitarian theological terms, namely, from its differentiated reference to creation and to the reality of reconciliation of Jesus Christ. As the Third in the divine covenant, the Holy Spirit in person ensures that the divine Father-Son relation is not closed into itself, but rather opened to humanity and the world. Therefore, the Spirit does not leave the event in Jesus Christ which became the occurrence of fulfillment for the end-times, precisely in that He glorifies it in its perfect definiteness "not yet complete" (ST III, 550), but leaves it rather open to be for God's creatures, in order to give creation and especially humans independent shares in the sonship of Jesus Christ. This is also in order to lead them to the end-times Kingdom commonly as individuals and as belonging to God for their own sake as children of God. Through the Spirit of creation and completion, creatures receive a share in the eternal life of God as creatures in the differentiated nature of their temporal existence. With this, they are acknowledged in their present as different from the future of God, and completed in a manner that ends time. "The fact that the independence of the creature is still preserved in its eschatological consummation before God, that the creature is not swallowed up by the presence of God, will prove to be the point of the tension and relation between the present and the future of the Spirit, between the reconciliation and consummation of the creature, between pneumatology and eschatology." (ST III, 555) The tense connection of pneumatology and eschatology demonstrates at the same time the differentiated unity of individual and general eschatology. The Creator-Spirit of creaturely completion is, after all, the same who gives Himself as a gift to the faithful, in order to lead them to their destiny and unite them in their individual difference, even in the confirmation of that. A pneumatologically appropriate eschatology cannot thus deal with the salvific completion of the individual life beyond death without taking into account the completion of humanity and the world in the Kingdom of God, and vice-versa.[17]

With the presupposition of the inseparable connection between the two forms of Christian future-hope, Pannenberg treats first the *individual eschatology*. Faith, whose hope is continually connected to love, expects the fulfillment of human destiny beyond death from the coming of the Kingdom of

---

17 To the differentiated connection of the eschatological aspects of the Kingdom of God and the resurrection of the dead, cf. among others "Die Auferstehung Jesu und die Zukunft des Menschen", in: KuD 24 (1978), 104–117; reprinted in GSTh 2, 174–187.

God. It does this in the manner of the hope of resurrection. In order to appropriately describe the content of such a hope, one must first examine the anthropological meaning of death. The human as a creature is differentiated from God, and in this differentiation from the infinite, finite. From the finitude of the human, it would appear that death belongs to the creaturely nature of humans. Not seldom has Christian theology made this conclusion, and differentiated between natural death as an event grounded in the creaturely nature of the creature and the death of judgment as a result of sin. "Yet is finitude always linked to mortality and death? If it is, then the incorruptible life of the risen Christ should have devoured and outdated the finitude of human existence. In opposition to Monophysitism, however, the church confesses that even the risen Christ, too, remained a man, and therefore a finite being distinct from God, even though he will never die again. Thus the Christian hope is the same for believers who will in the future share in the new life of the risen lord. It follows, then, that we must distinguish between finitude and mortality. But if so, the thesis that death belongs to our nature as finite beings loses its plausibility." (ST III, 560)

Pannenberg's thesis to the contrary, according to which death does not belong to the creaturely destiny of humans or to their creaturely finitude as such, presupposes a clarification of the relationship between finitude and time, in order to be appropriately developed. "The finite life of creatures is a life in time. For that reason, however, it did not have to be lived in the brokenness of our experience of time for which all life is torn apart by the separateness of past, present, and future. In life the present the past is no more and the future has not yet come. This separateness means that the totality of our life constantly evades us. Hence time is no more a theologically neutral thing than death. Instead, in the brokenness of our experience of time temporality is of a piece with the structural sinfulness of our life." (ST III, 561) It is first the disunity of our temporal experience in past, present and future that finitude can become transience and end in death. This disunity of time is connected with the self-centeredness of our existence, the form of existence of which is time, and is structurally caused by this self-centeredness. It is precisely the self-centered refusal to accept one's own finitude which lets time become an antagonistic conflict of past, present, and future. This delivers up temporal existence to transience and death, which allows the revelation of what the self-centered finite is: a transient, ending, invalid something which is given over to death from the beginning and ultimately something dead, something which lacks to fullness of its finite existence, which it is seeking in itself. "It would not have been this could we have lived out life as a totality in acceptance of our own finitude and hence with reference to the reality of God that transcends our finitude and that both links our own existence to that of all other creatures and at the same time limits it by them." (ST III, 563) As a result of this, Pannenberg sees death as such and not first the – differentiated from a so-called natural, belonging to the creaturely nature of the human and thus to the goodness of creation death – death of judgment as conditioned by the structural wickedness of sin. However, an existence which lives as the integrated entirety of its temporal being need not die, and need not taste death.

Prior to unfolding the content of the Christian hope of resurrection[18] on the background of this understanding of death, Pannenberg determines the relation of such a hope to other forms of faith in a future of the individual beyond death, such as to a doctrine of reincarnation or the idea of the transmigration of the soul. While both have been traditionally rejected, the Christian hope of resurrection made the Platonic thought of the immortality of the soul its own. This could not occur without critical modification: "In distinction from Plato's view of the deity of the soul Christian theology views us as creatures in both body and soul, destined indeed for immortality in fellowship with God, yet not possessing it of ourselves, nor able to secure it for ourselves, but receiving it only as a gift of grace from God.

Closely related is a second distinction. The soul is not on its own the true person as though the body were simply a burdensome appendage or a prison to which the soul is tied so long as it has its being on earth. Instead, the person is a unity of body and soul, so that we can think of a future after death only as bodily renewal as well…

A third distinction between the Judeo-Christian hope of resurrection and the ancient Greek idea of the immortality of the soul arises from the fact that the soul whose immortality Plato taught in *Phaedo* is not identical with the individual whose history ruse once and for all between birth and death." (ST III, 571 – 572)

The question why Christian hope of resurrection wanted to take up the thought of immortality in the face of such fundamental differences is to be answered with reference to a problem posed in this hope internally and to the desire for a means to solve this problem. How is it that one can think of the identity of the future resurrected life, regardless of all presupposed, granted changes, along with the present bodily existence of an individual person and their history in time? If one did not wish to take refuge in an unconvincing assumption of identity-preservation through material leftovers of earthly bodyliness, then the idea of an immortal soul separated from the body at death offered itself to function as a principle of the continuity between this and the future life. "For the sake of this function early Christian theology took over the Greek idea of the immortality of the soul but modified it in such a way that the soul is defined as the vital principle only of the one individual." (ST III, 575) While one opined, on one hand, that the concept of the individual soul and its duration must be expanded by the thought of the resurrection of the body, on the other hand the theoretically superior alternative of the soul as the principle of the form of the nature offered itself, that is, of the nature of the individual

---

18 Cf. "Tod und Auferstehung in der Sicht christlicher Dogmatik" in: KuD 20 (1974), 167 – 180; reprinted in GSTh 2, 146 – 159.

embodiedness, such that the soul contains the schema for the body in the sense of a construction plan, in order to preserve the identity of the future body with the present body in its peculiar particularity. The lasting difficulties of the latter concept come, according to Pannenberg, from the fact that "our life history is constitutive for our identity. A different history would mean a different individuality. On the premise that after death the human soul lives on up to the resurrection of the dead, the question arises whether it also has new experiences during the intervening period." (ST III, 576) In the case of the obvious and, according to Pannenberg, nearly impossible to avoid affirmation of this question, the idea ends in an apparent aporia, which drives one to the conclusion: "Precisely in relation to the time between death and resurrection the concept of the soul cannot, then, guarantee the identity of the future life with this earthly life that the idea of the resurrection of the dead seems to demand, for according to this idea our present life will be subject to change only as it is confronted by the divine eternity at the end of this earthly existence." (ST III, 577) Thus, it remains an open problem, how it is that the identity between the future resurrected life of the individual and their present individual existence can be thought without dissolving the body-soul connection and without dissolution of the internal unity of individual and general eschatology. Prior to returning to this point in the framework of his considerations of the relation between eternity and time, Pannenberg turns first to the *general eschatology* and, with this, the problem of the completion of humanity – a problem which can be so little separated from the completion of the human as an individual as the other way round.

The considerations of the eschatological theme of the Kingdom of God as the completion of human society take their beginning from the insight of creation theology that the creative will of God is towards the independence of the creature, which allows creation to be a matter of something not always already completed, but structured towards future completion. That creatures can become themselves in their creaturely nature, they require time as a form of existence and as a condition of independent formation of existence. With the temporal for of existence is in no case already present the necessity of an inevitable failure to fulfill creaturely destiny. At the same time, this failure cannot be excluded with inevitable necessity by the creative will of God, due to the desire independence of the creature, which belongs to the goodness of creation. Although the self-failure which cannot be excluded with necessary inevitability through God's creative will due to the desired independence of the creature has become factual in a universal manner, the economy of God's action in His creation, proved by the appearance of the Son and the sending of the Spirit, remains oriented on the salvation of creatures and the goal for which they are structured: to take part through being children of God by the power of the Spirit in the communion of the Father and the Son. According to Pannenberg, not only a conversion of the human in his moral depravity, but also a radical change of the natural conditions of human existence itself is obliged, for the sake of the reaching of the goal, and for the sake of the erection of the justice and love of God. "Nothing less than a new heaven and a new earth…is demanded as a prerequisite for the definitive actualizing of the kingdom of God. For human conflict, on account of the dominion of sin in human relations, is deeply rooted in the natural conditions of existence as it now is. The independence for which we are created, and which we are actively to achieve by our conduct, becomes in fact the self-seeking of each individual vis-à-vis the rest of the world hence the hope of the coming of God's kingdom necessarily goes hand in hand with the expectation of a cosmic renewal of the world. Included is also the resurrection of the dead." (ST III, 584) This is furthermore soteriologically indispensable, because only the connection of the idea of the completion of the kingdom of God with the general resurrection of the dead preserves the participation of all individuals of humanity in the completion of their destiny and thus the eschatological reconciliation of individuality and society.

The thought of a completion which finally removes the antagonism of individuals and society in human destiny is, according to Pannenberg, unthinkable without assuming an end to history. Indeed, there could be a end without completion, but no completion without an end. One must hold fast to the idea of the kingdom of God as the end of history, as it is distinctive in the Jewish apocalyptic writings and further developed in the New Testament witness, despite the modern tendency to make a problem of it. This dedication is in no sense an act of blind decision: for in distinction to physical cosmology, which cannot verify but of course also cannot falsify it, the peculiar claim of Christian eschatology of an eschatological end of world history a quite solid foundation in the internal logic of the historic nature of human awareness of meaning. For every sense experience of a human which is connected to a determinate meaning presupposes a whole of meaning as a condition of its possibility, and is referential to this in an anticipating manner. "Since, then, we have to think of the totality of the real, and also of our experience of it, as an incomplete process in time, it follows that each individual experience presupposes as a condition of its definite nature an end of history that makes of the history of the universe as well as humanity a total process. Naturally we do not have to link reflection on this presupposition to any knowledge as to how the end of history might come about. We can know the sheer facticity of the end, or, more accurately, the fact that the world is moving on to an end, only as an implication of the concept of reality in its totality as a once-for-all process, a history." (ST III, 590–591) Pannenberg notes himself the formal nearness of this argument to transcendental-philosophical and –theological considerations, but not without noting the remaining incompatibilities: "We might call the postulate of an end of history a transcendental condition (a condition of the possibility9 of experience in general as regards its historicity if it were not for objections relative to the strict differentiation of transcendental functions (in Kant's sense) from empirical data and above all the fact that for Kant all transcendental forms of experience are simply an expression of the unity of the subject of knowledge." (Ibid.) Regarding the theoretical difficulties which are connected with the assumption of an end to world history, Pannenberg opines that they can only be put aside when it is considered "that *God and not nothing is the end of time*. As the finite is bounded by the infinite, so are time and the temporal by eternity. The end of the temporal, of time and history in general, thus means transition to eternity." (ST III, 594)

Just as in the carrying out of individual eschatology, that of the general finds its peak less in the thought of the end of life of the individual and much more at the end of history of humanity and with world, an eschatology oriented on the *problem of the relation between time and eternity*. This is a matter of "the crucial problem in eschatology, and its solution has implications for all parts of Christian doctrine. The identity of those who will be raised with those who are now alive; the relation of the future of God's kingdom at the end of history to its being present in the work of Jesus; the relation of the general resurrection of the dead at the return of Jesus Christ to the fact that even at death those who sleep in him are already with him , so that their fellowship with him is not broken; the relation of the return of Jesus himself to his earthly work; and last but not last the relation of the eternal kingship of God and his world government to the futurity of his kingdom – all these are question and themes that are without answers, and the substance of which cannot be understood, so long as we do not clarify the relation between time and eternity. But the answers that we give here affect also our understanding of human creaturliness in distinction from its corruption by sin, and they obviously have ramifications also for our understanding of God's economy of salvation as a whole in its relation to the inner trinitarian life of God." (ST III, 595 – 596) Even more important is to give a precise determination of the relationship between time and eternity. The initial point that Pannenberg offers here is the idea of duration. "The duration of time is decisive for the independent existence of creatures. only by their own, if limited duration do they have their own existence in distinction from God and each other. Life is present for us, as for other creatures, as we sense it in its indefinite totality. This presence of the sensed totality, which is constitutive for the temporal sense of duration, is vague when considered in isolation. It acquires definite contours only by means of recollection and expectation, so far as these go. In this regard expectation takes precedence, for the totality of life is defined only by the future that completes it, just as we grasp the totality of a song only as we think ahead to the ending that has not yet been reached." (ST III, 597 – 598) If then, according to this, the "today" of the human and the present awareness of its duration structurally provided with the tension of remembrance and expectation, among which the primacy of the future of the lifespan of the human dictates its direction, then it sheds light on the fact that the ego of the human, bound to the transient and changing "now" of the time stream, can neither ground its duration nor the entirety of its existence in its own momentary presence, nor can it preserve the same through this. For this, one requires – as Pannenberg makes clear against diverse attempts to base the idea of time on the subjectivity of awareness – the eternity of God as the ground of constitution and preservation for the durative cohesion of creaturely moments of time in their succession.

If the divine foundation of eternity becomes contrafactual for the unity and continuity of creaturely time, that is, if it is denied to be presupposed as it always necessarily must be claimed, the creaturely existence and its temporal form of existence perverts itself. In this, the differentiated unity of the modes of time is torn, and past, present, and future end up on a self-contradictory relation of mutual destruction, as it not only fails to correspond to creaturely determination of time, but contradicts it. For the determination of time as the creaturely form of existence is structured towards the integral unity of time in the differentiation of the modes of time, which themselves are structured towards the Kingdom of God. To this disposition of time, which makes up its destiny according to creation, belongs both the objective duration of limited lifetime as well as the temporal feeling of duration in the wandering of the "now" through time, with the inclusion of remembrance and expectance. The differentiated nature of the modes of time is thus not already as such an indication of fallen creation. For a life, which extends through the course of time from the past through the present and into the future can absolutely be collected entirely in God, as the true humanness of the second Adam proves? Neither the differentiation of the modes of time in reference to the present of creatures nor the multiplicity of self-replacing temporal moments which belong to every sequence of events are *eo ipso* of a "postlapsarian" nature. After all, the yet-to-occur future of the completed whole of human life is also not as such a sign of alienated existence and an awareness that is unhappy in and of itself. The primacy of the future accords much more to the creaturely destiny of humans insofar as this is not intended to remain and linger in its own self-present presence, but rather to extend itself toward God and God's accomodationary approach. The advancement of human time, according to which the entirety of the human life is only to be awaited from an future that integrates the multiplicity of life-moments to a unity, lets itself in a completely salvific manner be thought of along with the accommodating, approaching being of the Creator-God, who fulfills His work eschatologically. The time of humans is only a hopeless situation, when the human loses faith in God's arrival and with that the love for God, self, and the world of humans, including all consistent hope. While for the eccentricity of faith which relies on the accommodation of God the eschatological future already comes into view, the wicked perverseness of unbelief must not only appear as indecent but also as resistant, namely as hopeless death and ominous judgment. It remains to be added, that the God-desired finitude of creaturely being does exclude the limitlessness of existence, which would mean nothing more than infinite boredom, "but not the present of the whole of this limited existence in the form of duration as full participation in eternity. Nor does it contradict the finitude of creaturely existence that his participation in eternity is held fast by it as an element of its own and thus itself preserved as imperishable." (ST III, 601, fn. 244) One may thus hope for a perpetuation of the life-history of the individual human as well as the history of humanity as a whole in eternity, in the expectation that the differentiation of times are in good keeping in God's eternity.

If one can expect that the difference of times are in good keeping in God's eternity, then from this follows a "solution to the much discussed problem whether individuals go immediately at death into God's eternity for participation in his eternal life, or will rise again only at the end of history." (ST III, 606) Both views have, according to Pannenberg, their correctness, and yet such that they give up the supposed opposition to one another under the conditions of the awaited sublation of the temporal into God's eternity. If, namely, that which occurs in time remains unlost in eternity, and God remains present to all that was present in its temporal existence, then the resurrection of the dead and the renewal of creation present themselves as the act "by which God through his Spirit restores to the creatures' existence that is preserved in his eternity the form of being-for-themselves. Herein the identity of creatures needs no continuity of their being on the time line but is ensured by the fact that their existence is not lost in God's eternal present." (*Ibid.*) Because, however, in the event of the sublation of time into eternity the identity of the individual creature is remembered through God's memory and made known along with that of all other creatures in the context of a commonly given creaturely world, one must think of the (unimaginable in the merely chronological aspect of an iterating timeline) simultaneity of the non-simultaneous, which is the prerequisite to think of individual and general eschatology as a differentiated unity, as it is theologically demanded.

The eschaton, as one sees, is the *becoming sublated of time in eternity*. With this, eternity marks an end of time and history also and precisely when this end, on which faith sets all its hope, will be the completion of time and history. Whether the eschatological end of time and history has the positive meaning of completion through participation in God's own eternal life, is decided in judgment, the judgment in which eternity encounters the time which it negates and raises up in itself critically. With this, it is characteristic for the Christian expectation of final judgment "that its execution relates to the person of Jesus" (ST III, 610), even when this allocation is not nearly so emphasized in the New Testament as in later theological and historical-piety traditions, for which the return of Christ and the Day of Judgment build a context of conception. In what way the carrying out of judgment and the verdict might be determined in detail, decisive is "that the message of Jesus is the standard of judgment." (ST III, 615) The factual concordance or discord with the will of God as proclaimed by Jesus Christ in the power of the Holy Spirit and not the coincidental fact, dependant on history or personal life conditions, of a personal encounter with Jesus through ecclesial proclamation will be the criterion of the eschatological verdict of God. Thus have "all people, whether Christians or not...the chance of participation in the kingdom of God that Jesus proclaimed." (ST III,616) The advantage of the Christian is merely in "that in the person of Jesus they *know* the standard for participation in eternal salvation and hence also the standard of judgment. By relating their lives to Jesus Christ in baptism and faith they can also be sure already of future participation in salvation. "

Although those who are destined to eternal salvation in the eschatological judgment will persevere and not be destroyed, thanks to their aware and unaware participation on the filial relation of Jesus Christ to the divine Father, as worked out by the Holy Spirit (cf. ST III, 622 – 626), they require also a cleansing from sin and its consequences. This fact is introduced in the idea of purifying fire (cf. 1 Cor. 3:12 ff.) which is to be differentiated from purgatory insofar as it is not necessarily connected with the assumption of an intermediate state of the soul between death and completion, as it had become in the middle ages the foundation for the institution of indulgences. Once removed from this condition, which was correctly criticized in the Reformation, the thought of cleansing is not only acceptable, but a non-negotiable moment, indeed, a constitutive moment for the idea of eschatological judgment in connection with the return of Christ. Pannenberg underscores the latter aspect through the fact that he speaks to the problem of a possible eternal damnation in the context of the idea of cleansing and purifying, an idea which apparently is neither limited to those who are destined to eternal salvation, nor can be identified with the assumption of an ultimate retrieval of all (*apokatastasis panton*). According to the witness of the New Testament, one cannot exclude that the cleansing and purifying process occurring in the Last Judgment effects the total destruction of those "who persist irreconcilably in turning aside from God...in certain cases nothing may remain when the fire of the divine glory has purged away all that is incompatible with God's presence." (ST III, 620) This relationship, today also held in Roman Catholic eschatology (J. Ratzinger), of the purifying fire of 1 Cor. 3:12 ff. to the Last Judgment instead of an intermediate state of souls between death and Last Judgment makes possible an understanding of the connection between the fire of judgment and the glorification of the faithful: the fire of judgment is the other side of the coin to the light of divine glory which transforms the believers, so that they are preserved in the light of the eternal God and must not pass away.

As the idea of eschatological judgment fire is tightly connected in the metaphorical speech (cf. ST III, 621 f.) of Christian eschatology with the reality of the returning Christ, so can it analogously never be separated from the work of the Spirit. In this, the scope of the Spirit-worked return of Christ to the eschatological judgment is the glorification of the resurrected crucified One and the elation of all who participate, in the power of the Spirit, in His filial relation to the divine Father and thus in the eternal life of God Himself. The eschatological work of the Spirit will thus glorify Jesus Christ precisely in that it gives a general share of His reality of reconciliation, in order to fulfill it in this manner. The eternal life, which was granted to Jesus Christ at Easter, will become the life of all which have communion with Him in the Spirit. In this every separation of individual will cease, without the loss of individual difference. In self-differentiation from God they will be one with Him, and as those made eschatologically eternal in Jesus Christ through the power of the divine Spirit they will be connected among one another in such a manner that their difference, without ceasing, will lose all separating character.

The completed richness of relation, which the Spirit opens up by the means of the eschatological return of Christ, proves and effects also an ultimate justification of the Creator-God, that the almighty Creator of heaven and earth is nothing but pure fatherly love in His being. With this, the open (and under earthly conditions best initially solvable) *problem of evil* will be given an ultimate soteriological solution from God himself. In a detailed treatment of the attempts at an argumentative solution to the problem of evil, among which the attempts of Leibniz and German Idealism stand out, Pannenberg makes clear "that we cannot master this theme merely by theoretical clarifications. Also needed is the real history of reconciliation. The issue in such a history is the future of the world that will mean both its end and its transfiguration." (ST III, 636) It is first from the completion of the active process of salvation economy of the triune God with His creation that the general unity of this process can be grasped and ultimately understood, which is manifest in an anticipatory manner in the resurrection of the crucified One: that God namely desires the salvation and nothing but the salvation of His creatures which are destined to independent communion with God. It is first the light of eschatology which throws light, in glorious splendor and in a fully unobscured manner, what God is. Without eschatology, there can thus be no Christian theology. For the idea of God itself, under the aspect of which theology unfolds in all its parts, is, as every idea, only an anticipation of the reality which it claims to grasp – and it requires the definitive self-proof, in order to have validity. After all, the salvific event of Jesus Christ is a matter of a "real anticipation that calls for a final enforcement on which its own power and truth retrospectively depend because it always derives already from this future of God's salvation and is to be understood as its inbreaking into this present world." (ST III, 637) The same is true for Christian faith as it is called forth from the *heilsgeschichte* of Jesus Christ: He knows His truth to be absolutely connected to God, on whom He relies and from whose coming Kingdom He expects the eschatological overcoming of evil and wickedness.

Neither the wickedness of the world nor the evil of sin match up with to the creative intention of God. Their allowance merely "expresses the roust that is involved in the freedom with which God willed to endow his creatures, angels and humans." (ST III, 642) It is the divine will for the independence of creatures, which cannot exclude the possibility of sin and its consequences with absolute necessity – a possibility which is, in itself, impossible, as it destroys all meaningful possibility. The eschatological completion of the will of God for His creation fulfills itself, as much as it will bring wickedness and evil to disappearance, thus not in the elimination of the opposition of creatures to their Creator. God wants much more His human creatures as free beings, which are characterized through spontaneity in the relation to Him as to one another and the creaturely world, "Hence the glorification that accrues to them cannot imply their absorption into the life of God. Instead, the spontaneity of the glorification of the Father who is manifested in his glory by the Son is the medium in which the glorification of creatures themselves takes place by the Spirit." (ST III, 643) The eschatological community of the Kingdom of God, in which God is all in all, will thus not be indifference, but the fullness of eternal liveliness, in which the different as different are one and mutually enrich one another, in order to belong in this manner to the triune God whom they have in their life, whose unity of being is not to be thought of without personal differentiation, and whose personal differentiation is not to be thought of without His own being.

§8 Epilegomena

1. Theology and Philosophy

Anthropology is the leading science of the modern age. Without the evidence of the constitutive meaning of religion for the humanness of the human, the universal validity of it cannot be grounded. The Christian religion and its theology can also only do away with this evidence at the price of the loss of human plausibility, since it has lost its self-evident cultural validity since the Western faith splits which essentially caused the modern turn to anthropology. So non-negotiable as the anthropological demonstration of the religious nature of humans is for the plausibility of Christian faith-content under modern conditions, it does not suffice to ensure the truth of the Christian idea of God. For its claim hangs on the presupposition, that the world, as epitome of reality become objective to human experience, is at least thinkable as God's creation. The thought of God and the idea of the world belong together. Theology is thus connected essentially with philosophy, which in the sense of its classical tradition has the understanding of the reality of humans and that of the world as a whole as a topic – a function in which it cannot be replaced by any other individual science.

Because an understanding of God and an understanding of the world do not let themselves be separates, but rather belong inalienably together, theology and philosophy are in a mutual relation of correlation according to their own nature. Pannenberg made this emphatically clear in his final regular lecture at the evangelisch-theologischen Fakultät of the Ludwig-Maximilians-Universität on February 22nd 1994. The lecture is the final chapter of the monograph "Theologie und Philosophie" from 1996, in which it is examined the relation between both sciences in the light of their common history – from Platonism, Aristotelianism, and Stoicism to the anthropological turn in post-Hegelian philosophy, with particular attrition to the history of the reception of the various philosophical systems into theology. The beginning chapter is dedicated to the *types of determining the relation between philosophy and theology*, not only as is abstractly possible, but how they have been on the stage of history in their relationships factually. The thesis that theology and philosophy are pure opposites is rejected right at the beginning as excessive and pragmatically untenable. For on one hand, theology is elementarily dependant on the use of reason, and already due to this not straightforwardly dissolvable from philosophy; on the other hand, the traditional task of philosophy, to think of reality in its entirety, connects it in its essence with theology, which, according to its own concept, is structured for thinking of

God as the all-determining reality. A merely alternative definition of the relation between philosophy and theology thus does not let itself be held, indeed for objective reasons which can call for philosophical as well as theological legitimation.

However, a direct identification of both sciences also does not come into question for Pannenberg. Indeed, philosophy is connected to the ideas of religious tradition not only in its historical origin but in its original themes. Yet it fulfills its task not in affirmation without critique, but rather in critical reflection on that which is claimed from religious tradition. The other way round, the claim of theology to be true philosophy cannot be directly held theologically, but only in treatment of philosophy and the critical standards it has developed for the thought of God as the all-determining reality. "Where God and the totality of all that is real are not thought in this, their belonging together and mutual dependence on one another, there it is that speech about God remains an empty word or an objectively ungrounded imagination, as it is interpreted, for example, as an anthropomorphism, as the product of religious projection. If one knows, what one says, when one speaks of 'God', then one cannot longer think of the reality of world and man without thinking of God as their origin, and conversely, one can only think of God so, such that one at the same time thinks of the entirety of reality as that which is brought forth by Him." (ThuPh 16).

On the condition of the demonstrated correlation of the idea of God and the idea of the world as the epitome of all that is real, the relation between theology and philosophy can neither be defined as alternatives nor as an indifferent identity. The former is excluded through the common task of thinking of reality in its entirety, the latter through the commanded differentiation of perception in this task. An unabridged quote of the final passage of Pannenberg's farewell lecture: "Philosophy and theology have a common topic in their labor for an understanding of the reality of man and the world as a whole. One can, of course, do theology as well as philosophy in all sorts of manners, which remain behind this task. However, philosophy accords to its great tradition only when it faces this task, and only then does it perceive its function, in which it cannot be replaced by any of the other individual sciences. Theology, for its part, can only speak properly of God and his revelation, when it takes it as a matter of the Creator of the world and man, and thus relates its speech of God to an understanding of the entirety of the reality of man and the world. In this, theology needs the interlocutor of critical and orienting reflection in philosophy, and philosophy for its own part cannot come to full understanding of man in the world without taking religion and its meaning or the nature of man into account, as well as taking into account the constitution of the entirety of man and the world out of divine reality, which thematizes religion. Philosophy must, in this, not desire to replace religion through a purely philosophical doctrine of God. Indeed, even when this does not occur, there remains enough tension between theology and philosophy, because the theology has the task of thinking of the whole of human existence and the world from the point of God and His revelation, which philosophical thought traces the ground in the absolute from the experiences of man and world." (ThuPh 637)[1]

The differentiated connection with philosophy is non-negotiable for theology. Even when philosophical disciplines today only in exceptions take the task of their classical idea seriously, that is, to transcend the limits of the given world of experience of human to the absolute and to consider the whole of reality, the metaphysical reference remains indispensable for theology. Instead of being satisfied with the results of the individual sciences, or pulling back into the internal relationships of its own science, theology must thus, according to Pannenberg, take this given deficit of philosophical orientation as an occasion to more strongly "engage with the history of philosophy, in order to se how philosophy in earlier times perceived the unsolved tasks still today of extensive orientation regarding reality, and what the problems of these solutions are." (ThuPh, 19) The studies on the relation of theology and philosophy offer selected examples for this.

In the beginning was *Plato*. In Platonic thought, it is not only the pre-Socratic origins of western philosophy that culminates, at the same time it was Platonism in the three main phases of its school-development, the third of which is perhaps best represented by Plotinus, that influenced Christian theology in the age of its formation and first development as deeply as no other philosophy of the antique world (cf. ThuPh, 37–68). In this, it is not merely a matter of external influences, but rather a "process of productive reception" (ThuPh, 37)[2], the essential moment of which Pannenberg presents in relation to three thematic circles: the Platonic doctrine of God and principles (cf. ThuPh, 40–50), the Platonic life ideal of becoming like God, including the psychological presuppositions which affect the doctrine of souls (cf. ThuPh, 50–55) and the context of epistemology and grace (cf. ThuPh, 56–58), which was determinative for the Platonic thought of enlightenment. In this it is shown that the process of Christian reception of Platonism was from the beginning on filled with tension. The Christian corrections and reformulations of Platonic doctrine (cf. ThuPh, 58–65) were primarily the definition of the relation between God and the world as well as anthropological foundations: the Neo-Platonic idea of a stair-like transition from the first

---

1 Cf. "Christliche Theologie und philosophische Kritik", in: Gottesgedanke und menschliche Freiheit, 1972, 48–77, here: 76 f.: "Philosophical critique dissolves the authoritative tradition-strucutre of religion. It forces that which comes through tradition to change, where it has become unable to grasp the present reality of life. With this, both religion and theology are presented with a challenge, but one such that both are given in this challenge the chance to impact their own nature more clearly."

2 Pannenberg has presented this process of reception paradigmatically in "The Appropriation o the philosophical concept of God as a Dogmatic Problem of Early Christian Theology" in BQiTh 2, 119–183.

principle to the material cosmos is rejected, the free opposite of the personally conceived Creator-God the creature is as emphasized as is the created nature of material. The Trinitarian-theological criticism of the thought of the pure One as well as the idea of the world-soul belongs in this context. Anthropologically, Christian theology insists on the created nature of the soul and the unity of body and soul, which can be made distinct but never divided, in denial of Plato's concept of the immortal divinity of the soul. This "has as a consequence another view and appreciation of the individuality of the single human in their unique life history, and in connection with this another view of personal immortality than was developed in the framework of Platonic thought. " (ThuPh, 62) As a consequence of this, the turn to history in the one enclosing understanding of the world-even in a reality of understanding which finds its basis in the historical uniqueness of the incarnation of Jesus. A transformation of cosmology into *heilsgeschichte* prepares its way, "which shall reach its high point in the thought of Augustine" (ThuPh, 65). Further Christian revisions of Platonism, for example regarding anamnesis, could be given.[3]

Although Platonic motifs remained effective in the Christian thought if the western middle ages and beyond that into the modern age (cf. ThuPh, 65 – 68), *Aristotle* became the absolute philosopher for Latin Christendom since the 13th century (cf. ThuPh, 69 – 89). Without going into detail regarding the relationship between the core of Aristotelian and Platonic thought, a difference which was felt less sharply in the philosophy of the late antique and patristic theology than in later times, it is merely maintained that the Christian reception of Aristotle was also in no case an uncritical, but rather a constructive process. Particular attention is earned in this by the Christian revision of the Aristotelian doctrine of the active intellect (essentially done for reason of faith in an individual resurrection), in which in contrast to the Philosopher is asserted to be a part of the human soul. Pannenberg interprets this process of revision, notably connected with the name of Albertus Magnus, as one of great consequence not only in theological history but also in that of philosophy, because with the assumption that the *intellectus agens* is an integral part of the human soul, the way is opened for the first time for the (in modern times, a matter of course) concept of the productive subjectivity of human knowledge acquisition, that is, the concept of an active human reason. The consequences of this process can be studied not least in the modern reformulation of the Aristotelian categories as, next to logic, one of the most

---

3 The critical reception of Plato by Augustine is handled in its importance for modern christian thought in "Chistentum und Platonismus", in: ZKG 96 (1985), 147 – 161; reprinted (also elsewhere) in BSTh 1, 58 – 73. A plea for the rationality of theology in the sense of the doctrine of conjecture from Nicholas Cusanus is found in "Die Rationalität der Theologie", in: M. Kessler, W. Pannenberg, and H. J. Pottmeyer (eds.), Fides quaerens intellectum. Beiträge zur Fundamentaltheology. Max Seckler zum 65. Geburtstag, 1992, 533 – 577; reprinted in BSTh 1, 74 – 84: "It is a matter of a conjectural thought in rational reconstruction, which, however, never exhausts the truth of God and thus remains correctable and surpassable." (BSTh 1, 78)

amazing and influential achievements of the Philosopher, as Kant's doctrine of the functions of understanding in the transcendental analytic of his "Critique of Pure Reason" proves.

As the third trend of antique thought which is particularly relevant for Christendom, next to Platonism and Aristotelianism, are the *stoic schools* (ThuPh, 90 – 105), although the relation between Christian theology and the Stoa is primarily determined by a fundamental opposition: "It was given through the transcendence of the biblical God to the world. The Stoics, however, claimed the complete immanence of the divine in the cosmos." (ThuPh, 93) Despite the immanent nature of the understanding of God and the world-piety of the Stoa, foreign to the spirit of Christendom, Christianity was able to take in stoic concepts in an remarkably large number of individual movements. Individually named are the idea of the *logos*, the idea of a creative *pneuma*, the thought of *pronoia* as well as aspects of epistemology, in particular the doctrines of natural knowledge of God, the natural law, the understanding of the conscience and general ethics. However, with all these noted aspects, one cannot miss the more-or-less decisive modifications. With this it is again confirmed that the relation of Christendom to antique thought can only be appropriately described as a process of productive reception. "Christian theology has received philosophical thoughts, but Christendom has also, for its part, changed philosophical awareness. This occurred through the fact that the Christian faith opened a new understanding of reality, the reality of the world and its divine origin as well as the reality of man. Particular aspects of this new understanding form man and world became not only topics of Christian theology, but also of philosophical contemplation, although one did not always remain aware of their Christian origins." (ThuPh, 106)

In summary, Pannenberg brings out the following topics individually, in reference to which Christendom has made a significant contribution to philosophy and general educational awareness (cf. ThuPh, 106 – 128): 1. The contingence of the world and all finite being; 2. The concentration on individuality of the human, in union with an understanding of his person mediated and based on Trinitarian theology, as well as the discovery of his mental subjectivity in the process of knowledge; 3. The understanding of the world as history in the sense of an irreversible process open to the future; 4. The positive evaluation of the infinite as being-determination of the divine origin of the world, and 5. A specific understanding of human freedom, and the ideas of love and reconciliation as effects of the Christian belief in the incarnation. "In all these cases, the affected topics along with Christendom are not simply fully immediately appeared in the awareness of man. This shows itself already in their prehistory, which reaches back to pre-Christian roots. However, each of these topics has received a decisive imprint through the spirit of Christendom." (ThuPh, 106)

In an epochally new stage of development for its history, in comparison to the antique world and the Middle Ages, Christendom encountered *modernity*.

The epochal turn of the modern age resulted largely from the confessional wars of the 16th and 17th centuries, and their undecided result.[4] Not only and not primarily was the break determined by motifs of intellectual history, but rather through experiences with the religious wars following the reformation and counter-reformation? The end of these, ultimately for all involved devastating, forced society in the middle of the 17th century to "determine the foundations of the systems of society in state, right, and morals anew, on a foundation untouched by confessional opposites. As such a basis, the general nature of man offered itself, and on this foundation that what Dilthey called a 'natural system' of humanities was achieved: a rational natural law, an idea of the state grounded on natural law, and ethics grounded in the nature of man – ultimately, a theory of religion arising from the same." (ThuPh, 138). The recourse to stoic traditions played no small role in this (cf. ThuPh, 102 – 105). While this meant a distancing from the confessional oppositions of doctrine and the anthropological concentration in their context, at the beginning it was in no case a turning-away from Christendom. As little as the renewal of the antique in the renaissance philosophy of the 15th century intended a break with Christian tradition, so little was the turn to anthropology in the 17th century originally intended as an opposing position to theology. It was first in a second phase that it came to a turn away from not only the controversial doctrines of the confession but from Christendom itself (cf. in detail ThuPh, 129–141).

Pannenberg shows that the fresh approaches of philosophy which defined the early modern period (cf. ThuPh, 142 – 173) were, as a rule, not at all hostile to Christendom and religion, in particular with the example of Descartes, whose renewal of metaphysics is acknowledged as (in his time) an epoch-making event, along with the founding of philosophical empiricism by John Locke. While *Descartes* appears in the common view of German history of philosophy as a "precursor of Kant and his epistemological subjectivism" (ThuPh, 143), Pannenberg sees him essentially as a re-founder of philosophical doctrines of God, who claimed the foundational function of his famous "*cogito ergo sum*" as not only sufficient in itself, but lifted it up in a higher ground of knowledge, as he gave with the intuitive idea of the infinite as the condition of possibility of the inclusion of every finite content, including one's own ego. "The introduction of the self-certainty of the thinking ego, which plays off of Augustine, opens access to the idea of God, but this is factually foundation for the self-understanding of the ego as well as for knowledge

---

4 "European modernism is not a consequence of the Reformation, it has not been the worldly realization of the Reformation principle of Christian freedom, as Hegel opined. It has arisen from the unintentional consequences of the Reformation, from the schism and the folliwng age of religious war after it as well as from the requirement to neutralize the political effects of confessional opposition after such experiences, in order to make possible societal peace." (Reformation und Kirchenspaltung, in: W.-D- Hauschild [ed., among others], Kirchengemeinschaft – Anspruch und Wirklichkeit [*festschrift* for G. Kretschmar], 1986, 137 – 148; reprinted in BSTh 3, 160 – 172, here: 171)

about things in the world. All that is finite, including one's own ego, can only be thought of as a limitation of the infinite" (ThuPh, 144). From this, it is not surprising that Descartes was perceived in his time as a renewer of a metaphysics which built on the intuition of the infinite, instead of being seen as the founder of an anthropological philosophy which bases itself on the purported direct evidence of the ego-certainty. As different as the interpretations of and deviations from Descartes in their evaluation of the distinction between *res cogitans* and *res extensa* are, Descartes' metaphysical fresh start with the intuition of the absolute as the highest condition of all content of human awareness was followed by Henry More, so influential for Newton, as well as Malebranche, Spinoza, and Leibniz, if with various accents.

In Pannenberg's judgment it remained for *Kant* (cf. ThuPh, 174–215) to divorce human reason from its reference to theological concepts, which were foundational for itself and its functions, and to reduce the idea of God to a limiting idea of theoretical reason, something which is no longer constitutive for human awareness of its self-relation and its relation to the world. In Kant's critique of reason the theistically grounded metaphysics of the enlightenment are accordingly dissolved in an anthropocentric description of the awareness of experience. With this, the process of modern emancipation had stepped into its phase of manifest criticism of religion, Christendom, and theology. Kant's ethics and his philosophy of religion change nothing in this. Despite his wide theological effects in supernaturalism, awakening theology, on Ritschl and his school and all the way to transcendental Thomism (cf. ThuPh, 203–215), the Königsberg thinker is seen rightly as the destroyer of metaphysics. He has, in opposition to his leading intention, but as a factual result of his philosophizing, "loosed the ego of reason and of the awareness of experience from every connection to God. Through the failure of the moral-philosophical re-founding of faith in God, this result came that much more impressively into view. Kant has factually, as Hegel has objected against him later, handled the finite ego as the absolute basis of experience, and thus, against his intention, set it in the place of God." (ThuPh, 201)

2. *"History of Problems in the Modern Protestant Theology in Germany"*

The relationship between theology and philosophy presents itself as a differentiated connection, which excludes an alternative opposition as well as indifferent equation, but also which cannot be appropriately understood in the long run in models of precedence or subordination. While the subordination of philosophy to theology characterized the Christian Aristotelianism of the Middle Ages, the reverse of this relation was characteristic for the enlightened thought of the modern age which arose from the demise of the medieval world. "from the Enlightenment, then, two further definitions for the relationship have taken their cue, namely, first the attempt to remove theology, faith, from subordination to the authority of reason, and the other, the attempt of philosophy to stake a claim itself for the content of faith through the sublation of religious concepts into the philosophical idea. Both tendencies presuppose the autonomy of philosophical reason, and insofar they presuppose the foundational position of the Enlightenment." (ThuPh, 30).

For the attempt of theology to make itself independent as a science of faith, Schleiermacher is exemplary, with his labors to secure for religion an own province in the soul beyond metaphysics and morals. The attempts of philosophy, in turn, to sublate the concepts of religion and Christian faith into the philosophical idea are connected typically with the name of Hegel. It is not without good reason that these two receive a key role in Pannenberg's "Problemgeschichte der neueren evangelischen Theologie in Deutschland" from 1997, a role which is not least decisive for the conceptional formation of the historiographical presentation. Significantly, this deviates "in one place from the orientation on the temporal advancement of the history" (Probl., 6) in order, after presentation of Schleiermacher's new foundation of theology as a theory of subjectivity and its radicalization in theologies of awakening, after examinations of Albrecht Ritschl and Wilhelm Hermann, and after the theocentric turn of Erich Schaeder and its peak in dialectic theology, to return to Hegel's initiation of a renewal of the doctrine of God and its resolution. After all, the problem which is connected with the task of theological concentration on the thought of the sovereignty of God and His revelation can be studied paradigmatically in the process of the relation of the speculative theology based on Hegel's philosophy of religion. That the perception of this task is non-negotiable for a theology that is true to itself is underscored by Pannenberg in chorus with both Hegel and Barth in disassociation from the diverse forms of faith-subjectivism in the history of modern theology, even when he sees the solution of this task neither in the thought of the former nor of the latter.

To go in order, that we might at least achieve a certain impression of the theological-historical course of the modern age as presented by Pannenberg: at the beginning is Schleiermacher (cf. Probl., 46–76; ThuPh, 239–256), because he was the one who grounded theology anew as a theory of subjectivity and prescribed the paradigmatic structural model for the thought of German Protestant theology in the 19th century, with the thesis of the constitution of human subject-nature from the relation to God. With his fundamental-anthropological theology of religion, Schleiermacher summed up not only the development of Protestant theology in the post-reformation, post-confessional epoch following the wars of religion, as was characterized by the increasing independence of state and right through recourse to the idea of the "nature" of man and through an advancing privatization of religious confession and, as a consequence of this, an increasingly developing secular cultural awareness (cf. Probl., 25 ff.); revealed for German Protestant theology at the same time that unity of problem-awareness that characterizes it beyond the 19th century and into the present, even in all its positional distinctions and internal differences.

As large as the importance is that Pannenberg acknowledges to the church father of the 19th century in the independence of Christendom in the modern world, so critically does he judge at the same time the tendency of Schleiermacher's anthropocentric thought towards subjectivism. This becomes more apparent in the course of his development from the 1799 edition of the speeches "On Religion", to the "Christian Faith" of 1821/22 and 1830/31. Not that Pannenberg evaluates the process of modern emancipation, and thus the cultural framing conditions of newer theology as a whole, as less positive as was for example the case in the magnum opus of Emanuel Hirsch to the modern "remodeling circles" of Christendom after the results of the wars of religion; it is thoroughly Schleiermacher's theology itself and in the specific sense in which it influenced the unity of the awareness of problems in modern Christianity against which he has elemental reservations. Indeed, Pannenberg is not pleading for an anti-modern retreat, which desires to fix theology directly on a level that is its, so to speak, mythical original history, be it that of the Reformation or be it that of the early church. Such a suggestion is in contrast not only evaluated as reactionary, but as pragmatically impossible. In the awareness that the question of the universal validity of Christendom in the modern age can only be raised on the level of the question regarding the nature of human existence, Pannenberg knows himself as connected not only with the modern situation in distinction to the antique and medieval in general, but along with Schleiermacher in the particular. However, what brings forth a decisive objection is the trend to a subjectivism which is prone to disconnect religious internality from world experience, as Pannenberg sees, among other places, in the surrender of the original primacy of notion in the idea of religion and the retreat to feeling and immediate self-awareness.[5]

This objection becomes sharper against the radicalization of subjectivity in awakening theology, which is introduced with the example of F.A.G. Tholuck (cf. Probl, 78 – 79). Though the Herrnhuter Schleiermacher tried to ground the subjectivity of religion in a full theory of human subjectivity in order to prove

---

5 Pannenberg expressed his criticism of Schleiermacher even more sharply in "Religiöse Erfahrung und christlicher Glaube" in A. Kreiner and P. Schmidt-Leuket (eds.), Religiöse Erfahrung und theologische Reflexion (festschrift for Heinrich Döring), 1993, 113 – 123; reprinted in BSTh 1, 132 – 144. According to this, "Schleiermacher's description of religious experiences in the second speech on religion [remains] on the level of natural religion, in which the divine power is perceived in its appearance in a finite medium, but is not thematized in its distinction from the medium" (BSTh 1, 136). To the difficulties with creation, cf. "Schleiermachers' Schwierigkeiten mit dem Schöpfungsgedanken" in the report of this name published by the Bavarian Academy of Sciences, Philosophical-Historical class (München 1996).

religion as an anthropological universal, the late pietist Tholuck radicalized the principle of subjectivity such that only individual experience could still function as a criterion of verification. As much as Tholuck's theology claimed to be a theology of revelation and scripture, so much was it also based always on the conviction of an immediate coincidence of knowledge of God and knowledge of self in the heart: the self-experience of the sinful human, his awareness of guilt and need for salvation are as a result not only indispensable moments, but also foundational for knowledge of God, not only a medium to perceive personal guilt, but at the same time a means to overcome it. From this internal tension, it can be explained why it is that Tholuck could be taken as initiator of extremely different theological movements. For Tholuck, the possibility to allow faith to be taken up into subjective self-experience is calculated as much as the possibility of connecting everything to the positive authority of revelation, as manifested in the authentically interpreted word of scripture in the confessions. With the examples of the new confessional theology from Erlanger Lutheranism from Adolf von Harleß to Ludwig Ihmels (cf. Probl., 89 – 100) the ambivalence of the tradition of awakening theology is shown as it comes to light in the history of influence, as well as the new Bible-theology of Julius Müller, Hermann Cremer, and Martin Kähler (cf. Probl., 100 – 120), which connects to Johann Tobias Beck. In particular it is Kähler who provides Pannenberg with an instructive example for ambivalences and limitations which are connected to the awakening-theology correlation principle of faith and scripture, faith and gospel. However, here is not the place to examine this in such detail.

A remarkable fresh start of modern theology marks, in Pannenberg's judgment, the theology of Albrecht Ritschl (cf. Probl., 121 – 136), whose inspiring topic became the evidence of Christian continuity in its history. The importance of Ritschl, which even led to the building of a whole school of thought, is essentially conditions by the fact "that he grounded the confidence to historical Christendom on its historical examination itself and thus opened a middle way between simple faith in authority in scripture and confession on one side and the subjectivism of awakening theology on the other." (Probl., 121). There were three major problems which Ritschl attempted to solve out of interest in the historical continuity of Christendom: the problem of the transition of ancient Christianity into the developing early catholic church, that of the internal unity of the reformation, and ultimately the continuity of the effects through history of reformation-based Christendom. Ritschl's major individual monographs as well as his entire work are calculated towards the solution of these problems. This is not explained by Pannenberg without sympathy, though one can demonstrate positive conceptions influences on the own system-building, for example, in the case of the allocation of justification and reconciliation. Even the discovery of the eschatological meaning of Jesus' message by Johannes Weiß, the ignoring of which over the long-term damaged Ritschl and his school the most, would have been, according to Pannenberg, combinable with Ritschl's theological foundational intentions. For the connection between the Kingdom of God and ethics, which was particularly important for Ritschl as a result of his Kant reception, which reminds one of the older supernaturalism (cf. Probl., 37 ff.), was first with Jesus not to be denied and also in a systematic sense not to be rejected. "It must merely be formulated differently than was the case with Ritschl. The Kingdom of God must not be understood as the extension of human action and their completion, but rather His coming must be understood as God's own initiative. This can quite well occur in connection with the philosophical thought of the highest good, which had been connected since Kant – and so, with Ritschl – with the thought of the Kingdom of God. This thought of the highest good is in itself complex, as Kant knew well: the highest Good in a genuinely Platonic sense (thought as an origin) precedes all human actions and desire for happiness. The highest good that can be brought about by human action in the world can, as Kant explicitly noted, only be called the highest good in a derivative sense. The original highest good, however, that is God Himself, is able to inspire humans to act, to lift them to freedom, and to make them capable of conceiving of the idea of a good which can be made real through their actions, a good which lets itself be described as the anticipation of the future of God Himself as the highest food for the world. (Probl., 135 f.) Pannenberg continues: "Ritschl's school unfortunately has not had the strength to develop Ritschl's thought of the Kingdom of God further in the direction suggested by the discovery of the eschatological character of the Kingdom in the message of Jesus. Much more, already Weiß and following him Harnack and Hermann pulled back from the eschatology of Jesus to His word regarding the presence of the Kingdom of God "in us" (Lk. 17:21). The questionable translation of this word, that actually means that the Kingdom of God already is dawning "among us", that is in the presence of the contemporaries and hearers of Jesus, with the expression "in you", which pointed towards the internality of man and allowed theology a clear conscience in returning to a subjectivist understanding of faith, one which even weighed down the beginnings of dialectical theology." (Probl., 136). With the example of Wilhelm Herrmann the bent towards awakening theology from Ritschl's theology is presented, in exhaustive detail (cf. Probl. 163 – 166).

   In Pannenberg's presentation of the history of theology, Hermann and the forced retreat of his theology from objective historical facts to a subjectivism of pure experience marks not only the end of the Ritschl school, but also the transition to *dialectical theology*. Instead of reforming the historical method-ical awareness in the critique of positivism and instead of developing it further to a universal theory of the history of tradition (which would include the difference from facts and meaning), Hermann released the objectivity of the world of history and with it the objective world of nature from the area of responsibility for theology, in order to take theology and with it the Christian religion back to an abstractly conceived subjectivity of pure internality. The emptiness of its feeling of guild and the in general remaining faith in forgiveness, which loses all content definition like the feeling of guilt does, characterizes this as a late pietistic declining form of that subjectivity which appeared in Schleiermacher in its devout first bloom of youth. From this regressive situation in modern theology, in which religious awareness reduces itself in flight to the point of individual subjectivity, comes, according to Pannenberg, the transition to the early form of dialectical theology, as it can be encountered in the beginnings of Rudolf Bultmann and Karl Barth. "In the thought of both the God-world opposites, already claimed by Hermann, were brought to such a peak, that it no longer coincided with the opposites of the spiritual to the naturally given, but was understood even as the opposite of the spiritual life reality of man. This, however, had as a consequence that the independence of one's judgment, emphasized by Hermann, regarding the tradition had to be given up in its central place. The kerygma in the sense of Bultmann demanded, as did the Word of God in Barth's sense, an obedience of faith without critical inquiry regarding the legitimacy of the call to faith. This could occur because neither Bultmann nor Barth returned to Hermann's original topic of certainty in the historical ground of faith in the person of Jesus Christ, but rather both completed the independence of theology from such a connection to a historical ground of faith." (Probl., 161)

With this, the essential grounds for Pannenberg's doubts are named, whether one can overcome the aporias of Wilhelm Hermann's theology through sharpening the dualism between God and the world and the opposition of God and the world and all that is present to humans without compromise. Nonetheless, the theo-centric return from Hermann's anthro-pocentricism prepared through Erich Schaeder (cf. Probl., 168–176) in no case denied their foundational correctness as a whole. Not only the fact that Hermann's interest in preserving the freedom of faith, which is obligated to one's own judgment, has failed in the subjective tightening of his idea of experience gives the new start in theo-centricism a momentary right. A moment of truth is beyond this also not fundamentally denied in the respect of its extensive criticism of the religio-theological concentration on humanity, characteristic for modern theology as a whole. In particular Barth's turn to a new grounding of dogmatics on the doctrine of the Trinity, in consequence of which he at least modified some of the diastatic positions he took at the beginning, is something which it is possible for Pannenberg to judge as positive and helpful. Barth's theo-centricism as such, to say nothing of the Trinitarian organization of his systematics, do not offer occasion for criticism. It is much more the unmediated beginning with the subjectivity of God in His revelation and the revealed unity of God and man in Jesus Christ, which itself impedes the Trinitarian-theological intention, and which draws Pannenberg's objections. "We are fooling ourselves, when we say that the words 'God' and 'man' are first able to be given meaning in with the thesis of the unity of God and man in Jesus Christ. Theology cannot begin straight from zero with the

Christological confession, as the insight of Barth in the sovereignty of God in His revelation, belonging to the Godhood of God, seems to demand. The sovereignty of God in His revelation must rather much more be thought of as the raising up of these, its inevitable presuppositions." (Probl., 197)

Where one fails to do such theoretical work of mediating ideas, or where one intentionally avoids it, the thought of revelation loses necessarily its content-determination and degenerates into a formal term that at last must appear as random settlement. Speech about God and His revelation takes on, under these conditions, the character of mere assurance, which in its lack of theoretical demonstrability is based on pure decision or sheer authority. "And therein lies the main problem of Barth's radically theo-centric approach. For the grounding of his speech about God remained to him…only the way of direct settlement, which, meant as the self-setting of God, must present itself as an arbitrary setting of the subjectivity of the theologian, at least in the fact of the contentious nature of divine reality." (Probl., 199) instead of overcoming the anthropocentricism in theology which he criticized, Barth drove it into its most extreme consequence. "it is a deeply ironic phenomenon that precisely the decided theo-centricism of Barth, which should overcome all anthropocentricism and subjectivism in modern theology, ends up in an extreme escalation of this same subjectivism, so resisted by Barth. The anthropological grounding of theology by Schleiermacher could at least show up with the claim to universal validity, and something similar is true – with limitations – yet of the ethical grounding of the truth of Christian revelation in the awakening theology from Tholuck to Wilhelm Hermann's description of the 'way to religion'." (Probl., 201). In Barth's thought, as Pannenberg says, comes in the place of theological theory of human subjectivity the subjective decision of the theologian, which still remains in the foundation after the re-acquisition of the decisiveness of ecclesial authority, as succeeded in Barth's later development. The observation that the connection between decisionism and the thought of authority belonged to the larger context of the cultural situation at the time takes nothing away from the sharpness of Pannenberg's criticism. Indeed, Barth's theology made possible resistance against the *zeitgeist*, and brought this resistance about, but it was a matter of "resistance on the level of the same principle, of the same form of thought" (Probl., 204).

No less sharp and serious than the criticism of Barth are the objections against Bultmann. His development from the starting position of dialectical theology moved in a different direction that that of Barth, much like that of Emil Brunner and Friedrich Gogarten, whose theological personalism receives its own observation which will not be repeated here (cf. Probl., 323 – 247). "In this it was precisely the problems of the relation of the God-proclamation of the church to the situation of man, pushed aside by Barth, and the conditions of understanding which must be presupposed in the use of the word "God", and ultimately the historical questions which are inevitably connected to reference to Jesus Christ, which became motifs of distancing oneself from

Barth's theological path." (Probl., 205) In this context Pannenberg can value Bultmann's program of demythologization, despite the problem of the presupposed idea of mythos, as a justified reflex to Barth's unhistorical exegesis. Also is the demand of existential interpretation justified, insofar as one cannot speak appropriately of God without taking into account the human and his existential constitution. "However, also and precisely the proper awareness and speech of God will always differentiate God from man, as man in his finitude is infinitely inferior, as the infinite opposite of man and all finite things and appearances." (Probl., 214 f.). insofar as the existential interpretation and the wholesale prohibition on objectification could not sufficiently accommodate this differentiation, and in connection with this tended to blend out the elemental world-reference of the content of religious tradition and de-historicize the kerygma according, Bultmann's approach led to a reduction of theological statement about God as well as of those about the world to statements about possibilities of human self-understanding. This anthropological reduction could lead to that dissolution of the opposites of God-man and God world, contrary to the original intention of dialectical theology, just as it is factually the case in the currently fashionable "death of God" theology, but also as is seen in a Bultmann student like Herbert Braun, indeed, already in Bultmann's own later phases. "Insofar as this is not a matter of an unintentional derailing, but of the most extreme consequence of the demand for demythologization of the idea of God itself, connected with existential interpretation, the theological-historical function of Bultmann's theology can be understood as the dissolution of dialectical theology. As Bultmann thematized the relativity of God-certainty, suppressed by Barth and intentionally cut off, into the self-understanding of man, but now in the sense of a reduction to the understanding of existence, he had as a result to come to the dissolution of the opposition of the reality of God to that of man." (Probl., 226). It is on this background that the view of the fact that Bultmann's dissolution of the opposition between God and the world with his sublation of history into the kerygma hangs tightly together that the inquiry which arose in the Bultmann school regarding the origin of the early Christian kerygma in the historical Jesus Himself is valued as a new beginning that is as necessary as it is requiring of development (cf. Probl., 226 ff.).

Despite the critical judgment of Barth and Bultmann, which leaves nothing to be desired in its clarity, Pannenberg opines that the emergence of dialectical theology has not been in vain: "It has demonstrated the necessity, but also the difficulty, of a theology which takes the sovereignty of God in His revelation seriously. Here lies in particular the continuing service of Karl Barth's theology. Through Bultmann and his school are the problems pushed aside by the particular shape of Barth's theo-centric method in the thought of God, the understanding of man, and the historical problem of the early Christian message of Christ in its relation to Jesus of Nazareth again brought into awareness. That is its function in the history of theology. However, with this, the theocentric approach has fallen victim to demythologization. One does have to take this result as historical fate. It is merely a matter of the failure of Bultmann's specific concept of dialectical theology, with its approach from the sovereignty of God. The partner to this remains the renewal of the theo-centric approach in Barth and his Trinitarian execution of the same, despite the defects in Barth's theology – and it remains pioneering." (Probl., 231 f.), With this, the essential determinations for the task for the current concept of systematic theology are named.

3. Rationality of Faith

According to Pannenberg, the essential function of modern history of theology as a discipline of systematic theology is "to hold erect the awareness of the unified situation of problems for Christian theology in modern times." (Probl., 16). This is in order to be able to order the currently defended positions into a unified frame of reference and at the same time to define them, the future task of which is given from the present context of problems. In reference to the "theology of crisis", which itself is at least since the middle of the 20th century in a crisis, and as which dialectical theology was originally called, the demand is given as the determination of a task for every further phase of development in theology that the agenda, developed primarily by Barth, to think of the sovereignty of and Godhood of God as such, and not to let them fall by the wayside, but to continue to think of them, "in order to free this central agenda from the aporias in which it became stuck in Barth's thought" (Probl., 247). The emphases of dialectical theology next to Barth help, in Pannenberg's opinion, "not much further" (Ibid.). "To clear up and overcome the aporias of Barth's theo-centric approach would rather be helped by the question, from whence the thought-motifs of Barth come which he has used to work out the thought of the sovereignty of God. This question leads to the importance of speculative theology in the development of Barth's thought." (Ibid.)

Pannenberg dedicates the closing chapter of his history of problems in modern Protestant theology to the answering of this question, which deals with the renewal of the doctrine of God in speculative theology and its dissolution, in deviance from the chronological order. The factual nearness of Barth's theo-centric position to that of speculative theology, which goes out from Schelling and before all from *Hegel*, and of which Barth is aware in reference primarily to I.A. Dorner, comes particularly explicitly to light in the effort to develop theology from the subject-hood of God. This effort it still characteristic for Barth's doctrine of the Trinity, which locates itself entirely within the tradition of speculative theology. Indeed, Barth said himself that he wanted to ground the doctrine of the Trinity from the historical revelation of

God in Jesus Christ. "But factually, he developed his argument from the mere thought of the subject-hood of God as the self-revealing Lord, and with this, it might connect, that Barth, despite his objection to Hegel in the aspect of the freedom of God, could not pull away from the Hegelian form of thought in which subjectivity is the principle of the understanding of God in His revelation and His Trinitarian differentiation." (Probl., 259)

The objection against Hegel and parts of speculative theology that the sovereignty of God's freedom transcends all necessary thought is only expressed under very limited conditions in Barth's unfolding of the doctrine of the Trinity, insofar as this comes not from exegetical results but from the internal logic of the idea of revelation or the subjectivity of God. While this is the case, in the Trinitarian beginnings this objections is quite clear: Barth gave a form to the access of the otherwise speculatively grounded idea of God a decisionistic, from thought- and reflection- mediated manners of under- standing separated, "in demanding of theology the courage to begin with a certainty of God. For Barth, then, the standpoint should be reached through an act of subjective decision from whence the self-explication of God in His revelation – and in God Himself as the ground of His revelation – should be developed in the manner of speculative theology." (Probl., 260). Pannenberg's criticism is focused on the aspect of the decisionistic beginning. This decisionism has allowed Barth's theo-centricism to fall back into the merely subjective individual piety in the position of Wilhelm Herrmann. In this sense is Barth's dialectical theology consumed in a self-destructive dialectic. In opposition to this, the speculative theology of Hegel and his students has earned the clear advantage, when also the accusation that Hegel had placed the limits of necessary thought around the freedom of God is not taken from thin air.

Here is not the place to unfold the genesis of idealistic philosophy (cf. ThuPh, 216–239) or the grounds for the extreme importance which Pannenberg acknowledges of Hegel's systematic thought had for religion and Christianity in the history of theology (cf. Probl., 206–276 and ThuPh, 257–276). Instead, we draw immediately the mentioned problem of Hegel's idea of God (cf. Probl., 276–289), which is mediated though the speculative support of religious elevation. As little as this as this is affected by the sweeping accusation of pantheism, as is claimed by the so-called left-Hegelians and not seldom taken up by theologians (cf. in detail ThuPh, 276–284), as justified is the critique for Pannenberg "that Hegel had thought of the reality of God as a process of His self-unfolding in the sense of the logical necessity of human thought-execution." (Probl., 282) With this, he handled neither the individ- uality of the individual finite, not from the logic of the idea to be grasped, in the contingence of its existence, nor the creative freedom of God correctly. This creative freedom has brought for the world contingently and not with necessity, that is not in the manner of a necessary process of thought. Indeed, with this Hegel's efforts are not at all criticized, when he tries to understand the reality of God in the medium of thought, but rather the insertion of finite thinking- and thought-determinations into the absolute reality of God, as it was done with the thought of the spirit as subject and the structural equivalence of the subject- or ego-idea with the idea of ideas as the highest thought of logic. If one wished to criticize Hegel's assumption of a logically necessary self-unfolding of God from its idea in a meaningful manner, one would have to subject his definition of God to the criticism which comes along with the thought of the early Fichte from a self-setting of the ego, and which shares its theological aporias. Holding fast to the thought of a self-setting of the subjects is to be judged the actual limitation of Hegel's philosophy, and in particular his idea of God, which cannot be appropriately thought of in the logic of a self-setting and self-realizing subjectivity, as the unity of God is "living reality only in the three Persons and their mutual mediation." (Probl., 289)

The idea of subject taken from the early Fichte (cf. in detail ThuPh, 216 – 226)[6], which was merely expanded in reference to objectivity, marks for Pannenberg not only the aporetic point upon which serious objection to Hegel's philosophical doctrine of God are concentrated, but also it marks the starting point for the historical dissolution of the Hegelian idea of God in the historical process of reflection by his student. Ludwig Feuerbach, Bruno Bauer and David Friedrich Strauß are given as examples (cf. Probl., 289 – 302): the first stands for the sublation of the individual into nature, the second for the reduction of the infinite to the finite subject, and the third ultimately for the thought of collective God-humanity, in which he meant to bring the Christian central idea of divine-human unity in Jesus Christ in the sense of Hegel. Although this, as in both of the former cases, is a matter of fundamentally false interpretation of the philosophical theology of Hegel, the thesis of the subject-

---

6 For the development of ego-philosophy cf. also "Fichte und die Metaphysik des Unendlichen", in: Zeitschrift für philosophische Forschung 46 (1992), 348 – 362; reprinted in BSTh 1, 32 – 44. In connection with Dieter Heinrich's examination of 1967 on the development of Fichte between 1794 and the beginning of the new century, particular attention is given to the question, to what extent the return to a pre-Kantian metaphysic can claim relevance after the Kantian criticism of metaphysics. This is made topical in the Spinoza-reception of Fichte and his relation to Descartes. "Fichte accepted, in his later philosophy, the thesis of Spinoza regarding God as sole substance. However, his philosophical view is in many respects nearer that of Descartes than Spinoza. Fichte, as Descartes, but also differently than Spinoza, developed his thought of the infinite as that of absolute being from a description of the ego and its awareness." (BSTh 1, 41). With the later Fichte, a new level of grounding the thought of God as non-recourse intuition of the infinite as the condition of possibility for the awareness of finitude was reached, even under post-Kantian conditions. The critical reservations which Pannenberg has even against the later Fichte are connected to the question, whether the Absolute is accessible as the constitution ground of self-awareness through transcendental reflection, that is, directly through entrance into the self-awareness, or only through the detour of world experience. While Fichte's philosophy of religion assumes a mystical turning into the self, in order to consummate in the self, Pannenberg sees the Infinite present to man in the ground of self-awareness as first identifiably through the revelation of God in history.

hood of God brought about by Feuerbach, Bauer and Strauß and its transferral into anthropology brought about "an element of pragmatic inevitability – at least for a time which proved itself unable to overcome the insufficient forms of execution from the foundational insights of Hegel's philosophy. For this, however, a deep revision of the Hegelian understanding of the absolute as a subject, and thus the foundation of his entire philosophy, would have been necessary. The movements within his school which made an effort to preserve Hegel's philosophy, in particular his philosophy of religion, could not understand this, and thus Hegel's concept of the absolute must fall to criticism. His idea of the subject is literally a result of a transferral of the finite subjectivity of man to the absolute. It is the idea of subject in the ego-philosophy of the early Fichte, simply expanded by the inclusion of objectivity in the movement of the self-realization of the ego. This ego is already as an absolute ego, in the sense of Fichte, the limitless form of human subjectivity, the finite ego. The removal of limits from the concept of the subjectivity of the ego led already in Fichte's thought of a self-setting of the ego in its action to aporias which were repeated I Hegel's doctrine of the self-unfolding of the absolute subject in the process of its revelation. Through this insufficiency of his idea of God as a subject, Hegel brought out a criticism which exposed this idea in one form or another as a mere projection of the finite subjectivity of man." (Probl., 304 f.)

The anthropologization of not only cosmology, but also the thought of God and the absolute is characteristic for *the post-Hegelian situation of thought*, in which the turn to anthropology (cf. ThuPh, 294 – 358) has determined both the philosophy and theology of the time. In philosophy, it is frequently not a matter of the fact "that man is the starting point for the awareness of God, but rather God is reduced to being a thought of man." (ThuPh, 294) Not only in the thought of Feuerbach, but also of Stirner, Marx and Nietzsche did "the replacement of God by man become programmatic" (ThuPh, 295).[7] The latter has grasped the anti-Christian and anti-theistic sense of the post-Hegelian turn to humanity as no other, and brought it to its nihilistic consequences (cf. ThuPh, 315 – 325). This has become the starting point of diverse gestalts of a new determination of human existence after the death of God. Among the various existential philosophies which arose between the two world wars, stands out next to that of Jaspers the philosophy of Martin Heidegger (ThuPh, 325 – 337), in whose main work "Time and Being" despite intentions beyond this, the ontological topic is factually taken back into the understanding of being in the carrying out of human existence. This is valid in a certain sense also already for Søren Kierkegaard, although according to his thesis, against

---

7 Cf. "Types of Atheism and their Theological Significance" in BQiTh 2, 184 – 200. Cf. further: Reden von Gott angesichts atheistischer Kritik, in: EvKomm 2 (1969), 442 – 446; reprinted in Gottesgedanke und menschliche Freiheit, 1972, 29 – 47.

Nietzsche and Heidegger, "the individual human is already always referred to
the eternal in the dialectic of his self-understanding" (ThuPh, 305).

The turn to anthropology characteristic in the dissolution from Hegel in
many philosophical new starts since the middle of the 19th century, which
gained its radicalism in comparison to the two preceding centuries which
considered the nature of human existence through its tendency towards often
open criticism of religion and theology, is in a comparable manner identifiable
with the post-Hegelian history of theology. As a paradigmatic case of a
theology of immanence we are shown A.E. Biedermann, whose works show
"that in the train of the left-Hegelian Hegel critique religion was only available
as a topic as a subjective behavior of man and in any case as such to be
defended in its justification against criticisms of religion." (Probl., 310).
Pannenberg continues: the criticism of Hegel's idea of the absolute subject and
its logical self-unfolding has as a consequence that in liberal theology religion
was once again a central topic as life-execution of man in the place of the reality
of the absolute (Ibid.). Using the example of the religion-psychology of Otto
Pfleiderer and the concept of Richard Adelbert Lipisus this is made clear.
Especially with the latter it becomes completely clear "that the idea of religion
in liberal theology after the surrender of Hegel's dialectical logic and his
thought of the self-unfolding of the absolute once again was limited to the
subjectivity of religious experience. The objective reality of the awareness of
God appeared not to be provable on the basis of a psychology of religious
experience without a falling back into pre-Kantian metaphysics. It is
remarkable how close liberal theology comes to the theological subjectivism
which came from pietism and awakening theology. The difference lay only in
that the liberal theory of religions did not restrict the religion theme to moral
awareness, but rather saw it as a given with the finite of man as such. But it was
no longer seen that with the awareness of finitude the thought of infinitude is
always already present, and indeed as a condition for the possibility of
understanding finite content at all, such that also philosophy of religion cannot
limit itself to the description of the finitude of religious awareness without
bringing onto itself Hegel's accusation of making finite subjectivity absolute."
(Probl., 313 f.)

Pannenberg's "Problemgeschichte" closes with an examination of the topic
"history and the question after the truth of religion" (Probl., 314–349) which
takes particular reference to F.C. Baur's speculative draft pf the history of
Christendom, upon which the ethico-theology of Ernst Troeltsch[8] and the

---

8 In the history of the relation between dogmatics and ethics, Pannenberg sees a key role in Ernst
   Troeltsch, insofar he completes the ethical intention in a certain sense by expanding ethics to a
   universal philosophy of culture and society, but also takes it to its limits: "the insight in this fact
   makes legitimate the return which occurred in dialectical theology away from the priority of
   ethics to dogmatics which Troeltsch claimed despite all criticism of the insufficiency of how this
   turn was carried out in dialectical theology." Cf. also the foreword to EuE, in which the debate
   between Troeltsch and W. Hermann regarding the grounding of ethics at the beginning of the 20th

theonomy-concept of Paul Tillich take reference, and at the same time which points to Pannenberg's own system. These references can be taken from the final passage of the study on the relationship of theology and philosophy in the light of their common history. This is true for the examination of the so-called philosophical anthropology (cf. ThuPh, 337 – 345), of the natural-philosoph-ical expansion of its perspective from Henri Bergson, Samuel Alexander, and Alfred North Whitehead (cf. ThuPh, 345 – 358) as well as not least the comments on Wilhelm Dilthey (cf. ThuPh, 307 – 315) whose reflections on the historicity of metaphysic in the frame of a historicity valid for all appearances of life, despite the questions that he leaves open about the whole of life, mean, according to Pannenberg "a quite important advancement of philosophical insight, also beyond Hegel" (ThuPh, 315).[9] Hegel has indeed principally

century is acknowledged: "The difference which is come to expression in the opposition of these two concepts of the situation has not been reached by the later awareness of theological ethics and certainly not bettered. In my judgment, the most fruitful perspective is opened not by the fascinating ethics of Hermann, who focuses on Christian subjectivity, but the ethic of the highest Good in Troeltsch, who connects on to Schleiermacher. This must be, in critical connection with the argumentation of Troeltsch – with consideration of the turn in the relation of ethics and dogmatics made by Barth – oriented on the thought of the Kingdom of God as the future of God which confronts both individual and society, but not as a postulated theocentrism, but rather through the mediation of a criticism of the various philosophical expositions of the question of the good. In the execution of such an ethic precedence will be given, in the sense of Troeltsch' argumentation, to the 'objective' ethics of social institution over the otherwise abstract theme of individual ethics of personality." (EuE, 5.f) For the relation of dogmatics and ethics cf. further the detailed examinations in: Grundlagen der Ethik. Philosophisch-theologische Perspektiven, 1996, in particular 101 – 103. Although Pannenberg accords to dogmatics a grounding function for ethics, he does not deny its relative independence, which should be acknowledged within Christian theology in the relation to dogmatics. This relative independence arises from the necessity to ground ethical arguments on an anthropological basis. At the same time, the inde-pendence of ethics from dogmatics remains a relative one. In the necessity and factuality of specific Christian modifications of the anthropological foundations of ethical arguments, "the dogmatic presuppositions of Christian ethics become concrete in reference to the anthropolo-gical foundation itself, upon which ethical arguments must move" (op. cit. 104). The first im-portant anthropological aspect for Christian ethics is the destiny of man to communion with God as the basis of the value of the individual as well as for a life order in justice and freedom of communal life; the second aspect is marked by the topic of sin.

9 Cf. to this the comment in the lecture "Ein theologiscer Rückblick auf die Metaphyisk" in: Heidelberger Jahrbücher 39 (1995), 19 – 23; reprinted in BSTh 1, 27 – 31: "The deepest critique of the formation of metaphysical systems appears to me…to be that of Dilthey, that the meta-phyisical thinker has not or has not sufficiently thought the historicity of one's own though as the thought of a finite ego along with the concept. With this, the hermeneutic of human experience in its historicity become the ground for the interpretation of the thought-history of metaphysics." (BSTh 1, 30). Pannenberg confirms that he sees the importance of Dilthey's thought for his own as greater than that of Hegel in: M. Baumann, Roundatble. Conversations with European Theolo-gians, Grand Rapids, 1990, 43 – 53, here: 48: "I am not a Hegelian. I just happen to think that Hegel was one of the outstanding minds in the history of modern thought, one whose work sets a high standard for us to follow. That is why I believe that theology after Hegel should strive to rise to his level of sophistication and rigor. But very few of my ideas did I actually get from Hegel – very few. I feel much more closely related and indebted to thinkers other than Hegel. His ideas, for example,

overcome the relativization of all experience to the awareness of the finite subject, which largely determined the developments of modern philosophy since Kant and beyond this the secularized world and the theology of the time after the Enlightenment, thought the demonstration of the constitutive function of the infinite and absolute for the self-and world-experience of the human. And yet, he – not least as a consequence of the continuing predominance of the subject idea and the remaining virulence of the Fichtean self-setting aporia – is in tension through the thesis of yet-to-be-achieved sublation of religious concepts in the philosophical idea, indeed in contradiction "to his own insight in toe dependence of philosophical understanding of the absolute true from historically given religion. From this latter, a consideration of the thoroughgoing historicity and thus the finitude of philosophical understanding, even in relation to absolute truth, could have been suggested, with the consequence of a sublation of philosophical theology into revelatory theology or philosophy of religion, the latter of which just as that other makes the presupposition of the historical givenness of the object explicit." (ThuPh, 35)

Thus, the direction for Pannenberg's approach in his own systematic conception is given. It is valid: "Theology must deal appropriately with the historicity of the situation of faith as well as of theological thought itself, given the fact of an open future and together with the historicity of its object, within the framework of a hermeneutic of historical experience without surrendering the trust in the ultimate truth of the revelation of God in Jesus of Nazareth." (Probl., 352). As theology thinks of God and the future of His Kingdom as the cause and completion of that whole upon which all human world- and self-experience is proleptically referential, it becomes not only aware of the point toward which the history of humanity is going; it perceives at the same time that faith, in its trust in the eschatological coming of the God of reason, can assist its own rationality through hindering its own self-totalization and takes occasion to appropriately differentiate itself from its divine ground and goal. The reason which has come to awareness of itself and of its destiny understands itself as an anticipation. The idea of ideas, by means of this reason knows itself truly, is an anticipation and cannot be removed from religious relationship.[10]

are not as good as those of Wilhelm Dilthey, to whose assumptions in the area of hermeneutics I am indebted."

10 "Faith can confirm itself as the criterion for the rationality of reason just by its orientation toward a final, eschatological future." (Faith and Reason, in BQiTh 2, 46 – 64, here. 64)

Bibliography of Wolfhart Pannenberg's Publications 1998 – 2012

1998

599. Review of Markwart Herzog: Descensus ad Inferos (Frankfurt, Knecht 1997), in: ThLZ 122, 1997, 1151 – 1153.
600. The Historical Jesus as a Challenge to Christology, in: Dialog 37, 1998, 22 – 27.
601. Neue Konsense, entschärfte Gegensätze und protestantische Ängste, in: Idea Informationsdienst 16, 1998 vom 5.2.1998, I – IV.
602. Übereinstimmung in christlichen Grundwahrheiten. Thesen zur "Gemeinsamen Erklärung zur Rechtfertigungslehre", in: Evang. Gemeindeblatt für Württemberg 93, 1998, 6 (8. Febr. 1998), 4.
603. When Everything is permitted, in: First Things 80, 1998, 26 – 30.
604. Evangelische Überlegungen zum Petrusdienst des römischen Bischofs, in: Zeitwende 69, 998, 13 – 25 (cf. Nr. 593).
605. Fondamenti dell' etica. Prospettive filosofico-teologiche (ital. Translation of Nr. 556 by Marco Zanini), Editrice Queriuiana, Brescia 1998, 214 pp.
606. Eine Antwort, in: Lo Statuto della Teologia Morale Fondamentale, Pontificia Università Lateranense 1997 a cura die Livio Melina, Città del Vaticano 1997, 71 – 80. (op.tit.) in: Anthropotes 13, 1997, 485 – 492.
607. Ostersonntag. 1. Korinther 15,1 – 11. Exegetisch-systematische Besinnung und Predigt, in Homilet. Liturgisches Korrespondenzblatt NF 15, 1997/98, 58, 197 – 203.
608. Ecumenical Anxieties, in: First Things 84, 1998, 68 – 70.
609. Die Bedeutung des Alten Testaments für den christlichen Glauben, in: Jahrbuch für Biblische Theologie 12, 1997, 181 – 192.
610. Il significato cristiano del dolore, in: KOS Rivista di medicina, cultura e science umane 152, 1998, 42 – 45.
611. Leserbrief (Antwort auf Leserbrief von Prof. Jüngel, FAZ 29.1.98) in: epd-Dokumentation 11 vom 9.3.1998, 48.
612. Lutherans and Episcopy, in: Colin Podmore (ed.): Community – Unity – Communion, Essais in Honour of Mary Tanner, Church House Publishing, London 1998, 183 – 188.
613. Masao Abe in my encounter with Buddhism, in: D.W. Mitchell: Masao Abe, a Zen Life of Dialogue, Boston etc. 1988, 208 – 210.
614. Human Life: Creation versus Evolution?, in Ted Peters (ed.), Science and Theology. The New Consonance, Boulder Colorado (Westview) 1998, 137 – 148.
615. (op.tit.), in: University of Pennsylvania. The Boardman Lectureship in Christian Ethics XXXV, 1998, 21 – 28.

616. Die lutherische Tradition und die Frage eines Petrusdienstes an der Einheit der Christen, in: Il Primato del Successore di Pietro. Atti del Simposio teologico, Roma dicembre 1996, Libreria Editrice Vaticana, Città del Vaticano 1998, 472–475.

617. A Lutheran's Reflections on the Petrine Ministry of the Bishop of Rome, in: Communio. International Catholic Review XXV,4 (1998), 604–618.

1999

618. The Resurrection of Jesus: History and Theology (transl. Gabriele Schroeder), Dialog 38 (1999), 20–25 (cf. Nr. 520).

619. Review of J. Ratzinder, Vom Wiederauffinden der Mitte. Grundorientierungen. Texte aus vier Jahrzehnten, hg. vom Schülerkreis, Freiburg (Herder) 1997, in: ThLZ 124 (1999), 20–22.

620. Teologia e filosofia. Il lore rapporto a la luce della storia commune, trraduz. G. Sansonetti, Brescia (Queriniana) 1999 (Italian translation of Nr. 568).

621. Die Gemeinsame Erklärung zur Rechtfertigungslehre aus evangelischer Sicht, in: J.B. Hilberath und W. Pannenberg (eds.), Zur Zukunft der Ökumene. Die "Gemeinsame Erklärung zur Rechtfertigungslehre", Regensburg 1999, 70–78.

622. Unbekümmert um die Moden der Zeit, in: Alexa Läng (ed.), Worauf ich hoffe. Gedanken und Wünsche an der Schwelle zum neuen Jahrtausend, Wuppertal 1999 (RB Taschenbuch 566), 64–67.

623. Das christliche Inkarnationsdogma als Thema der Philosophie, in: M. Olivetti (ed.), Incarnation (Biblotheca dell' Alchivio di Filosofia), Padua (CEDAM) 1999, 503–508.

624. "Uno è buono" (Mt 19,17), in: L. Melina/J. Noriega, Domanda sul bene e domanda sul Dio, Mursia (Pontificia Universita Lateranense) 1999, 25–33.

625. The Rationality of Christian Theism, in: G. Brüntrup/R. Tacelli (eds.), The Rationality of Theism, Kluwer 1999, 11–19.

626. Teologia Systematica vol. III. romanian Translation by George Remete, Alba Julia 1999.

627. Bibel und Philosophie in der protestantischen Theologie, in: Euntes Docete 111 (1999), 123–131.

628. Philosophie, Religion, Offenbarung. Beiträge zur Systematischen Theologie Bd. 1, Göttingen 1999.

629. Die Ökumene als Wirken des Hl. Geistes, in: St. Leimgruber (Ed.), Gottes Geist bei den Menschen. Grundfragen und spirituelle Anstöße, München 1999, 68–77.

630. Gemeinsame Erklärung zur Rechtfertigungslehre, in: Stimmen der Zeit 217 (1999), 723–726.

631. La contribucion di Martin Luthero a la espiritualidad cristiana, in: Miscellánea Comillas. Rivista de Teologia y Ciencias Humanas 57, 469–474.

632. Il linguaggio teologico tra la prospettiva di totalità ontologica e la frammentarieta del sapere, in: Protestantesimo Rivista trimestrale publicata dalla Facolta Valdese di teologia, vol. 54 (1999), 357–366.

2000

633. Chinese Translation from Grundzüge der Christologie (Nr. 82) Kap. 1: Der Ausgangspunkt, in: Logos & Pneuma. Chinese Journal of Theology 12 (2000), 89–152.

634. Natur und Mensch – und die Zukunft der Schöpfung. Beiträge zur systematischen Theologie Bd. 2, Göttingen 2000.

635. Die Gerechtigkeit des Glaubens, in: Roger Liggenstorfer u. B. Muth-Oelschner (Eds.), Anleitungen und Rezepte für eine Kirche der Hoffnung, FS für Kurt Koch, Freiburg 2000, 20–23.

636. Eternity, Time and the Trinitarian God, in: Dialog. A Journal of Theology 39 (2000), 9–14.

637. A Trinitarian Synthesis (R. Jensons Systematic Theology I & II), in: First Things 103 (2000), 40–53.

638. Review of Werner Beierwaltes, Platonismus und Christentum, Frankfurt am Main 1998, in: Theologische Revue 96 (2000), 150–151.

639. Hintergründe des Streites um die Rechtfertigungslehre in der evangelischen Theologie, Sitzungsberichte der Bayerischen Akademie der Wissenschaften, Philosophisch-historische Klasse, Heft 3 (2000).

640. Evangelische Überlegungen zum Petrusdienst des römischen Bischofs, in: H. Schütte (Ed.), Im Dienst der einen Kirche. Ökumenische Überlegungen zur Reform des Papstamtes, Frankfurt/Paderborn 2000, 173–187 (cf. Nr. 599).

641. Dab og identitet. Danish partial translation of Systematische Theologie Bd. 3, Kap. 3,1 by Hans E. Kons u. a., Dialogcentrets Forlag, Aarhus 2000, 62 Seiten.

642. Kirche und Ökumene. Beiträge zur Systematischen Theologie Bd. 3, Göttingen 2000.

643. Eternity, Time and the Trinitarian God, in: C.E. Gunton (ed.), Trinity, Time and Church. A Response to the Theology of Robert W. Jenson, Grand Rapids (Eerdmans) 2000, 62–70 (cf. Nr. 635).

644. Storia i problemi della teologia evangelica contemporanca in Germania. Da Schleiermacher fino a Barth e Tillich, trad. di G. Sansonetti, Brescia (Queriniana) 2000.

645. Senza Dio tutto e leeito, inervista a Wolfhart Pannenberg a cura die Mauricio Pagani, in: G. Cingolani/O. Urpii (a cura di), Luei sull' immortalità (Futuribili 2–3, 1999), Milano 2000 (Franco Angeli), 24–27.

2001

646. Präsentische Eschatologie in Hegels Geschichtsphilosophie, in: R. Bubner/W. Mesch (eds.),: Die Weltgeschichte – das Weltgericht? Stuttgarter Hegelkongreß 1999, Stuttgart 2001, 312–322.

647. Una historia de la filosofia desde la idea de Dios. Teologia y filosofia (Spanish translation of Nr. 571 by R. F. de Mururi Duque), Salamanca 2001.

648. Freude des Glaubens: Predigten, München 2001.

649. Metafisica e idea de Dios (Spanish translation of 437 by M. Abella) Caparros Editores Madrid 1999.

650. The Christian Interpretation of Suffering, in: B Ars (ed.): The Meaning of Medicie. The Human Person, den Haag 2001 m 119–129 (cf. Nr. 655).

651. Die religiöse Erhebung über das endliche Dasein zu Gott, in: Euntes Focete 54, 2001, 15–23.

652. die Einzigkeit Jesu Christi und die Einheit der kirche. Anmerkungen zu der Erklärung der vatikanischen Glaubenskongregation "Dominus Jesus" in: Kerygma und Dogma 47, 2001, 203–209; Polish translation as "Jesus chrsitus i jednosc Kosciola" in: Znak LIII, 552, 2001, 48–55.

653. Theology in the Context of Modern Culture, Seoul 2001 (A Series of Special Lectures by Distinguished Scholars), English and Korean.

654. Article "Unendlichkeit" in: Historisches Wörterbuch der Philosophie 11, Basel 2001, 140–146.

655. The Christian Interpretation of Suffering, in: A.T. Tymieniecka / E. Agazzi (eds.): Life – Interpretation and the Sense of Illness within the Human Condition. Medicine and Philosophy in dialogue (Analecta Hesserliana LXXII), Dordrecht 2001, 203–224 (cf. Nr. 650).

656. Treeinigheden og vor evige skabelse (Danish selected translaion of volumes 1 and 3 of the Systematic Theology by H.E. Kongsø and others, cf. Nrs. 436 and 503) Aarhus 2001.

657. God as Spirit – and Natural Science, in: Zygon 36, 2001, 783–794.

658. Response to John Polkinghorne, in: Zygon 36, 2001, 799–800.

659. "Extra nos". Ein Beitrag zur christlichen Frömmigkeit, in: A. Raffelt (ed.): Weg und Weite (*festschrift* for K. lehmann), Freiburg i.Br. 2001, 197–205.

660. Review of: Johannes Duns Scotus: Über die Erkennbarkeit Gottes, herausgegeben und übersetzs von H. Kraml, in: theologische literaturzeitung 127, 2002, 214–215.

2002

661. Fortschritt und Vollendung der Geschichte, Weiterleben nach dem Tode und Auferstehung des Menschen im Christentum, in: P. Koslowski (ed.): Fortschritt, Apokalyptik und Vollendung der Geschichte und Weiterleben des Menschen nach dem Tode in den Weltreligionen (Diskurs der Weltreligionen 4), München 2002, 103–113.

662. Una historia filosofica desda la idea de Dios (Spanish translation of Nr. 571), Salamanca 2002.

663. The Task of Christian Eschatology, in: C.E. Braaten / R. Jenson (eds.): The Last Things. Biblical and Theological Perspectives on Eschatology, Grand Rapids 2002, 1–13.

664. La recerche dogmatique aujourd'hui, in: F. Bousquet (and others): La responsabilité des Theologiens. Mélanges offerts a Josepf Doré, Paris 2002, 827–835.

665. Foreword, in A. Stirling (ed.): The Trinity. An Essential Faith in our Time, Nappunee 2002, VII–X.

666. Resurrection – the Ultimate Hope, in: K. Tanner / Chr. A. Hall (eds.): Ancient

and Postmodern Christianity. Essays in Honor of Thomas C. Oden, downers Grove Ill. 2002, 254–262.

667. Dìo come spirit e le science natural, in: Lateranum LXVIII, 1, 2002, 9–21.

668. A Symposium on Dabru Emet. Wolfhart Panennberg, in Pro Ecclesia. A Journal of Catholic and Evangelical Theology 11, 2002,8–9.

669. Anglikanismus und Ökumene, in: Kerygma und dogma 48, 2002,197–202.

670. The Concept of Miracle, in: Zygon 37, 2002, 759–762.

671. Review of A. E. McGrath: A Scientific Theology, Vol. 1: Nature, Grand Rapids 2001, in: Theology Today 59 (2002), 312–316.

672. Bestimmung und Transzendenz des Menschen, in: Leben und Wissen. Symposium zu Ehren von Hans Tuppy, ed. by der Österreichischen Forschungsgemeinschaft, Wien 2002, 37–48.

673. Wir werden ihn sehen von Angesicht (1. Joh. 3,2), in: Il volto dei Volti. Christo, a cura dell'Istituto Internazionale di ricerca sul volto di Cristo, Gorle 2002, 47–52.

674. Review of: Facing Up: Science and its Cultural Adversaries, by Steven Weinberg, in: First Things 125 (2002), 64–66.

675. Cristianesimo e filosofia, in: Filosofia e Teologia XVI (2002), 431–437.

676. Tod und Sünde, in: Mysterium Redemptionis, Congresso de Fatima (9.–12. May 2001), Fatima 2002, 31–45.

2003

677. Letter from Germany, in: First Things 131 (2003), 8–11.

678. Japanese Translation of Nr. 557 durch Kyo Bun Kwan, Toyko 2003.

679. Die Auferstehung als historische Tatsache. Ausschlaggebend sind die Augenzeugen, in: Bayernkurier Jg. 53 (2003) Nr. 16 vom 17.4.2003, 18.

680. God en de opstanding – een antwoord aan Sjoerd L. Bonting .. door Wolfhart Pannenberg, in: Gamma, Stichting Teilhard de Chardin, Heiloo (NL), Jg. 10 (2003) Nr. 2, 10–14.

681. Tod und Sünde, in: Berliner Theologische Zeitschrift 20 (2003), 103–110.

682. Die weltgründende Funktion des Mythos und der christliche Offenbarungsglaube, in: W. Barner / A. Detken / J. Wesche (Eds.): Texte zur modernen Mythentheorie, Stuttgart 2003, 265–276.

683. Geschichtliche Offenbarung Gottes und ewige Trinität, in: KuD 49 (2003), 236–246.

684. A Symposium on Dabru Emet, in: C. E. Braaten / R. Jenson (eds.): Jews and Christians – people of God, Grand Rapids 2003, 183–185 (cf. Nr. 668).

685. Chinese Translation of Nr. 41, in: Logos & Pneuma, Chinese Journal of Theology 19 (2003), 44–68.

686. Teologia della creazione, in: Il Regno 48 (2003), Bologna, 508–514.

687. Il linguaggio Teologico tra la prospettiva di totalità ontologica e la frammentarietà del sapere, in: Linguaggi dell' ontologia. Atti del VIII Colloquio su filosofia e religione, Macerata, 13–15 maggio 1999, a cura di Giovanni Ferretti, Macerata 2003, 67–77 (cf. Nr. 631).

2004

688. Der eine Gott als der wahrhaft Unendliche und die Trinitätslehre, in: F. Menegoni / L. Illetterati (Eds.): Das Endliche und das Unendliche in Hegels Denken. Hegelkongress in Padua und Montegrotto Terme 2001 (Veröffentlichungen der Internationalen Hegel-Vereinigung 23), Stuttgart 2004, 175 – 185.

689. Der ökumenische Weg seit dem II. Vatikanischen Konzil – aus evangelischer Sicht, in: KuD 50 (2004), 17 – 24.

690. Death and Sin, in: Theology Digest 51 (2004), 35 – 40.

691. Korean Translation of Nr. 222 by Sung-Soo Choi, 2004.

692. "Fundamentaltheologie" als anthropologische Grundlegung einer Theologie der Religion und der Religionen?, in: M. Petzoldt (ed.), Evangelische Fundamentaltheologie in der Diskussion, Leipzig 2004, 195 – 204.

693. Beiträge zur Ethik, Göttingen 2004.

694. Das Verhältnis unserer Begriffe von Raum und Zeit zum Gedanken der Ewigkeit, in: O. Reinke (ed.): Ewigkeit? Klärungsversuche aus Natur- und Geisteswissenschaften, Göttingen 2004, 102 – 109.

695. Defectus ordinis? Zum Verhältnis von Bischofsamt und Pfarramt aus lutherischer Sicht, KNA Ökumenische Information 35 (2004), 3 – 5.

696. Fine della metafisica? in: Humanitas 59 (2004), 425 – 433.

697. "Outside us" – Luther's Contribution to Christian Piety, in: Luther Digest 12 (2004), 65 – 69.

698. Luther's Contribution to Christian Spirituality, in: Luther Digest 12 (2004), 70 – 73.

699. Ein Nachwort als Dank, in: K. Koschorke / J. Moltmann / W. Pannenberg: Wege zu einer trinitarischen Eschatologie, München 2004, 23 – 26.

700. Die Frage nach Gott als Schöpfer der Welt und die Kosmologie, in: H. A. Müller (Ed.): Kosmologie. Fragen nach einer Evolution und Eschatologie der Welt, Göttingen 2004, 197 – 208.

701. Der eine Gott als der wahrhaft Unendliche und die Trinitätslehre, in: I. U. Dahlferth u. a. (eds.): Denkwürdiges Geheimnis. Beiträge zur Gotteslehre (FS Eberhard Jüngel zum 70. Geburtstag), Tübingen 2004, 417 – 426 (cf. Nr. 688).

702. Ökumenische Aufgaben im Verhältnis zur römisch-katholischen Kirche, in: KuD 50 (2004), 260 – 270.

703. Geist und Bewusstsein, in: Theologie und Philosophie 79 (2004), 481 – 490.

704. Teologie della creazione e scienze naturali, in: Valentino Maraldi (ed.): Teologie della creazione e scienze della natura. Atti del Convegno "Teologie della creazione e scienze della natura. Vie per un dialogo in prospettiva interreligiosa", Trento, 28 – 29 maggio 2003, Bologna 2004, 101 – 116.

2005

705. Eternity, Time and Space, in: Zygon 40 (2005), 97 – 106.

706. Versöhnung mit Gott, in: Bayernkurier Jg. 56 (2005) Nr. 11 vom 1.3.2005, 18.

707. Vorwort zur Neuausgabe der "Ökumenischen Dogmatik" von Edmund Schlink

(= Edmund Schlink, Schriften zu Ökumene und Bekenntnis 2), Göttingen 2005, VII – IX.

708. Notes on the Alleged Conflict between Religion and Science, in: Zygon 40 (2005), 585 – 588.

709. Japanese translation of Nr. 477, Tokyo 2005.

710. Die Freiheit eines Christenmenschen und das Problem der Wahlfreiheit, in: N. Elsner / G. Luer (eds.): "sind eben alles Menschen". Verhalten zwischen Zwang, Freiheit und Verantwortung, Göttingen 2005, 281 – 293.

711. Tareas ecuménicas en relación con la iglesia católica romana (Spanish translation of Nr. 702), in: Selecciones de Teologia 44 (2005) Nr. 176, 331 – 338.

712. Rendszeres Teológia 1 (Hungarian translation of Nr. 436 by Osiris Kiadó), Budapest 2005.

713. Apostolsko vjerovanje pred pitanjima današnjice (Croatian translation of Nr. 185), Zagreb 2005.

2006

714. Die bleibende Relevanz der Erkenntnislehre des Kusaners, in: Nicolai de Cusa Opera Omnia. Symposium zum Abschluß der Heidelberger Akademie-Ausgabe (Heidelberg 11. und 12. Februar 2005), ed. by W. Beierwaltes and H. G. Senger, Heidelberg 2006, 147 – 162.

715. Problems between Science and Theology in Modern History, in: Zygon 41 (2006), 105 – 112.

716. Der Glaube an Gott und die Welt der Natur, in: ThLZ 113 (2006), 123 – 130.

717. Raum, Zeit und Ewigkeit, in: Chr. Böttigheimer / H. Filser (eds.): Kircheneinheit und Weltverantwortung (FS Peter Neuner), Regensburg 2006, 209 – 219.

718. An Intellectual Pilgrimage (Plenary Address at AAR Meeting at Philadelphia Nov. 18, 2005), in: Dialog 45 (2006), 184 – 191.

719. Morality, Ethics and God, in: A. J. Torrance / M. Banner: The Doctrine of God and Theological Ethics, London 2006, 47 – 54.

720. Der offenbarungstheologische Ansatz in der Trinitätslehre, in: M. Welker / M. Volf (eds.): Der lebendige Gott als Trinität. Jürgen Moltmann zum 80. Geburtstag, Gütersloh 2006, 13 – 22.

721. Ecumenical Tasks in Relationship to the Roman Catholic Church, in: Pro Ecclesia XV (2006), 161 – 171.

722. Der Glaube an Gott und die Welt der Natur, in: S. J. Lederhilger (ed.): Mit Gott rechnen. Die Grenzen der Naturwissenschaft und Theologie, Frankfurt a.M. 2006, 15 – 24 (cf. Nr. 716).

723. Contributions from Systematic Theology, in: Ph. Clayton (ed.): The Oxford Handbook of Religion and Science, Oxford 2006, 359 – 371.

724. La resurrezione come speranza umana e come evento storico, in: La resurrezione – mistero del desiderio. Un dialogo interdisciplinare. Atti del X Colloquio su filosofia e religione, Macerata, 27 – 29 maggio 2004, a cura di Giovanni Ferretti, Macerata 2006, 31 – 42.

725. Eine Einführung zu den christlichen Bildgehalten, Review by F. A. v. Metzsch

(ed.): Bild und Botschaft I–III, München, in: Das Münster. Zeitschrift für christliche Kunst und Kunstwissenschaft 59 (2006), 308 f.

726. Metaphysik und Offenbarung. Eine Betrachtung aus reformatorischer Sicht, in: PATH (Pontificia Accademia di Teologia) 5 (2006), 425–433.

727. Chinese translation of Nr. 571 by the Institute of Sino-Christian Studies, Hongkong 2006.

728. Metafizika és istengondolat (Hungarian translation of Nr. 437), Budapest 2006.

729. Rendszeres Teológia 2 (Hungarian translation of Nr. 482 by Osiris Kiadó), Budapest 2006.

2007

730. Analogie und Offenbarung. Eine kritische Untersuchung zur Geschichte des Analogiebegriffs in der Lehre von der Gotteserkenntnis, Göttingen 2007.

731. Predigt über Lk 13,1–5: Glaube an Gottes rettenden Willen, in: H. Schneider (ed.), Gebete und Predigten zu Ehren des seligen Johannes Duns Scotus, Mönchengladbach 2007, 52–55.

732. Divine Economy and Eternal Trinity, in: D. H. Knight (Ed.): The Theology of John Zizioulas. Personhood and the Church, Hampshire 2007, 79–86 (cf. Nr. 683).

733. Der Glaube an Gott und die Welt der Natur, in: Confessio Augustana. Das lutherische Magazin für Religion, Gesellschaft und Kultur I/2007, 21–29 (cf. Nr. 716 and Nr. 722).

734. God of the Philosophers, in: First Things 174 (2007), 31–34.

735. Was konstituiert das Ich und seine Identität? Überlegungen zu Erik H. Erikson, in: U. Schwab (ed.), Erikson und die Religion. Beiträge zur Rezeption der Theorie Erik H. Eriksons in der Gegenwart, Berlin 2007, 96–98.

736. Afterword: Faith in God and the World of Nature, in: Intelligent Design, ed. Robert B. Stewart, Minneapolis 2007, 210–218.

737. Neutralität des Staates gegenüber der Religion? Vortrag vor dem politischen Club Tutzing (12.3.2005), in: Ph. Jenninger / R. Peter / H. Seubert (eds.): Tamen! Gegen den Strom. Günter Rohrmesser zum 80. Geburtstag, Stuttgart 2007, 381–389.

2008

738. Filosofia e Teologia. Tensões e convergências de uma busca comum (Portuguese translation of Nr. 571), São Paulo 2008.

739. The Historicity of Nature. Essays on Science and Theology, ed. by Niels Henrik Gregersen, West Conshohocken 2008.

740. Sergio Rondinara (ed.): Dio come Spirito e le scienze della natura. In dialogo con Wolfhart Pannenberg, Rom 2008.

741. Japanese translation of Nr. 358 Tokyo 2008.

742. Théologie systématique Paris 2008; French translation of nos. 436, 482, 503.

2009
743. Defectus ordinis? Zum Verhältnis von Bischofsamt und Pfarramt aus lutherischer Sicht, in: KuD 55 (2009), 342 – 346.
744. Teología sistimática vol. III; Spanish translation of Nr. 503.

Selected English Secondary Literature
on the Work of Wolfhart Pannenberg

Adams, N.: Eschatology Sacred and Profane. The Effects of Philosophy on theology in Pannenberg, Rahner, and Moltmann, in: International Journal of Systematic Theology 2, 200, 283 – 306.

Ahlers, R.: Theolgoy of God and Theological method, in: dialog 22, 1983, 235 – 240.

Albright, Cr.R / Haugen, J. (eds.): Beginning with the End. God, Science, and Wolfhart Pannenberg, Chicago 1997.

Alpern, B.D.: The Logic of Doxological Language. A Reinterpretation of Aquinas and Pannenberg on Analogy and doxology, Pittsburg 1980.

Alsford, M.: The Notion of Coadunacy and the Problem of self/other Relationality in Theology with Special Reference to Kant, Fichte, Hegel, Barth, and Pannenberg, University of Durham 1990.

Apczynski, J.V.: Truth in Religion. A Polanyian Appraisal of Wolfhart Pannenberg's Theological Program, in: Zygon 17, 1982, 49 – 73.

Beam, J.N.: A Critical Assessment of Wolfhart Pannenberg's Relation to Process Thought, Baylor University 1985.

Beeching, B.: Antitheism and Eschatological Theology. W. Pannenberg's Indictment of Thirteenth Century Theology, Ottawa 1978.

Beechler, D.J.: the Centrality of Jesus" Resurrection in W. Pannenberg's Christology "From Below", Roma 1973.

Betz, H.D.: The Concept of Apocalyptic in the theology of the Pannenberg Group, in: Journal for Theology and Church 6, 1969, 192 – 207.

Blanco, C.: God, the Future, and the *Fundamentum* of history in Wolfhart Panenneberg, in: The Heythrop Journal, prepublished online May 2012.

Bollinger, G.: Panneberg's Theology of the Religions and the Claim to Christian Superiority, in: Encounter 43, 1982, 273 – 285.

Borowitz, E.B.: anti-Semitism and the Christologies of Barth, Berkouwer and Pannenberg, in: Dialog 16, 1977, 38 – 41.

Boutwell, W.S.: The Eschatology of Wolfhart Pannenberg, in: Southwestern Journal of Theology 36, 1994, 25.

Braaten C.E. / Clayton, P. (eds.): The Theology of Wolfhart Pannenberg. Twelve American Critiques, with an Autobiographical Essay and Response, Minneapolis 1988.

Braaten, C.E.: History and Hermeneutics (New Directions in Theology Today II), Philadelphia 1966.

Braaten, C.E.: The Current Controversy in Revelation. Pannenberg and His Critics, in: Journal of Religion 45, 1965, 225 – 237.

Braaten, C.E.: Wolfhart Pannenberg, in: Marty, M.E. / Peerman, D. (eds.): A Handbook of Christian Theologians, Nashville 1984.

Bradley, H.: Hope and Participation in Christ. A Study in the Theology of Barth and Pannenberg, Princeton, no year.

Bradshaw, T.: Trinity and Ontology. A Comparative Study of the Theologies of Karl Barth and Wolfhart Pannenberg, Edinburg 1988.

Bridges, J.T.: Human Destiny and Resurrection in Pannenberg and Rahner, New York 1987.

Buller, C.A.: The unity of Nature and History in Pannenberg's Theology, Langham 1996.

Burhenn, H.: Pannenberg's Argument for the Historicity of the Resurrection, in: Journal of the American Academy of Religion 40, 1972, 368–379.

Burhenn, H.: Pannenberg's Doctrine of God, in: Scottish Journal of Theology 28, 1975, 535–549.

Clark, W.R.: The Relation of Present Experience to Eschatology and Christological Uniqueness in Schleiermacher, Tillich and Pannenberg, Iowa 1973.

Clayton, P.: Anticipation and Theological Method, in: Braaten, C.E. /Clayton, P. (eds.): The Theology of Wolfhart Pannenberg. Twelve American Critiques, with an Autobiographical Essay and Response, Minneapolis 1988.

Clayton, P.: The God of History and the Presence of the Future, in: Journal of Religion 65, 1985, 98–105.

Cobb, J.B.: Pannenberg and Process Theology, in: The theology of Wolfhart Pannenberg. Twelve American Critiques, with an Autobiographical Essay and Response, Minneapolis 1988.

Cobb, J.B.: The Resurrection of Jesus in the Theology of W. Pannenberg, South Western Baptist Theological Seminary 1972.

Colombo, J.A.: An Essay on Theology and History. Studies in Pannenberg, Metz, and the Frankfurt School, Atlanta 1990.

Cook, P.J. A.: Pannenberg. A Post-Enlightenment Theologian, in: Churchman 30, 1976, 245–264.

Craig, W.L: The Historical Argument for the Resurrection of Jesus. Its Rise, Decline, and Contribution, München 1979.

Culpepper, G.M.: Ecclesial Being and one Theologian. Pannenberg's Doctrine of Faith in its Sacramental Context, in: The Thomist 63, 1999, 283–306.

Dickenson, C.: Pre-Existence, Resurrection and Recapitulation. An Examination of the Pre-Existence of Christ in K. Barth, W. Pannenberg and the New Testament, Pittsburg 1973.

Dietterich, I.T.: Toward a Contemporary Theology of the Holy Spirit. An Inquiry into the Thought of Wolfhart Pannenberg and john B. Cobb, University of Chicago 1987.

Dobbin, E.: Pannenberg on Theological Method, in: Proceedings of the Catholic Theological Society of America 32, 1977, 202–220.

Dobbin, E. Reflections on W. Pannenberg's Revelation Theology, in: Louvain Studies 4, 1972, 13–37.

Dobbin, E: Revelation as History, A Study of W. Pannenberg's Theology of Revelation, Lovania 1971.

Dupuis, K.: Jesus, God and Man. Some Reflections on W. Pannenberg's Christology, in: Indian Journal of Theology 20, 1971, 213–220.

Ebel, B.: The Pannenbergzan Retroactive Significance of Resurrection, in: The Asbury Journal 66, 2011, 47–63.

Edwards, D.: the Ecological Significance of God-Language, in: Theological Studies 60, 1999, 708–722.

Equina, L.: Faith and History. The Significance of the Historical Jesus in the Systematic Theologies of Paul Tillich, Wolfhart Pannenberg, and Jon Sobrino, Regensburg 1998.

Erickson, M.J.: Pannenberg's Use of History as a Solution to the Religious Language Problem, in: Journal of the Evangelical Theological Society 17, 1974, 99–104.

Fizgerald, G.: Revelation in the Theology of Wolfhart Pannenberg, Roma 1971.

Ford, L.S.: A Whiteheadian Basis for Pannenberg's Theology, in: Encounter 39, 1977, 307–317.

Ford, L.S.: The Nature of the Power of the Future, in: Braaten, C.E. /Clayton, P. (eds.): The theology of Wolfhart Pannenberg. Twelve American Critiques, with an Autobiographical Essay and Response, Minneapolis 1988.

Foster, D.: Pannenberg's Polanyianism. A Response to John V. Apczynscki, in: Zygon 17, 1982, 75–81.

Fulljames, P.: God and Creation in Intercultural Perspective. Dialogue between the Theologies of Barth, Dickson, Pobee, Nyamiti and Pannenberg, Frankfurt a.M. 1993.

Galloway, A.: Wolfhart Pannenberg, London 1973.

Gilbertson, M.R.: "See I am making all things new". God and Human History in the Book of Revelation and in Twentieth-century Theology, with particular Reference to Wolfhart Pannenberg and Jürgen Moltmann.

Gingrich, J.: The Structure of Faith in the Theology of W. Pannenberg, Claremont 1973.

Gnanakan, K.R.: Pannenberg's Quest for Universal History, in: Asia Theological Association Journal 5, 1997, 3–40.

Goff, R.: The Resurrection of Jesus as a Basis for Hope for the Future in the Theologies of Pannenberg and Moltmann. A Theological Dialogue, Wesley Theological Seminary, 1974.

Gray, D.P.: Response to Wolfhart Pannenberg, in: Cousin, E.H. (ed.): Hope and the Future of Man, Philadelphia 1972.

Greence, C.J.D.: The Doctrine of God in the Theology of Wolfhart Pannenberg, University of Nottingham 1982.

Grenz, S.J.: "Scientific" Theology / "Theological" Science. Pannenberg and the Dialogue between Theology and Science, in. Zygon 34, 1999, 159–166.

Grenz, S.J.: Pannenberg and Evangelical Theology. Sympathy and Caution, in: Christian Scholar's Review 20, 1991, 272–285.

Grenz, S.J.:Reson for Hope. The Systematic Theology of Wolfhart Panenneberg, New York – Oxford 1990.

Grenz, S.J.: The Appraisal of Pannenberg. A Survey of the Literature, in: Braaten, C.E. /Clayton, P. (eds.): The Theology of Wolfhart Pannenberg. Twelve American Critiques, with an Autobiographical Essay and Response, Minneapolis 1988.

Grenz, S.J.: The Irrelevancy of Theology. Pannenberg and the Quest for Truth, in: Calvin Theological Journal 27, 1992, 307 – 311.

Grenz, S.J.: Wolfhart Pannenberg. Reason, Hope and Transcendence, in: The Ashbury Theological Journal 46, 1991, 73 – 90.

Gunton, C.: Time, Eternity and the Doctrine of the Incarnation, in: Dialog 21, 1982, 263 – 268.

Gutenson, C.E.: Can Belief in the Christian God be Properly Basic? A Pannenbergian Perspective on Plantinga and Basic Beliefs, in: Christian Scholar's Review 29, 1999, 49 – 72.

Hackmann, D.W.: Validation and Truth. Wolfhart Pannenberg and the Scientific Status of Theology, University of Iowa 1989.

Hasley, J.S.: history, Language and Hermeneutic. The Synthesis of Wolfhart Pannenberg, in: Westminster Theological Journal 41, 1979, 269 – 290.

Hamilton, W: The Character of Pannenberg's Theology, in: Robinson J.M. / Cobb, J.B. (eds.): Theology as History, New York – Evanston – London, 1967, 176 – 196.

Hanson, B.: Hope and Participation in Christ. A Study in the Theology of Barth and Pannenberg, Princeton 1970.

Harder, H.G. / Stevenson, W.T.: The Continuity of History and Faith in the Theology of Wolfhart Pannenberg. Toward an Erotics of History, in: Journal of Religion 51, 1971, 34 – 56.

Harder, H.G.: Continuity Between Method and Content in Contemporary Theology. The Achievement of Wolfhart Pannenberg, Toronto 1971.

Hasel, F.M.: Scripture in the Theologies of W. Pannenberg and D.G. Bloesch. An Investigation and Assessment of its Origin, Nature, and Use, Frankfurt a.M. 1996.

Hefner, P.: Pannenberg's Fundamental Challenges to Theology and Science, in: Zygon 36, 2001, 801 – 808.

Hefner, P.: The concreteness of God's Kingdom. A Problem for Christian Life, in: Journal of Religion 51, 1971, 188 – 205.

Hefner, P.: The Role of Science in Pannenberg's Theological Thinking, in: Zygon 24, 1989, 135 – 151.

Hefner, P.: Theological Reflections. Questions for Moltmann and Pannenberg, in: Una Sancta 25, 1968, 32 – 51.

Heinitz, K.: Pannenberg. Theology 'from Below' and the Virgin Birth, in: Lutheran Quarterly 28, 1976, 173 – 182.

Hendrickson, M.L.: Behold the Man! An Anthropological Comparison of the Christologies of John Macquarrie and of Wolfhart Pannenberg, Lanham 1998.

Hick, J.: A Note on Pannenberg's Eschatology, in: Harvard Theological Review 77, 421 – 423.

Hinton, R.A.: Pannenberg on the Truth of Christian Discourse. A Logical Response, in: Calvin Theological Journal 27, 1992, 312–318.

Hogan, J.P: The Historical Imagination and the New Hermeneutic. Collingwood and Pannenberg, in, Masson, R. (ed.): The pedagogy of God's Image, Decatur 1982, 9–30.

Holwerda, D.: Faith, Reason and the Resurrection in the Theology of Wolfhart Pannenberg, in: Plantinga, A. / Wolterstorff, N. (egs.): Faith and Rationality, Notre Dame 1983.

Hyslop, A. The Theology of Image and Imagination in the theology of W. Pannenberg, Milwaukee 1977.

Hentz, A.H.: Personal Freedom and the Futurity of God. Some Reflections on Pannenberg's "God of Hope", in: Reformed Review 31, 1978, 148–154.

Jackson, M.B.: An Interpretation of Wolfhart Pannenberg's Theory of Knowledge as Creative Subjectivity, Union Theological Seminary virgina 1973.

Jackson, M.B.: How True is God-Language. W. Pannenberg, in: Cumberland Seminary 19, 1981, 21–27.

Jacobs, A: The Creative Power of the Future: Wolfhart Pannenberg, Modern Science, and the Metaphysics of Divine Action, in: ETD Collection for Fordham University, 2009.

Johnson, E.A.: Analogy, Doxology and their Connection with Christology in the Thought of Wolfhart Pannenberg, Washington 1981.

Johnson, E.A.: Resurrection and Reality in the Thought of Wolfhart Pannenberg, in: Heythrop Journal 24, 1983, 1–18.

Johnson, E.A.: The Ongoing Christology of Wolfhart Pannenberg, in: Horizons 9, 1982, 237–250.

Johnson, E.A.: The Right Way to Speak about God? Pannenberg on Analogy, in: Theological Studies 43, 1982, 673–692.

Keen, C.S.: "Dominus Jesus Novus". An Experiment in the Conception of the Transcendence of God from the Theologies of Karl Barth and Wolfhart Pannenberg, Claremont 1985.

Kehm, G.H.: Pannenberg's Theological Program, in: Perspective 9, 1968, 245–266.

Kim, J: Toward a Comprehensive Theology of Divine Action, in: Theology and Science 1, 2012, 95–101.

Klooster, F.H.: Aspects of Historical Method in Pannenberg's Theology, in: Bakker, J.T. et. al. (ed.): Septuagesimo Anno (festschrift G.C. Berkhouwer), Kampen 1973, 112–128.

Kolden, M.: Panneberg's Attempt to Base Theology on History, Chicago 1976.

Kondo, K.: Revelation and History in Pannenberg and Moltmann, in: Journal of Theology 33, 1970, 70–112.

Lösel, S.: Wolfhart Pannenberg's Response to the Challenge of Religious Pluralism. The Anticipation of Divine Absoluteness?', in: Journal of Ecumenical Studies 34, 1997, 499–519.

MacCulloh, G.W.: Creation to Consummation. The Theology of Wolfhart Pannenberg, in: Anglican Theological Review 83, 2001, 115–128.

MacHann, J.C.: The Three Horizons. A Study in Biblical Hermeneutics with Special Reference to Wolfhart Pannenberg, Aberdeen 1987.

Maloney, M.: Wolfhart Pannenberg's Use of the Concept of the True Infinite: A Critical Inquiry, in: ETD Collection for Fordham University 2009.

McClean, J.-A.: Anticipation in the Thought of Wolfhart Pannenberg, Melbourne College of Divinity 2010.

McCoy, J.: Soteriology and the Doctrine of God. A Historical Typology and an Analysis of the Theologies of K. Rahner and W. Pannenberg, Princeton 1979.

McDermott, B.O::: Pannenberg's Resurrection Christology. A Critique, in: Theological Studies 35, 1974, 711–721.

McDermott, B.O.: The Personal Unity of Jesus and God according to Wolfhart Pannenberg, St. Ottilien 1973.

McGrath, A.: Christology and Soteriology. A Response to Wolfhart Pannenberg's Critique of the Soteriological Approach to Christology, in: Theologische Zeitschrift 42, 1986, 222–236.

McKenzie, D.: Panneberg on Faith and Reason, in: Dialog 18, 1979, 222–224.

McKenzie, D.: Pannenberg on God and Freedom, in: Journal of Religion 60, 1980, 307–329.

McKenzie, D.: The Rational Theology of Wolfhart Pannenberg. A Philosophical Critique, Austin 1977.

McKenzie, D.: Wolfhart Pannenberg and Religious Philosophy, Lanham 1980.

Michalson, G.E: Pannenberg on the Resurrection and Historical Method, in: Scottish Journal of Theology 33, 1980, 345–359.

Mikelic, P: Universal History within the Christologies of Hegel and Pannenbeg, union Theological Seminary in Virigina 1981.

Miller, E.L::: Salvation-history. Pannenberg's Critique of Cullmann, in: The Iliff Review 37, 1980, 21–25.

Molnar, P.D.: Some Problems with Pannenberg's Solution to Barth's 'Faith Subjectivism', In: Scottish Journal of Theology 48, 1995, 315–339.

Mostert, C.: From Eschatology to Trinity. Pannenberg's Doctrine of God, In: Pacifica 10, 1997, 70–83.

Mostert, C.: God and the Future. Wolfhart Pannenberg's Eschatological Doctrine of God.

Neie, H.: The Doctrine of the Atonement in the Theology of Wolfhart Pannenberg, Berlin – New York 1979.

Neuhaus, R.J.: Pannenberg Jousts with the World Council of Churches, in: Christian Century 99, 1982, 74–76.

Nicol, I.G.: Facts and Meanings. Wolfhart Pannenberg's Theology as History and the Role of the Historical-Critical Method, in: Religious Studies 12, 1976, 129–139.

North, R.: Pannenberg's Historicizing Exegesis, in: The Heythrop Journal 12, 1971, 377–400.

Noyalis, W.: The Resurrection of Jesus as Metaphor in the Theology of W. Pannenberg, Indiana 1979.

O'Collings, G.: The Christology of Wolfhart Pannenberg, in: The Heythrop journal 7, 1966, 394–406.

O'Collins, G.: The Theology of Revelation in some Recent Discussion. A study of W. Pannenberg, E. Fuchs, j. Moltmann and G. Downey, Cambridge 1967.

O'Donnell, J.: Pannenberg's Doctrine of God, in: Gregorianum 72, 1991, 73–98.

Obayashi, H.: Future and Responsibility. A Critique of Pannenberg's Eschatology, in: Studies in Religion 1, 1971, 191–203.

Obayashi, H.: Pannenberg and Troeltsch. History and Religion, in: journal of The American Academy of Religion 38, 1970, 401–419.

O'Callaghan, P.: Whose Future? Pannenberg's Eschatological Verification of Theological Truth, in: The Irish Theological Quarterly 66, 2001, 19–49.

Olive, D.H.: Wolfhart Pannenberg, Waco 1973.

Olson, R.E.: The Human Self-Realization of God. Hegelian Elements in Pannenberg's Christology, in: Perspectives in Religious Studies 13, 1986, 207–223.

Olson, R.E.: Trinity and Eschatology. The Historical Being of God in Jürgen Moltmann and Wolfhart Pannenberg, in: Scottish Journal of Theology 36, 1983, 213–227.

Olson, R.E.: Trinity and Eschatology. The Historical Being of God in Jürgen Moltmann and Wolfhart Pannenberg, Houston 1984.

Olson, R.E: Wolfhart Pannenberg's Doctrine of the Trinity, in: Scottish Journal of Theology 43, 1990, 175–206.

Olthius, J.H: God as True Infinite. Concerns about Wolfhart Pannenberg's Systematic Theology, I, in: Calvin Theological Journal 27, 1992, 318–325.

Onah, G.I.: Self-Transcendence and Human History in Wolfhart Pannenberg, Lanham – New York – Oxford 1999.

Osborn, R.: Pannenberg's Program, in: Canadian Journal of Theology 13, 1967, 109–122.

Owen, J.M.: A First Look at Pannenberg's Christology, in: Reformed Theological Review 25, 1966, 52–64.

Page, J.S.: Critical Realism and the Theological Science of Wolfhart Pannenberg: Exploring the Commonalities, in: Bridges: An Interdisciplinary Journal of Philosophy, Theology, History and Science 10, 2003, 71–84.

Park, A.P.: Christian Hope According to Bultmann, Pannenberg and Moltman, in: Westminster Theological Journal 33, 1971, 153–174.

Parks, L.A.: Fulles by a Coming Kingdom. The Phenomenon of Projection in Pannenberg's Theology, St. Mary's Seminary and University 1984.

Pasquariello, R.D.: Pannenberg's Philosophical Foundations, in: Journal of Religion 56, 1976, 338–347.

Pasquariello, R.D.: Reality as History. An Investigation of W. Pannenberg's Understanding of Reality, New York 1972.

Peters, T.: Method and Truth. An Inquiry into the Philosophical Hermeneutics of Hans Georg Gadamer, and the Theology of Wolfhart Pannenberg, Chicago 1973.

Peters, T.: Truth in History. Gadamer's Hermeneutics and Pannenberg's Apologetic Method, in: Journal of Religion 55, 1975, 36–56.

Placher, W.C.: History and Faith in the Theology of Wolfhart Pannenberg, Yale 1975.

Placher, W.C.: Pannenberg on History and Revelation, in: Reformed Review 30, 1976, 39 – 47.

Placher, W.C.: The Present Absence of Christ. Some thoughts on Pannenberg and Moltmann, in: Encounter 40 ,1979, 169 – 179.

Polk, D.P.: God who Comes. The Future of God's Mode of Being in the Thought of W. Pannenberg, Claremont 1983.

Polk, D.P.: On the Way to God. An Exploration into the Theology of Wolfhart Pannenberg, Lanham 1989.

Polkinghorne, J.C.: Fields and Theology. A Response to Wolfhart Pannenberg, in Zygon 36, 2001, 795,797.

Polkinghorne, J.C.: Wolfhart Pannenberg's Engagement with the Natural Sciences, in: Zygon 34, 1999, 151 – 158.

Powell, S.M.: History and Eschatology in the Thought of Wolfhart Pannenberg, in: Fides et historia 32, 2000, 19 – 32.

Priebe, D.: History and Kerygma. A Study of the Concept of Revelation in the Theology of W. Pannenberg, Claremont 1965.

Ratliff, F. Shapes of Mystery. An Analysis of Selected Models of Transcendence in the Theologies of Macquarrie, Ogden, Pannenberg and Kaufmann, Louisville 1975.

Rhem, R.A.: A Theological Conception of Reality as History. Some Aspects of the Thinking of Wolfhart Pannenberg, in: Reformed Review 26, 1972, 179 – 188, 212 – 223.

Rice, R.: Wolfhart Pannenberg's Crowning Achievement. A Review of his "Systematic Theology", in: Andrews University Seminary studies 37, 1999, 55 – 72.

Rise, S.: The Christology of Wolfhart Pannenberg. Identity and Relevance, Lewiston – New York 1997.

Robinson, J.M. / Cobb, J.B.: Theology as History, New York 1967.

Russell, J.M.: Pannenberg on Verification in Theology. An Epistemic Response, in: the Iliff Review 43, 1986, 37 – 55.

Russell, R.J.: Contingency in Physics and Cosmology. A Critique of the Theology of Wolfhart Pannenberg, in: Zygon 23, 1988, 23 – 43.

Salai, H.A.: The doctrine of Creation in the Theology of Barth, Moltmann, and Pannenberg. Creation in Theological, Ecological, and Philosophical-Scientific Perspective, Regensburg 1998.

Schmidt, L: historical Process and Hermeneutical Method in the Theologies of John Macquarrie, Schubert Ogden and Wolfhart Pannenberg, Toronto 1975.

Schott, F.: Comparing Eberhard Jüngel and Wolfhart Pannenberg on Theological Method and Religious Pluralism, in: Dialog 31, 1992, 129 – 135.

Schwöbel, C.: Rational Theology in Trinitarian Perspective. Wolfhart Pannenberg's Systematic Theology, in: Journal of Theological Studies 47, 498 – 527.

Sharam, E.S.: Person and Community. The Corporate Identity of Christ in the Theology of Dietrich Bonhoeffer and Wolfhart Pannenberg, University of Oxford 1995.

Shouse, J.W.: Incarnation and Christological Construction in Wolfhart Pannenberg,

Russel Aldwinckle and Geoffrey Lampe, The Southern Baptist Theological Seminary 1980.

Shults, F.L.: A Theology of Everything? Evaluating Pannenberg's Interdisciplinary Method, in: Christian Scholar's Review 28, 1998, 155–163.

Shults, F.L: Constitutive Relationality in Anthropology and Trinity. The Shaping of the *Imago Dei* doctrine in Barth and Pannenberg, in: Neue Zeitschrift für Systematische Theologie und Religionsphilosophie 39, 1997, 304–322.

Shults, F.L.: The Postfoundationalist Task of Theology. Wolfhart Pannenberg and the New Theological Rationality, Grand Rapids – Michigan – Cambridge 1999.

Shults, F.L.: Theology, Science, and Relationality. Interdisciplinary Reciprocity in the Work of Wolfhart Pannenberg, in: Zygon 36, 2001, 809–825.

Simpson, G.M: Reciprocity and Political Theology. Wolfhart Pannenberg and three Americans – John B. Cobb, Jr., Carl E. Braaten, and Richard John Neuhaus, St. Louis 1983.

Simpson, G.M.: Whither Wolfhart Pannenberg? Reciprocity and Political Theology, in: Journal of Religion 67, 1987, 33–49.

Stewart, J.A.: Reconstructing Science and Theology in Postmodernity. Pannenberg, Ethics, and the Human Sciences, Aldershot 2000.

Stewart, J.A.: Some Problems with the Theological Appropriation of Biology by W. Pannenberg, in: Studies in Science and Theology 4, 1996, 118–127.

Stewart, J.: Does Pannenberg's View of Culture and Social Theory have Ethical Implications?, in: Studies in Christian Ethics 13, 2000, 32–48.

Summer, G.: Pannenberg and the Religions. Conflictuality and the Demonstration of Power in a Christian Theology of the Religions, Yale 1994.

Tatum, W.B.: The Resurrection and Historical Evidence, in: Foundations and Facets Forum 10, 1994, 249–254.

Tipler, F.J.: The Omega Point as Eschaton. Answers to Pannenberg's Questions for Scientists, in: Zygon 24, 1989, 217–253.

Tripole, M.R.: Philosophy and Theology. Are they Compatible? A Comparison of Barth, Moltmann and Pannenberg with Rahner, in: Thought 53, 1978, 24–54.

Tupper, E.F.: The Christology of Wolfhart Pannenberg, in: Exegetical Review 71, 1974, 9–73.

Tupper, E.F.: The Theology of Wolfhart Pannenberg, Philadelphia 1973.

Turner, G.: Wolfhart Pannenberg and the Hermeneutical Problem, in: Irish Theological Quarterly 39, 1972, 107–129.

Vekathanam, M: Christology in the Indian Anthropological Context. An Evaluative Encounter with K. Rahner and W. Pannenberg, Frankfurt a.M. 2001.

Venema, C.P.: History, Human Freedom and the Idea of God in the Theology of Wolfhart Pannenberg, in: Calvin Theological Journal 17, 1982, 53–77.

Vettikkattil, B.: Role of Modern Science in the Creation Theology of Wolfhart Pannenberg. Analysis and Critical Assessment, Universität Leuven 1999.

Villa-Vicencio, C.: History in the Thought of Reinhold Niebuhr and Wolfhart Pannenberg, Drew University 1975.

Vigulak, F.E.: The Death of Christ According to Wolfhart Pannenberg. An Exposition and Criticism of Pannenberg's Theology of the Cross, Roma 1977.

Walsh, B.J.: A Critical Review of Pannenberg's Anthropology in Theological Perspective, in: Christian Scholar's Review 15, 1986, 247 – 259.

Walsh, B.J.: Futurity and Creation. Explorations in the Eschatological Theology of Wolfhart Pannenberg, Toronto 1979.

Walsh, B.J.: Introduction to Pannenberg's Systematic Theology, I, A Symposium, in: Calvin Theological Journal 27, 1992, 304 – 306.

Walsh, B.J.: Pannenberg's Eschatological Ontology, in: Christian Scholar's Review 11, 1982, 229 – 249.

Watts, G.J.: Revelation and the Spirit. A Comparative Study of the Relationship between the Doctrine of Revelation and Pneumatology in the Theology of Eberhard Jüngel and Wolfhart Pannenberg, University of London 1998.

West, J. M.: The Eclipse of Meaning. Religion and Self-Discovery in Pannenberg's Recent Thought, in: Harvard Divinity Bulliten 14, 1974, 10 – 12.

Westphal, M: Hegel, Pannenberg, and Hermeneutics, in: Man and World 4, 1971, 276 – 293.

White, H.W.: A Critique of Pannenberg's "Theology and the Philosophy of Science", in: Studies in Religion 11, 1982, 419 – 436.

Wilken, R.L.: Who is Wolfhart Pannenberg?, in: Dialog 4, 1965, 140 – 142.

Williams, D.D.: Response to Wolfhart Pannenberg, in: Cousin, E. (ed.) Hope and the Future of Man, Philadelphia 1972, 84 – 88.

Wood, L.W.: Above, Within or Ahead of? Pannenberg's Eschatologicalism as a Replacement for Supernaturalism, in: Asbury Theological Journal 46, 1991, 43 – 72.

Wood, L.W.: Defining the Modern Concepts of Self-Revelation. Toward a Synthesis of Barth and Pannenberg, in: Asbury Theological Journal 41, 1986, 85 – 105.

Wood, L.W.: History and Hermeneutics. A Pannenbergian Perspective, in: Wesley Theological Journal 16, 1981, 7 – 22.

Worthing, M.W.: Foundations and Functions of Theology as Universal Science. Theological Method and Apologetic Praxis in Wolfhart Pannenberg and Karl Rahner, Frankfurt a.M. 1996.